Texts and Monographs in Computer Science

Texts and Monographs in Computer Science

Suad Alagić
Object-Oriented Database Programming
1989. XV, 320 pages, 84 illus.

Suad Alagić
Relational Database Technology
1986. XI, 259 pages, 114 illus.

Suad Alagić and Michael A. Arbib
The Design of Well-Structured and Correct Programs
1978. X, 292 pages, 68 illus.

S. Thomas Alexander
Adaptive Signal Processing: Theory and Applications
1986. IX, 179 pages, 42 illus.

Michael A. Arbib, A.J. Kfoury, and Robert N. Moll
A Basis for Theoretical Computer Science
1981. VIII, 220 pages, 49 illus.

Friedrich L. Bauer and Hans Wössner
Algorithmic Language and Program Development
1982. XVI, 497 pages, 109 illus.

Kaare Christian
A Guide to Modula-2
1986. XIX, 436 pages, 46 illus.

Edsger W. Dijkstra
Selected Writings on Computing: A Personal Perspective
1982. XVII, 362 pages, 13 illus.

Edsger W. Dijkstra and Carel S. Scholten
Predicate Calculus and Program Semantics
1990. XII, 220 pages

W.H.J. Feijen, A.J.M. van Gasteren, D. Gries, and J. Misra, Eds.
Beauty Is Our Business: A Birthday Salute to Edsger W. Dijkstra
1990. XX, 453 pages, 21 illus.

Melvin Fitting
First-Order Logic and Automated Theorem Proving
1990. XIV, 242 pages, 26 illus.

Nissim Francez
Fairness
1986. XIII, 295 pages, 147 illus.

continued after index

Programming with Specifications

An Introduction to ANNA, A Language for Specifying Ada Programs

David Luckham

Springer-Verlag
New York Berlin Heidelberg London
Paris Tokyo Hong Kong Barcelona

David Luckham
Computer Science Laboartory
Stanford University
Stanford, CA 94305-4055
USA

Series Editor

David Gries
Department of Computer Science
Cornell University
Ithaca, NY 14853
USA

Printed on acid-free paper.

Photocomposed copy prepared by the author using the author's LATEX file.
Printed and bound by R.R. Donnelley & Sons, Harrisonburg, Virginia.
Printed in the United States of America.

9 8 7 6 5 4 3 2 1

ISBN 0-387-97254-4 Springer-Verlag New York Berlin Heidelberg
ISBN 3-540-97254-4 Springer-Verlag Berlin Heidelberg New York

These pages are dedicated
to those who sat by
and watched them grow:
Susannah and Brian

Preface

Topics

- *what this book is about,*
- *its intended audience,*
- *what the reader ought to know,*
- *how the book is organized,*
- *acknowledgements.*

Specifications express information about a program that is not normally part of the program, and often cannot be expressed in a programming language. In the past, the word "specification" has sometimes been used to refer to somewhat vague documentation written in English. But today it indicates a precise statement, written in a machine processable language, about the purpose and behavior of a program. Specifications are written in languages that are just as precise as programming languages, but have additional capabilities that increase their power of expression. The terminology *formal specification* is sometimes used to emphasize the modern meaning. For us, all specifications are formal.

The use of specifications as an integral part of a program opens up a whole new area of programming — *programming with specifications*. This book describes how to use specifications in the process of building programs, debugging them, and interfacing them with other programs. It deals with a new trend in programming — the evolution of specification languages from the current generation of programming languages. And it describes new strategies and styles of programming that utilize specifications. The trend is just beginning, and the reader, having finished this book, will certainly see that there is much yet to be done and to be discovered about programming with specifications.

This is a book for people who have attained some experience with programming languages and have already written some significant programs. Better yet, the reader should have tried to understand or modify someone else's programs. Such readers will have concluded from their own experience that the current methods of programming have to become more disciplined. Now they are ready to explore programming with specifications.

In writing the book, I have had in mind primarily two groups of people: professional software engineers and college undergraduates and graduates taking courses in computer science or software engineering. But in this age of the home computer, people who have the sort of experience I have just alluded to can come from almost any age group and many different backgrounds.

What precisely should the reader know already? There are two prerequisites, which I will describe by telling you just a little about the book.

The book deals with the use of specifications to develop Ada programs. Specifications are written in a formal language called Anna. Anna is a specification language. It is no harder to learn than programming languages such as Pascal or Modula2 or Ada. In fact, Anna is an extension of the Ada language. It allows annotations to be included as part of an Ada program. Annotations can be processed by tools "like" compilers, and by very different kinds of tools as well. Anna stands for "ANNotated Ada."

Ideally, the reader should already know Ada. This is the first prerequisite, but it is not absolutely necessary. A reader who knows Modula2 or more advanced dialects of Pascal, or C^{++}, can use this book as a way of simultaneously learning Ada as well as Anna. This is possible because the concepts and methods of programming with specifications are independent of any particular programming language. They apply equally well to any language containing constructs similar to Ada. Anna could just as easily have been based on Modula2, for example.

Why choose to study programming with specifications in the context of Ada — or any particular programming language? My answer is this. In order to develop new ways of programming that are really practical, it is absolutely essential to deal with the real problems that are faced by the real programmer in the use of a real programming language. And since Ada is certainly the most ambitious Algol-like language of the time, it is a logical choice upon which to base the development of new programming methods. Of course, some of the details involved in specifying programs written in any of today's programming languages are quite messy. Indeed, these messy details have an annoying way of complicating methods that are really very simple. But, if we are successful in developing new methods of programming, the ultimate consequence will be the evolution of more advanced languages that make those methods easy to apply. By exposing the messy details, they will eventually disappear!

The second prerequisite is a little background in the theory of computer science — not a lot, just a little. This involves three things that are normally part of an undergraduate curriculum: (1) basic data structures (lists, trees, sets, stacks, and queues); (2) formal logic, usually called Propositional and Predicate Logic (you should know about Boolean operators, what a quantifier is, and what a formal proof looks like); and (3) an undergraduate course in abstract algebra (a knowledge of axioms for linear ordering, groups, a little of that sort of thing).

Anna and methods of programming with specifications are presented informally. They are described in much the same way as most books describe programming languages or algorithms and data structures. The idea is not to demand a lot of background from the reader. So the book is really an experiment to see if the use of specifications in programming can be taught just like the use of advanced programming constructs and structures are taught now. As readers progress in the methods of writing and using specifications, they may become interested in exploring the foundational theories. These can be found in other books on the mathematical semantics of specifications and programs, and on axiomatic proof systems.

This book does two things: it explains Anna and it describes possible ways of using it. The book alternates between explaining Anna constructs and giving examples describing methods of programming with specifications. I have used four devices to help this alternation: (1) **commentaries** on examples, (2) **guidelines** on constructing specifications, (3) **recipes** for describing methods of applying specifications, and (4) the star (*).

Examples nearly always include a **commentary** that encapsulates various details of methodology. Our examples aren't perfect either; their imperfections are used to illustrate the compromises and choices one may face in the practical world of imperfect languages and too little time. Commentaries also include a lot of the details that are specific to Ada. Those interested in a general overview of Anna can skip commentaries, but I don't advise it.

Guidelines are common-sense rules of thumb about how to construct specifications, and what kinds of information to express in them. They are prominently displayed at various points in the discussion of applications of specifications.

Recipes really are cookery. Sometimes I want to describe an algorithm for applying specifications that really is too complicated for humans to do in general. I give a rather vague outline called a recipe. Recipes give the reader a taste of the method as it applies to simple examples. Good cooks should be able to reconstruct a complete algorithm, with variations to taste. Future environments will contain tools that automate such algorithms. So eventually, users will need to know only *what* a recipe produces, and not *how* to cook it.

Some parts of the book are hard to read. They contain complicated formulas, or go into messy details. These sections and chapters are **starred**

(*). Starred sections can be passed over on a first reading.

It is important to read this book in conjunction with other books and research papers as well. I have included reading lists at the end of some chapters. The lists are short — to encourage the reader. They provide an overview of some of the prior work upon which programming with specifications is based, and also how it fits in with other current work and perceived problems in the software area.

The structure of the book is as follows.

Chapter 0 describes how modern programming languages are gradually evolving into specification languages and why this is happening. It gives a short general description of applications of formal specifications to the programming process.

Chapters 1, 2, and 7 deal with annotations of the Pascal-like subset of Ada — called *simple annotations*. A description of simple annotations is in Chapter 1. The basic concepts needed to define the meaning of formal annotations and the correctness of programs are introduced and discussed as the need for them becomes obvious. This way, a lengthy preliminary chapter on formal semantics and correctness is avoided. Applications of simple annotations are described in Chapter 2. More advanced annotations for composite data structures, together with examples of applications are in Chapter 7.

Chapter 3 describes annotations for programs with exceptions and a method of specifying exceptional behavior in Ada programs.

Chapters 4 and 5 deal with specification of packages. These chapters are the heart of programming with specifications. Chapter 4 explains the annotation constructs for package specifications. Chapter 5 describes methods of specifying packages and analyzing the consequences of package specifications. The methods and examples given here are only a small introduction to the science of building formal specifications for software packages. This is an area where more powerful methods and languages need to be developed. Many topics, such as incompleteness of specifications, are only mentioned in passing. These two chapters could easily have taken the entire book.

Chapter 6 describes annotation of Ada generic units and how such annotations are relevant to building reusable software.

Chapters 8, 9, and 10 are devoted to annotation and construction of package bodies. The crucial problem is construction of a package body that is consistent with a given package specification. There are three parts to this problem, each part being assigned a separate chapter. Chapter 8 explains package body annotations. Chapter 9 illustrates ways to analyze whether the body, as it is being implemented, is (or will be) consistent with the original specification. This chapter is starred since it involves rather lengthy annotations. Chapter 10 describes new methods of utilizing a package specification as a guide in implementing a body. These methods are examples of *rigorous* software development methods. They integrate techniques such as runtime checking of specifications into the process of building packages so that implementation errors are caught as early as possible and certain kinds of errors never happen.

As mentioned earlier, this book is an introduction to programming with specifications. This area is just emerging. The use of specifications is a logical development from recent trends in programming languages, and it is being explored as an approach to dealing with increasing problems in software production. There is much still to be done. I hope the reader will be encouraged to improve upon what is in these pages, and if so, I shall consider the book a success.

Acknowledgements

The research leading to the development of Anna and its support tools has been sponsored by the Defense Advanced Research Projects Agency. I am indebted to DARPA for the opportunity to do this work in the first place.

Many patient people have read various versions of this book during its evolution, and their comments have been helpful and influential. Some of them were good enough to review more than one version! Particularly, I am indebted to past and present members of the Program Analysis and Verification Group at Stanford who have reviewed the book and developed the Anna toolset: Doug Bryan, John Kenny, Neel Madhav, Walter Mann, Geoff Mendal, Randy Neff, Wolfgang Polak, David Rosenblum, Sriram Sankar, Will Tracz, and Friedrich von Henke. In addition, it gives me great pleasure to thank David Gries for a detailed review beyond the duty of any editor, and Jennifer Anderson, David Guaspari, and Norman Ramsey for detailed comments. And there are many others to whom my thanks are also due, especially the students in my *"Topics in Ada Programming"* courses at Stanford. The book is much better as a result of everyone's efforts to help me, but of course I'm responsible for whatever is wrong with it.

Certainly, the book would not exist without Rosemary Brock, who of all patient people has been the most patient, dealing with many versions in Scribe and TEX and LATEX over several years. So, Rosemary, thank you too.

D. C. L.
Palo Alto
1989

Contents

0

What Anna Is

Topics:

- *extending programming languages to specification languages;*
- *formal annotations;*
- *applying annotations in the process of programming, two activities: specification and annotation;*
- *environments for programming with specifications.*

We can do a lot more with modern programming languages than we currently do. Normally, we use them simply to write programs. But programs have become problematic in so many ways — bugs, size, cost, and incompatibility, to mention but four — that attention is shifting from the program itself to the *processes* of writing programs. What are the processes we refer to as "programming"? How can we turn programming into a precise science?

To get a feel for part of the answer, reflect for a moment on the kinds of questions that come to mind whenever we read someone else's program — sometimes one of our own programs too! "What is he doing here?" "Why do it that way?" "If we changed this, wouldn't it work better?" And, when we ask these kinds of questions, why don't we find the answers in the comments and documentation?

These questions stem from trying to understand the reasoning that went on during the programming process and eventually led to the program. This reasoning uses the goals of the program and knowledge about the problem domain. It enables us to argue that the program satisfies those goals. We do not find the reasoning written in the program text or comments because there is no precise notation for expressing it. We need a language that is just as precise as the programming language itself — a language a machine can understand, but one a human can understand too. Such a language must be more powerful than the programming language in the sense that it can be used to describe not only the program, but also its goals and the reasoning leading to it. We refer to these kinds of languages as *Specification Languages*.

Anna is a step towards developing specification languages. The first fundamental thesis behind Anna is that we do not yet understand all the component activities of our programming processes. So we cannot design the ultimate specification language in one leap. We must design a language that is capable of expressing some of the things we already know are related to programming. We must experiment with primitive specification languages, and, by using them, gain the insight to develop more powerful ones. This is an evolutionary approach to specification languages.

The second fundamental thesis of Anna is that we start with the programming language itself. Many simple things that influence the development of a program, and the understanding of it later on, can be described in the programming language, perhaps with a few extra features added to it. With very few additions, we can describe mathematically what the program is supposed to do, how its variables are related to one another, and the mathematical facts that led to the program being written the way it was. Already, the possible applications of such extra information, expressed in machine-processable form, to improving and maintaining the program are enormous.

Anna is a language extension of Ada. It includes Ada and adds facilities that are useful in specifying the intended behavior of Ada programs. Many of the extensions are more general versions of features that are already in Ada. Some Anna features are entirely new. The new features are based on well-established theories of formal specification and documentation of programs. Similar extensions can be made to other programming languages such as Pascal and Modula2.

Let us look briefly at some examples of how Anna extends Ada.

0.1 From Informal Comments to Formal Annotations

Anna is the result of a few simple observations. First of all, programs nearly always contain informal English comments. In fact, this is such a universal practice that all programming languages provide a comment convention. We call these comments *informal* because they are not used in the processing or execution of the program. Simply put, informal comments are intended to guide human readers, not to be understood by the machine.

Another observation is that most informal comments can be expressed in a formal language similar to the programming language itself. It is called *formal* because precise rules define its syntax and semantics. Comments written in a formal language are called *formal comments*. They can be parsed, checked for semantic validity, and translated into an executable form by techniques similar to those used in compiling a program.

A third observation is that many programming languages already contain simple kinds of formal comments. The strong typing of Algol, Pascal, and Ada is really a particular kind of formal comment. In fact, the rationale for introducing types, subtypes, and constraints in Ada is to prevent errors and improve the reliability of programs. Subtype declarations with range constraints, for example, are used to check the values of variables during a computation, but are not needed to execute the program.

A natural conclusion from these observations is that many informal comments can be expressed formally in a language with the following properties: (1) it uses existing features of a programming language together with a few new features, and (2) it uses the position of comments to relate them to the program. This new kind of formal language is called an *Annotation Language*, and formal comments written in it are called *annotations*. An annotation language is a particular kind of specification language, one that uses textual position to relate specifications and program.

Let us illustrate three basic extensions of Ada. The first is an annotation that generalizes the Ada concept of a *constraint*. Consider the type TARGET declared in a program that computes target practice scores:

```
    type TARGET is
        record
            BULLS_EYE : REAL range 1.0 .. 10.0;
            INNER_CIRCLE : REAL range 3.0 .. 30.0;
            OUTER_CIRCLE : REAL range 9.0 .. 90.0;
        end record;
    -- the inner circle must be twice as wide as the bulls-eye,
    -- the outer circle must be twice as wide as the inner circle.
```

The Ada range constraints place bounds on the individual components of a target. A bulls-eye, for example, must lie between 1.0 and 10.0 units. When the program is executed, an error results if an attempt is made to construct a target that does not satisfy the constraints.

The informal comments in English give more information about targets. Unfortunately they cannot be expressed as Ada constraints, so they cannot be used to check that the program is computing with valid targets. Indeed, the two comments are not only informal, they are ambiguous. What does "twice as wide" mean? Is the bulls-eye part of the inner circle?

The Anna concept of *type constraint* generalizes Ada range constraints. Type constraints are Boolean expressions that can be applied to types and subtypes. They are more general than Ada constraints in several ways. One way is that they can constrain a type by relating its components, whereas Ada constraints can only apply to individual components. Thus,

```
        type TARGET is
            record
                BULLS_EYE : REAL range 1.0 .. 10.0;
                INNER_CIRCLE : REAL range 3.0 .. 30.0;
                OUTER_CIRCLE : REAL range 9.0 .. 90.0;
            end record;
--|         where T : TARGET =>
--|             T.INNER_CIRCLE = 3*T.BULLS_EYE and
--|             T.OUTER_CIRCLE = 3*T.INNER_CIRCLE;
```

The informal comments have been replaced by a precise annotation of the type — the annotation is a comment in the Ada program, but the vertical bar "|" indicates that it is a formal Anna annotation. Every value of type TARGET is constrained to have components that satisfy the equalities on the right of the "=>" symbol. "Twice as wide" has been given a precise definition.

The annotation can be processed by compiler-like tools that recognize formal comments. One kind of tool, called an *Annotation Transformer*, can translate the annotation into runtime checks that are executed whenever a target value is computed. The formal annotation can then be used to check the program, just as Ada uses the range constraints. The components of target then satisfy both the Ada range constraints and the Anna type constraint. Another kind of tool, called a *Verifier*, analyzes the program to see if it will always behave consistently with the annotation. Verification usually involves formal proof methods.

We can make another extension of programming languages by noticing that many concepts in informal comments can be computed. These concepts are used to talk about *what* the program is doing rather than *how* it does it, so they appear only in the comments. The human reader is expected to understand them, but beyond that the concepts have no use. Why not define these concepts as pieces of program? If we do this, so their values can be computed, then we can use them to check the program automatically — not just talk about it. We must take care to keep these concept definitions separate from the actual program. Definitions of annotation concepts will be formal comments too. This leads us to the idea of *virtual* program text.

The idea of virtual text is very simple: "write a program to describe a program, but keep the two programs separate." Virtual text is the separating feature.

To illustrate a use of virtual text, suppose there is another comment in our target practice program:

```
   ...
-- Score 10 for a bulls-eye, score 5 for an inner circle, score 1 for an outer circle.
   ...
```

The new comment tells us how the components of a target are to be interpreted in target practice. But it still lacks precision. Is a component of a target record to be viewed as a radius or a diameter or a circumference?

The concept "score" may be expressed formally by an Ada function declaration:

```
--: function SCORE(X, Y : REAL; T : TARGET)
--: return INTEGER;
--|   where return
--|       if X*X+Y*Y <= T.BULLS_EYE ** 2 then 10
--|       elsif X*X+Y*Y <= T.INNER_CIRCLE ** 2 then 5
--|       elsif X*X+Y*Y <= T.OUTER_CIRCLE ** 2 then 1
--|       else
--|           0
--|       end if;
```

The symbol "--:" indicates virtual Ada text. The function appears as a formal comment. It is a virtual Ada function, which means it can be used only in annotations or other virtual functions — it is not visible to the actual target practice program.

The values of SCORE are specified by a *result annotation*. In this example the result annotation is a conditional expression defining the values under various conditions. We could also give a virtual Ada body for SCORE that computes these values — it would have to be consistent with the annotation, which is easily done in this example.

Note, by the way, that the result annotation of SCORE makes it clear that the components of a target can be modeled geometrically as radii of concentric circles. In fact, until we know the operations on the target type, we can't "model" or "picture" the type. If the actual program is treating the target as if it is composed of squares or triangles, its results will conflict with annotations using SCORE. Again, we see that if the annotations using SCORE are translated into runtime checks, conflicts between the program and the annotations will be detected automatically. Alternatively, the process of trying to prove consistency between the program and its annotations can be automated by verification tools.

A third Anna extension to Ada concerns the problem of defining precisely the interfaces between programs. In Ada, interfaces are represented by package declarations. However, in all but the simplest examples, the Ada package declaration contains too little information to play an adequate role as an interface. A user of a package must look at the package body to see what the interface really provides. By including annotations, the Ada/Anna package declaration can contain enough information to enable a user to understand the package without looking at its body.

What kinds of annotations should be included in package declarations? Imagine that the target practice program is a package of facilities for computing scores. Here's a possible Ada package declaration for it.

```
generic
   T : TARGET;
package SCORE_BOARD is
```

```
    function TOTAL return NATURAL;
       -- Total score since cleaning.
    procedure SHOOT (X, Y : REAL);      -- Enter a shot, X, Y.
    procedure CLEAN;                    -- Clean the score board.
    BUZZER : exception;
       -- Raised by SHOOT when shot is off target.

end SCORE_BOARD;
```

This package declaration presents an interface to a body of subprograms that keep score during a shooting session at a particular target. The interface is general in that it works on any target (in Ada we say that it has a generic object parameter of type TARGET). To use this interface, it must first be instantiated to fit a particular target. One simply writes

```
package MY_BOARD is new SCORE_BOARD (MY_TARGET);
```

and one gets a score board that works on MY_TARGET. The interface should be understandable independently of the actual target size.

The informal comments probably would satisfy most casual users. Three operations can be performed on score boards, and we might get an exception. The interface tells us all we need to know. We do not have to worry about how the total is actually computed — it could be cumulative or it could be recomputed each time from a stored list of previous shots. But can we be sure that the body will work according to our understanding of the comments? In fact, are we sure we understand the comments? The cryptic phrase "since cleaning" implies a history of operations.

Here's one possible Anna interface that expresses the informal comments by formal annotations. Let's look at it first; then we will explain a few things about it.

```
--: with SCORE;
    generic
        T : TARGET;
    package SCORE_BOARD is

        BUZZER : exception;
           -- Raised by SHOOT when shot is off target.
        function TOTAL return NATURAL;
           -- Total score since cleaning.
        procedure SHOOT (X, Y : REAL);     -- Enter a shot, X, Y.
--|        where T.OUTER_CIRCLE ** 2 ≤ X*X+Y*Y =>
--|                                                raise BUZZER,
--|            raise BUZZER =>
--|                          SCORE_BOARD = in SCORE_BOARD;

        procedure CLEAN;                   -- Clean the score board.
```

```
--|       axiom
--|           SCORE_BOARD'INITIAL.TOTAL = 0;
--|       axiom
--|           for all B : SCORE_BOARD'TYPE; X, Y : REAL =>
--|               B[CLEAN].TOTAL = 0,
--|               B[SHOOT(X, Y)].TOTAL =
--|                                       SCORE(X, Y, T)+B.TOTAL;

    end SCORE_BOARD;
```

The virtual concept SCORE is imported into the specification for use in annotations — that is the meaning of the virtual **with** clause. The declaration of exception BUZZER has been placed first, so that it can be used in annotations of SHOOT. The declaration of SHOOT has two propagation annotations specifying when it propagates BUZZER. The first one captures the "off target" behavior. The second one expresses that SCORE_BOARD remains in its input state when SHOOT propagates a BUZZER.

Axiomatic annotations may be included in package declarations. They specify behavior on which the user of the package can rely. Thus, it is assumed that the package operations satisfy the axioms. SCORE_BOARD contains two **axiom** declarations, the second one having two clauses (or axioms). The first axiom says that the initial state of a SCORE_BOARD has a zero total. The second one says the same thing for any SCORE_BOARD state that results from a CLEAN operation. The third axiom says that the score of a shot is added to the previous total. The second and third axioms together imply the property that the total is the sum of the scores of shots after the last CLEAN.

SCORE_BOARD gives the flavor of the extensions to Ada for specifying packages. However, we have used several new annotation concepts and new notation, without explanation. In Anna, packages are treated as typed objects, their values being called *states*. States that result from sequences of operations are expressed in a special sequence notation. Axiomatic annotations are used to express algebraic relationships between package operations. Exception propagation annotations are used to specify exceptional behavior.

All this will be explained in the book. The point to be made here is that the Anna package specification defines the semantics of the Ada operations, whereas the Ada package declaration by itself defines only their syntax and their parameter types. The implementation details mentioned previously are still hidden. (We still do not know if a call to TOTAL will recompute the sum of all the previous shots, or simply use the previous total; we do know that whatever method is used must satisfy the third axiom.) All the information necessary to use the package should be in the Anna specification. The Ada/Anna package declaration can be used as an interface to combine programs, without one programmer having to understand the other's program during the combination process.

The application of this kind of interface definition to checking, debugging, and verification goes two ways. It defines a set of assumptions for checking or verifying the user's program, and it defines a set of constraints to be satisfied by all possible package bodies. As documentation, it provides a formal standard — all SCORE_BOARDs must satisfy the package declaration.

Notice that we have not deleted the informal comments from the Anna specification of SCORE_BOARD. Formal annotations need explanation too. Indeed, this book is based on the principle that we will always start with informal concepts and comments in our programming process. A fundamental part of programming with specifications is formalizing the informal knowledge.

0.2 Adding Annotations to Ada

In Anna, a program is specified by means of annotations and virtual text. Anna extends Ada by adding a different kind of annotation for each kind of entity in Ada. Here is a short outline of the kinds of annotations, going top-down with respect to program structure.

- **Dependencies between units.**
  Ada contexts define dependencies between separately compiled units. "Unit" usually means "package." Often, a dependent unit does not use all the facilities that are provided by its Ada context. Anna *context annotations* allow accurate identification of the facilities of a separately compiled unit that are actually used in a dependent unit, and also those elements that are not.
- **Generic units.**
  Ada generic parameters allow a unit to be parameterized for use in a set of different contexts. For any particular application, the unit is instantiated by providing values for the generic parameters. Annotations of a generic unit are also generic — they are instantiated to become annotations of each instance of the Ada unit. Also, a generic unit often makes assumptions about its generic parameters that are not expressible in Ada. *Annotations of generic parameters* can be used to express constraints to ensure the generic unit will be instantiated correctly.
- **Specification of packages.**
  The Ada package declaration defines an abstract interface between a user and a package body. But it almost never contains adequate information to be used as an interface. *Axiomatic annotations* as well as annotations of types and subprograms are used to specify packages. Typically, when packages represent abstract types and objects, their properties are most conveniently expressed algebraically by axiomatic annotations. Attributes of packages such as their *state* and *type* are

also provided in Anna. In annotations and virtual text, the Anna package is treated as a type.

- **Specification of subprograms.**
  In Ada, the subprogram declaration, given separately from the subprogram body, acts as an abstract interface to that subprogram. Again, as with packages, there is a need to supply information defining the subprogram independently of any of its bodies. This is done by *subprogram annotations*. Relationships between input and output values of parameters may be specified, and also conditions for exception propagation.
- **Exceptions.**
  Conditions under which exceptions are propagated are specified by *exception propagation annotations*. Usually, propagation annotations apply to subprograms, but they may also apply to blocks and more local scopes.
- **Types.**
  Constraints on types, extending the kinds of constraints expressible in Ada, are expressed by *type annotations*.
- **Objects.**
  Constraints on variables and sets of variables are expressed by *object annotations*.
- **Statements.**
  The behavior of a program may be specified at a local level, generally in a sequence of statements, by *statement annotations*. The simplest of these are *assertions*.
- **Assertions.**

This modest list of additions to Ada adds a great deal of expressive power. It follows the philosophy of making small extensions of the programming language to learn more about the kinds of annotations that are most useful.

Here are a few more facts about Anna.

No special annotations are associated with tasking constructs. Even so, Anna can be used in programs that contain tasks. Entries, for example, may be annotated by subprogram annotations. The reason for not including tasking annotations is that there are not enough research results about specifying concurrent and distributed programs. At present, it is not obvious what kinds of annotations would be useful in the process of designing and specifying tasking programs.

The expressions that may be used in Anna are a superset of the Ada expressions. Addition of new kinds of expressions, such as quantified and conditional expressions, is motivated by the need to express functional properties while omitting computational details.

Annotations in Anna are subject to the same computational hazards as expressions in Ada. For example, expressions in annotations may be undefined, and may even propagate exceptions such as numerical errors. Most mathematically oriented notations used in theories of programming turn a blind eye to such annoying possibilities. They complicate the nice theory! Unfortunately, if one is going to develop machine-aided support for specification languages, one must allow for these complications. So the semantics of Anna defines the meaning of annotations in the abnormal case when they are undefined as well as the normal case where they are defined.

We have mentioned that background knowledge is regarded as part of the specification of a program. The reader may wonder how this is expressed in Anna, since there appears to be no obvious kind of annotation for it. The answer is to build virtual packages that define the theory (i. e., types and operations) of a particular problem domain by axiomatic annotations. This gives us the ability to define axiomatic theories. Libraries of theory packages can be constructed. This ability is very important since we want to use previous specifications whenever possible on a new problem. Theories may be built up by combining simpler theories. To do this, Anna relies on Ada features for combining compilation units, such as context clauses and generic instantiation. Experience may show that we need new language features to combine theories for various problem domains.

0.3 Applying Anna

Using formal annotations should be viewed as an opportunity to develop new ways of programming. Of course, this is a rather large opportunity, and we should approach it by addressing specific facets of the programming process. Can we find better methods of specifying module interfaces and new ways of using interfaces, better methods of testing and debugging programs, more accurate documentation, and more powerful methods of ensuring that programs posses required properties? These are just a few facets.

To encourage experimentation, Anna does not enforce any particular process of programming. Formal annotations may be used whenever, and however, the programmer sees fit during the development of a program.

There are four general applications of annotations during the programming process. Each assumes that the concepts used in annotations are defined formally during the process — recall how the concept of a "score" of a shot at a target was formalized by the function SCORE. Ideally, there will be libraries of virtual functions (with subprogram annotations and/or virtual bodies) that define programming concepts. There will also be concepts unique to a particular problem. So part of programming with specifications is to understand the concepts of a problem well enough to define them formally at some stage.

The four general applications are:

1. **Specification of programs prior to implementation.** Annotations are used to express formally behavior and properties of a program before it is implemented. In this application, package, type, and subprogram annotations are most often used.
2. **Goal-oriented programming.** Annotations are used to define the goals of each major step of a program. This may be done at any level: the declarative region, package declaration or body, subprogram body, or block. The assumptions and objectives of each step are formally written as annotations using the concepts of the problem domain. A plan is represented as a tree with directed branches and annotations at the nodes — a sequence of annotations is the simplest kind of a plan. Code to be implemented on any branch assumes annotations at the start node and achieves those at the end node. All kinds of annotations are useful in planning. Various methods of actually producing executable code may be used with a plan. Some new methods are emerging from current research. Two examples are automatic transformation of goals to code and proof-theoretic programming, whereby a proof that the code satisfies the goals is constructed along with the code.
3. **Definition of runtime checks.** Checks may be intended either for temporary use for debugging or to be incorporated permanently into the program. Programs with permanent runtime checks are called self-checking programs. Checks are expressed as annotations. Most annotations may be used to define runtime checks. Subprogram annotations and lower level annotations such as assertions are particularly useful. Package axioms can be used to express checks of invariant properties of packages — e. g., messages received by a mailer package are delivered in first-in, first-out order. This use of annotations has two advantages. Very powerful checks can be expressed in Anna, and checks are clearly separated by syntax from the program being checked. Anna rules ensure that checks do not affect the program being checked.
4. **Documentation.** All annotations have the role of providing formal documentation of the underlying program once it is completed. If a formal plan is written to guide implementation, it usually constitutes most of the formal documentation when the program is finished.

The first two applications may be classified as *specification* processes — properties of a program are defined *before* constructing the program. The last two applications may be classified as *annotation* processes — properties of a program are defined *after* it is expressed in the programming language. The distinction between "specification" and "annotation" refers to the *use* of annotations during the programming process. We shall use both words to refer to annotations, but to indicate different uses of them.

Which kind of application we choose depends on the particular situation. If one is faced with a brand new requirement in English, then specification and goal-oriented programming using Ada/Anna are appropriate. If a completed Ada program already exists, then testing and documentation are appropriate uses of Anna.

Top–Down, from specifications to code.

One approach to programming with specifications is to apply each of the four general methods in succession. The programmer begins by expressing the concepts behind the program formally. The steps of (1) specification, (2) goal-oriented program development, (3) testing, and (4) documentation are then carried out with annotations that use the basic set of concept definitions.

At each step, the fact that the annotations are expressed formally allows us to automate various kinds of analysis. For example, the consequences of a formal specification can be deduced or computed to see if it conforms to requirements. Mismatches between the consequences of the specification and the informal requirements may lead either to changes in the specification or to revisions in the requirements — or both! This kind of specification analysis is sometimes called prototyping, because it is done *before* the program that implements the specification is constructed. The goal here is to avoid misunderstandings that persist from early steps in the programming process and are often never caught until the program is actually finished and delivered.[1]

At the next step, consistency between annotations and code may be proved during program development. This involves proving the correctness of small local pieces of code as they are developed to satisfy goals on particular branches of the program plan. On some branches it may be possible to transform the goal annotations into executable code automatically.

A completed program can be tested against its formal specifications. To do this, we must be able to check that annotations are satisfied by the computation when we run the Ada program on test data. Methods of doing this have been developed for most annotations in Anna, so this application is already an accomplished fact.

Throughout this process, an annotation may play different roles at different steps, being first a specification, then a goal, then a check, and finally part of the documentation.

Of course, faced with a new problem, this approach is rather "ideal." Its practice may be somewhat haphazard, with changes of mind, and goings back. But at each step the use of annotations should give us new ways to judge correctness, discover misunderstandings early, communicate accurately, and generally minimize our wanderings in the wilderness. The final

[1] See the paper by Brooks cited at the end of this chapter.

product, with its basis of formal definitions and documentation, should look as though we have not wandered around at all. It should be a *process map*, telling others who follow after us how to do it again.[2]

Specification compilation.

Another approach to programming with specifications views the process as a gradual transformation of specifications into executable forms. A succession of small transformations is applied to a specification. Each transformation guarantees consistency between the specification that is input to it and the specification that it outputs. The choice of transformations will usually be made by the programmer, but their application is automated. If this approach is successfully developed for wide classes of programs, *and* it turns out to be completely automatable, *and* to produce efficient code, the result will be a new generation of specification compilers. However, that is rather a lot of "if"s, which brings us to our next concern.

0.4 Environments for Programming with Specifications

These days, any high-level programming language comes with an environment of support tools. A compiler is essential, and other tools such as a debugger or syntax-directed editor are often included. What kind of tools can we expect for supporting applications of Anna?

Anna environments are being constructed at present. Our own environment [3] has reached a stage that may be called "experimental." That is, it can be used by fairly sophisticated users (who have some knowledge of the shortcomings of the tools) to study the feasibility of new ways of programming with specifications.

An Anna environment is built around an Ada environment. It contains a suite of tools that operate on a common data representation of Ada and Anna. Any of these tools may be invoked to process a program at any stage of its development. Each tool performs a specific service. No longer is there a rather large service, like compilation. Instead compilation is performed by invoking a sequence of tools that do parsing, semantic analysis, and code generation. So, when we sit down at the console of our new programming environment, we should expect a suite of "atomic" tools, many of which may be applied usefully at various stages of the programming process.

The Ada parser and semantic analyzer are extended to operate on Anna as well as Ada. So the environment allows us to start by checking that

[2]See the paper by Parnas and Clements cited at the end of this chapter.

[3]See Appendix B.

annotations are correctly written, and provides error messages if they are not.

Next, it is possible to check if a program satisfies some kinds of annotations, such as context annotations, without running the program. Such checking is often called "static" because people have in mind the kind of semantic rule checking done by compilers. However, in the case of Anna, we may be able to do static checking either because a particular kind of annotation is easy to check or because the checking tools employ sophisticated methods such as automated deduction. Static checking tools allow annotations to be integrated very closely into the programming process. At any stage, even before the program is completed, the programmer can invoke static checking to ask, "have I violated any of these kinds of annotations so far?"

Tools to aid analysis of specifications are being developed. When would we want to use such a tool? Consider a stage where we have constructed a module specification that consists of an Ada package declaration with annotations of subprograms, and axiomatic annotations. It is like the SCORE_BOARD, but a hundred times more complicated. Our problem is to decide if the specification is "right" before we implement it. We need to answer questions such as "is the specification consistent?" or "what would happen if this particular sequence of package subprograms was called?" A specification analyzer will answer such questions. It uses the annotations to find the answers. Currently, analyzers are being developed as experimental prototypes. We can expect them to be part of standard environments in the next five to ten years.

A specification analyzer opens up a number of possible changes in the programming process. It will quite likely influence that fuzzy area that involves going from English requirements for a program, which are usually vague, to a formal specification. Currently, all manner of rather interesting review processes are practiced, attempting to avoid misunderstandings from percolating into the implementation; but formal specifications are seldom constructed at all. On the other hand, an Anna formal specification can be quite a formidable document — not light reading. But, if questions about it can be answered automatically, then it becomes a negotiation document. Trade-offs involved in changing specifications can be analyzed. And the intentions of the requirements can be compared against the logical implications of the specification. Some day in the future, specifications could become legal contracts, if we have such automated legal clerks at our fingertips.

Most annotations can be transformed into runtime consistency checks. A tool that performs this kind of transformation is perhaps the Anna tool that is closest to a code generator in a conventional compiler. This kind of tool has already been developed to a stage where it provides a new, powerful testing and debugging capability in our Anna environment. It allows us to compile Anna as well as Ada, and to run Ada programs in comparison with their annotations. If an annotation is violated, a very precise error message is given specifying which annotation was violated, and exactly where the violation occurred.

There are two main applications of runtime checking of annotations. The first is to test and debug programs using the concepts that were used to design and construct the programs. If a high-level annotation such as a subprogram specification is violated, we can use lower level annotations, such as assertions in the subprogram body, to find out exactly what caused the inconsistency. Violations are reported automatically. Low-level, detailed annotations are used to zero-in on bugs. We have shown experimentally that this capability gives us a great improvement over current debugging practices. The programmer no longer has to recognize bugs by inspection, nor understand the organization of the runtime environment — which may be distributed over several processors. Instead, errors are analyzed using the concepts that were used to think about the program and construct it.

The second application is the construction of self-checking programs. Normally, the execution of runtime checks for consistency with annotations requires a significant runtime penalty. It is a reasonable penalty for debugging. But often we may not be willing to check annotations permanently during the normal use of a program. Suppose, however, that we have a few spare processors in a multiprocessor system. Then the penalty may be worth paying for the added confidence. The annotation checking can be dumped off on a watchdog processor, and permanent checking for consistency becomes a possibility. Checking of annotations in this way is currently a research topic.

In the course of explaining annotations in this book, we illustrate the use of the tools outlined here, and we describe the principles behind the tools. Appendix B describes some current Anna support tools in detail.

0.5 Future Developments

Anna represents a beginning in the evolutionary development of specification languages. There are many areas where Anna needs strengthening. Here are three examples.

- **Tasking**.
  Extending Anna to include annotations for tasks will not be straightforward. Merely annotating rendezvous constructs such as entries, entry calls, and select statements, while useful, is insufficient. Ada tasks can communicate through global objects, notably global packages such as buffers and mailboxes, without ever entering a rendezvous. An *abstract task* construct is needed that specifies more general kinds of actions than Ada entries. For example, an *abstract action* of a task could represent accessing an array shared with other

tasks. Or it might represent a pattern of more atomic interactions between tasks. Indeed, we believe that patterns will play a fundamental role in specification languages for concurrent programs.[4]

However, when new tasking annotations based on abstract tasks and actions are added to Anna, it is quite likely that we will need to change the annotations for packages. After all, package annotations should be a special case of task annotations, since it is logical to think of a sequential program as a single task. It is possible that package annotations, and the Ada package design itself, will need to be changed.

- **Manipulating annotations.**
  As we begin to develop techniques of programming with specifications, we will need more powerful ways of combining annotations than Anna provides. One possibility would be methods for reusing old specifications to build new ones — perhaps methods similar to those in SmallTalk.[5]

  New ways of naming, parameterizing, and instantiating annotations will be popular requests. The problem for a language designer will be to satisfy all the requests with a few elegant and easily understood constructs.

- **Abstraction.**
  The constructs defining abstract interfaces between programs in Ada (or Modula2, or any other programming language at present) have deficiencies that are not corrected by adding annotations. Ada sometimes enforces interpretations of abstractions in packages that are inconsistent with their implementation in the package body — as the programmer constructed it. However, annotated packages are adequate for most abstractions used in practical applications today. The question is, how abstract will modules in real programs become in the future? Programming with specifications may result in more abstract modules that have many more possible interpretations than one sees at present. Then, we will need more powerful constructs to support abstraction than the package specification and body constructs provided by Ada and Anna.

  One popular prediction is that Ada package specifications, together with algebraic annotations as allowed in Anna, will play the role of type declarations in future languages. Another is that new languages will have "mapping" constructs for defining correspondence between abstract interfaces and executable code.

These examples address two parts of the programming process. The

[4]See the reference to Task Sequencing Language in the Bibliography.

[5]See the book by Goldberg and Robson in the Bibliography.

abstraction issues are related to expressing what is often called *design*. The manipulation of annotations is related to *reasoning* — how to express knowledge and how to use it. In the future, languages will be needed that allow us to express more about these two parts of our programming process. They must provide more for design and reasoning, and perhaps less for computation. Smart environment tools will do more of the computational decisions.

As we said at the beginning, the plan we are adopting is to start by experimenting with small extensions of the programming languages we have now. Our first step is to explore how to use Anna, and where its deficiencies lie. That is what the rest of this book is about.

0.6 Terminology and Notation

Alternative symbols in expressions.

Anna permits some widely used mathematical symbols for operators and quantifiers. They may be used to improve the readability of annotations. These special symbols are:

$$\neg \quad \wedge \quad \vee \quad \rightarrow \quad \leftrightarrow \quad \forall \quad \exists \quad \neq \quad \leq \quad \geq$$

Their names are as follows:

Symbol	*Name*	*Symbol*	*Name*
$\neg$	not	$\forall$	for all
$\wedge$	and	$\exists$	there exists
$\vee$	or	$\neq$	not equal
$\rightarrow$	implies	$\leq$	less or equal
$\leftrightarrow$	if and only if	$\geq$	greater or equal

They are interchangeable with Anna reserved words, or combinations of ASCII symbols as follows:

Symbol		*Symbol*	
$\neg$	**not**	$\forall$	**for all**
$\wedge$	**and**	$\exists$	**exist**
$\vee$	**or**	$\neq$	/=
$\rightarrow$	->	$\leq$	<=
$\leftrightarrow$	<->	$\geq$	>=

These mathematical symbols are often used in this book, especially $\leftrightarrow$ for logical equivalence in place of the standard ASCII symbol <->, $\rightarrow$ for logical implication in place of ->, and $\leq$ for the less or equal operator in place of <=.

A summary of Anna syntax is given in Appendix A.

Terminology is introduced in the text by italics: a new term is placed in italics when it is first introduced and defined. We try to make definitions of new terms stand out from surrounding text without being too formal about it.

Further Reading

The first two references are the language manuals for Ada and Anna. These will be needed if the reader gets serious about programming in Ada with Anna specifications. Reading either of the books by John Barnes or Grady Booch is a good way to get the basics of Ada. Norman Cohen's book is a larger, more comprehensive text-book. There is also a more recent Ada book by Doug Bryan and Geoff Mendal. The *"Fake It"* paper by Parnas and Clements is a very readable classic on the advantages of using formal specifications, even if they are not really used according to the most rational software development methodology. The paper by Brooks describes the kinds of problems in software production that we need to overcome by new, more scientific programming processes.

1. Jean Ichbiah et al. *The Programming Language Ada*, Reference Manual. ANSI/MIL–STD–1815A, Lecture Notes in Computer Science No. 155, Springer-Verlag, 1983.
2. D. C. Luckham, F. W. von Henke, B. Krieg-Brückner, O. Owe. *Anna, A Language for Annotating Ada Programs*. Reference Manual, Lecture Notes in Computer Science No. 260, Springer-Verlag, 1987.
3. J. G. P. Barnes. *Programming in Ada*. Addison-Wesley, 1982.
4. G. Booch. *Software Engineering with Ada*. Benjamin Cummings, 1986.
5. N. Cohen. *Ada as a Second Language*. McGraw Hill, 1984.
6. D. Bryan and G. Mendal. *Exploring Ada*. Vol 1, Prentice Hall, 1989.
7. D. L. Parnas and P. C. Clements. The Rational Design Process: How and Why to Fake It. IEEE Transactions on Software Engineering, Vol. SE–12, No. 2, February 1986, pp. 251–257.
8. F. P. Brooks, Jr. No Silver Bullet — Essence and Accidents of Software Engineering. Information Processing '86, H. J. Kugler (ed.), Elsevier Science Publishers B. V. (North Holland) 1986.

1

Simple Annotations

Topics:

- *annotations: scopes, observable states, and satisfiability;*
- *Anna expressions, quantifiers, modifiers;*
- *statement annotations;*
- *object annotations;*
- *subprogram annotations;*
- *type and subtype annotations;*
- *elaboration of annotations;*
- *proper annotations.*

This chapter describes *simple annotations*. These are annotations that apply to the Pascal-like subset of Ada: statement, object, subprogram, type and subtype annotations. We must first explain these annotations and how they are related, before going on to annotations of exceptions, packages, and generic units.

To begin, let us first recall a basic concept in Ada, the *object*. Objects are those elements of a program that can contain (or have) values. In Ada, objects include not only those elements declared explicitly by object declarations, but also other elements such as formal parameters of subprograms and task entries, loop parameters, and so on. Objects that are not declared by an explicit **constant** declaration are called *variables*.

In Anna, objects are the most basic entity. The behavior of a program is described by annotating values of objects. As we shall see later, Anna contains some new kinds of objects that are not objects in Ada. A non-generic package, for example, is treated as an object in Anna, and it has a new type called a package state type. So, bear in mind that Anna concepts apply to a wider class of objects that includes all the Ada objects and some new ones.

1.1 Annotations

An *Anna program* is an Ada program with annotations. *Annotations* are Boolean expressions placed at certain positions in the program. They are always stated as comments in the Ada program. Since annotations are formal expressions, they are called *formal comments* and are preceded by a special formal comment symbol, --|. The Ada program is often referred to as the *underlying program*.

An annotation may refer to any entity of the Ada program that is visible at the position of the annotation. This includes, for example, the variables of the Ada program. The variables of the Ada program that occur in an annotation are called *program variables* to distinguish them from other kinds of variables in the annotation.

In most cases, annotations restrict the values of program variables; such annotations are also called *constraints*, an analogy with the standard kinds of Ada constraints, which can be viewed as simple kinds of constraining annotations.

In some cases, however, the meaning of an annotation is more complex. An annotation may act as a "go-between" for two parts of a program, such as a package specification and a package body. In this case an annotation can play a dual role. It can be a guarantee (or promise) to users of a package that subprograms in the package possess a stated property; simultaneously, it is a constraint on the package body to implement the property.

The meaning of an annotation is determined by its boolean expression (i. e., *what* it says) together with its position in the program (i. e., *where* it is said). The meaning of some annotations is also indicated by Anna keywords.[1] Keywords in annotations may either bind an annotation to a declaration or statement in the Ada program or restrict its application in some way.

Here is a short list of examples of most kinds of simple annotations. The reader can probably guess what they mean, even before we explain them.

1. *A type annotation:*

```
        type SQUARE is record
              X, Y : NATURAL;
        end record;
   --|     where S : SQUARE => S.X = S.Y;
```

2. *A result annotation of a function:*

```
        function SQUARE(X : NATURAL) return NATURAL;
   --|     where return X*X;
```

Examples of simple annotations

[1] Also called reserved words.

3. *An* **out** *annotation of a procedure:*

```
    procedure QUICKSORT (A : in out VECTOR);
--|    where out (A = SORTED (in A));
```

4. *An object annotation:*

```
    S : SQUARE;
--| S.X > 0 and S.Y > 0;
```

5. *An assertion:*

```
    S := (3, 3);
--| SQUARE (S.X) = 9;
```

Examples of simple annotations

1.2 The Meaning of Simple Annotations

The meaning of simple annotations depends on two concepts, *scope* and *observable computation state*. So we must first describe these concepts.

- **Scope of an annotation**

An annotation is always placed within an Anna program in the position of either an Ada declaration or an Ada statement. Its position determines the region of the Anna program where the annotation applies — i. e., its *scope*. In general, when an annotation is in a declaration position, its scope is the same as the scope of an Ada declaration at the same position. When it is the position of a statement, its scope is defined by Anna rules.

The following example compares the scopes of an Ada range constraint and an annotation that is placed in the same sequence of declarations as the range constraint.

Example: Scopes of declarative annotations.

```
    declare
        X : INTEGER range 1 .. 10;        -- Ada range constraint.
--|     X mod 2 = 0;             -- Annotation constraining X to be even.
-- (A)                           The annotation applies from (A) to (B).
        ...
```

```
    begin
       ...
-- (B)                          Both constraints cease to apply here.
    end;
```

In the example, program variable X is declared with a range constraint. Throughout the scope of its Ada declaration it must have values between 1 and 10. The annotation immediately follows the declaration of X. In fact it is the first thing in the scope of X. The scope of the annotation includes everything following it, i. e., from the position marked (A) to the end of the declarative region (B). The scopes of the declaration of X and the annotation cover the same region of the underlying Ada program.[2] So the values of X are constrained to be the even integers between 1 and 10.

Actually, the Ada range constraint in

```
    declare
        X : INTEGER range 1 .. 10;
```

is interchangeable with an Anna declarative constraint

```
    declare
        X : INTEGER;
--|     1 ≤ X ≤ 10;
```

The only difference is what happens when X strays out of its range. The first case propagates Ada CONSTRAINT_ERROR, whereas the second case propagates ANNA_ERROR.[3]

• Visibility

The elements of an Anna program that are visible to an annotation are those that would be visible in an Ada declaration or statement at the same position. Certain additional predefined Anna entities are also visible in annotations. An annotation may contain the types, variables, constants, functions, exceptions, and attributes that are visible to it.

• Observable states

A *computation state* is a mapping from program variables to values of the corresponding types. A state associates a unique value with each program variable at a particular point in a computation. A computation of a program is a sequence of states.

An *observable state* is a state that results from the normal termination of

[2] The annotation is not part of the underlying program.

[3] Anna predefined exceptions are discussed in Chapter 3.

an Ada simple statement or the normal termination of the elaboration of an Ada declaration. That is, a single simple statement or a single declaration is taken as the finest computational step at which a state can be observed.

Note that our definition of observable state implies that a computation state may change not only when statements are executed, but also when declarations are elaborated. In Ada, elaboration is the process by which a declaration is made ready for computation. This process itself can involve computation. For example, the expression E in the declaration

```
X : INTEGER := E;
```

is evaluated when the declaration is elaborated. This could have a side effect that changes the computation state.

When a scope is executed, a particular sequence of observable computation states results. Not all states that may occur during that computation are observable from that scope. For example, an assignment is a simple statement in Ada. Therefore any states that occur during execution of an assignment statement X := E; are not observable; only the states before and after the assignment are observable. Similarly, a procedure call is a simple statement in Ada. Therefore, in a scope that executes a procedure call P (X), the states before the call begins and after the call terminates are observable. Intermediate states during the call P (X) are not observable. The inner workings of P can only be observed in the scope of the procedure body.

One more thing: observable states, as we define them here, result when steps in computing a program terminate normally. A step terminates *abnormally* by propagating an exception. We will deal with the states resulting from abnormal termination later.

• States constrained by an annotation

Most annotations apply to all observable states in their scope. In the previous example in the beginning of Section 1.2, the annotation X **mod** 2 = 0 applies to all observable states in its scope. So it constrains X in each state after elaboration of each declaration following position (A), and in each state after execution of a simple statement in the block. Some annotations, as we shall see, apply to only some of the observable states in their scope.

• Satisfying an annotation

A state satisfies an annotation if, when each program variable in the annotation is replaced by the value associated with it in that state, the resulting boolean expression has the value TRUE. If the boolean expression has the value FALSE or is undefined (does not have a value), then the annotation is not satisfied by that state.

A program satisfies an annotation if the annotation is satisfied by all observable states that it constrains that can ever arise in any computation.

• Consistency between annotations and programs

An annotation is consistent with the underlying program if it is satisfied by the program.

For an annotation to be consistent with an underlying program, it must be defined and true on every computation state that it constrains. We will discuss methods of checking and proving consistency later.

If we look back at the list of annotations at the end of the previous section, we can do a little guesswork, anticipating the rest of this chapter. Let us try to guess what the annotations mean from descriptions of their scopes and what they apply to.

1. The type annotation applies to all variables of the type. It has the same scope as the type declaration. It must be satisfied in every state in which the value of a SQUARE object can be observed. So, the annotation means that all values of the type SQUARE must be records with X and Y components that are equal.
2. The result annotation of function SQUARE has the same scope as the declaration of the function. It applies to values returned by the function. It constrains all those states in which calls to SQUARE terminate normally. So, every time we observe the result of a call to the function SQUARE, that value will be the square of the input parameter. The annotation constrains function SQUARE to return values that are squares of natural numbers.
3. The subprogram annotation of QUICKSORT has the same scope as the declaration of QUICKSORT. It applies to parameter A. It constrains states after calls to QUICKSORT terminate, so its effect is to constrain the value of parameter A in those states. So, the annotation constrains procedure QUICKSORT as follows: calls to QUICKSORT must return **out** parameter values that are equal to SORTED versions of the **in** values of actual parameters. Here SORTED must be a function that is visible at the QUICKSORT declaration so that it can be used in the annotation.
4. The object annotation of S has the same scope as S. It constrains all observable states in its scope. So, the annotation places another constraint on S in addition to the type constraint on type SQUARE. Variable S must not only be a square record (previous type annotation), but it must have nonzero components.
5. The assertion is placed in a statement position. It applies to program variable S and it constrains observable computation states that occur at its position. Therefore, it must be satisfied each time the assignment to S is executed and terminates normally. Actually, if function

SQUARE satisfies its annotation, then we can prove logically that the assertion is always satisfied.

- **Terminology**

In discussing an annotation A, say, we will sometimes write informally, "A is true" meaning that A is defined in some state and has the boolean value TRUE; similarly for "A is false".

1.3 Anna Expressions

To make it easier to formalize properties of programs, Anna provides more powerful expressions than Ada. Anna extends Ada expressions by adding some new names and operators that are not in Ada.

The new names are Anna attributes and include states of packages and of collections (attributes of access types). These new attributes will be described in later chapters.

The new logical operators are implication ($\rightarrow$ or −>) and equivalence ($\leftrightarrow$ or <−>). They have the usual meaning and relationship with the other logical operators, **and**, **or**, and **not**. They have the lowest precedence of operators in boolean expressions. There are also the following operators, which are described in later sections of this chapter: the quantifiers **for all** and **exist**; the modifiers **in** and **out**, which associate annotations with specific computation states in their scope; and the Anna membership test **isin** and its negation, **not isin**.

Anna expressions include conditional expressions. The syntax of a conditional expression is similar to an Ada **if** statement except that there must always be an **else** part.

Example: A conditional expression.

if X $\neq$ 0 **then** Y/X **else** Y **end if**
-- *This conditional expression is always defined. It is* Y/X *if* X *is nonzero and*
-- *is* Y *otherwise.*

Note that terminating semicolons are not used in conditional expressions (here the analogy with Ada conditional statements breaks down). The whole "**if** ... **end if**" is an *expression* as opposed to a statement.

A conditional expression selects one of a number of expressions for evaluation, depending on the truth value of one or more conditions. The conditions are evaluated in sequence in the same way as an **if** statement in Ada, and the expression corresponding to the first true condition is selected. The expressions defining the possible values of a conditional expression must all have the same type, which is the type of the conditional expression.

Example: Legal and illegal conditional expressions.

```
        A : BOOLEAN;
        B, C : INTEGER;
        D : CHARACTER;
    function F(X : INTEGER; Y : CHARACTER)
        return BOOLEAN is ...
        ...

--|     F (if A then B else C end if, D);                   -- Legal
--|     F (if A then B else D end if, D);                   -- Illegal
```

The requirement that an **else** part must always be included encourages writing expressions that will always have a value even when the **if** condition and all of the succeeding (optional) **elsif** conditions are false. This is important because annotations that are undefined for some values of their program variables are, by definition, inconsistent with the underlying program.

Conditional expressions are also useful when we want to specify values by simple recursive annotations. For example:

Example: A recursive annotation.

```
--| F(N) = if N = 0 then 1 else N*F(N-1) end if;
--    A conditional expression is used to specify that F satisfies
--    a recursive equation.
```

1.4 Quantified Expressions

Boolean-valued expressions include the two quantifiers **for all** (universal quantifier) and **exist** (existential quantifier) and their negations. The mathematical symbols ∀ and ∃ are also allowed. Quantifiers permit us to formalize properties of sets of values.

A quantified expression consists of a quantifier declaration followed by the compound symbol => and then the boolean expression that is being quantified. This boolean expression is called the *scope* of the quantifier.

Examples: Quantified expressions and their meaning.

```
--| for all X : T => P(X);
--    For each value X in T, the property P(X) is true or else is not
--    defined.
--    Informally read: "for all X in T, when P(X) is defined then P
--    is true".
```

```
--| exist X : T => P(X);
--   There exists a value X in T such that P(X) is true.
--   Informally read: "there is an X in T such that P is true."
```

In these expressions, the quantifier declaration declares a *logical variable* X and a subtype or range T of values of X. T is called the *domain* of values of the quantifier. X is a *name* for any arbitrary value in T. T can be any type.

Variables declared by quantifiers are called logical variables to distinguish them from program variables. They allow us to build annotations that express properties about "some" or "all" of the values of a type. Although we call them "variables" because of tradition in Predicate Logic, they are names denoting unspecified values. The rules of logical inference of Predicate Logic may be applied to logical variables, thus allowing us to construct other annotations that are logical consequences of a given annotation. But they cannot be treated like program variables — e. g., a logical variable cannot be assigned a value because it *is* a value (unspecified).

The scope and visibility rules for logical variables are as follows. The expression P following the symbol => must be a boolean expression. P may also contain quantifiers, which means that quantifiers may be nested. The scope of X extends from its declaration to the end of the quantified expression — i. e., the scope of the quantifier. It is visible only after the symbol => but it hides any outer use of the same name throughout its scope.

Note that the symbol => associates a quantifier declaration with a boolean expression that is the scope of the quantifier. It is not a logical operator, and it must not be confused with logical implication $\rightarrow$.

In the examples above, the meaning of the quantified expressions is described in the comments. A **for all** quantifier expresses that a property P is true for all the values in the subtype or range, T, for which it is defined. The quantifier declaration declares the set of values; the boolean-valued condition, P, defines the property that must be true for every value for which it is defined.

An **exist** quantifier expresses that there is some value in the subtype or range T that satisfies the property P. Consequently, it is possible for a program variable of type T to have property P.

• Universal quantifiers

Examples: *Universally quantified expressions.*

```
     type DAY is (SUN, MON, TUE, WED, THU, FRI, SAT);

--     Every value of DAY has length 3.
--|     for all X : DAY => DAY'IMAGE(X)'LENGTH = 3;
```

```
--      Names of weekdays do not contain 'S'.
--|      for all X : DAY range MON .. FRI =>
--|           for all I : 1 .. DAY'WIDTH =>
                                        DAY'IMAGE(X)(I) /= 'S';

--|      for all X : DAY range MON .. FRI;
--|          I : 1 .. DAY'WIDTH => DAY'IMAGE(X)(I) /= 'S';
```

Commentary

In the examples, the informal comments about DAY are formalized as the universally-quantified expressions. The second example contains two universal quantifiers, an outer one declaring X and an inner one declaring I, nested within the scope of the outer one. So we can read it intuitively as saying, for all weekdays X, it is true that all components I of X are not equal to 'S'.

The second version of this example shows a shorthand that omits repetition of two or more adjacent universal quantifiers or two or more adjacent existential quantifiers. The two quantifiers are combined into one **for all** by a syntax simplification rule called *vanishing of quantifiers*.

• Vanishing of quantifiers

The Anna syntax permits nested quantifiers of the same kind that are not separated by an opposite quantifier to be represented by a single quantifier. For example,

```
for all X : T => (for all Y : S => ... )
```

may be written in a shorter form as

```
for all X : T; Y : S => ... .
```

When vanishing is used, the scope and visibility rules for logical variables are the rules that apply to the unvanished form of the quantified expressions, e. g., X is visible in the declaration of Y and could appear in S as a range parameter.

• Existential quantifiers

Examples: Existentially quantified expressions.

```
-- 1. There is a least natural number.
--| exist X : NATURAL; for all Y : NATURAL => Y ≥ X;
```

```
-- Type declarations.
   type PERSON;
   type PERSON_NAME is access PERSON;
   type CAR is
      record
         NUMBER : INTEGER;
         OWNER  : PERSON_NAME;
      end record;
   type PERSON is
      record
         NAME : STRING(1 .. 5);
            ...
      end record;

-- 2. There is a car whose owner is SMITH.
--| exist X : CAR => X.OWNER.NAME = "SMITH";
```

Commentary

The existentially quantified expressions formalize the informal comments above them. In the first example, quantification is over the natural numbers. It is true because 0 is an example of a member of the set of natural numbers that can be substituted for X so that the expression is true.

In the second example, quantification is over a nondiscrete type, CAR (a record type), which is given as an example in the Ada reference manual (Ada83, 3.8.1). X is a logical variable. The example expresses that there is a value in the set of all possible values of type CAR that has a particular component. It is true because the set of all possible CAR values includes a CAR record aggregate with an OWNER component that designates a PERSON record with the NAME component "SMITH".

The second example is a quantified annotation of the domain of values of type CAR. It says nothing about the particular values that might exist in some DATA constructed during a computation. To express that a car owned by SMITH has actually shown up, we write

```
exist X : CAR =>
                X ∈ DATA and X.OWNER.NAME = "SMITH";
```

Here DATA is a program variable containing CAR components, and "ϵ" stands for some kind of membership test.

• Definedness of quantified expressions

There is one important difference between quantifiers in Anna and in classical logic. In Anna, quantifiers may be applied to expressions that may not be defined for all values in the quantifier domain. For example, **for all** allows P to be undefined for some values in T. Thus,

```
for all X : T => P(X);
```

has the value TRUE if for every value of X in T, whenever P(X) is defined then it has the value TRUE. In particular, it will be true if P is undefined for all values in T. If, on the other hand, there is a value V in T such that P(V) is false, then the quantified expression has the value FALSE.

In the case of an existential quantifier, if P is undefined for all values of T, then the expression

```
exist X : T => P(X);
```

is false.

The reason for this treatment of undefinedness is to make quantified expressions easier to write when they involve program variables that may be uninitialized or computations that may not terminate.

```
for all X : INTEGER => X*X ≥ X;
```

is true in Anna even though X∗X may propagate an exception on some values of X. We are not forced to write,

```
for all X : INTEGER => X not isin S → X*X ≥ X;
```

where S is some set of values that has to vary with each Ada compiler to ensure that computing X∗X does not raise NUMERIC_ERROR. The exceptional situations can be specified more conveniently by other kinds of annotations. However,

```
for all X : INTEGER => X*X > X;
```

is false.

- **A fully quantified expression is always defined**

A quantified expression is called *fully quantified* if it has no program variables — all of its variables are logical variables.

A fully quantified expression always has a value (TRUE or FALSE) even when the property being quantified is undefined. This is a consequence of our definitions of quantifiers.

- **Quantification over nondiscrete types**

Quantification over nondiscrete types is permitted. This is useful in specifications where the order of enumeration of values of a type is not important. The previous example of an existential quantifier over type CAR is one such example. Here is another one.

Example: Quantification over a nondiscrete type.

```
        subtype INDEX is POSITIVE;

        type SQUARE_MATRIX is array(INDEX, INDEX) of INTEGER;

        type UPPER_PAIR is record
                                    FIRST, SECOND : INDEX;
                                end record;
--|        where X : UPPER_PAIR => X.FIRST < X.SECOND;
--         Type annotations are described in Section 1.10.

        A : SQUARE_MATRIX(N, N);

--         An annotation constraining A: A must be a lower
--         triangular matrix.
--| for all X : UPPER_PAIR => A(X.FIRST, X.SECOND) = 0;
```

Commentary

In this example type UPPER_PAIR is the set of pairs of positive integers such that the first member of a pair is less than the second member. This is not a discrete type, and its pairs of integers are not ordered a priori — Ada does not define an order of enumeration.

The annotation on A formalizes the comment about A. Essentially, it says that *all* the components of A above the diagonal must be 0. A universal quantifier over type UPPER_PAIR is used. An explicit order of enumeration of the components of A is not given. During specification such details ought to be ignored.

Note that, because the universally quantified annotation is not affected by undefined values in the scope of the quantifier, we do not need to express restrictions on X so that A(X.FIRST, X.SECOND) does not raise an Ada constraint error. That would clutter the annotation and make it confusing.

Here is another example where use of quantifiers allows us to suppress details that are irrelevant at a particular level in specifications.

Example: Existential annotation of a function.

```
        function LOOKAHEAD(S : STRING) return BOOLEAN;
--|        where
--|            return (exist I : S'FIRST .. S'LAST-2 =>
--|                                          S(I .. I+2) = "KEY");
```

Commentary

This example gets a little ahead of our exposition since it uses a result annotation to specify a function — but never mind, it is easy to explain.

The result annotation following **return** constrains the values returned by LOOKAHEAD. S, the parameter of function LOOKAHEAD, is a program variable in this annotation. The boolean values returned by LOOKAHEAD are specified by an existentially quantified boolean condition on its parameter.

The annotation expresses: if "KEY" occurs in string S, then LOOKAHEAD is true, otherwise it is false. The details of how LOOKAHEAD looks for "KEY" are irrelevant in the specification. Those details are "hidden" in the existential quantifier.[4]

• Rule of negation of quantifiers

Quantifiers in Anna may be applied to boolean expressions that are not defined for all values in the quantifier domain. Even so, the rules of negation that relate quantifiers in classical logic are still true for Anna quantifiers. For example,

```
for all X : T => P(X)
```

is equivalent to

```
not exist X : T => not P(X).
```

However, in general we must be careful about applying other rules of classical logic in using quantifiers in annotations. Most classical rules only hold for annotations if all expressions have defined values. It is possible for a program to satisfy

```
for all X : T => P(X) and Q(X)
```

but violate

```
for all X : T => P(X) and
for all X : T => Q(X)
```

unless P(X) and Q(X) are defined for all values of X. For example, if P(V) is false and Q(V) undefined for the same value V, then the first annotation could be true but the second one must be false.

---

[4]The quantifier hides some interesting papers on efficient implementations.

1.5 Modifiers

Certain computation states of a scope are particularly important. These are the *initial state*, when execution of the scope begins, and the *final state*, when the scope is terminated — or, more accurately, when it is exited *normally*, which is by any means (end of block or body, return statement, etc.) other than propagation of an exception.

It is helpful to be able to refer to these states explicitly in annotations. For example, an annotation will often compare values of variables during a computation with their values in the initial or final states. For this purpose, Anna provides the two modifiers, **in** and **out**.

The modifier **in** indicates values of expressions in an initial state. If we want to indicate the initial value of a variable X we modify it by **in**, thus: **in** X. For a more complex expression that is not a simple name, E, say, the parenthesized expression is modified: **in** (E). The parentheses are used to avoid ambiguity as to which expression is modified (see examples below). Initial names and initial expressions — i. e., names and expressions modified by **in** — are expressions in Anna.

Examples: **in** *modifiers in annotations.*

1. *Annotation of variables* X *and* Y:

```
--| X ** 2 + Y ** 2 ≤ in X ** 2 + in Y ** 2;

--      Throughout the scope of the annotation, the sum of the
--      squares of X and Y is bounded by the sum of
--      the squares of their initial values.
```

2. *Annotations of array variable* A *and index variable* I:

```
--| in A(I) = 0;        means     --| (in A)(I) = 0;

--      The component of the initial value of A selected at the
--      current value of I is 0.

--| in (A(I) = 0);      means     --| (in A)(in I) = 0;

--      The component of the initial value of A selected at the
--      current value of initial value of SEARCH requires
--      ORDERED (in A (in I .. in J))
--      to be satisfied whenever it is called.
```

There is a simple rule about the modifier **in**İf exceptions are not propagated during the evaluation of **in** (E), then **in** can be distributed inwards until it modifies only simple names. That is, we can write **in** (E) equivalently as E′, which is obtained by deleting the outermost **in** and modifying every program variable of E by **in**.

The modifier **out** indicates values of expressions in a final state.

Examples: **out** *modifiers in annotations.*

```
--|   out (X = in X+1);
--    The final value of X is obtained by incrementing
--    its initial value.

--|   out (ORDERED(A(in I .. in J));
--    The output value of A is ordered in the array slice bounded
--    by the input values of I and J.
```

If **out** appears anywhere in an annotation, then that annotation refers only to a final state of its scope. This is simply because some of its constituent values are not known until a final state is reached. This poses a language design problem in the syntax of annotations as to whether or not to treat **out** as an expression constructor like **in**. The problem is this. While the meaning of an annotation such as

```
out X < in Y+1;
```

is intuitively clear, the same meaning can be expressed in a confusing way by

```
in (out X < Y+1);
```

if **out** is an expression constructor. This looks like an **in** annotation, but it is in fact an **out** annotation. To avoid this kind of confusing annotation, **out** may only appear at the beginning of an annotation — called an **out** annotation. Thus, to specify a "less than" relationship between the final value of X and the initial value of Y, we must write

```
out (X < in Y + 1);
```

When **in** (E) appears in an **out** annotation, it means that the input value of E is to be used in evaluating the annotation in the final state of the scope. The general rule is that **out in** (E) means **in** (E).

The use of modifiers in each kind of annotation is given later in the descriptions of those annotations.

1.6 Assertions

The simplest kind of statement annotation is an *assertion*. This is a boolean-valued expression placed in the position of a statement. If it follows a statement then its scope is that statement; if it has the first position in a sequence of statements, or if it comes immediately after a label, then its scope is empty. It constrains the values of program variables in exactly one computation state — the state in which it would be executed if it were a statement.

Example: An assertion.

```
    X := A;
    Y := X+1;                    -- the value of Y is A+1.
--| Y = A+1;
```

Commentary

In the example, the scope of the assertion is the assignment, Y := X+1. The annotation constrains the value of program variable Y in the state following execution of the assignment. Note that the assertion formalizes the informal comment. It could have been placed in that same position — i. e., on the same line as the assignment. The traditional practice of placing a comment on the same line as the statement can be applied to an assertion — i. e., it must be positioned immediately after the statement that it annotates, but not necessarily on a new line.

Example: An assertion annotating the final state of a compound statement.

```
    if A (X) > A (X+1) then
        Y := A (X);                            -- Position A.
        A (X) := A (X+1);                      -- Position B.
        A (X+1) := Y;                          -- Position C.
    end if;
--| A (X) <= A (X+1);
```

Commentary

The example shows an assertion annotating an **if** statement. The **if** statement is its scope and the annotation constrains the values of A (X) and A (X+1) following execution; it must be true whether or not the **then** part of the statement is executed. Consider the other possible positions of the annotation in this example. It could be placed in position C so as to annotate the third assignment; it would be true but less effective there, since it would not apply when the **if** test is false. In position B it would also be a true annotation of the second assignment but not useful since a stronger condition, A (X) = A (X+1), is true. In position A, it would annotate the first assignment; it would always be false and inconsistent with the Ada text.

Assertions have the same meaning as if they were modified by **out**. That is, they apply to the final state in the computation of the statement in their scope, if that computation terminates normally. Even so, it is often useful to use **out** to modify an assertion for clarity, especially when it indicates a relation between values of program variables *before* and *after* execution of a compound statement.

• Lists of assertions

An assertion may be a list of boolean expressions. Each expression in the list is an assertion annotating the statement.

A list of assertions following a statement,

```
      S;
--|   A, B, C;                                  -- A list of assertions.
```

is equivalent to a single assertion that is the conjunction of the list,

```
      S;
--|   A and B and C;                            -- An equivalent assertion.
```

Example: A list of assertions.

```
      if A(X) > A(X+1) then
          Y := A(X);
          A(X) := A(X+1);
          A(X+1) := Y;
      end if;
--|   out (A(X) ≤ in A(X+1)),
--|   out (for all I : INDEX_RANGE =>
--|                        I /= X and I /= X+1 → A(I) = in A(I));
```

Commentary

Successive annotations of the same statement are written in a convenient form as a list. Here, the first annotation relates the *before* and *after* values of the array A at the relevant component positions; the second annotation is an example of a "frame" specification, expressing that A(X) and A(X+1) are the only components affected.

Here is another example of an assertion written as a list of annotations.

Example: Assertions checking correct initialization of an array.

```
      type SQUARE_MATRIX is array (1 .. N, 1 .. N) of REAL;
      A : SQUARE_MATRIX;
          ...
      for I in 1 .. N loop
          A(I) := (1 .. I-1 => 0, others => 1);
      end loop;
```

```
--| A'DEFINED,
--    Test that all components of A are initialized.
--| TRIANGULAR(A);
--    A call to a function testing if A is triangular.
```

Commentary

The annotations use the Anna 'DEFINED attribute and assume that function TRIANGULAR has already been defined. Often, assertions like triangularity must be true at a particular point, but may not be preserved by subsequent computation, and therefore must be expressed locally.

1.7 Compound Statement Annotations

A statement may also be annotated by a *compound statement annotation*. This is an annotation (or list of annotations) that precedes the statement and is bound to it by the reserved word **with**. Its scope is the statement following it. The scope may be either a simple statement or a compound statement. In other words, a "compound statement annotation" can be used to annotate any kind of statement, even though its intended use is for compound statements.

Example: *A compound statement annotation.*

```
     ...          -- Preceding statements.
--| with
--| A;            -- Compound statement annotation.
    S;            -- Statement in the scope of A.
...               -- Following statements.
```

Suppose that the scope is a compound statement S. Computations of S must satisfy the compound statement annotation A at all observable states. This means that a compound statement annotation A must be satisfied initially before S begins execution, and then after each of the simple statements of S is executed. The annotation is called an *invariant* of the compound statement.

Example: *A compound statement annotation of a binary search loop.*

```
-- These annotations constrain execution of the loop body.
--| with
--|     in LOW ≤ LOW and HIGH ≤ in HIGH,
--|     LOW ≤ MID+1 and MID ≤ HIGH,
--|     ORDERED(A(in LOW .. in HIGH)),
--|     IN_INTERVAL(X, A (in LOW .. in HIGH))
--|                       → IN_INTERVAL(X, A(LOW .. HIGH));
```

```
while LOW < HIGH loop
    MID := (LOW+HIGH)/ 2;
    if X > A(MID) then
        LOW := MID+1;
    else
        HIGH := MID;
    end if;
end loop;
```

Commentary

In this example, the annotations in the list must remain true throughout execution of the loop body. They are *invariants* of the loop. They impose constraints on program variables LOW, MID, HIGH, A, and X. For example, LOW, MID, and HIGH must remain bounded by the initial values of LOW and HIGH. Array A must remain ORDERED in the slice A (**in** LOW .. **in** HIGH). And if X is a component of A in this initial slice, then it is always a component of the slice of A between any observable pair of values of LOW and HIGH. These constraints express properties of the way the loop works and are important in checking or proving that the loop achieves its goal.

One of the important points of this example is that the compound statement annotation is an *invariant* of the statement. An *invariant* is a constraint that must be satisfied at *all observable states* during the execution of the statement. This example constrains every assignment to LOW, MID and HIGH during the execution of the loop. It is therefore much stronger than an assertion made after the loop terminates. Another invariant of the binary search loop is,

A = **in** A.

Note that these compound statement annotations express only invariant properties and do not say what the goal of the loop is, — e.g., eventually, A (MID) = X or A (HIGH) = X. Obviously, the goal is not an invariant.

Compound statement annotations can be modified by **in** and **out**. When they are modified, they constrain the input and output states of a statement. Modified compound statement annotations are equivalent to assertions, but are written before the statement to which they apply instead of after it.

The two main uses of compound statement annotations are (1) to express invariants of sections of code such as blocks and loops within procedure bodies, and (2) to specify sections of code prior to implementation — e.g., planning a procedure body.

Invariants, as illustrated above for a binary search loop, are useful in constraining pointer manipulations so that there are no side effects. We shall see examples of this in Chapter 7.

In the second use, a compound statement annotation is written prior to implementation of a section of a program. It expresses a plan of what the code will do. It may be part of a logical proof that the program will be correct if that section of code is correct. Often a combination of modified and unmodified annotations will appear in a compound statement annotation used as a specification. Their use for specification is the main reason why compound statement annotations are placed *before* the statement.

Example: A specification to be implemented by a compound statement.

```
--| with
--|    ORDERED (in A (in LOW .. in HIGH)),    -- Input condition.
--|    A = in A, X = in X,                    -- Loop invariants.
--|    out (IN_INTERVAL (in X, in A (in LOW .. in HIGH)) →
--|              A (MID) = in X);                  -- Loop goal.

       ...                         -- Loop construct to be completed.
```

Commentary

We assume that variables LOW, MID, HIGH are previously declared and visible here. The first annotation is simply an input condition. The second and third annotations specify an invariant property of the loop; the values of array A and key X must remain unchanged throughout the loop. The last annotation specifies the goal of the loop. The loop may now be constructed to meet these specifications. The standard binary "divide and conquer" method used in the previous example is one possible implementation. Other loops also satisfy the specifications — e.g., a simple linear search. The specifications, even though they are strong in the sense that they are invariants, do not determine the computational method by which they are implemented. The use of compound statement annotations for specification should be compared with the use of subprogram annotations (coming soon).

1.8 Object Annotations

A *declarative object annotation* is a boolean expression placed in a list of declarations — in the same position as a declaration. Its scope is the declarative region associated with its position. It constrains its program variables throughout its scope, which means that it must be satisfied at every observable state in its scope. This includes the states after elaborations of declarations in its scope.

Declarative object annotations allow restrictions on values of program variables to be factored out and expressed at the earliest possible position in the program. They should normally be positioned immediately following the declarations of the program variables.

Example: An object annotation.

```
      declare
         A : array (1 .. 10) of INTEGER;

--  Components of A are less than function F of their index position.
--|        for all J : A'RANGE => A(J) < F(J);
           ...
--  Any side effect on A caused by elaborating a declaration must satisfy the
--  annotation.

      begin
         ...
--       Computations in this block must satisfy the annotation on A.
         ...
      end;
```

Commentary

The informal comment about A is formalized by the object annotation, which constrains A by placing a bound on its components. It must be true throughout its scope, which is from the annotation to the end of the block.

Sometimes a variable may obey different constraints in different regions of the program. These can usually be expressed conveniently by object annotations placed in different blocks. Continuing the example above, suppose that in some inner region the components of A are ordered.

If this region can be contained within a local block, a second annotation of A can be given that applies within that block.

Example: Successive object annotations of the same variable.

```
      declare
         A : array (1 .. 10) of INTEGER;

--  Components of A are less than function F of their index position.

--|        for all J : A'RANGE => A(J) < F(J);
      begin
         ...          -- Here the upper bound annotation constrains A.
```

```
        declare
--|         for all I, J : A'RANGE => (I <= J →
--|                                             A(I) <= A(J));
        begin
              ...  -- Here both upper bound and ordering annotations
                   -- of A must be true.
        end;
        ...      -- Here only the upper bound annotation constrains A.

    end;
```

Commentary

This example illustrates the use of successive object annotations to specify different properties of a global object within different scopes. To do this, the operations on the object must be organized so that the object takes on the different properties in sections that can be represented as local blocks.

Note that object annotations are cumulative — i. e., at any position, an object is constrained by *all* the annotations referring to it that have that position in their scope. The cumulative constraint applying to an object at a particular state includes constraints on any Ada renamings of the object. That is, an object designated by more than one name is constrained by all the constraints referring to all its names.

Example: *Constraints using different names of an object.*

```
    X : T := A;
--| C(X);          -- The value of X is constrained by C.
    Y : T renames X;
--| D(Y);          -- The value of X, which is also the value of Y, is
                   -- constrained by C and D.
```

Annotations may apply to more than one program variable. Let us clarify what this implies in the case of object constraints that generally apply to many states. Suppose C (X, Y) is an annotation of two program variables X and Y. This means that those pairs of values of X and Y that occur together at the same state during the computation are constrained to satisfy C — not every value of X and every value of Y.

Example: *Consistency of an object annotation of two program variables.*

```
    declare
        U, V : INTEGER := 1;
--|     U <= V; -- U is always bounded by V; the annotation
                -- is initially true.
```

```
begin
    U := 0;              -- Annotation is true: U = 0 and V = 1.
    V := 5;              -- Annotation is true: U = 0 and V = 5.
    U := 4;              -- Annotation is true: U = 4 and V = 5.
end;
```

An object constraint can be applied to a constant, in which case the value of the initializing expression is constrained.

1.9 Subprogram Annotations

Subprogram annotations are annotations of the specification part of a subprogram. They are placed immediately after a subprogram name and its formal parameter list, and are preceded by **where**. They may be used to annotate either a subprogram declaration or the specification part of a subprogram body. In the case of a body, the subprogram annotations are placed before the reserved word **is**.

Examples: Position of subprogram annotations.

1. *A subprogram declaration.*

```
    procedure P(X : T1; Y : in out T2; Z : out T3);
--|     where
--|         ...;                      -- List of subprogram annotations.
```

2. *A subprogram body.*

```
    procedure P(X : T1; Y : in out T2; Z : out T3)
--|     where
--|         ...;                      -- List of subprogram annotations.
    is
        ...                  -- Subprogram body with other
    end P;                   -- annotations.
```

An Ada subprogram declaration is an interface specification defining the legal syntax for calling the subprogram. It contains some minimal information about the subprogram, such as the types or subtypes of parameters and their modes, but nothing else. Anna extends the syntax of subprogram declarations so that annotations may be associated with a declaration in order to define properties of a subprogram independently of any implementation. Subprogram annotations define the values of parameters and the results of functions. They may also define situations when the subprogram will propagate an exception — these latter kinds of annotation will be described in Chapter 3. It may be necessary to give several annotations in order to specify a subprogram adequately. Therefore Anna permits a list of annotations of a subprogram.

In this section we describe three kinds of annotations of subprogram declarations:

1. *In* annotations — used to specify the values required of **in** and **in out** parameters when a call is made,
2. *Out* annotations — used to specify the values of **in out** and **out** parameters of procedures when a call terminates normally,
3. *Result* annotations — used to specify the value returned by a function when a call terminates normally.

• In and Out annotations of subprograms

An *in* annotation is a boolean expression in which all parameters of the subprogram that appear in it are modified by **in**. This means that the annotation refers to the values of those parameters in the state when the subprogram is called — the initial state. It must be true of the initial state whenever the subprogram is called.

An *out* annotation is a boolean expression of the subprogram parameters prefixed by the modifier **out**. It refers to the values of parameters in the final state when a call to the subprogram terminates normally. It must be true of any normal final state. An *out* annotation does not apply to states when a call is terminated abnormally by exception propagation — we emphasize this by using the phrase, *normal termination*.

Example: Input and output annotations of a procedure.

```
      procedure P(X : T1; Y : in out T2; Z : out T3);
--|      where
--|         in (A(X, Y)),
--|         out (B(X, in Y, Y, Z));
```

Commentary

In this example A(X, Y) is an input condition constraining the values of X and Y whenever P is called. The **in** modifier can be distributed inwards so that it modifies the individual parameters — sometimes this adds emphasis and makes the annotation more readable.

out (B(X, **in** Y, Y, Z)) is an output condition constraining the values of Y and Z whenever a call to P terminates normally. It expresses a relationship between the **out** values of Y, Z and the **in** values of X, Y. A reference to the **in** value of Y in B is explicitly written as **in** Y because Y is an **in out** mode parameter of P. A reference to Y in an **out** annotation means **out** Y. But we do not have to write **in** X, although we can do so for emphasis, since X is an **in** mode parameter of P — its value cannot change. Two examples of B that express different constraints by either including or omitting an **in** modifier on Y are:

```
out (Z = X + in Y);        out (Z = X + Y);
```

• **Parameter modes**

A subprogram parameter with the Ada mode **in** can only be modified by **in** when it is used in annotations of the subprogram. The **in** modifier is assumed by default if the parameter has mode **in**.

Similarly, a mode **out** parameter is required to have a value, by Ada rules, only upon normal termination of a subprogram call. Therefore, we should expect that it can only appear in *out* annotations. However, some types of **out** mode parameters have Ada attributes that must be defined at input.[5] So what is actually true in Anna is that the value of a mode **out** parameter cannot be modified by **in**. But certain *attributes* of **out** parameters can be constrained at input by *in* annotations — an example is coming.

Parameters of mode **in out** can be modified by either **in** or **out**.

We can use subprogram annotations to specify properties of the output values without defining them completely. This facility for incomplete specification is often useful, as in the next example.

Example: *Specification of a procedure for sorting vectors of integers.*

```
-- ORDERED and PERMUTATION are previously declared virtual functions.

     procedure SORT (V : in out INTEGER_VECTOR);
--|     where
--|        out PERMUTATION (V, in V),
--|        out ORDERED (V);
-- The result is a sorted version of the input vector.
```

Commentary

The first annotation expresses that the output value of V is a permutation of its input value; the second that its output value is such that its integer components are ordered. Note that the output value of V is not defined explicitly; crucial properties are specified. In general, properties of the final values of parameters of subprograms will be specified as a relationship with their initial values, as in the first annotation here. In such cases both of the modifiers **in** and **out** will be used in the annotation; **in** will modify parameters and expressions to designate their input values, whereas a single **out** will modify the entire annotation

[5]We sometimes refer to these kinds of complexities of Ada as "Ada-isms".

to refer only to the output state. In formalizing the first annotation, it is tempting to write

```
PERMUTATION (out V, in V).
```

Anna does not allow this for reasons given in Section 1.5 even though, in this very simple case, the tempting form is perhaps a little more natural.

Example: *Annotation of a procedure declaration* – READ_LINE.

```
with TEXT_IO; use TEXT_IO;
procedure READ_LINE (FILE : in FILE_TYPE;
                     LINE : out STRING;
                     LAST : out NATURAL);
--|   where
--|      IS_OPEN (in FILE),
--|      in (LINE'LENGTH) >= 80,
--|      out (LINE(LAST) = ASCII.LF),
--|      out (for all I : LINE'RANGE =>
--|                   I <= LAST → LINE (I)'DEFINED);
```

Commentary

We suppose READ_LINE is implemented using TEXT_IO.

The first annotation specifies that parameter FILE must be open on all calls to READ_LINE. The requirement can be checked by calling function IS_OPEN of the Ada TEXT_IO package. Note also that, since FILE is an **in** mode parameter, it cannot be changed; the modifier **in** would be assumed by default in the annotation — it has been used here for emphasis.

The second annotation constrains the actual parameter passed for LINE to have a length of at least 80 characters on input. Even though LINE is an **out** mode parameter, its length is determined by the caller of READ_LINE. This annotation constrains only the LENGTH attribute and not the value of LINE.

The third annotation is an **out** annotation on the values of LINE and LAST. It specifies that a line feed always occurs in the LAST position.

The fourth annotation uses an Anna attribute, the 'DEFINED attribute, which we discuss later on. Its use here expresses that all components of LINE up to LAST are defined on output — i. e., a character occupies each position of the string up to LAST. The actual value of LINE is not specified, but that is to be expected in specifying an input routine like READ_LINE. The ability to make incomplete specifications is necessary.

From the point of view of the caller, **in** and **out** annotations express different kinds of information. An **in** annotation is a constraint placed on the caller. It must be met by the actual parameters being passed in any call to the procedure or function. An **out** annotation is a promise to the caller. When the call is completed, the caller may assume that the final values will satisfy each **out** annotation.

From the point of view of the subprogram body, the roles of **in** and **out** annotations are the reverse of their roles for the caller. An **in** annotation expresses a property of the **in** values of parameters that may be assumed on entering the body. An **out** annotation is a constraint on the **out** values that must be satisfied by the body upon normal termination. In the example of READ_LINE above, the procedure body may assume that FILE is open and that LINE has at least 80 characters; it must then output a value for LINE that contains a line feed and a defined character in each position up to the line feed.

• Result annotations of functions

Result annotations specify the values returned by functions when calls complete normally. There are two forms, result expressions and result annotations. Actual values may be specified by giving a **return** expression. Thus, example (1) below defines the values returned by F as an expression E (X).

Examples: Annotations of functions.

1. *A return expression.*

```
    function F (X : T) return T';
--|     where return E (X);
```

2. *A return annotation.*

```
    function F (X : T) return T';
--|     where return Y : T' => C (X, Y);
--  Read: "return a Y such that C (X, Y)."
```

Alternatively, a property that any returned value must satisfy can be specified; in the latter form (Example 2), the result annotation need not specify a unique value.

In example (2) of a result annotation, Y is a logical variable. Its scope extends from its declaration to the end of the annotation. The result of F is specified to be any value Y that satisfies C (X, Y).

Examples: Result annotations of functions.

```
    function SQUARE (N : INTEGER) return INTEGER;
--|     where return N*N;
```

```
      function SQUARE_ROOT (N : NATURAL) return NATURAL;
--|     where
--|        N ≥ 0,
--|        return S : NATURAL => S ** 2 ≤ N < (S+1) ** 2;
--    Read "return S natural such that ... "

      function FACTORIAL (N : NATURAL) return POSITIVE;
--|     where return
--|        (if N = 0 then 1 else N*FACTORIAL (N−1) end if);
```

Commentary

The first example gives a result expression defining the value returned by each call. The second gives a boolean condition (actually, two conditions in a short notation permitted by Anna) that any returned value must satisfy. S is a logical variable ranging over type NATURAL; its scope extends from its declaration to the end of the annotation. SQUARE_ROOT may return any value S satisfying the annotation. In this case, there is a unique solution. Note also the **in** annotation of the second example. Since function parameters always have mode **in**, annotations of functions like this one are always **in** annotations.[6] The third example of a result annotation is a conditional expression that defines FACTORIAL recursively. The name FACTORIAL is visible after the end of the Ada specification (Ada rules), which means that it is visible in its annotations.

A result annotation is a promise to the caller. Also, it is a constraint on the function body to be satisfied when the body terminates normally. For example, if we provide a body for FACTORIAL, say one that computes iteratively, it will be constrained by the recursively defined result annotation (above).

1.9.1 OUT VALUES OF PROCEDURE PARAMETERS *

Quite often, we need to write expressions that refer to the **out** values of parameters of procedure calls. This gets us into a messy detail of finding a decent notation. Consider the procedure,

```
      procedure READ_LINE (FILE : in FILE_TYPE;
                           LINE : out STRING);
```

Suppose that a call on a particular file F always yields a LINE in which the first character is a dollar sign. How can we express this fact as an assertion? Perhaps we would like to write

[6]Actually, this **in** annotation is implied by the type NATURAL.

```
FIRST_CHARACTER (READ_LINE (F)) = '$'
```

but unfortunately we can't because READ_LINE is not a function of a file returning a line. It is a procedure and cannot be used in expressions.

Ada provides notation for many properties of things by means of attributes, such as the E'COUNT attribute that gives the length of the queue of calls to an entry E. Similarly, the **out** value of a parameter of a procedure call can be viewed as an attribute of the call.

Anna provides a new attribute of procedures, the 'OUT attribute, for use in annotations. Every procedure, say,

```
procedure P (X : in T1; Y : in out T2; Z : out T3);
```

has an Anna attribute that is a virtual function P'OUT and that behaves as if it were declared as

```
--: function P'OUT (X : in T1; Y : in T2; Z : in T3 := A)
--: return R;
```

Parameters of P having mode **in out** or **out** are mode **in** parameters of attribute P'OUT. The **in** values of those parameters of P'OUT that correspond to **out** parameters of P, such as Z, do not affect the value of P'OUT; their only purpose is to resolve Ada overloadings.

P'OUT returns a record containing the **out** values of the **in out** and **out** parameters resulting from a call to P. The type R can be viewed as having a record declaration whose component types are the types of the **in out** and **out** parameters of P

```
type R is
    record
        Y : T2;
        Z : T3;
    end record;
```

although, strictly speaking, this view does not satisfy Ada record rules since the constraints on the components vary from call to call.

In Anna, the **out** values of parameters Y and Z resulting from a call, P (A, B, C) can be referenced by selection on the result of the attribute

```
P'OUT (A, B, C).Y        and        P'OUT (A, B, C).Z.
```

Revisiting our assertion about READ_LINE, we can express "a call with file F as parameter always yields a LINE with "$" as the first character" by

```
READ_LINE'OUT (F, S).LINE
        (READ_LINE'OUT (F, S).LINE'FIRST) = '$'.          (1)
```

The call, READ_LINE'OUT (F, S) returns a record with a single component: the **out** value of the actual parameter S that results from the call to the procedure READ_LINE (F, S) — not to be confused with the dummy **in** value of S in the call to the attribute. ". LINE" selects this component, which is a string. The index selects its first character.

As we can see, this notation can get a bit long-winded. But once we have it, we can introduce shorter notation, e. g.,

```
    function FIRST_CHARACTER (S : STRING)
    return CHARACTER;
--|     where return S (S'FIRST);
```

Assertion (1) can be rewritten as

```
    FIRST_CHARACTER (READ_LINE'OUT (F, S) . LINE) = '$'.
```

1.9.2 Conformance of subprogram annotations *

Ada allows a subprogram declaration to be given separately from the subprogram body. This separation allows a similar separation of package specifications and bodies, and it permits mutually recursive subprograms.

Whenever a subprogram declaration and body are given separately, Ada requires the specification parts to *conform* [Ada83, 6.3.1]. This means that they can vary in some minor ways but have to be essentially the same.

Following Ada, annotations may be given separately for a subprogram declaration and then later on for the specification part of the body. The two sets of annotations must conform in the Ada sense, except in one case. When the subprogram specification is in a package declaration and the body is in the package body, the two sets of subprogram annotations must be logically consistent, but they do not have to conform.[7]

1.10 Type Annotations

In Ada, a type characterizes the set of values that objects of the type may have and the set of operations that may be performed on them. A subtype defines a subset of the values of a type that satisfy a constraint. Unfortunately, the kinds of constraints that can be expressed in Ada subtypes are limited. In many programs the restrictions that are actually assumed on values of variables are not fully expressed by the subtype declarations.

Anna type annotations permit the more powerful class of Anna boolean expressions to be used to define subsets of values of an Ada type. This

[7] See Chapter 9.

means, for example, that the class of subsets of a scalar type definable using annotations is much richer. And, going beyond the Ada facilities altogether, annotations may define constraints that relate various components of a composite type.

A type annotation is an annotation of a type or subtype declaration. It consists of a boolean expression bound to the immediately preceding type or subtype declaration by the keyword **where**.

Example: *Syntax of type annotations.*

```
      subtype S is T;
--|      where X : S => C(X);
```

In the example, X is a logical variable, whose type is the base type T. The annotation may be read intuitively as saying

> "where S contains those values X of type T that satisfy constraint C".

The annotation defines a subset of the values of T. It has the same scope as the subtype declaration. Therefore, any object of the subtype S must have only values of type T that satisfy the constraint C. The underlying Ada program will be consistent with the subtype annotation if the value V of any object of type S at every observable state satisfies C (V).

There are some restrictions to prevent the most obvious circularities in type annotations:

1. The type name, S, cannot occur in constraint C.

2. All type names in C must be the names of types that have complete Ada declarations prior to the declaration of S.

Example: *A noncontiguous subset of integer values.*

```
      subtype SMALL_EVEN_INTEGER is INTEGER range 1 .. 100;
--|      where X : SMALL_EVEN_INTEGER => X mod 2 = 0;
```

Commentary

Here the Ada range constraint defines a contiguous interval of small values — typically the kind of subset an Ada range constraint can define. The annotation picks out the noncontiguous subset of even values. The two constraints together have the effect of defining the intersection of two subsets of the integers.

Example: The subset of letters in the type character.

```
      subtype LETTERS is CHARACTER;
--|      where S : LETTERS =>
--|         S isin CHARACTER range 'A' .. 'Z' or
--|         S isin CHARACTER range 'a' .. 'z';
```

Commentary

The annotation constrains LETTERS to be a union of two subranges of the Ada standard type CHARACTER. We will explain **isin** later. It is similar to the Ada membership test, **in**, but Anna requires **isin** to be used in annotations.

• Annotations of composite types

Example: An annotation relating components of a record.

```
      type INTERVAL is
         record
            LEFT_POINT, RIGHT_POINT : REAL;
         end record;
--|      where X : INTERVAL =>
--|                              X.LEFT_POINT ≤ X.RIGHT_POINT;
```

Commentary

The set of values of the INTERVAL type is restricted to those pairs of reals in which the left point is not "to the right" of the right point. This annotation constrains intervals so that their components satisfy a relationship that is intuitively implied by their names. Consistency with the underlying program can be checked at runtime or verified by proof methods.

It is not possible to define a subtype in Ada with this domain of values. The intuitive property encoded in the names is not checked by Ada runtime checking, and may be a source of errors. Typically, programs using type INTERVAL may assume that input values of intervals have this property, without checking for it, and may also be required to generate intervals satisfying it. The annotation, together with checking or proof of annotations, will ensure that such intuitive assumptions do not lead to errors.

Constraints relating components of composite types can be arbitrarily complex. There is no general way to express such subtypes in Ada, although it is sometimes possible to use variant records to define unions of subtypes. Type DATE below can be defined using variant records (the reader should try this), but it will not be as clear and readable as the annotated type:

```
      type DATE is
         record
            DAY : INTEGER range 1 .. 31;
            MONTH : MONTH_NAME;
            YEAR : INTEGER range 1 .. 4000;
         end record;
--|      where X : DATE => X.MONTH = "FEBRUARY" →
--|                                             X.DAY ≤ 29;
```

The annotation can be made more accurate so that it expresses the old song, "30 days hath September, ..." (hint: define a function that maps months to maximum dates).

A type denoting the set of values of DOSSIER as annotated below cannot be defined in Ada because of the complex functional relationship between the components.

```
      type DOSSIER is
         record
            REAL_NAME, CODE_NAME : STRING(1 .. N);
               ...
         end record;
--|      where X : DOSSIER =>
--|                  X.CODE_NAME = ENCRYPT(X.REAL_NAME);
--    Assume ENCRYPT is a previously specified function.
```

• Updating composite types

Now the question arises: how do we update values of a composite type when the components are related by a constraint? Any variable of the type must have a value satisfying the constraint at any observable state. The usual component-wise assignment will often temporarily violate the constraint, until the update is completed.

There are some simple methods of getting around this problem. We can assign complete aggregates that satisfy the constraint. If this is too inefficient, we can define an updating function. This must be defined on the base type so that its body is outside the scope of the subtype constraint. Calls to an updating function are simple statements, so they are checked after updates — the actual updating operations executed by the call are not subject to the subtype constraint. However, this requires a subprogram call, and again may be regarded as inefficient.

Example: An update function for a composite type annotation.

```
      type BASE_TYPE is ...;

      function UPDATE(X : BASE_TYPE; A : COMPONENT_LIST)
```

```
        return BASE_TYPE;
--|        where return V : BASE_TYPE => C(V);
        is
           ...                                         -- Body of UPDATE.
        end UPDATE:

        subtype T is BASE_TYPE;
--|        where X : T => C(X);

        U : T;                                  -- Values of U must satisfy C.
           ...

        U := UPDATE(U, B);
```

Commentary

The intermediate values of U during execution of the call to UPDATE are not observable in the scope of the subtype declaration of T. Only the final value, when the updating is completed, is subject to the check C(U). This solution is viable for some kinds of composite type constraints.

A final solution to the updating problem is to exclude "updating regions" from the annotation checking. Anna provides a way to do this by using a modified type annotation associated with a package. Composite type annotations are most advantageously used to specify the hidden structure of private types. Since the package body has complete control over the updating of variables of a private type, the annotation checking can be restricted to entering and exiting the package operations. This is discussed in Chapter 8.

- **Successive subtypes**

A type or subtype declaration may have only one type annotation. To strengthen the constraint on a subtype requires a new subtype. Subtypes may be defined successively, each one being declared as a subtype of the previous one. Suppose T is the base type, S1 is a subtype of T, and S2 is a subtype of S1. Values of S2 must satisfy the constraints on S1 and on S2.

Example: *Successive subtype annotations.*

```
        subtype S is T;
--|        where X : S => C(X);

        subtype U is S;
--|        where X : U => D(X);

           X : U := A;                  -- A must satisfy C(A) and D(A).
```

1.10.1 Anna membership test

The Ada membership test **in** is evaluated without regard for Anna type annotations, which are merely comments as far as Ada is concerned. Therefore it may yield the value TRUE in cases where the Anna constraint is FALSE. For example, within the scope of type INTERVAL the Ada test

```
(3.0, 2.0) in INTERVAL,
```

has the value TRUE. The Anna type annotation requires $3.0 \leq 2.0$, which is FALSE.

If a membership test is used in an annotation, it should be consistent with any (sub)type annotation. Obviously, it has to be different from the Ada test. Therefore, Anna introduces a new membership test, **isin**, which is evaluated in conjunction with type annotations. For example, if we have a type annotation

```
    type T is ... ;
--|     where X : T => C(X);
```

then

```
(X isin T) = ((X in T) and then C(X)).
```

Thus, (3.0, 2.0) **isin** INTERVAL = FALSE.

The negation of the Anna membership test is **not isin**.

• Remark

The choice of notation **isin** for the Anna membership test is not entirely pleasing. Previously we had considered **is in** and the negation **is not in**. However, this choice causes a syntax ambiguity with the Ada case statement.

1.11 Elaboration of Annotations *

The concept of *elaboration* is used to explain the meaning of Ada declarations when they contain parameters whose values are defined at runtime. Elaboration can be thought of as a little "precomputation" that happens before the main computation whenever a scope is entered. Parameters of a declaration are evaluated and the declaration is converted to a state in which it can be used. For example, expressions defining the bounds of a range constraint in a subtype declaration are evaluated when the declaration is elaborated. The resulting constraint, using the values of the expressions at that time as bounds, is applied in the computation.

Annotations are capable of expressing any Ada constraint, and in order to do so, they may also contain parameters whose values are not known until the scope of the annotation is entered at runtime. Elaboration therefore also applies to annotations.

We describe briefly *when* annotations are elaborated and *what* happens.

Elaboration rules

- **An assertion or compound statement annotation** is elaborated each time control reaches its position in a sequence of statements. All expressions that are modified by **in** are replaced by their values.
- **An object annotation** in a sequence of Ada declarations is elaborated at the same time as the declarations. All expressions that are modified by **in** are replaced by their values.
- **A subprogram annotation** is elaborated at each call to the subprogram. All expressions that are modified by **in** are replaced by their values.
- **A type annotation** is elaborated whenever the type or subtype declaration to which it applies is elaborated. All program variables in the annotation are replaced by their values at that point. So program variables in type annotations are treated as **in** parameters of the annotation.

Examples: *Elaboration of annotations.*

1. **Before elaboration**:

```
-- X is bounded by the square of the initial value of Y.
     X : T;     --| X <= in Y * in Y;

-- All SQUARES must fit inside a circle with radius R.
     type SQUARE is record
                        X, Y : REAL;
                    end record;
--|       where S : SQUARE => S.X = S.Y and
--|                             S.X*S.X <= PI*R*R;
```

2. **After elaboration**:

```
--   If the value of Y is 3 when the declaration of X is elaborated:
     X : T;     --| X <= 9;

-- If the value of R is 2 when the declaration of SQUARE is elaborated:
     type SQUARE is record
                        X, Y : REAL;
                    end record;
--|       where S : SQUARE => S.X = S.Y and
--|                               S.X*S.X <= 4*PI;
```

Commentary

Elaboration takes place each time control enters the declarative region containing these examples. In the case of the declaration of X, **in** Y is replaced by its value, 3, at that point. The values of X are then constrained to be at most 9. If Y was not modified by **in** no replacement would be made, and all pairs of values of X and Y would be constrained.

In the case of the type declaration of SQUARE, program variable R is replaced by its value at the time of elaboration.

Generally speaking, elaboration of annotations resembles the Ada rules for elaborating similar kinds of constraints. However, in the case of type annotations, there is a difference. Elaboration of type annotations is analogous to the first step in the Ada elaboration of a type constraint. But the second Ada step, checking compatibility of the current constraint with any already imposed constraint, is *not* carried out in Anna. The Ada concept of compatibility is meaningful only for simple kinds of type constraints, such as Ada range constraints. In general, successive type (or subtype) annotations may well be incompatible in the sense that a later one does not logically imply an earlier one — e.g., X **in range** 1 .. 100 and X **mod** 2 = 0 might be considered incompatible, but together they define a subset of small even integers. If two successive type annotations are logically inconsistent, they specify an empty subtype.

1.12 Proper Annotations

Two important restrictions on annotations are required by Anna language rules.

First, annotations must not change the values of variables in the underlying Ada program. To do this would be a gross violation of the philosophy that an annotation is an explanation of a program and not part of the program itself. A meaningful definition of consistency between annotations and underlying program would be impossible.

Secondly, the meaning of an annotation should depend only on the variables explicitly mentioned in the annotation, and not on any hidden implicit parameters. If implicit variables are allowed, it is not clear from the text of the annotation which program variables it constrains.

Therefore expressions in annotations must satisfy two general restrictions:[8]

1. **No Side Effects.**
   Evaluation of expressions in an annotation must not change the value of any program variable.

[8]We discuss how these restrictions are enforced later.

2. **No Implicit Global Variables.**
   The values of expressions in an annotation must not depend on program variables that are not explicit variables of the annotation.

Annotations satisfying these two conditions are called *proper annotations*. All Anna annotations must be proper.

Example: *An illegal annotation with a side effect.*

```
X : INTEGER := 10;

function EQUAL(U, V : INTEGER) return BOOLEAN is
begin
    X := U;
    return U = V;
end EQUAL;

declare
    Z : INTEGER; --| EQUAL(Z, X);                      -- Illegal.
    ...
```

Commentary

The annotation has a side effect and is therefore illegal. If it was legal it would always be true since it changes X to the current value of Z. Clearly, the intention of such an annotation is to specify that the underlying program maintains equality of Z and X. Instead it changes the program.

Example: *Legal and illegal use of global variables in annotations.*

```
X : INTEGER := 10;

function CHECK return INTEGER is
begin return X;
end CHECK;

function LESS(A, B : INTEGER) return BOOLEAN is
begin return A < B;
end LESS;

declare
    Z : INTEGER := 0;  --| Z < CHECK;                  -- Illegal.
    W : INTEGER := 11; --| LESS(W, X);                 -- Legal.
begin X := 5;
      Z := 9;
      W := 9;
end;
```

Commentary

The object constraint on Z is illegal because its expression, CHECK, depends on global variable X, which is not a variable in the annotation. If it was legal, the annotation could be interpreted as meaning that Z must be less than a constant CHECK which is computed when Z is elaborated. One might guess that it was intended to mean Z < 10, in which case the assignment of 9 to Z would satisfy it. In fact, the runtime check at the assignment to Z would require a value less than 5. On the other hand, W is constrained explicitly to be less than X. This constraint refers explicitly to all the program variables involved. The assignment to W does not satisfy LESS(W, X).

Both of these restrictions on expressions in annotations can be enforced by *strong checks*. A strong check is a sufficient condition but not a necessary condition for a particular restriction. If an annotation passes the check then it satisfies the restriction, but some annotations may satisfy the restriction and still not pass the check. Strong checks must be used for these kinds of restrictions because the classical undecidability theorems of mathematical logic tell us that tests that are both necessary and sufficient do not exist. Generally, strong checks can be automated along similar lines to type checking in compilers.

We assume in all of our discussions that annotations are proper, unless explicitly stated otherwise.

Further Reading

Details about classical logic (i. e., the Propositional and Predicate Logic), which we have often referred to in this chapter, can be found in the books below. The first part of David Gries' book contains an elementary introduction to logic. Zohar Manna and Richard Waldinger also give a readable basic introduction to logic. The book by Herb Enderton is a mathematical approach to first order logic and the classical metatheorems about it.

1. D. Gries. *The Science of Programming*. Texts and Monographs in Computer Science, Springer-Verlag, New York, 1981.
2. Z. Manna and R. Waldinger. *The Logical Basis for Computer Programming*. Vol. 1, Addison-Wesley, 1985.
3. H. B. Enderton. *A Mathematical Introduction to Logic*. Academic Press, New York, 1972.

2

Using Simple Annotations

Topics:

- *three activities: formalization, specification, and annotation;*
- *virtual Ada text;*
- *using statement annotations: assertions, assertions in loops, inductive assertions, and invariants;*
- *checking and proving assertions;*
- *using object annotations: maximizing the scope of an annotation;*
- *specifying subprograms;*
- *organizing annotation concepts, theory packages.*

This chapter describes some applications of simple annotations in the programming process. It deals with general questions concerning their use, e. g., what can they be used for, which kind of annotation to choose, how to reduce the number of annotations, when to write annotations, and so on. The examples given here are intended to be suggestive, and are not exhaustive or complete in any sense.

We begin by discussing some of the general activities involved in using annotations. Then we describe the *virtual Ada text* feature of Anna and how it is used to define executable annotations. The rest of the chapter is devoted to examples. Chapter 7 deals with the applications of simple annotations to programs that manipulate arrays, records and access types. It can be read immediately after this chapter.

In presenting example applications of simple annotations, the lower level annotations such as assertions are discussed before higher level subprogram annotations. This order is adopted because the discussion of higher level annotations leads into new topics such as organization of concepts used in annotations. In practice, however, the various techniques illustrated here will be applied in reverse order. Higher level annotations will be applied in early stages of the programming process such as specification. Then lower level annotations will be applied in later stages such as testing and verification of finished programs.

2.1 Three General Activities

There are three general activities in applying annotations: *formalization*, *specification*, and *annotation*.

• Formalization

A formal specification of a program is constructed by expressing informal, intuitively described properties as annotations. Usually, a property can be formalized as an annotation in many ways. In Anna, annotations are constructed out of expressions. The first step, therefore, is to find an expression or function that "captures" or "expresses" the property as simply as possible. We call this step *formalization*.

informal description	$\Longrightarrow$	Anna formal expression or Anna function declaration

If we do not expect to use a property in many annotations, we may choose to express it formally as an expression. On the other hand, if we expect to use a property often, we should declare a function with a **return** annotation that expresses the property. Then we can use the property in different annotations simply by calling the function.

Examples: *Formalization.*

1. **Informal description**:

```
--   The first component of the array Q_SPACE has a least priority.
```

Formalization:

```
--|      for all I : INTEGER range Q_SPACE'RANGE =>
--|                                Q_SPACE(1).P ≤ Q_SPACE(I).P;
```

2. **Informal description**:

```
--   A maximal element of a VECTOR.
```

Formalization:

```
--:      function MAX(X : COMPONENT; V : VECTOR)
--:      return BOOLEAN;
--|          where return exist I : V'RANGE =>
--|             X = V(I) and for all J : V'RANGE => V(J) ≤ X;
```

Suppose we have chosen an expression or function that formalizes a property. The next step is to choose the best kind of annotation using that expression or function to formalize how the property relates to the program. The annotation indicates where the property applies in the underlying program.

• **Specification**

Specification is the activity of defining the behavior of a program by annotations prior to implementation. A specification should define *what* the behavior is and omit details about *how* to achieve that behavior. Generally, many different implementations will satisfy the same specification.

Specification using Anna usually involves making Ada declarations with annotations. It is done prior to writing Ada bodies for the program units that are declared.

Here are typical specification activities — we have already mentioned them — and the kinds of simple annotations that are used in them:

1. **Formalization of concepts.**
   Concepts to be used in specifying a program are formalized before construction of the program starts. Function declarations with result annotations are used.
2. **Specification of programs prior to implementation.**
   Types, subprograms, and packages are declared with annotations. The annotations are used to define the behavior of subprograms and packages before bodies are implemented. Details of particular methods of implementation are omitted. In this activity, subprogram, type, and subtype annotations are the most appropriate simple annotations. Later on we shall see this as the principal role of package annotations.
3. **Goal-oriented programming.**
   Annotations are used to plan bodies of subprograms and packages before Ada code is written. The idea is to plan the implementation as a succession of small steps towards achieving a global specification that is already given. The goal of each step in the plan is specified by an annotation. In planning a body for a subprogram, object annotations and assertions will be most often used.

• **Annotation**

Annotation is the activity of choosing annotations as the underlying program is being implemented or after it is finished — i. e., at the same time as Ada bodies for subprograms and packages are being written, or after they are written.

The kinds of simple annotations used in typical annotation activities are:

1. **Definition of runtime tests.**
   Runtime tests may be intended either for temporary use for debugging or for incorporation permanently into the program. Statement annotations, especially assertions, are the most useful annotations for expressing runtime tests.
2. **Documentation of a completed program.**
   All annotations have the role of providing formal documentation of

the underlying Ada program, once it is completed.

There is some fuzziness as to whether a particular use of annotations is a specification or an annotation activity. Goal-oriented programming, for example, might fall under either heading. And annotations produced during specification will certainly wind up being used as formal documentation in the end. Never mind! This terminology is widely used and serves to indicate roughly which stage of the programming process is being discussed.

2.2 Virtual Text

Virtual text is Ada text placed in comments. It is not part of the underlying Ada program, which is why it is called *virtual* (possessing all the properties but not formally recognized or admitted). In fact, the computation of the underlying program must be entirely independent of, and unaffected by, any virtual Anna text.

Virtual text must obey (with a few exceptions mentioned later) the Ada syntax and semantic rules — particularly the scope and visibility rules — just as though the comment symbols were removed and it was considered part of the underlying Ada program. As a consequence, entities in the underlying Ada program are visible in virtual text, but not conversely.

Virtual types, objects, and subprograms are visible in annotations and in other virtual text.

In Anna programs, virtual text is a second kind of formal comment. Since it is not an annotation, it is always preceded by a different formal comment symbol, --: . Text of the underlying Ada program is often referred to as *actual text* to distinguish it from Anna virtual text.

Examples: *Virtual declarations.*

1. *A virtual type*:

```
--: type HISTORY_SEQUENCE is array (POSITIVE) of VALUE;
```

2. *A virtual subprogram declaration*:

```
--: procedure CATENATE(C : CHARACTER; S : in out STRING);
--|     where out (S = C & (in S));
```

Commentary

In the first example, VALUE must be a type that is visible at this point. It can be an actual or virtual type. Variables of type HISTORY_SEQUENCE must be declared in virtual text since this type is not visible in actual text.

In the second example, CATENATE can only be called from virtual text or annotations — for example it can be called in expressions in an annotation. In any call, the parameter for

C can be any expression that has a character value — it can contain calls to actual and virtual functions. Any parameter for S, however, must be a virtual variable since its value may be changed by the call and virtual text may not affect actual values.

Virtual text has been introduced in Anna for three purposes:

- *To make a clear distinction between actual facilities of an Ada program and additional features introduced for some purpose other than as part of the actual computation.*
  Virtual text may be included for testing, debugging, tracing, and so on. Anna rules for virtual text support this distinction by ensuring that virtual text cannot influence the actual computation.
- *To introduce new Anna attributes.*
  Examples are the 'OUT attribute, the state of a package, and the the collection associated with an access type. These Anna attributes must be clearly separated from the standard Ada attributes. Virtual attributes can only be referred to in annotations and virtual text.
- *To provide a simple programming language notation for naming and parameterizing expressions.*
  Typically, one would like to write, "let F (X) be defined as EXPR (X)". Towards this end, one of the Ada language rules is not enforced on virtual subprograms: a virtual subprogram declaration need not have a corresponding virtual body.

Examples: *Two virtual definitions of equality of shots in target practice.*

```
--: function TIE (SHOT1, SHOT2 : PAIR; T : TARGET)
--: return BOOLEAN;
--|    where return SCORE (SHOT1, T) = SCORE (SHOT2, T);

--: function EQUAL (SHOT1, SHOT2 : PAIR) return BOOLEAN;
--|    where return SHOT1.X ** 2 + SHOT1.Y ** 2 =
--|                              SHOT2.X ** 2 + SHOT2.Y ** 2;
```

Commentary

Here, PAIR is a pair of real coordinates X, Y, and TARGET and SCORE are discussed in Section 0.1. Bodies for TIE and EQUAL do not have to be provided.

The two definitions can be viewed as originating from two different domains of discourse, target practice and plain geometry. Informal descriptions of the same concept will often lead to different formal definitions. We can analyze formal definitions logically, and in this case, prove their equivalence.

2.2.1 FORMALIZING CONCEPTS

The most important use of virtual text is to define concepts used in annotations. Concepts are defined formally by Ada declarations of types and functions. Most often, when a concept is used only in annotations, the defining Ada declaration is virtual.

Usually we start out with concepts that have been used in informal comments, often without any kind of definition. To illustrate the process of formalization, let us start with some informal documentation.

Example: *A stack manager package with informal comments.*

```
      package STACK_MANAGER is

         type STACK is private;

         procedure PUSH(X : in ITEM; S in out STACK);
--       Increase the length of S by one and place X on top.

         procedure POP(Y : out ITEM; S in out STACK);
--       Decrease the length of S by one, remove the top and return it
--       in Y.
      private
         ...

      end STACK_MANAGER;
```

The comments describe the effects of PUSH and POP using concepts "length" and "top". These concepts are not declared in the package, nor anywhere else in the actual program. This is a common practice in documentation of programs. Because we are already familiar with the ideas of stacks, the mnemonics "length" and "top" enable us to understand the comments. But if the names were changed, or if we were not familiar with stacks, they would give us little information.

To express these informal comments as formal annotations, "length" and "top" are declared as virtual functions and used in subprogram annotations for PUSH and POP:

Example: *Virtual declarations in formal specifications.*

```
      package STACK_MANAGER is

         type STACK is private;
--:      function LENGTH(S : STACK) return NATURAL;
--:      function TOP(S : STACK) return ITEM;

         procedure PUSH(X : in ITEM; S : in out STACK);
--|         where out (LENGTH(S) = LENGTH(in S)+1),
--|               out (TOP(S) = X);
```

```
        procedure POP (Y : out ITEM; S in out STACK);
--|        where out (LENGTH (S) = LENGTH (in S) -1),
--|              out (Y = TOP (in S));

    private ...

    end STACK_MANAGER;
```

Now what have we gained? Let us look at some of the advantages of the second specification of STACK_MANAGER over the first one with informal comments.

First of all, we have given precise declarations of the informal concepts. The virtual declarations tell us that "length" and "top" are functions returning values of types NATURAL and ITEM, respectively. This information is now represented formally and is available independently of any meaning implied by the actual names. The fact that the functions are virtual indicates that they are not part of the actual Ada program, and can only be used in annotations or other virtual text. The separation between actual text and text used in annotations is clearly defined.

The annotations describe the effects of PUSH and POP in terms of calls to the virtual functions made before and after those operations. For example,

```
    out (LENGTH (S) = LENGTH (in S) +1)
```

expresses that upon normal termination of a call to PUSH, the length of the final value of stack S is one greater than the length of its initial value — PUSH increases the length of the stack by one. The second specification of PUSH,

```
    out (TOP (S) = X)
```

expresses that X is on top of the stack.

Secondly, we can apply mathematical reasoning to the formal specification, which may enable us to improve the specification. Let us see what happens when we specify properties of the virtual functions.

Virtual Ada text may be annotated in exactly the same way as actual text. For example, a virtual subprogram declaration can be annotated. In the stack manager we could specify a property of LENGTH using a **return** annotation (Chapter 1):

```
--: function LENGTH (S : STACK) return NATURAL;
--|    where return X : NATURAL => (0 <= X <= MAX);
--  Length must return a value between 0 and MAX.
```

Now the concept LENGTH is defined as a function whose values lie between the bounds 0 and MAX. Any other subprogram whose annotations use LENGTH must be consistent with the constraint that the values of

LENGTH lie between 0 and MAX. We can prove that the annotations of PUSH and POP are inconsistent with the **return** annotation of LENGTH. For example, if S = MAX before a call PUSH (X, S), then the **out** annotation of PUSH implies LENGTH(S) = MAX+1 after the call terminates normally.

Consequently, if we annotate LENGTH in this way, the other annotations of STACK_MANAGER must be extended to specify exceptional conditions for PUSH and POP so that the bounds are maintained. For example, we could declare an exception OVERFLOW and extend the specification of PUSH with a propagation annotation:[1]

```
       procedure PUSH (X : in ITEM; S : in out STACK);
--|       where LENGTH (S) = MAX => raise OVERFLOW,
--|           out (LENGTH (S) = LENGTH (in S) +1),
--|           out (TOP (S) = X);
```

Thirdly, the use of virtual declarations in annotations also eliminates some kinds of bad practices that can occur in informal comments. For example, annotations are subject to Ada scope and visibility rules. Therefore any virtual concepts appearing in them must be visible in the specification part of the package. Implementation details of the STACK_MANAGER body cannot be used. This, however, is not true of informal comments. There is no automated checking that informal comments in a specification do not refer to a particular implementation. For example, consider

```
       procedure PUSH (X : in ITEM; S : in out STACK);
--     Increase INDEX by one and place X in SPACE (INDEX).
```

Here, the informal comment implies that the stack should be implemented as an array. This is contrary to the fundamental principle of hiding implementation details in package bodies.

2.2.2 Rules for virtual text *

The presence of virtual text in an Ada program should not result in any difference in the behavior of the program, except possibly that the processor on which the program is running may appear to slow down.

Anna rules for virtual text serve three purposes. First, since virtual text is intended for specification and need not be executable, certain Ada rules are not enforced. Second, when it is executable, virtual text is not permitted to affect the values computed by the underlying program. This second rule supports the construction of executable proper annotations using virtual functions that can be executed.[2] Third, certain Ada declarations are not

[1] Propagation annotations are described in Chapter 3.

[2] See restrictions on annotations in Section 1.12.

allowed as virtual declarations if they result in a name having different meanings in actual and virtual text.

These rules are summarized below (see [Anna87, 11]):

- Virtual text must be legal Ada, with the following exceptions:

  1. It is allowed to contain some additional Anna attributes and operations.
  2. Bodies corresponding to virtual declarations of program units may be omitted.

- Virtual text must not influence the computation of the actual program by changing the value of an actual object or the state of an actual package, or by altering the flow of control of the actual program. Anna therefore places restrictions on virtual text so that any reference to an actual object or package is "read only." Moreover, a virtual exception may not be raised in an actual unit or block unless an inconsistency is indicated.
- Virtual declarations may not hide or overload entities declared in the actual Ada text *if* there is a use of the actual entity in the scope of the virtual declaration. Without this restriction, the same name might have different meanings in the same context, depending on whether it appears in actual or virtual text.

These restrictions can be enforced by strong compile-time checks as discussed at the end of Section 1.12 — i.e., checks that disallow programs violating a rule, but that may also disallow some programs that do not violate the rule.

Example: *Illegal virtual declaration.*

```
     declare
        X : INTEGER := 1;
        ...
        declare
--      Illegal virtual declaration hiding the actual X.
--:         X : INTEGER := 1;
              ...    --  Virtual X is not visible in actual text.

        begin
            X := 2;  --  Assignment to the actual X.
--|         X = 2;   --  A false assertion referring to the virtual
            ...      --  X.
```

The example illustrates the kinds of confusions that can arise if the virtual declaration of X hiding the actual X was allowed.

2.3 Assertions as Tests and Documentation

The most obvious use of an assertion is to constrain a computation state at a particular point in the underlying program. The assertion must be satisfied whenever control reaches that point. It is a specialized and local annotation. Generally, this kind of annotation is added when the underlying text is being written, or afterwards, and is used for testing, debugging, and documentation of local details.

Example: *Use of assertions to test an operation in a priority queue package.*

```
    package body QUEUE is

--      Type and object declarations local to the package body.
        type Q_ITEM is
            record
                D : DATA;
                P : PRIORITY;
            end record;

        Q_SPACE : array (1 .. MAXSIZE) of Q_ITEM;
        LAST : INTEGER range 0 .. MAXSIZE := 0;

--  Insert procedure body within the priority queue package body.
        procedure INSERT (NEW_ITEM : Q_ITEM) is
            I, J : INTEGER;
            TEMP : Q_ITEM;
        begin
            if LAST = MAXSIZE then raise Q_FULL; end if;
            LAST := LAST+1;
            Q_SPACE (LAST) := NEW_ITEM;
-- Restore the heap property of the array by bubbling up the new element as
-- far as possible.
            I := LAST;
            while (I>1) and (Q_SPACE (I) . P < Q_SPACE (I/2) . P)
            loop
                TEMP := Q_SPACE (I);
                J := I/2;
                Q_SPACE (I) := Q_SPACE (J);
                Q_SPACE (J) := TEMP;
                I := J;
            end loop;
```

```
-- Assertion: priorities are ordered by a binary tree organization of Q_SPACE.
--|          for all I : INTEGER range 2 .. LAST =>
--|              Q_SPACE(I/2).P ≤ Q_SPACE(I).P;
        end INSERT;
        ...                  -- Other operations of QUEUE package.

    end QUEUE;
```

Commentary

Procedure INSERT is one of a number of operations of a priority queue package. The example shows the local data of the package body, the procedure body, and a local assertion in the procedure body.

The assertion constrains the output state of the "insertion loop." For each value of I, it requires the priority of component Q_SPACE(I/2) to be lower or equal to the priority of component Q_SPACE(I). The assertion must hold after the reordering loop has completed. It expresses the goal of the loop.

The assertion can be viewed as local documentation. As documentation it expresses the intended outcome of the loop. Other package operations should satisfy similar assertions placed appropriately.

It is also quite natural to view this assertion as defining a runtime test that may be used during testing and debugging of the package to check that the loop is working as intended. Of course, since this assertion involves a quantifier, each runtime test might require a nontrivial amount of computation. So we may be tempted to try proof methods to establish consistency between the assertion and the loop. We will give examples of proofs later. For now we pursue the runtime checking of assertions.

This example raises two subtle questions about the use of assertions:

1. How to choose an assertion.
2. Whether to use an Anna assertion or Ada code to express a test.

We discuss these questions, as illustrated by our QUEUE example, in the next two sections.

2.3.1 Choosing assertions

The first question involves identifying which properties are intended to hold at some important local points in a program. The key to solving this problem is to understand the plan or reasoning behind the program — i.e., why it is correct.

- **Guideline: Choosing assertions.**

  An assertion should express a subgoal achieved locally towards attaining a higher level annotation.

Let us discuss some of the factors involved in choosing the assertion in the QUEUE example. We view this assertion as part of a plan to prove or check that the whole package body is consistent with its annotations. So, first consider a little more of the overall plan for the package body.

There is a higher level property of the data of the QUEUE that has not been expressed in the example: whenever any of the priority queue package operations (e. g., INSERT or REMOVE) terminates, then the local data, Q_SPACE and LAST, must satisfy a constraint:

```
Q_SPACE : array (1 .. MAXSIZE) of Q_ITEM;       -- the queue
LAST : INTEGER range 0 .. MAXSIZE := 0;         -- last element

-- After each operation of QUEUE, Q_SPACE and LAST form a heap:
--   for all I : INTEGER range 2 .. LAST =>                     (1)
--                        Q_SPACE(I/2).P ≤ Q_SPACE(I).P;
```

We have placed the formal constraint in an informal comment because it is not an object constraint that must hold at all observable states. It is typical of the kind of constraint that is placed on data local to a package body, usually for efficiency — called a stability constraint (Chapter 8). It expresses that the components of Q_SPACE from 1 to LAST must be a heap. The constraint need not hold during the execution of a call to INSERT or REMOVE. But it must hold each time a call terminates normally. So, the constraint may be assumed at the start of a call, and must be satisfied when the call terminates. Otherwise the next operation may not work correctly.

The assertion in the body of INSERT is related to achieving this higher level property of the queue data. If we want to prove that the whole package body is correct, we must certainly prove that the data satisfies this constraint when INSERT terminates. Next, let's look at the plan for the body of INSERT:

1. Insert a NEW_ITEM.
2. Restore the heap property.

Restoring the heap property is the goal of the loop. The assertion at the end of the loop expresses this goal. After the loop, INSERT terminates. Therefore, if the assertion is satisfied, then the heap constraint on the package data will be satisfied when INSERT terminates.

Another question involves choosing between assertions that could be made at a particular point.

- **Guideline: Reducing the number of assertions.**

  If one assertion can be proved from other assertions, then the first assertion can be eliminated.[3]

By considering all the properties of the program variables that must be true at some point, we may be led to make a number of assertions at that point. Each assertion is a boolean expression. We should therefore try to see if any of them are logical consequences of the others. Also, in proving that one assertion is a consequence of another, we may assume any other assertions that we have already proved hold at the position.

Consider the QUEUE example again. Another property of the data that must hold whenever a package operation terminates is:

```
--   The data item in the first position has a least priority.
--|  for all I : INTEGER range 1 .. LAST =>                      (2)
--|               Q_SPACE(1).P ≤ Q_SPACE(I).P;
```

This property is assumed to be true whenever operation REMOVE of the package is called — that is, the implementation of REMOVE simply removes the first component of Q_SPACE. Now, REMOVE must return a data item of lowest priority. So REMOVE won't work unless the data satisfies this property when it is called. Therefore property (2) must also be true when INSERT terminates.

We might be tempted to make a second assertion at the end of the INSERT loop to express data constraint (2). However, the chosen assertion (1) logically implies (2). Here's a sketch of a proof:

From (1) we can deduce a sequence of inequalities by substituting values for I over the range 2 .. LAST:

```
Q_SPACE(1).P ≤ Q_SPACE(2).P,
Q_SPACE(1).P ≤ Q_SPACE(3).P,
Q_SPACE(2).P ≤ Q_SPACE(4).P,
Q_SPACE(2).P ≤ Q_SPACE(5).P,
    ...
```

This follows from the Anna meaning of the universal quantifier, but it assumes that the components of Q_SPACE in the range are defined. To meet this assumption, we can require the data to satisfy another constraint, which can be expressed in Anna using the 'DEFINED attribute:

```
Q_SPACE(1 .. LAST)'DEFINED
```

[3]Of course, if a dependent assertion is helpful it does not have to be removed — just as corollaries to a theorem are often stated in mathematics.

- **Attribute** 'DEFINED.

  'DEFINED is an Anna attribute of an object that is true if a scalar object has a value, or if the attribute is true for all components of a composite object.

Next, if we make a second assumption that operations $<$ and $=$ of type PRIORITY are transitive, then we can deduce

$$\begin{aligned} \text{Q\_SPACE}(1).\text{P} &\leq \text{Q\_SPACE}(4).\text{P}, \\ \text{Q\_SPACE}(1).\text{P} &\leq \text{Q\_SPACE}(5).\text{P}, \\ \text{Q\_SPACE}(1).\text{P} &\leq \ldots, \end{aligned}$$

and assertion (2) follows from the Predicate Logic rules for quantifiers — but we do need the definedness assumption mentioned above.

So our proof eliminates a possible second assertion. It also uncovers two more basic assumptions made by the programmer — definedness of the data within an array slice and transitivity of type operations. The transitivity assumption will be satisfied if PRIORITY is a scalar Ada type. This ends our sketch of a proof.

Note that (2) does not imply (1), so we cannot use the second assertion in place of the first one.

- **Guideline: Remembering forgotten assumptions.**

  Trying to prove logical relationships between assertions often uncovers assumptions about the program that we have forgotten to formalize.

In fact, our proof has uncovered that we want the queue components in the range between *1* and LAST to be defined. So, finally, our assertion at the end of the INSERT loop should be:

```
--|   (for all I : INTEGER range 2 .. LAST =>
--|          Q_SPACE(I/2).P <= Q_SPACE(I).P) and
--|          Q_SPACE(1 .. LAST)'DEFINED;
```

The guideline stresses an important practical reason for trying to prove logical relationships between annotations. We have illustrated it only in the case of assertions, so far. It is a theme that will recur in later chapters.

2.3.2 When to use assertions to express tests

The second question involves the choice between using an Anna assertion and inserting actual Ada code to test the underlying program. The latter can be done by a conditional statement that raises an Ada exception.

For example, we could replace the assertion in the QUEUE example by the actual loop:

```
for I in 2 .. LAST loop
    if Q_SPACE(I/2).P > Q_SPACE(I).P then
        raise ERROR;
    end if;
end loop;
```

What should we do — use the Anna assertion or the Ada loop?

In making this choice it is important to emphasize the need to make a clear syntactic distinction between a *termination condition*, which is what an Ada exception signifies, and a *test for inconsistency* between the computation state and the intended behavior, which is what an Anna assertion signifies. Not only is there a syntactic distinction, but also a runtime check for an assertion will not have a side effect on the underlying program unless an inconsistency arises.[4]

- **Guideline: Choosing between assertions and actual code.**

  A runtime test should be expressed as an assertion whenever the test is not part of the normal processing of the underlying program.

If a test can be removed after testing, it should be expressed in Anna and not Ada text. Such a test is to be viewed as distinct from the normal exception raising and handling of the program.

In the QUEUE example, the conditional **raise** statement at the beginning of INSERT is part of the specified behavior of the insert procedure: Q_FULL is propagated if the queue is full. A calling program can take appropriate action to handle the exception. On the other hand, the assertion expresses a constraint that INSERT should always satisfy, and therefore should not test in normal operation. The Anna assertion syntactically distinguishes the constraint from the Ada program. It is intended for documentation as well as for testing.

2.4 Assertions and Timing

One application of assertions is in formalizing real-time behavior of programs. Often the time taken for a computation must lie within given bounds. Current practice is to insert Ada code to check if timing specifications are being met. This checking code is usually removed after testing.

There are several advantages to using assertions to express timing. Constraints on the timing of the underlying program can be expressed clearly in Anna. A clear separation between the underlying code being timed and the assertions is thereby maintained. Various methods of analysis can be

---

[4]Virtual Ada text can be written instead of the assertion, but this is equivalent to compiling the assertion by hand.

applied. We can try to prove that the timing assertions are satisfied, or we can check the assertions at runtime. If we use runtime checking, the Anna restrictions on virtual text and annotations will prevent side effects on the values computed by the underlying program. However, the checks themselves will take time, which must be allowed for in the assertions.[5]

Here is a simple sketch of one way to use assertions to express timing constraints.

Example: Virtual text and assertions expressing timing constraints.

```
--: with CALENDAR;
--: use CALENDAR;
        ...
    declare
          ...
--:       TEST_TIME : TIME := CLOCK;
          ...
    begin
        ...                                  -- Actual code to be timed.
--|       CLOCK-TEST_TIME ≤ 0.1;
--:       TEST_TIME := CLOCK;
        ...
    end;
```

Commentary

CALENDAR is the standard Ada predefined package that provides various types and functions for timing, including function CLOCK for reading the time. CALENDAR is used by the timing assertion and is therefore declared in a virtual context clause. TEST_TIME is a virtual variable used to store CLOCK readings. It is updated to the current time in a virtual assignment after each assertion.

The assertion in the example expresses that not more than 0.1 seconds has elapsed since TEST_TIME was last updated. If it is satisfied, the underlying program between successive assignments to TEST_TIME must execute in no more than 0.1 seconds.

Note that the CALENDAR package changes state independently of the operations performed on it by the using program — the implementation of CALENDAR behaves as if a hidden task is computing in its body — the clock task. So this example is really a multi-tasking program. CLOCK is a function of CALENDAR and therefore may be assumed not to have a side effect on the state of the CALENDAR package. This is important, because if

[5]This is also true if Ada code is inserted to do timing.

CLOCK did have a side effect we could not use it in the timing annotation — a call to it in an annotation would be disallowed by the Anna rules.
Finally, we mention that if CALENDAR is already a compilation unit of the actual program, the virtual context clause is omitted.

This example of expressing timing constraints by assertions is deceptively simple. In practice, it requires a more sophisticated timing environment than CALENDAR — as does the traditional method of inserting code to do the timing. A special Anna predefined library package will be needed — let's call it STOP_WATCH. We touch briefly on some reasons for this.

First, there is a problem of accuracy. Function CLOCK in the standard Ada CALENDAR package ([Ada83], C–5) is not required by the Ada environment definition to provide the accuracy necessary for most tests. So STOP_WATCH would contain a more accurate clock function.

Secondly, CALENDAR does not supply adequate facilities to allow timing constraints to be expressed in a way that makes them easy to check. There is often a problem of proliferation of cases to be checked. Suppose, for example, we want to constrain the period during which the tests are run to be less than one day. It would be tempting to initialize a new variable DAY_ONE and place a global constraint on the block being tested:

```
            ...
--|         with                        -- Compound statement annotation.
--|             DAY(CLOCK) = DAY_ONE;
            begin
                ...                                -- Timing test as before.
            end;
```

Here, DAY is the function of CALENDAR that returns the day of the month corresponding to a given time. The annotation expresses that DAY must not change during the block.

Unfortunately, any constraint involving calls to CALENDAR must be checked (proved) at every observable state in the program because CALENDAR contains tasks — and therefore may change independently of what the program is doing. This would require too many tests (or indeed proofs) to show that CALENDAR.DAY(CLOCK) has not changed value.

The package STOP_WATCH will have to provide facilities to report if our global constraint of "same day testing" is ever violated — then we do not have to test for it. This could be a procedure, SAME_DAY, a call to which puts the package into a special state so that any subsequent call to the CLOCK function will propagate an exception on any other day.

Summary

We are suggesting, in this short section, that annotation methods can be utilized in performance analysis. Checking of real-time performance should be viewed as a particular case of the problem of establishing that a program satisfies formal annotations.

2.5 Assertions in Loops

Assertions may be used to annotate the bodies of loops. At first sight, this appears to be just another application of assertions — to constrain states during the execution of a sequence of statements. But a loop, generally speaking, depends on some instance of a principle of induction to achieve its goals. One of the assertions in a loop should express that induction step. We shall give some simple examples, and also illustrate how we can prove that assertions are satisfied by loops.

To simplify matters in this section, we assume that our loops do not contain **exit** or **goto** statements. So a typical example loop with an assertion A will have this form:

```
     while TEST loop
         S1;
--|      A;
         S2;
     end loop;
```

where S1 and S2 are code segments of the loop body and TEST is the loop test.

- **Guideline: Using virtual variables to construct loop assertions.**

  Virtual variables are often needed to save old values of actual program variables on one iteration of a loop body for use in loop assertions on the next iteration.

Suppose we want to make an assertion that relates values of loop variables on successive executions of the loop body. The problem is that the values of those variables on the previous execution are overwritten when the assertion is reached on the next execution. The guideline suggests using virtual variables to save the previous values.

Example: *Loop assertions for bubble sort.*

```
--   Assume the types:

     subtype INDEX_TYPE is INTEGER;
     type VECTOR is array (INDEX_TYPE range <>)
                                                 of INTEGER;

-- Specification of a block to sort a one-dimensional vector A of integers.

--|  with
--|      out (PERMUTATION(A, in A) and ORDERED(A));
```

```
--   Block implementing a bubble sort on A.
     declare
        TEMP : INTEGER;
--:     IN_A : constant VECTOR := A;
     begin
        for I in reverse A'FIRST .. A'LAST loop
--|        PERMUTATION (A, IN_A) and                    -- (1)
--|           ORDERED (A (I .. A'LAST)) and PARTITIONED (A, I);
           for J in A'FIRST .. I-1 loop
              if A (J) > A (J+1) then
                 TEMP := A (J);
                 A (J) := A (J+1);
                 A (J+1) := TEMP;
              end if;
--|           PERMUTATION (A, IN_A) and                 -- (2)
--|              MAX_IN_SLICE (A (J+1), A (A'FIRST .. J+1));
           end loop;
        end loop;
     end;
```

Commentary

Each loop contains an assertion, which must be satisfied by the computation states whenever control reaches their positions. There is also an output assertion that must be satisfied when the block terminates — the compound statement annotation, which is modified by **out**, specifies the output of the block.

Loop assertions are seldom uniquely determined, and can often be expressed by different (but related) concepts. The concepts used in this example are those in the specification (*permutation* and *ordered*) together with concepts used in explaining the implementation (*partitioning* and *maximum component in a slice of a vector*):

PERMUTATION (A, B)	=	"A is a permutation of B",
ORDERED (A)	=	"components of A are in increasing order",
PARTITIONED (A, I)	=	"every component of A (A'FIRST . . I) is less than or equal to every component of A (I+1 . . A'LAST)",
MAX_IN_SLICE (X, A)	=	"X is greater than or equal to every component of A".

These concepts are defined in textbooks on the theory of sorting.[6] To use them in annotations, they must be defined

[6]See, e. g., Knuth's book listed at the end of this chapter.

by virtual declarations of boolean-valued functions prior to use (see Section 2.1). The virtual function declarations will be specified by boolean expressions (possibly with quantifiers). They may also be implemented by virtual bodies if we want the annotations to be executable (more about this later).

The Ada array slice operation gives us a convenient way to apply these functions to slices of a vector. For example, we can express that X is a maximum among the components A (I), A (I+1), ..., A (J) where I $\leq$ J by,

```
MAX_IN_SLICE(X, A(I .. J)).
```

Assertion (1) for the outer loop requires A to be a permutation of its input value, to be ordered in the slice A (I .. A'LAST), and to be partitioned by I.

Virtual variable IN_A is used to save the initial input value of A for the permutation assertion. Note that using **in** A instead of IN_A in assertion (1), e. g.,

```
PERMUTATION(A, in A)
```

expresses a weaker constraint. IN_A contains the value of A upon entering the block and is constant during execution of the block, whereas **in** A refers to the value of A each time the assertion is evaluated. Because the scope of this assertion is empty, **in** A = A, the PERMUTATION (A, **in** A) is always true.

The inner loop actually changes the array, so the permutation property is an important assertion on each iteration. It is certainly not true during execution of the **if** statement in the loop body. But we must be able to show that it is true when the loop terminates if we want to prove that the permutation assertion on the outer loop is true. Loop assertion (2) states that the permutation property is true each time the inner loop body terminates. The *maximum in a slice* concept is crucial in explaining how the bubble loop works; the ordering and partitioning assertions on the outer loop depend on the inner loop satisfying this assertion. It expresses that on the Jth iteration, A (J+1) is a maximum value of all components in the slice, A (A'FIRST .. J+1).

The loop assertions in the bubble sort example express, intuitively speaking, *what* the loops are doing. We have omitted one or two details that are so obvious that they would not normally be documented or tested, although they are crucial in proving that the program is consistent with the loop assertions.

- **Frame annotations**

A *frame annotation* is an annotation that expresses that an object does not change value.

Typically, a frame annotation is omitted when the program variable concerned is not a parameter of a program operation in the scope being considered. For example, we have neglected to mention in bubble sort that the inner loop does not alter the slice, A (I .. A'LAST). Since the inner loop only changes the Jth and (J+1)th components of A, this should be "obvious," and we want to keep our assertions short.

Frame assertions like this one are examples of those "obvious" properties that are needed in consistency proofs. However, the example illustrates that it may be convenient to omit some of the details needed for proof. One should always be aware of omissions like these. Sometimes it is easy to be fooled into thinking they are satisfied when they are not — e. g., if side effects are possible in the underlying program.

2.5.1 SUCCESSOR FUNCTIONS

A simple path between two assertions A and B is a path through the program that starts at A, ends at B, and has no intermediate occurrence of either A or B. In simple examples, there are a small finite number of simple paths; in complex examples, e.g., where A and B are separated by a loop, there can be lots of simple paths. We will stick to simple examples.

A *successor function* is a function that computes how the value of a program variable changes along the simple paths between two points in a program. In general it may be a function of (i. e., have as parameters) many of the program variables — those related to the variable whose changes in value it computes. Successor functions are important, particularly when we are dealing with loops, because they allow us to construct the history of values of variables during a computation.

Let's look at an example of a successor function. Consider the inner loop of the bubble sort program. This loop is successively swapping elements that are out of order in an array A.

```
        for J in A'FIRST .. I-1 loop
           if A(J) > A(J+1) then
              TEMP := A(J);
              A(J) := A(J+1);
              A(J+1) := TEMP;
           end if;
--|        PERMUTATION(A, IN_A) and                      -- (2)
--|              MAX_IN_SLICE(A(J+1), A(A'FIRST .. J+1));
        end loop;
```

Consider two successive points in a computation at which assertion (2) is evaluated. How does A change between these two points? There are two (simple) control paths that start at (2) and end at (2). On one path, the Jth and (J+1)th components are swapped; on the other path, A is not changed. So a successor function for A will be a function of A and J, and it will be a conditional expression each branch of which defines a value change on one path. Here it is:

```
f (A, J) = if J ≤ I−1 and then A(J) > A(J+1) then
               SWAP (A, J, J+1)
           else
               A
           end if;
```

where SWAP(A, J, J+1) is the function that returns the array value that is A with its Jth and (J+1)th components swapped. (Note that I is treated as a constant in this definition.)

If A has the value a and J has the value j when the computation is at (2), then A will have the value f (a, j) the next time the computation reaches (2).

The simplest method of constructing a successor function, as above, is to use our intuitive understanding of the intended changes to the variables as control moves between the assertions. A reliable method is to use the program operations that are performed on a variable to construct a functional expression that computes the successive changes made to that variable along a path — rules for doing this can be defined formally, but we do not do that here.[7]

2.5.2 Related assertions

First of all, we should always try to write assertions that express what the program should satisfy at particular points. But we can go further and try to make assertions that are relevant to the surrounding assertions and contribute to proving or checking them. So, not only should an assertion formalize what we want to be true at a point, but it should be "relevant" to surrounding assertions too. One notion of relevance is *support* between assertions.

We give a rather simple definition of *support* between assertions. Suppose we have two assertions A (U) and B (U) in a program such that there is a control path from A to B:

```
--|     A (U);   --   If U = Ui here
        S;
--|     B (U);   --   then U = f(Ui) here.
```

and let f be the successor function that computes that values of U at B from the values of U at A when S is executed. Let LEMMAS denote a set

[7]See the book by McGettrick listed at the end of this chapter.

of properties satisfied by the functions used in assertions A and B, and in the code S.

- A *supports* B if for all values of program variable U the following implication is true:

$$\text{A(U) } \mathbf{and} \text{ LEMMAS } \rightarrow \text{ B}(f(\text{U})).$$

If A supports B we know the following. If we can show that the program satisfies A (which means that A is always true of the values at its position), then the program also satisfies B because the implication shows that B must be true of the values when control reaches its position.

The notion of support between assertions takes into account properties of the formal concepts used in the assertions. Properties can be formalized as boolean expressions in Anna — called lemmas or axioms. They may be used to prove one assertion from another. Consequently, assertions do not have to repeat standard properties of concepts in order to support one another.

Examples: *Lemmas for sorting and searching concepts.*

```
--   Transitivity of PERMUTATION.

     for all A, B, C : VECTOR =>
        PERMUTATION(A, B) and PERMUTATION(B, C) →
                                       PERMUTATION(A, C);

--   The partitioning lemma.

     for all A : VECTOR; I : NATURAL =>
        PARTITIONED(A, I) and A'FIRST < I and
        MAX_IN_SLICE(A(I-1), A(1 .. I-1)) →
                                       PARTITIONED(A, I-1);
```

- **Guideline: Constructing related assertions.**

  Assertions should formalize sufficient information that is true of the computation state at their positions to support assertions at later points in the flow of control.

In the previous bubble sort example, the lower level assertion (2) supports assertion (1), and assertion (1) supports the output assertion of the block. Also, assertion (1) supports assertion (2).

Showing that one assertion supports another involves detailed arguments using successor functions and lemmas. These arguments are just what we do subconsciously when we construct a loop — figuring out how values change, and what will be true later in the flow of control — but we do not usually write down all the details. Here we give an example.[8]

[8]Skip the rest of this subsection on first reading if it gets too detailed.

Let us convince ourselves that assertion (1) supports assertion (2). Here is the relevant part of bubble sort again.

```
--|         PERMUTATION (A, IN_A) and                              -- (1)
--|            ORDERED (A (I..A'LAST)) and PARTITIONED (A, I);
            for J in A'FIRST .. I-1 loop
               if A (J) > A (J+1) then
                  TEMP := A (J);
                  A (J) := A (J+1);
                  A (J+1) := TEMP;
               end if;
--|            PERMUTATION (A, IN_A) and                           -- (2)
--|               MAX_IN_SLICE (A (J+1), A (A'FIRST .. J+1));
            end loop;
```

First of all, the successor function from assertion (1) to (2) for A is:

```
f (A) = if A'FIRST ≤ I-1 and then
              A(A'FIRST) > A(A'FIRST+1) then
              SWAP (A, A'FIRST, A'FIRST+1)
           else
              A
           end if;
```

This successor function defines the change in value of A along the simple paths from assertion (1) to assertion (2). There are two paths which can be executed when the inner loop variable J has value A'FIRST and the iteration range of the inner loop is nonempty. Then, if the **if** test is true, the new value of A results from swapping two components of the initial value of A; otherwise A is unchanged.

Next, we want to show that assertion (1) supports (2). To keep things short, we will only show that the permutation parts of the assertions are related. We assume assertion (1) is true initially and we want to prove (2) is true when control reaches that position, i.e.,

```
PERMUTATION (A, IN_A) and LEMMAS →
                                   PERMUTATION (f (A), IN_A).
```

Substituting the conditional expression for f,

```
PERMUTATION (A, IN_A) and LEMMAS →
   if A'FIRST ≤ I-1 and then
          A(A'FIRST) > A(A'FIRST+1) then
      PERMUTATION (SWAP (A, A'FIRST, A'FIRST+1), IN_A)
   else
      PERMUTATION (A, IN_A)
   end if.
```

Since the value of A is not changed under some conditions, we have to prove only one thing — under those conditions where swapping takes place, the result of swapping two components in an array is a permutation of that array. This can be proved using another lemma about permutation, namely:

for all I, J : A'RANGE => PERMUTATION (SWAP (A, I, J), A)

The lemma says that the result of swapping two elements of an array is always a permutation of the array. Now we use our assumption PERMUTATION (A, IN_A) and the previous lemma about transitivity of PERMUTATION to complete the argument.

Note that we can assume that all the **if** tests are true because we want to show that if assertion (1) is true and control takes a simple path to position (2), then assertion (2) is true.

If we want to prove that control will actually reach position (2) we have to prove that the **if** tests do not result in CONSTRAINT_ERROR.

Showing that assertion (1) supports the MAX_IN_SLICE part of assertion (2) uses also the successor function for J which is simply A'FIRST. We must show:

PERMUTATION (A, IN_A) **and** ORDERED (A (I . . A'LAST))
and PARTITIONED (A, I) **and** LEMMAS
→
MAX_IN_SLICE (*f* (A) (A'FIRST+1), *f* (A) (A'FIRST . . A'FIRST+1)).

We leave the details of this one to the reader.

2.5.3 Structuring testing and proof

The idea behind the guideline on constructing related assertions is to use relationships between assertions to structure the processes of *runtime checking* and *proving consistency* of annotations and programs. We want to organize these processes into small steps. At each step only a few assertions are tested or proved consistent.

There are two techniques for studying whether or not assertions are satisfied by (or consistent with) the underlying program.[9] The first is *runtime checking* and the second is *consistency proof*.

- **Runtime checking.**
  An assertion is translated into Ada code that will check if the assertion is satisfied by the computation state each time it is reached during a computation (Section 2.9).
- **Consistency proof.**
  An assertion is proved to be satisfied by every observable computation state to which it can ever apply.

---

[9]See Chapter 1 for definitions of satisfaction and consistency.

Both techniques can be supported by automated tools, such as assertion translators that generate checking code, and theorem provers. Both techniques apply to all kinds of annotations, and we will discuss them more generally later. Here we describe a top-down strategy for applying these techniques to assertions.

- **Runtime checking**

  A program is tested by first suppressing the runtime checking of assertions in inner scopes (lower level assertions). If a higher level annotation or assertion is violated, then the lower level assertions are tested with the same input data.

In the bubble sort example we would proceed as follows:

1. First the loop assertions (1) and (2) would be suppressed, and the output assertion only would be checked. Inconsistency is indicated by violation of the output assertion on some input data.
2. If there is an inconsistency, testing of the loop assertions would be turned on. The support relationship between the assertions tells us that *either* the loop assertions must also fail *or* the error results from violating local frame assertions that were "too obvious" to express in the assertions. In either case, we will be given more detailed information indicating the cause of the failure of the output assertion. The information will be in terms of the concepts used in the assertions. For example, violation of assertion (2) would yield an explanation such as "partitioning has failed for value I_0 of I."

- **Consistency proof**

  Proving the consistency of an assertion at one level should be first attempted assuming that the lower level assertions are satisfied. Then the lower level assertions should be proved.

This technique of breaking down big consistency proofs into sets of smaller proofs can only work if the lower level assertions support the higher level assertions.

In the bubble sort example, the overall consistency proof can be broken into three small proofs:

1. Prove the **out** assertion assuming the loop assertion (1) for the outer loop.
2. Prove assertion (1) by the principle of loop induction[10] assuming the inner loop assertion (2).
3. Prove the inner assertion (2) by loop induction.

[10]See the next section.

2.5.4 LOOP INDUCTION *

This section[11] deals with proving that loop assertions are *inductive* — a special form of "self–support."

The following induction principle is given for assertion A on a single program variable U. Similar principles can be given for assertions involving several program variables.

• Loop induction principle

Let A (U) be an assertion about a program variable U in a loop. Suppose A is placed at the top level of the statements in the loop body[12] so that it is evaluated on each iteration. Let TEST (U) be the control test of the loop.

Let U_0 be the value of U on entry to the loop. For positive i, let U_i be the value of U when A is reached on the ith execution of the loop. Let f be the successor function for U along the simple paths from the position of the assertion A to A again. Ignoring other parameters of the successor functions, it follows that for all positive i, $f(U_i) = U_{i+1}$.

- *Premises:* if the following two premises are true:
  1. TEST (U_0) **and** LEMMAS $\rightarrow$ A (U_1),
  2. for every value U_i, $i = 1, 2, \ldots$:
     A (U_i) **and** LEMMAS $\rightarrow$ A ($f(U_i)$),
- *Conclusion:* then the loop satisfies assertion A (U).

If the two premises of the induction principle are true, then the assertion A is called an *inductive assertion* for the loop. The principle tells us that an inductive assertion is always true when control reaches its position in the loop. The assertion must be placed at the top level of the statements in the loop so it will be reached on every execution — it must not be buried in some **if** statement. That way we know there are a small number of simple paths from A back to A.

LEMMAS stands for any true facts about the functions in the annotations and program. An inductive assertion is just a special case of *related assertions* (Section 2.5.2) when the assertion is in a loop. By the way, the induction principle does *not* conclude that an inductive assertion A(U) is true for all values of U — only those values f (U) when control reaches the position of the assertion.

Premise (1) is called the *base case* of the induction, and premise (2) is called the *inductive step*.

---

[11]It can be skipped without jeopardizing the understanding of the subsequent sections.

[12]That is, A is not nested inside another statement in the loop.

To prove that A is an inductive assertion at its position in a loop, we must do three things:

1. Define the successor function f for that position in the loop
2. Prove the base case
3. Prove the inductive step.

The successor function in the loop induction principle expresses how the loop modifies its variables between successive assertion points. If we get the successor function wrong, our use of loop induction won't apply to the given loop — quite a common error. The base case requires the assertion to be true on the first execution. The induction step requires us to prove that the assertion is true on every execution of the loop, assuming that it was true on the previous execution of the loop — usually the hard part.

A loop induction principle for assertions with several variables is almost identical to the one above — simply consider U to be a tuple of variables, and f to be a tuple of functions of the variables, each one computing the successor value of a particular variable in U.

In the following example, assume we have a library function, !.

Example: *An inductive assertion in a factorial function.*

```
    function FACTORIAL (N : NATURAL) return NATURAL
--|     where return N!
    is
        F : NATURAL := 1;
        I : NATURAL := 0;
    begin
        while I /= N loop
--|         F = I!;
            I := I+1;
            F := F*I;
        end loop;
        return F;
    end FACTORIAL;
```

Commentary

The assertion in the loop, F = I!, is an assertion on two program variables. It formalizes the idea that F always equals I! whenever control reaches that point in the loop body. We can prove that it is an inductive assertion by applying a loop induction principle for two variables.

The successor function for F, starting and ending at the assertion position, is:

```
f (F, I) = if I /= N then
               F * (I+1)
           else
               F
           end if;
```

The successor function for I is:

```
i (F, I) = if I /= N then
              I+1
           else
              I
           end if;
```

Now we can construct the induction premises:

Base case: 0 /= N **and** LEMMAS → 1 = 0!

Induction step: F = I! **and** LEMMAS →
f (F, I) = (i (F, I))!

The base case is true by definition of 0!.
The proof of the induction step is easy: Replacing f and i by their conditional expressions, and simplifying the resulting equation, the induction step is:

F = I! **and** LEMMAS **and** I /= N →
F * (I+1) = (I+1)!

Replacing F by I!, the right side is I! * (I+1) = (I+1)!, which is also true by definition of I!.
Having proved by loop induction that the body of the function is consistent with the assertion, it is simple to prove that the function itself satisfies its result annotation. The proof breaks into two cases, N = 0, and N > 0. In the case N = 0 the value 1 is returned. In the case N > 0 the loop test is true when I = N. The previous value of I is N-1, so the previous value of F is (N - 1)! because the loop satisfies the assertion. Therefore the final operation of the loop changes F to N!, which is the value returned.

The loop induction principle gives us a nice way to prove consistency between loops and assertions. There is an extensive literature on methods of constructing inductive assertions, but this goes beyond the scope of our discussion (see the books listed at the end of this chapter).

The main point for us is that inductive assertions can be expressed in Anna. They provide the most complete documentation of the local details of loops.

- **Guideline: Assertions in loops.**

  In general, inductive assertions are needed to annotate loops, and loop induction should be used to prove that the loops satisfy them.

Of course, not all assertions in loops need be inductive. But most assertions that express how values of loop variables are related to their previous values are inductive.

Sometimes it is reasonable to break this guideline and use a loop assertion which is not inductive according to our definition, for example by omitting frame properties from the assertion. We may want to do this to save having to write repetitious and trivial parts of assertions. If we do this, the incomplete assertions are not inductive although they are consistent with the loop. However we should always know what needs to be added to make them inductive.

- **Proving consistency of bubble sort**

It can be proved that the loops in the bubble sort example satisfy the assertions by showing that the assertions really are *inductive*. We start with the outer loop. Our proof will apply the loop induction principle. Step one is to define successor functions in the outer loop for the variables I, A in the loop assertion (1).

1. Successor function for I :

$$f_I(\mathrm{I}) = \textbf{if } \mathrm{I} > \mathrm{A'FIRST} \textbf{ then } \mathrm{I}-1 \textbf{ else } \mathrm{A'FIRST} \textbf{ end if};$$

2. Successor function for A :

$$f_A(\mathrm{A},\ \mathrm{I}) = \textbf{if } \mathrm{I} > \mathrm{A'FIRST} \textbf{ then } \mathrm{A}_1 \textbf{ else } \mathrm{A} \textbf{ end if};$$

   where

$$\mathrm{A}_1(\mathrm{I} \mathrel{..} \mathrm{A'LAST}) = \mathrm{A}(\mathrm{I} \mathrel{..} \mathrm{A'LAST}),$$
$$\mathrm{MAX\_IN\_SLICE}(\mathrm{A}_1(\mathrm{I}-1),\ \mathrm{A}_1(1 \mathrel{..} \mathrm{I}-1)),$$
$$\mathrm{PERMUTATION}(\mathrm{A}_1,\ \mathrm{IN\_A}).$$

What we have just said about the successor function for A assumes that inner loop assertion (2), with a *frame* property added, is inductive. The frame property we need is simply that the upper slice A (I .. A'LAST) is not changed by the inner loop. (As an exercise to see why this kind of omission is so tempting, try to extend assertion (2) so that you're sure it expresses that the upper slice remains constant. It is easier to add a third assertion about constancy after the inner loop.)

Assume that assertion (2) (extended with the frame property) is an inductive assertion for the inner loop. Then it must be true when the inner loop terminates because it is placed at the end of the inner loop body. Therefore it is true also when the outer loop assertion is reached. So it tells us properties of the outer loop successor functions that are written above.

Now we apply the loop induction principle.

Base case:

```
    PERMUTATION (IN_A, IN_A),
    ORDERED (IN_A (A'LAST .. A'LAST)),
    PARTITIONED (IN_A, A'LAST).
```

All these assertions can be easily proved from the descriptions of the concepts — the partitioning is true vacuously, for example, because the upper slice of the partition, A (A'LAST+1 .. A'LAST), is empty.

Induction step:

```
    PERMUTATION (A, IN_A) and                    -- Induction premises.
    ORDERED (A (I .. A'LAST)) and
    PARTITIONED (A, I) and
    A'FIRST ≤ I-1
    →
        PERMUTATION (A1, IN_A) and           -- Induction conclusions.
        ORDERED (A1 (I-1 .. A'LAST)) and
        PARTITIONED (A1, I-1).
```

These implications can be proved using the properties of A_1 together with properties of the concepts. To prove PARTITIONED(A_1, I−1), for example, we start with the premises,

```
--  The upper slice has not changed,
1.  A1 (I .. A'LAST) = A (I .. A'LAST),
--  Set of components has not changed,
2.  PERMUTATION (A1, IN_A),
--  Old value of A is partitioned,
3.  PARTITIONED (A, I),
--  New value of A satisfies assertion (2), our assumption,
4.  MAX_IN_SLICE (A1 (I-1), A1 (1 .. I-1)).
```

From the first two premises we deduce that the set of components in the lower slice has not changed either:

```
    PERMUTATION (A1 (A'FIRST .. I-1), A (A'FIRST .. I-1)).
```

This and premises (1) and (3) imply,

PARTITIONED (A_1, I).

So, using this with premise MAX_IN_SLICE,

PARTITIONED (A_1, I−1).

The other induction step conclusions can be proved similarly.

The inner assertion (2), with the frame property added, can also be shown to be inductive. This justifies our definitions of the successor functions for the outer loop. Finally, when the outer loop terminates, assertion (1) is true for the final value of I and implies the output assertion.

2.6 Invariants: Compound Statement Annotations

Compound statement annotations that are not modified by **in** or **out** constrain all observable states during execution of their scope. Whenever their scope is a compound statement such as a block, they express relationships between objects that must remain true over a number of consecutive states. We shall refer to them as *invariants*. (Note: Inductive assertions in loops are often called *loop invariants*. For us, a loop invariant is an annotation that must be satisfied by all states observable in the computation of a loop.)

- **Guideline: Use of invariants.**

  Invariants are best used locally over a block, loop, or case statement to document that something bad does not happen — or, more positively, that some good properties achieved earlier in the program remain invariant.

Invariants give us a convenient way of specifying how global variables are used. A particularly important application is their use to express constraints against side effects — especially so in the case of pointer manipulations (dealt with in Chapter 7).

Example: *An invariant over a loop.*

```
--   CUSTOMER_LIST_TYPE is an array of customer records.

--   Print customers in order of zip code.
     procedure REPORT_BY_ZIP
                              (CUSTOMERS : CUSTOMER_LIST_TYPE) is

         LIST : CUSTOMER_LIST_TYPE
                         (CUSTOMERS'FIRST .. CUSTOMERS'LAST)
              := CUSTOMERS;
         ...
```

```
    begin
        OPEN_REPORT;
        WRITE_REPORT_HEADER;
--      Sort LIST by zip code.
        SORT_BY_ZIP (LIST);
--|         for all C : LIST'FIRST .. LIST'LAST-1 =>
--|                                  LIST (C) . ZIP ≤ LIST (C+1) . ZIP;

--      Write LIST in order.
--|     with
--|         LIST = in LIST;              -- Invariant over the loop.
        for CUSTOMER in LIST'RANGE loop
            ...
            WRITE_RECORD (LIST (CUSTOMER) );
            ...
        end loop;
            ...
        CLOSE_REPORT;

    end REPORT_BY_ZIP;
```

Commentary

The procedure carries out two operations. First the list of customer records is sorted according to zip code; then each record is output by the loop. The invariant is expressed as a compound statement annotation of the output loop. It constrains LIST to remain constant throughout the loop. This implies that the loop cannot have a side effect on LIST while it is printing out the listing of customers, and thereby possibly disturb the order. The loop can't even have a temporary side effect[13] that is "undone" before it terminates. Therefore we can conclude without seeing any other details of the loop that the records must be output in their zip code order. Finally, when the loop terminates the list must be in zip code order.

2.7 Increasing the Scope of Annotations

The goal of the following guideline is to condense the formal description of the behavior of a program in as few annotations as possible and to present those annotations as early as possible in the text. Generally speaking, maximizing the scope of annotations improves clarity of documentation and minimizes the number of separate annotations of the same property.

[13] That is, one that can be observed between simple statements of the loop.

- **Guideline: Maximize the scope of annotations.**

  A program should be annotated so as to maximize the scope of its annotations.

The guideline is particularly relevent when trying to improve the annotations of a finished program. One should look out for annotations that were intended as local constraints but apply more globally.

Replacing an annotation applying to an inner scope by an annotation at a more global outer scope must be done without changing the consistency of the Anna program. Typically, an assertion or compound statement annotation is replaced by a declarative object constraint. The declarative constraint is placed in the declarative part of a body or block containing the statement annotation. This means that under certain conditions an annotation of form (1) below is consistent with the program if and only if an annotation of form (2) is consistent.

```
(1) declare
          ...                         -- Declarations.
      begin
          ...                         -- Other statements.
--|       with C(X);
          S                           -- C(X) applies to statement S.
          ...
      end;
```

or alternatively,

```
(2) declare
          ...                         -- Declarations.
--|       C(X);
          ...                         -- C(X) applies to declarations
      begin
          ...                         -- and other statements
          S                           -- as well as to S.
          ...
      end;
```

Alternative (2) is a stronger (or more global) constraint than (1). It holds if all the statements in the block, and the elaboration of all the declarations following C, satisfy C (X). Obviously, the correctness of (2) always implies (1). The guideline tells us to recognize when the converse holds and to choose (2) in those cases.

Equivalence, when it holds, must be proved. This involves showing invariance of C (X) over other statements and declarations surrounding S. Such proofs are usually easy — in the case when equivalence is true, the surrounding statements often only "read" the variables of C — or else counter-examples are obvious.

• Levels

We use the concept of *level* to refer to the "globalness" of the scope of an annotation. Higher level annotations have more global scopes than lower level annotations.

We won't define "levels" rigorously, but we can say the following things about them. Assertions always have the lowest level. Normally, object annotations are at a higher level than statement annotations, and subprogram annotations are the highest level simple annotations. But these rules of thumb may not hold if the underlying program has a complicated structure with the nested declarative regions and blocks. In general, to increase the level of annotations, we need to convert statement annotations to object annotations (as above), and sometimes conversely — object annotations to even higher level statement annotations such as invariants.

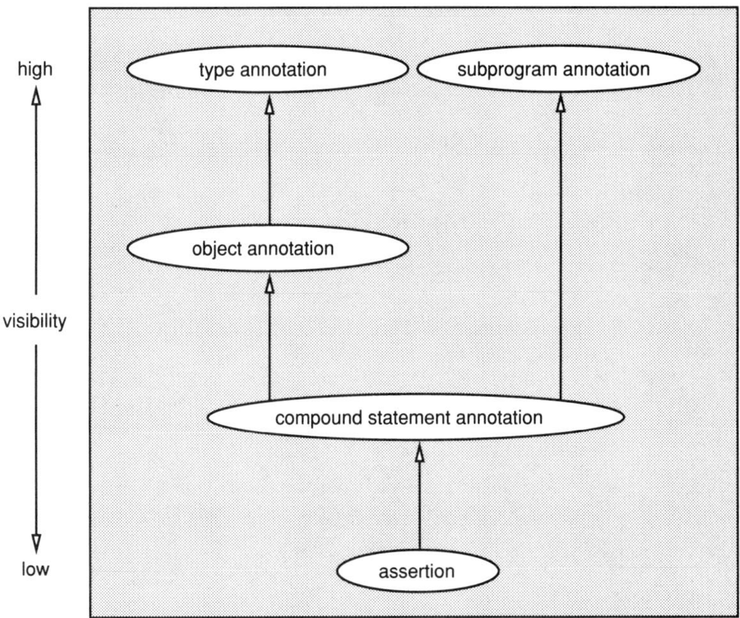

FIGURE 2.1. Typical conversions to increase scope of annotations.

Now let's discuss some examples of raising the levels of annotations. First, the example in Section 2.6 is an example where it can't be done. The invariance of the customer list, which is a compound statement annotation of the loop, cannot be raised to an object constraint over the whole procedure body. Why not? Because the list is sorted earlier in the block, and is altered there. The invariant simply does not imply a similar object constraint at a more global scope.

Compound statement annotations can be used to raise the level of assertions, often in conjunction with the trick of encapsulating hunks of code in subprogram bodies. Consider again the bubble sort example from Section 2.5. If we have a procedure SWAP that interchanges components,

```
      procedure SWAP (A : in out VECTOR;
                      X, Y : INDEX_TYPE);
--|      where
--|         out (A (X) = in A (Y) and A (Y) = in A (X)),
--|         out (for all I : A'RANGE =>
--|                   (I /= X and I /= Y => A (I) = in A (I)));
```

then we can replace the inner loop assignments by a call to it. The permutation property, which previously was part of both inductive assertions (1) and (2) at points in the loops, now becomes an invariant of the whole block.

Example: Factoring an invariant out of inductive loop assertions of bubble sort.

```
-- Compare with the example of bubble sort in Section 2.5.

-- Specification of a block to sort a one-dimensional vector A of integers.
--| with
--|    out (ORDERED (A)),
--|    PERMUTATION (A, in A);
    declare
       TEMP : INTEGER;
    begin
       for I in reverse A'FIRST .. A'LAST loop
--|       ORDERED (A (I ..  A'LAST)) and
--|       PARTITIONED (A, I);
          for J in A'FIRST .. INDEX_TYPE'PRED (I) loop
             if A (J) > A (J+1) then
                SWAP (A, J, J+1);
             end if;
--|          MAX_IN_SLICE (A (J+1), A (A'FIRST .. J+1));
          end loop;
       end loop;
    end;
```

Commentary

The compound statement annotation over the block consists of the previous **out** assertion and an invariant. The invariant is a new permutation constraint on variable A. It refers to all computation states of the block, including the elaboration of declarations. It expresses that any observable value of A is a permutation of the input value of A.

How do we argue that if the previous bubble sort example is consistent, then so is this one? In the first example the operations on A inside the inner loop destroy the permutation property,

temporarily. There, the permutation property has to be stated as inductive assertions in the loops, at points where operations on A have been completed.
In this example, a call to procedure SWAP hides the explicit reordering operations on A. The permutation property then applies over a larger scope. So the loop assertions for permutation can be replaced by an equivalent compound statement annotation over the entire block. This replacement can be thought of as taking place in two steps, each of which must be justified by a proof of equivalence. First, the permutation loop assertions are replaced by an object constraint on A placed at the end of the declarations of the block. Justification: SWAP is the only operation on A in the block, and one of the loop assertions containing PERMUTATION immediately follows the call to SWAP. Therefore, if the loop assertions are true, then the object constraint is true. Secondly, the declarative object constraint is replaced by an invariant over the block. Justification: the elaboration of the declaration of TEMP cannot affect A.
Note that there is no longer any need to save the input value of A in virtual variable IN_A. Also, the previous output assertion of permutation is an immediate consequence of the invariant.

One other point about this example should be noted: The semantics of procedure call are not altered by in-line expansion. If the Ada pragma INLINE is applied to SWAP, the internal computation states of the call do not become visible. Therefore the extra computation involved in the call can be avoided by using the INLINE pragma without altering the consistency of the program with its assertions.

Here is an example where the level of compound statement annotations documenting the effects of a local loop can be increased to global declarative constraints over the enclosing block.

Example: *Increasing the level of compound statement annotations.*

Before: *Binary search with compound statement annotations.*

```
-- If A is an ordered VECTOR and KEY is a component in the slice A(L ..
-- H) then the out value of Y will be one of the index positions of KEY.
--| with
--|     ORDERED(in A(L .. H)),
--|     out (L ≤ Y ≤ H),
--|     out (IS_IN_INTERVAL(KEY, A(L .. H)) → A(Y) = KEY);
 declare
     LOW, HIGH, MID : INTEGER;
```

```
     begin
          LOW    := L;
          HIGH   := H;
--   The loop keeps A invariant, and keeps KEY in the index range,
--   LOW .. HIGH.
--|       with
--|            A = in A,
--|            (IS_IN_INTERVAL (KEY, A (L .. H)) →
--|                          IS_IN_INTERVAL (KEY, A (LOW .. HIGH)));
          while LOW < HIGH loop
               MID := (LOW+HIGH)/2;
               if KEY > A (MID) then
                    LOW := MID+1;
               else
                    HIGH := MID;
               end if;
          end loop;

          if KEY = A (HIGH) then
               Y := HIGH;
          else
               raise NOT_FOUND;
          end if;
     end;
```

After: *Binary search with declarative object annotations.*

```
--|  with
--|       (ORDERED (in A)),
--|       out (L ≤ Y ≤ H),
--|       out (IS_IN_INTERVAL (KEY, A (L .. H)) → A (Y) = KEY);
     declare
--|       A = in A,
          LOW, HIGH, MID : INTEGER;
--|       IS_IN_INTERVAL (KEY, A (L .. H)) →
--|                          IS_IN_INTERVAL (KEY, A (LOW .. HIGH)));
     begin
          ...  -- Same body without the previous
               -- statement annotations.

     end;
```

Commentary

In the first version of this binary search algorithm, the invariants of the loop express that the loop does not change A, and that the interval between LOW and HIGH contains a KEY. An inductive assertion could also be used inside the loop to express another property, that the interval decreases on each iteration. In the second version, the loop invariants are replaced by object constraints over the whole block. This can be done because these annotations are satisfied not only by the loop, but also

by the assignments initializing LOW and HIGH and by the final **if** statement. It is now clear that the invariance of A could be used as an additional output specification of the block.
Note that the interval constraint

```
IS_IN_INTERVAL (KEY, A (L .. H)) →
          IS_IN_INTERVAL (KEY, A (LOW .. HIGH))
```

is true by default until LOW and HIGH are initialized (see [Anna87, 3.2]).

The process of raising the level of annotations is intended to improve formal documentation. It may appear, however, to make the problem of determining consistency more difficult — perhaps we would expect this since the annotations are being made more powerful. For example, an implementation of runtime checking of annotations must have "smarts" similar to the reasoning used to increase scope. It must be able to recognize that many of the checks over the increased scope of an annotation are redundant and do not need to be executed. (Ada compilers have similar problems in optimizing Ada runtime constraint checks.)

Higher level annotations can also be regarded as more difficult to prove consistent because of their greater scope. But raising levels of annotations can be viewed as a technique for structuring consistency proofs into small steps. Whenever we replace an annotation by one with greater scope, we must be able to prove that consistency is maintained — so one part of the overall consistency proof is required to make this step. As a result, local annotations are brought closer to global specifications. The proofs of specifications, which may assume consistency of the local annotations, are thereby easier (see Section 2.5.3).

2.8 Specification Using Subprogram Annotations

This section illustrates some applications of subprogram annotations to the process of specifying programs. What we are really doing is preparing for Chapters 4 and 5 on package specifications. Our examples here deal with two activities:

- Specifying subprograms
- Formalizing and organizing concepts

Ideally, the process of specification has four steps:

1. Choose concepts from among those normally used to explain the program informally.
2. Define the concepts formally by virtual subprogram declarations with annotations.
3. Organize formal concept definitions into theory packages.

4. Specify the actual program.

The first step of formalization, choosing which informal concepts to formalize, is the hardest one to give guidelines for. What usually happens is that, from previous experience, we already know some useful informal concepts that need to be formalized. Others become evident as we proceed through the later steps. In practice, there is a "feedback" loop in the formalization process.

Our first examples deal with the last step of specifying subprograms, assuming we can formalize the necessary concepts. Then we deal with the second and third steps of organizing formal definitions of concepts into theories.

2.8.1 Specifying subprograms

A subprogram is specified by annotating its Ada subprogram declaration. This is done before a subprogram body is constructed. The annotations of the subprogram declaration apply to any body that is eventually supplied for that subprogram. As we have seen previously (Section 1.9), subprogram annotations play a double role. They act both as formal documentation, which other units can assume when they call the subprogram, and as constraints to which subprogram bodies (implementations) must conform. In the latter role, they can be regarded as implementation guidelines. We shall refer to an annotated subprogram declaration as an *Anna subprogram specification.*

Consider specifying a transfer procedure in an electronic banking package. It allows the user to make transfers between bank accounts.

Example: *Specification of an electronic banking transfer procedure.*

```
   procedure
      TRANSFER ( AMOUNT  :  POSITIVE_DOLLARS_SUBTYPE;
                 OUT_ACCOUNT  :  in out  WITHDRAWAL_SUBTYPE;
                 IN_ACCOUNT  :  in out  DEPOSIT_SUBTYPE);
--|   where
--|      in (AMOUNT  ≤  BALANCE (OUT_ACCOUNT)),
--|      out  (BALANCE (OUT_ACCOUNT)  =
--|                     in  BALANCE (OUT_ACCOUNT) – AMOUNT),
--|      out  (BALANCE (IN_ACCOUNT)  =
--|                        in  BALANCE (IN_ACCOUNT) + AMOUNT),
--|      out  (for all  A  :  ACCOUNT_TYPE  =>
--|           A /= OUT_ACCOUNT  and  A /= IN_ACCOUNT →
--|                              BALANCE (A)  =  in  BALANCE (A));
```

Commentary

This specification uses the everyday concept of the *balance* in an account. The mnemonic name BALANCE acts as a guide

to the intended meaning. It enables us to make an intuitive association between the specifications and the familiar world of bank accounts. As a result we can understand the specification well enough to reason about it and to see its omissions.
The specification itself acts as a contract between the user and the bank (the implementor here). The first three annotations express what is normal in the everyday model of banking and need no explanation — at first glance. The last annotation specifies "no side effects" on other accounts. It expresses something that is so fundamental in the real world that it is taken for granted and goes unsaid in brochures on electronic banking. It is another example of a *frame* specification.[14]
The importance of the frame specification as a safety or security constraint on the bank cannot be overemphasized. And its appearance here may lead to a closer look at the first specification. Suppose the user violates the first input specification. Does the call simply hang up? Behavior of TRANSFER in case OUT_ACCOUNT is overdrawn is not specified, and the frame annotation disallows any overdrafts being automatically made up from a third account. So, after a little reasoning about the frame specification of TRANSFER, both a user and a bank may want to change it to allow more flexible options.
The formal specification requires a prior declaration of the concept BALANCE. This would normally be given by another subprogram specification,

```
function BALANCE(A : ACCOUNT_TYPE)
return DOLLAR_TYPE;
```

This subprogram may also have Anna specifications, or it may have a body. It may be virtual if it is used only in annotations. This declaration will constitute a definition of the formal concept BALANCE, and it is here that we will find out if accounts can be negative.
The double role played by a subprogram specification is illustrated here. A customer may assume that the act of performing a transfer (i.e., calling TRANSFER) will result in moving the AMOUNT between the named accounts, and will not affect any other account. A bank is required to provide a procedure body that satisfies the specified relationships between the **in** and **out** values of the BALANCE function on all accounts.
It is obvious that the frame specification could involve a large number of runtime checks in the checking approach to testing

[14]See also the mailing list example in Section 2.5.3.

consistency with annotations. A banking system should be designed from the beginning to be provably consistent with this kind of frame specification so that most checks are unnecessary. Finally, a slight digression. The "no side effects" annotation is a strong constraint, implying that no other account is changed during the execution of a TRANSFER call between two accounts. This would not be true in a multitasking model of electronic banking. But even so, this "simplified" specification is probably what a customer would be given. In the general multitasking case, a more sophisticated annotation would be needed, but this goes beyond the scope of our discussion.

A special application of subprogram specification arises in the situation where existing software is being revised, but is required to perform close to the original version in many respects. This will usually happen at the level of a program unit such as a package or subprogram. In the case of a subprogram, the original version is declared as a virtual unit and is used to specify the new version. Runtime checking to ensure the new version meets its specification will actually compare the two versions.

Example: *Specification of a new sine function using a standard algorithm.*

```
--    A standard power series algorithm.

--: function SINE_SERIES(X : FLOAT; CUT_OFF : INTEGER)
--: return FLOAT is
--:     Y : FLOAT := 0.0;
--: begin
--:     for I in 0 .. CUT_OFF loop
--:         Y := Y+FLOAT((-1) ** I) /
--:                     FLOAT(FACTORIAL(2*I+1))*X ** (2*I+1);
--:     end loop;
--:     return Y;
--: end SINE_SERIES;

--    Sine function to be implemented by a more efficient algorithm.

    function SIN(X : RADIANS_TYPE) return AMPLITUDE_TYPE;
--|     where return A : AMPLITUDE_TYPE =>
--|         abs (FLOAT(A)-SINE_SERIES(X, CUT)) <
--|                                                  MAX_DELTA;
```

Commentary

Obviously, differences between SIN and SINE_SERIES should be detected. The closeness of the comparison is controlled by the choice of values for CUT and MAX_DELTA. The specification can be altered to formalize accurately what differences are acceptable. The idea is to be able to test quickly for gross software errors, not for fine numerical analysis details.

2.8.2 Formalizing and organizing concepts

The choice of concepts is crucial in writing specifications. Recall that concepts used in annotations are formalized by declaring functions, usually virtual, and annotating their declarations (Sections 2.1 and 2.2.).

- **Guideline: Choosing formal concepts.**

  The concepts used to annotate a subprogram should formalize those informal concepts that are normally used to describe that subprogram.

The *organization* of concepts used in specifying related or similar programs is a second crucial issue.

Often, concepts will come from a theory of programs of the kind in question — sorting, data bases, list processing and so on. The operations and concepts of each theory should be encapsulated as a package. Let us refer to such packages as *theory packages*. A theory package will usually be virtual, signifying that it is used only in annotations. A theory package should be invoked when specifying a program in the general area of that theory, rather than attempting to define new concepts from scratch. Thus, arranging the principles of abstraction and separation into compilation units, which are applied to large programs, applies also to organizing specifications into theories.

- **Guideline: Packaging formal concepts.**

  The declarations of functions with annotations that formalize the concepts of a particular class of programs should be encapsulated in the visible specification part of a theory package.

Let us illustrate the use of theory packages as it applies to our previous example of a sorting procedure. First, the reader should review the bubble sort example of inductive assertions in Section 2.5.

Example: *Specification of a sorting procedure.*

```
--: with SORTING_CONCEPTS;
--: use SORTING_CONCEPTS;
-- Procedure to sort a vector A — a one-dimensional array of integers.

    procedure SORT (A : in out VECTOR);
--|     where
--|         out (PERMUTATION (A, in A)),
--|         out (ORDERED (A));
```

Commentary

The specification describes the behavior of SORT using well-known concepts from the theory of searching and sorting. The concepts are defined in a theory package, SORTING_CONCEPTS (below). The package is invoked by a context clause, indicating that SORT is dependent on it. The context clause is virtual, indicating that SORTING_CONCEPTS is used only in formal comments, and not in actual text.

No exceptional behavior is specified — because we do not deal with exceptions until Chapter 3.

Viewed "from the inside," the body of SORT must satisfy these specifications. The specifications of this subprogram declaration become **out** annotations constraining the body (or block). These specifications can be satisfied by many different possible bodies, each implementing a particular method of sorting. The block implementing a bubble sort (Sections 2.5 and 2.6) is one possibility. Note that in this particular example the **out** assertions constraining the bubble sort block logically imply the subprogram specifications. Other standard algorithms such as QuickSort (Section 7.2), Heapsort, etc. could be used as the body.

Now let's discuss organizing the sorting concepts. A window showing part of the declaration of a SORTING_CONCEPTS package is given below — later on we will give generic versions. This may be thought of as a library package in a library of specifications. Concepts usually have a hierarchical dependency structure. Higher level concepts are defined using lower level ones. This will be reflected in the order of declarations in a theory package. Indeed, packages specifying theories may themselves have a dependency structure analogous to a compilation dependency structure between Ada units.

Example: A theory package defining some standard searching and sorting concepts.

```
--: package SORTING_CONCEPTS is

--:     subtype INDEX_TYPE is INTEGER;
--:     type VECTOR is array (INDEX_TYPE range <>)
--:                                           of INTEGER;

--:         function ORDERED (A : VECTOR) return BOOLEAN;
--|             where
--|             return for all I, J : A'RANGE => I ≤ J →
--|                                           A (I) ≤ A (J);
```

```
--:     function PERMUTATION (A, B : VECTOR)
--:     return BOOLEAN;
--|         where
--|         in (A'LENGTH = B'LENGTH),
--|         return
--|             A'LENGTH = 0
--|                 or else
--|             (exist I : B'RANGE => A (A'FIRST) = B (I)
--|                     and
--|                     PERMUTATION (A (A'FIRST+1 .. A'LAST),
--|                                  B (B'FIRST .. I-1) &
--|                                  B (I+1 .. B'LAST) ) );

--:     function SORTED (A : VECTOR) return VECTOR;
--|         where return B : VECTOR =>
--|                     PERMUTATION (A, B) and ORDERED (B);

--:     function IS_IN_INTERVAL (X : ITEM; A : VECTOR)
--:     return BOOLEAN;
--|         where
--|           return (exist I : A'RANGE => X = A (I) );

--:     function PARTITIONED (A : VECTOR; I : INDEX_TYPE)
        return BOOLEAN;
--|         where return
--|             if I isin A'RANGE then
--|                 for all J : A'FIRST .. I => A (J) ≤ A (I) and
--|                 for all J : I .. A'LAST => A (I) ≤ A (J)
--|             else
--|                 FALSE
--|             end if;

          ...                 --  Other searching and sorting concepts.

--: end SORTING_CONCEPTS;
```

Commentary

Concepts are represented by function declarations and defined by subprogram annotations. Generally, they are represented by virtual functions. Virtual bodies may be provided for the concepts in a package body for SORTING_CONCEPTS. If annotations using them are to be checked at runtime, the checks will either execute the virtual bodies (if any) or utilize algorithms for checking the subprogram annotations that define the concepts.

The concept ordered vector is represented by the declaration of boolean function ORDERED. The annotation specifying it uses standard Ada predefined operations. The permutation concept is represented by boolean function PERMUTATION. It is spec-

ified recursively. Note that if logical variable I is B′FIRST then B (B′FIRST .. I−1) is a null slice — the fact that I−1 is not in B′RANGE does not lead to an Ada constraint error.
A "sorted vector" is defined using ordering and permutation. This is a simple example of dependency between concepts. The concept of an item being a component of a vector is represented by IS_IN_INTERVAL. An alternative recursive specification for this concept is

```
--| return X = A (A'FIRST) or else
--|        IS_IN_INTERVAL (X, A (A'FIRST+1 .. A'LAST));
```

Note that this package of concepts can be generalized to be generic in the index and component types, and the ordering relations on those types (see Section 6.3.3).

A theory package should provide the concepts necessary to specify many programs based on that theory. For example, SORTING_CONCEPTS can be used to specify a search procedure.

Example: *Specification of a search procedure.*

```
--: with SORTING_CONCEPTS;
--: use SORTING_CONCEPTS;
-- Procedure to search for an item in an ordered array A of integers.
   procedure SEARCH (X : ITEM;
                     A : VECTOR;
                     L, H : INTEGER;
                     Y : out INTEGER);
--|     where
--|        in  (ORDERED (A)),
--|        out (IS_IN_INTERVAL (X, A (L .. H)) →
--|                                             A (Y) = X);
```

Commentary

The binary search block (Section 2.6) is one possible body that satisfies the specifications of this procedure. Suppose we take the simple recursive definition of IS_IN_INTERVAL. Then what we really have done is to use a simple search algorithm as the specification, and implement it by a more complex and efficient algorithm. *The simple algorithm, which we have confidence in, can be used to check the sophisticated one* (see the next section).

- **Guideline: Confidence in annotation concepts.**

  Functions that formalize concepts should be defined as simply as possible, either by annotations or function bodies, even if the definitions are inefficient. Two alternative definitions should always be proved equivalent.

The guideline is aimed at maximizing our confidence that the definitions of concepts used in annotations express our intentions. Choose a simple, possibly recursive, return expression to define a concept function, instead of a tricky iterative body.

Let us digress from our main topic, theory packages, to discuss an example where the guideline might apply. The definition of PERMUTATION given in the sorting concepts package is a simple recursive one, using only the Ada array operations. It is a little unimaginative, but we will probably see any error in it immediately (e. g., possible constraint errors caused by array indexing). A more interesting definition can be given as follows.

```
--: function COUNT(A : VECTOR; X : ITEM)
--: return NATURAL;
--|     where return Y : NATURAL =>
--|         if A'LENGTH = 0 then
--|             0
--|         elsif A(A'FIRST) = X then
--|             1+COUNT(A(A'FIRST+1 .. A'LAST), X)
--|         else
--|             COUNT(A(A'FIRST+1 .. A'LAST), X)
--|         end if;

--: function PERMUTATION(A, B : VECTOR)
--: return BOOLEAN;
--|     where
--|         return (A'LENGTH = B'LENGTH) and then
--|             for all I : A'RANGE =>
--|                                 COUNT(A, A(I)) = COUNT(B, A(I));
```

The guideline given above does not say one definition is better than the other. It gives us a criterion for trying to choose — confidence. In fact, we should try to prove the two definitions equivalent. If successful, we will increase our confidence in both definitions. This ends the digression.

When a theory package does not contain all the concepts required to specify a subprogram, the extra concepts are declared separately and used in conjunction with the theory package. For example, our sorting concepts package may not contain a concept such as the catenation of two vectors. In specifying a merging operation, catenation will be defined separately. Catenation is a predefined operator in Ada; we give a formal definition corresponding to its informal English description in [Ada83(4.5.3)].[15]

---

[15]There is a simpler recursive definition of catenation.

Example: Specification of a merge function.

```
--: function "&" (U, V : VECTOR) return VECTOR;
--|     where
--|     return W : VECTOR =>
--|         W'LENGTH = U'LENGTH+V'LENGTH
--|         and
--|         W'FIRST = U'FIRST
--|         and
--|         for all I : W'RANGE =>
--|             W(I) = if I <= U'LAST then
--|                         U(I)
--|                     else
--|                         V(I- (U'LAST+1) +V'FIRST)
--|                     end if;

--  Function to merge two ordered vectors of integers.

--: with SORTING_CONCEPTS;
--: use SORTING_CONCEPTS;
    function MERGE(A, B : VECTOR) return VECTOR;
--|     where
--|         in (ORDERED(A) and ORDERED(B)),
--|         return C : VECTOR =>
--|                 PERMUTATION(C, A & B) and ORDERED(C);
```

Commentary

The new concept CATENATION or Ada "&" is declared first. The specification of MERGE uses catenation as well as ORDERED and PERMUTATION from the SORTING_CONCEPTS theory package.

An implementation may compare elements of A and B to decide which component is the next to be merged. The specification is nondeterministic in the sense that it specifies neither an order in which comparisons are made nor a preference in the case of equal components.

2.9 Runtime Checking of Simple Annotations

We end this chapter with a brief overview of runtime checking of annotations.

The essential idea is that annotations are evaluated in–line with the actual Ada program. Consistency between the annotations and computations of the Ada program on test data is checked automatically. Inconsistencies are detected and documented by Anna support tools.[16]

Runtime checking provides an automated aid to many applications of Anna. It can be used not only in testing and debugging, which is the most obvious application, but also in other software processes to be discussed later, such as specifying packages and implementing package bodies.

Anna annotations are designed to be executable, which is the reason for the elaboration rules in Chapter 1. Of course, it is not practical to execute the most general kinds of annotations, such as those containing quantifiers over large types like the integers. But most annotations can be transformed into Ada code that checks if the annotation is satisfied by the computation states of the Ada program.

Here is an outline of a basic method of transforming simple annotations into Ada code that checks whether or not the annotations are satisfied.

First of all, an annotation must obey some restrictions. The functions and operators (both virtual as well as actual) in an annotation must be executable. This means that the virtual functions must have bodies, even though Anna rules allow virtual bodies to be omitted. And certain kinds of Anna expressions, such as quantified expressions, should not appear in the annotation — although some quantified expressions can be transformed into executable code.

There are two main components to the basic transformation method:

1. Each annotation is transformed into a *checking function* that has as parameters the program variables of the annotation and that checks if their values satisfy the annotation. The checking function is declared in the underlying Ada program at the beginning of the scope of the annotation.

2. Calls to the checking function are inserted in the underlying Ada program at points where the annotation constrains program variables and the values of those variables are changed. The program variables are passed as parameters of a call.

Here is an example of the basic transformation for a subtype annotation. It contains a subtype annotation which constrains the Ada subtype EVEN to take on only those values that are divisible by 2. The procedure ADD_1 takes an **in out** integer parameter and adds one to it.

Example: Annotated Ada code.

```
    declare
        subtype EVEN is INTEGER;
--|         where X : EVEN => X mod 2 = 0;
        E : EVEN;
```

[16] Anna tools are described in Appendix B.

```
begin
      E := 4;
      ADD_1 ( E );
end;
```

The subtype annotation is transformed into a *checking function* and calls to this checking function are inserted at each of the operations on E. The above program fragment after transformation is shown below.

Example: Ada code with runtime checks for annotations.

```
declare
   subtype EVEN is INTEGER;
   E : EVEN;

   function EVEN_CHECKING_FUNCTION (X : T) return T is
   begin
      if not (X mod 2 = 0) then
         raise ANNA_ERROR;
      end if;
      return X;
   end EVEN_CHECKING_FUNCTION;

begin
   E := EVEN_CHECKING_FUNCTION (4);
   ADD_1 ( E );
   E := EVEN_CHECKING_FUNCTION (E);
end;
```

When the checking function EVEN_CHECKING_FUNCTION is called with a parameter value E, it will check if E satisfies the subtype annotation on EVEN. If yes, it returns E; otherwise, it propagates an exception ANNA_ERROR. At each point where the value of a variable of type EVEN is changed, the checking function is called with the new value. The reason for using checking functions rather than procedures lies in the need to position checks appropriately. (We will not go into further details of positioning calls to checking functions, which are quite complex due to various Ada rules.)

When the example above is executed, the test of the assignment statement is satisfied, but the test of the result of the call to ADD_1 detects an inconsistency.

Similar transformations apply to all simple annotations, and to most of the annotations discussed in the coming chapters. Subprogram annotations, for example, transform similarly into checking functions and calls to checking functions placed at appropriate points of the subprogram body. In general, an annotation such as a subprogram annotation or type constraint, which applies to a large scope, will be transformed into a single checking function, and many calls to it will be placed throughout the scope.

There are many variations of the basic method to deal with elimination of redundant checks, and optimization of checking. We omit details. The Anna user can simply assume that runtime checking is automated and need only make sure that annotations are executable in order to apply it.

• Why runtime checking

Software development processes based on runtime checking are simpler and more practical than processes based on formal consistency proof. Proof-based methods, however, yield more definitive results on appropriate applications, and can be applied to all annotations. Processes based on either technique can be used in applications of Anna.

A discussion of formal proof rules is beyond the scope of this book, although we shall describe some software processes based on consistency proof later (Chapter 10). Informal proof (i. e., reasoning without restriction to a particular set of formal rules, or proof steps), which all programmers use now and then, can be used in the proof-based software development processes as an alternative to formal proof. The results will be just as reliable until fully automated formal proof tools are available.

Fully automated tools are required to make the application of either technique practical — we shall see later examples of the kinds of formulas one must prove in order to establish consistency of package implementations by proof–based methods (Chapter 9). Automation of runtime checking has progressed to a level where it is feasible to use it on software development projects. Automation of formal proof is still mostly a research area.

Summary

Most of this chapter has dealt with the use of simple annotations in testing, verification, and documentation of programs. In these activities we have assumed that the specification concepts are defined correctly. In order to use the techniques to gain confidence in our programs, our specifications must express what we intend.

Good sets of formal concept definitions are only likely to result from trial and error through many iterations of the steps of formalizing and implementing concepts, together with analysis of consistency of sample programs using those concepts. This is a process of building up a special language for annotation of each particular class of programs.

In Section 2.8 we discussed the construction of packages of specification concepts as a way of encapsulating concept definitions and isolating the process of defining and implementing concepts from the process of developing actual programs. An important step towards evolving standard, widely accepted concepts is to organize concepts into theory packages.

In Chapter 5 we shall describe more restrictions on theory packages, and how they should be constructed from other theory packages, to ensure that they are "correct." This is the first half of the confidence problem: gaining confidence in our specifications.

Further Reading

Concepts we have used to define a theory of sorting will be found in Knuth's book. The paper by Hoare is a classic on proving the consistency of a program with its specifications. Gries' book discusses inductive assertions in detail, and gives examples of their use in building programs. It also gives some examples of goal–oriented programming. Principles of induction are discussed generally in Manna and Waldinger. The book by McGettrick is an exposition of the kinds of proof rules needed to apply Hoare's ideas to Ada programs (excluding tasking).

1. D. E. Knuth. *Sorting and Searching, The Art of Computer Programming*. Volume 3, Addison-Wesley, 1973.
2. D. Gries. *The Science of Programming*. Springer-Verlag, New York 1981.
3. C. A. R. Hoare. Proof of a program: find, pp. 101–115. In D. Gries, Editor, *Programming Methodology, A Collection of Articles by Members of IFIP WG2.3*, Springer-Verlag, New York 1978.
4. A. D. Mc Gettrick. *Program Verification Using Ada*. Cambridge Computer Science Texts No. 13, Chapters 2 and 3. Cambridge University Press, 1982.
5. Z. Manna, R. Waldinger. *The Logical Basis for Computer Programming*, Vol. 1, Addison-Wesley 1985.

3

Exceptions

Topics:

- *annotation of raise statements;*
- *annotation of exception handlers;*
- *propagation annotations;*
- *specifying exception propagation.*

Exceptions in Ada provide a facility for programming conditions under which the normal flow of control of a computation should be abandoned. When conditions for abandonment arise, exception handling provides a facility for programming the computations that should then take place.

Despite the elegant Ada syntactic separation of normal computation and exceptional computation, and Ada rules restricting propagation, it is still possible to write "spaghetti" using exceptions just as in the good old unrestricted **goto** days. Exceptional programming is clearly an area of Ada programming that requires additional specification, testing, and documentation techniques. From the viewpoint of annotating Ada programs, the raising, handling, and propagation of exceptions pose two main problems:

1. How to document the local raising and handling of exceptions within a program unit or block.
2. How to specify propagation of an exception out of a program unit.

The first problem can be handled adequately in Anna by applying statement annotations to **raise** statements and exception handlers. The second problem requires a new kind of annotation, *propagation annotations*.

3.1 Annotating Raising and Handling of Exceptions

First, we describe a method of annotating a single subprogram or block in which exceptions are raised and handled locally. We assume that the simple annotations discussed previously are used to annotate the normal computation states.

• Exceptional states

A computation state in which a **raise** statement is executed is called *an exceptional state*.

- **Guideline: Specifying exceptional states.**

  Exceptional states should be specified by assertions placed immediately before **raise** *statements. These assertions are called "raise conditions."*

An assertion placed before a **raise** statement specifies the conditions under which the exception is intended to be raised by it — of course, the same exception may also be raised elsewhere under different raise conditions. In Figure 3.1, assertions A and B specify different exceptional states for exception E.

Example: An assertion that specifies conditions for executing a **raise** *statement.*

```
--    Array A is searched for a component equal to KEY.
             ...
         if KEY = A(HIGH) then
              Y := HIGH;
          else
--|           for all I : A'RANGE => KEY /= A(I);
              raise NOT_FOUND;
          end if;
              ...
```

Commentary

The assertion before the **raise** statement constrains the exceptional state immediately before its execution. The value of array A must be such that KEY is not a component. This can be tested at runtime, or proved, just as any other annotation of a simple statement.

There is no **out** state after execution of a **raise** since its scope (which consists of that single statement) is terminated abnormally. The state in which a handler will then be reached is the exceptional state immediately before the **raise** was executed.

The next question is how to annotate a handler. The internal processing carried out by a handler, once it has been reached, can be documented by statement annotations. However, this by itself is usually insufficient for checking that exceptions are handled as intended, or for proof of consistency of the Anna program. Documentation of a handler should specify the initial state expected by the handler.

- **Expected initial states**

A computation state in which an exception handler is invoked is called the *initial state* of the handler. The initial states that a handler is intended to deal with are called *expected initial states*.

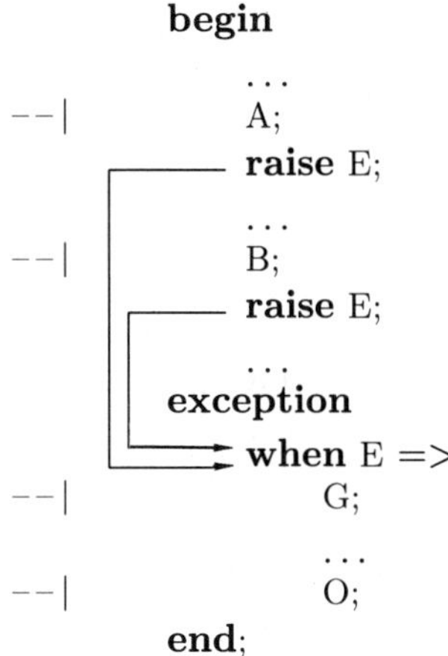

FIGURE 3.1. Raising and handling exceptions.

- **Guideline: Specifying expected initial states.**

  Expected initial states should be specified by an assertion at the beginning of a handler.

In Figure 3.1, G specifies an expected initial state for a handler for E.

Example: *Annotation of exception raising and handling within a block.*

```
-- The binary search of array A for a component equal to KEY as shown in
-- Section 2.7.
      begin
--|          (IS_IN_INTERVAL(KEY, A(L .. H)) →
--|                    IS_IN_INTERVAL(KEY, A(LOW .. HIGH)));
         while LOW < HIGH loop
            ...               -- Loop manipulating LOW and HIGH.
         end loop;
         if KEY = A(HIGH) then
            Y := HIGH;
         else
--|         HIGH ≤ LOW and KEY /= A(HIGH);                    (1)
            raise NOT_FOUND;
         end if;
            ...
      exception
         when NOT_FOUND =>
--|         for all I : L .. H => KEY /= A(I);                (2)
            TEXT_IO.PUT("The KEY is not in A");
            raise;
      end;
```

Commentary

The state in which the **raise** statement is executed is annotated by assertion (1) about local variables of the search loop — a raise condition. The expected initial state of the handler is constrained by assertion (2) so that KEY is not a component of A in the range L .. H. (Remember, there may be other statements raising NOT_FOUND with different raise conditions.) Whenever NOT_FOUND is raised by this particular **raise** statement, both assertions must be satisfied simultaneously because control will pass them successively without the state changing.

Despite Ada rules that carefully define the dynamic association of **raise** statements and exception handlers, the exceptional part of an Ada program can become complicated. This is true even without considering propagation. An exception can be raised in different places under different conditions, to be handled by the same local handler.

The idea of the previous guideline is to use expected initial state assertions to specify a boundary between exception raising and exception handling in the program. These assertions act as guards on the handlers.[1] When the program is constructed, these guards should be written *before* the handlers are written. This technique may be useful in breaking the program into two clearly separate pieces: the "normal processing" and the "exceptional condition processing."

3.1.1 Consistency of Raising and Handling Exceptions

Both runtime checking and consistency proof methods can be applied to programs that raise and handle exceptions.

Runtime Checking

Runtime checking methods translate assertions into tests. Assertions are tested as control reaches them. Raise conditions will be tested before **raise** statements are executed. Expected initial state guards will be tested immediately after a **raise** statement is executed and before a handler is invoked. Particular implementations of Anna runtime checking will raise the special ANNA_ERROR exception if either kind of assertion is violated. If a **raise** condition is violated, the ANNA_ERROR exception will be raised before the **raise** statement is executed.

Proving Consistency

In the presence of exceptional behavior, proofs of consistency can get complicated — e. g., if an exception is raised in several different places. In fact, complexity of consistency proof is a direct reflection of complexity

[1]We sometimes refer to expected initial state assertions as "guards".

of the program. One idea to simplify proofs, contained in the proof recipe below, relies on the previous guideline. If the guideline is followed, each handler will have an expected initial state guard. This is required to be complete enough to be used as a proof break point. The purpose is to break proofs into short pieces.

To simplify the discussion of proof methods, we assume that we are dealing with subprograms and blocks in which exceptions are raised and handled locally — we assume that exceptions are not propagated. Under these assumptions, proofs can usually be structured into three steps. The following recipe relies on the use of expected initial state guards.

• Recipe for proving consistency of subprograms that handle their exceptions

1. **Prove simple annotations that are not in exception handlers.** First we prove consistency of annotations and Ada text, excluding the handlers. This proof includes assertions that specify exceptional states of **raise** statements — they are treated as though they are **out** assertions at points at which the program terminates.
2. **Prove consistency of expected initial state assertions.** For each **raise** E statement, we must prove that some boolean expression satisfying its exceptional state logically implies the expected initial state assertion (or guard) of the handler for E in the same scope.[2]
3. **Prove consistency of handlers.** Finally, we prove the consistency of each handler with its annotations. This proof may assume the expected initial state guard for a handler in proving consistency of simple annotations within the handler.

When there is no exception propagation, the main problem to be faced in proofs is that an exception may be raised in more than one place. In general, a consistency proof for each handler will "branch" into cases, one for each raise statement. To prevent this, the recipe breaks the proof into two pieces at the expected initial state guard.

At Step 1, consistency of normal processing is proved; the raise conditions are treated as end conditions (or **out** annotations) that must be satisfied at those points. For example, in Figure 3.1 it must be proved that the block satisfies assertions A and B.

At Step 2, it is proved that the guard is satisfied by each exceptional state. Assertions that have already been proved to be true at an exceptional state, e. g., a raise condition, can be assumed in this proof. So, in Figure 3.1 it is proved that A implies G and that B implies G.

At Step 3, the guard may be assumed in proving consistency of a handler.

---

[2]Remember, for this discussion, we assume no propagation.

In Figure 3.1, we can assume G as an input condition in proving that the handler satisfies O when it terminates.

The wording of Step 2 in the recipe allows us to assume any assertion that is satisfied by the exceptional state of a **raise** statement in proving a handler's guard. If Step 1 is successful, we have proved that the raise conditions are all satisfied when exceptional states are reached. But raise conditions may be rather weak — they may express only some properties of an actual exceptional state. Other true facts may result from considering the computation that took place before the exceptional state was reached. Those facts may also be assumed in proving that a guard is satisfied by an exceptional state. Look back at the previous binary search example. Raise condition (1) expresses only the final situation when control reaches the exceptional state; other facts that must be true in order for the preceding computation to reach that point are needed to prove the guard (2).

Let's outline how our proof recipe would apply to the binary search example in Sections 3.1 and 2.7. Assume we have already proved consistency of the invariant over the loop (Step 1):

```
(IS_IN_INTERVAL(KEY, A(L .. H)) →                                (3)
                    IS_IN_INTERVAL(KEY, A(LOW .. HIGH)));
```

We must also prove consistency of the exceptional state assertion (1). The state in which the loop terminates is equal to the exceptional state since no values are changed between loop termination and the **raise** statement. Therefore, the loop test is false in the exceptional state: **not** LOW < HIGH. In fact, since the **if** test must be false to reach the **raise** statement, and the state is the same as when the loop terminates, we know that the exceptional state satisfies

HIGH $\leq$ LOW **and** KEY /= A(HIGH) **and** (3). (4)

Assertion (4) is a more complete formalization of the exceptional states, and perhaps we should have used it in place of (1).

At Step 2, we prove that the expected initial state guard of the handler for NOT_FOUND is satisfied by the states in which the handler is invoked. Control passes immediately from the **raise** statement to the handler, so the exceptional state is the handler's initial state. Therefore assertion (4) is true of the initial state. The values of LOW and HIGH have not changed since the loop terminated. Starting with (4), there are two cases to consider:

1. HIGH < LOW. The conclusion of (3) is false because the slice A(LOW .. HIGH) is empty. Therefore, the premise of (3) is false.
2. HIGH = LOW. The conclusion of (3) is false because the slice A(LOW .. HIGH) consists of one component, A(HIGH), which is not equal to KEY. Therefore, the premise of (3) is false.

In both cases,

not IS_IN_INTERVAL (KEY, A (L .. H))

is true of the initial state. This implies the expected initial state assertion — here we use the definition of IS_IN_INTERVAL given in our SORTING_CONCEPTS theory package (Section 2.8).

Finally, the exception handler itself is proved consistent, assuming the expected initial state assertion. This will entail proving consistency of local annotations in the handler.

Summary

The recipe for proving consistency is based on using a guard (expected initial state assertion) for each handler. A guard serves as a proof breakpoint to break a consistency proof into smaller proofs. It separates proof of the normal computation from the exception handling. It must express completely the expectations of the handler because it is the only assumption (or input condition) that is allowed in proving consistency of the handler. On the other hand, a guard must be true of all exceptional states. It should formalize properties common to all possible exceptional states of all the **raise** statements for the exception. Such weak properties are the only ones a handler may assume. Consequently, if we apply the recipe, we should follow this guideline:

- **Guideline: Choosing handler guards.**

  An expected initial state guard should be a **weakest** *raise condition for any of the* **raise** *statements that a handler is expected to handle. If this is insufficient to prove consistency of the handler, then the raise conditions must be strengthened.*

Note, however, that the recipe does not require raise conditions to specify exceptional states completely. Here, we have compromised so as not to require raise conditions to repeat all the assertions that are true before a **raise** — compare (1) and (4) above. Consequently, Step 2 in the binary search proof above requires information that is not expressed in (1).

This recipe for consistency proof is inadequate in more complicated examples where exceptions are propagated and handled at more global scopes instead of being raised and handled locally. Typically, the handler is situated in an outer scope and is separated from the inner context in which the exception may be raised and propagated. In these situations we may want to place more emphasis on the exceptional state assertions for documentation and proof (we return to this point in Section 3.3).

3.2 Propagation Annotations

Propagation of exceptions from subprograms constitutes a major part of their intended behavior. Obviously this behavior should be specified as part of a subprogram specification. The only method available to the Ada programmer is the use of informal comments. This situation is well illustrated in many examples from the Ada literature.

Example: *Informal specification of exceptional behavior of the* READ *operation of* DIRECT_IO.

```
-- This example is taken from [Ada83], Section 14.2.4.
   procedure READ (FILE : in FILE_TYPE;
                   ITEM : out ELEMENT_TYPE;
                   FROM : POSITIVE_COUNT);
```

Informal description of exceptional behavior:

The exception STATUS_ERROR is raised if any of the DIRECT_IO operations is attempted for a file that is not open. In addition, for READ:

- The exception MODE_ERROR is raised if the mode of the given file is OUT_FILE.
- The exception END_ERROR is raised if the index to be used exceeds the size of the external file.

This description is given in English text separately from the Ada specification of the DIRECT_IO package. The Ada specification of DIRECT_IO imports the exceptions by a context clause from another package, IO_EXCEPTIONS. The Ada specification does not associate the exceptions with operations that raise them. Nor does it give the conditions of propagation or the priorities between exceptions if more than one can be raised. Indeed, all the relationships between the DIRECT_IO operations and the exceptions are described in English at various points throughout Chapter 14 of the Ada Reference Manual [Ada83]. Consequently, in order to understand DIRECT_IO one must read most of Chapter 14.

In Anna, informal descriptions of propagation behavior such as those for DIRECT_IO can be expressed formally using propagation annotations. There are two kinds of propagation annotations, *weak* and *strong*. Propagation annotations may appear as subprogram annotations (i. e., as annotations of the specification part of a subprogram), as statement annotations, and as annotations over a declarative region. We will discuss their application in specifying subprograms, but the reader should bear in mind that they apply generally wherever a basic annotation can be made.

• Weak propagation annotations

A weak propagation annotation consists of the keyword **raise** followed by a sequence of exception names, the symbol =>, and a boolean expression (called the *propagation condition*).

A *weak* propagation annotation of a subprogram specifies exceptions that may be raised as a result of a call to that subprogram and a condition that will be satisfied by the state of the calling environment when the exceptions are propagated. That is, the boolean expression following the propagation condition will be true of the computation state of the calling environment at the point when the execution of the subprogram body is abandoned.

The annotation does not require any exception to be raised — which is why it is called *weak*.

Example: A weak propagation annotation.

```
    procedure INVERT (A : in out MATRIX_TYPE);
--|     where
--|         raise NUMERIC_ERROR | STORAGE_ERROR =>
--|                                            A = in A;
```

Commentary

A call to INVERT may propagate either NUMERIC_ERROR or STORAGE_ERROR. If it does so, then the current value of parameter A has to be equal to its input value.

A little more detail: **in** A refers to the value of A at the beginning of the call, and A refers to the value of A in the state when the execution of the call is abandoned. We do *not* use **out** A, which refers to the value of A on normal termination.

A weak propagation annotation may also be given without any condition; in this case it specifies (in the subprogram declaration) that an exception may be propagated from the body.

• Strong propagation annotations

A strong propagation annotation consists of the keyword **raise** followed by a boolean expression, the symbol =>, and a sequence of exception names.

A *strong* propagation annotation on a subprogram specifies a condition on the **in** values of parameters (and global variables) of a call under which an exception must be propagated; the condition need not be true after propagation. A boolean condition must be given in a strong propagation annotation.

Example: *A strong propagation annotation.*

```
    procedure INVERT (A : in out MATRIX_TYPE);
--|     where DET (in A) = 0 => raise NUMERIC_ERROR;
```

Commentary

A call to INVERT must propagate NUMERIC_ERROR if the **in** value of parameter A is singular. When it does, the value of A may have changed.

Weak and strong propagation annotations express different kinds of constraints on exception propagation. The two kinds of annotation may be compared as follows.

A weak annotation informs a caller what conditions to expect if a call propagates an exception. It provides information needed to construct an outer handler in the calling program. From the viewpoint of the implementor, it constrains the exceptional states in the subprogram body in which unhandled **raise** statements are executed.

A strong annotation specifies to a caller that certain conditions should be avoided when making a call — but the exception may be raised under other conditions as well. It also notifies an implementor of the subprogram body what input conditions must result in propagation of an exception.

These differences in semantics result in differences in the boolean conditions in the annotations. A weak propagation condition can refer to values of variables when propagation occurs. It is intended to constrain the values of parameters and variables upon abnormal termination. A strong propagation condition, on the other hand, can only refer to the **in** values of parameters and variables. It specifies a constraint on the input before the main computation starts.

Example: *Specification of exception propagation from a search procedure.*

```
--: with SORTING_CONCEPTS; use SORTING_CONCEPTS;
-- Search for an item in an ordered array A of integers.
        procedure SEARCH (KEY : ITEM;
                          A : in out VECTOR;
                          Y : out INTEGER);
--|       where
--|          in (ORDERED (A)),
--|          raise NOT_FOUND =>
--|             not IS_IN_INTERVAL (KEY, A)
--|                and A = in A,
--|          out (IS_IN_INTERVAL (KEY, A)),
--|          out (A = in A);
```

Commentary

The weak propagation annotation specifies that if the exception NOT_FOUND is propagated from a call to SEARCH, then KEY is not in A. However, the exception need not be propagated if KEY is not in A.

The weak propagation annotation also specifies that A remains unchanged. This specification is needed because A could be changed, since it has mode **in out** and the similar **out** annotation does not apply to abnormal termination.

We could also require strong propagation of NOT_FOUND whenever A does not contain KEY. To do this we could add

```
not IS_IN_INTERVAL (KEY, A) => raise NOT_FOUND
```

to the list of annotations of SEARCH. If the propagation condition is true, then NOT_FOUND must be propagated.

Example: *Formal specification of exception propagation of the* READ *operation of* DIRECT_IO.

```
-- Reordering of the declarations in DIRECT_IO [Ada83] is necessary: the ex-
-- ceptions and functions IS_OPEN, MODE, INDEX, ELEMENT_AT, and
-- SIZE should be declared prior to READ so as to be visible here.

   procedure READ (FILE  : in FILE_TYPE;
                   ITEM  : out ELEMENT_TYPE;
                   FROM  : POSITIVE_COUNT);
--|     where
--|        not IS_OPEN (FILE) => raise STATUS_ERROR,
--|        MODE (FILE) = OUT_FILE => raise MODE_ERROR,
--|        FROM > SIZE (FILE) => raise END_ERROR,
--|        out (ITEM = ELEMENT_AT (FILE, FROM)),
--|        out (INDEX (FILE) = FROM+1);
```

Commentary

The strong propagation annotations are used to specify the conditions on input parameters under which exceptions are propagated. They formalize the informal English descriptions in the earlier example of READ. This example also shows how the propagation behavior fits in with the normal termination cases. If an exception is propagated, the call is terminated abnormally and the **out** conditions do not apply; conversely, the **out** conditions constrain the state on normal termination. Virtual function ELEMENT_AT maps files and indices into elements (see Ada83, 14.2.4).

It should be mentioned that this example formalizes only the informal description given in [Ada83] (14.2.4). It is incomplete.

It does not say if the exceptions are only raised under the given conditions. If they are, this can be specified using weak propagation annotations that are the converses of the strong propagation annotations.
Also, the state of package DIRECT_IO after a propagation is not described — e. g., if an end error is propagated while reading a file, does the file remain open? These kinds of specifications will often use the Anna concept of package state, which is discussed in the next chapter.

When more than one strong propagation annotation applies to a subprogram, the Anna boolean conditions of propagation must be mutually exclusive. Strong propagation annotations are inconsistent whenever two or more conditions are true at the same time because two exceptions cannot be propagated simultaneously.

The specification of READ given previously is actually inconsistent. It is simple to make it consistent, and also to express that exceptions are propagated in the priority in which they are listed in the specification. To do this, we add the negation of each propagation condition to the conditions for propagating lower priority exceptions. Below, for example, exception QUIT_1 is given priority over QUIT_2 whenever conditions CASE_1 and CASE_2 hold simultaneously:

```
    procedure P;
--|     where
--|         CASE_1 => raise QUIT_1,
--|         not CASE_1 and CASE_2 => raise QUIT_2;
```

- **Combining weak and strong propagation annotations**

A combined propagation annotation, <=>, can be used as a shorthand notation for a pair of strong and weak propagation annotations for the same exception, provided they have the same condition[3]:

```
    procedure P;
--|     where
--|         CASE_1 <=> raise QUIT_1;
```

means

```
    procedure P;
--|     where
--|         CASE_1 => raise QUIT_1,
--|         raise QUIT_1 => CASE_1;
```

[3]This notation is not in the current Anna87 version.

This combined annotation ties an exception exclusively to one condition and does not permit it to be propagated under other conditions.

3.3 Annotating Exception Propagation

When exceptions are propagated out of a scope and handled elsewhere, there is a basic problem in providing understandable documentation and in proving consistency.

- **Bridging the context gap**

Consider a **raise** statement in an inner scope that propagates an exception to a handler in an outer scope. The expected initial state guard documenting the handler must use concepts visible at the global level. Local details of inner units are hidden and cannot be used to annotate the handler. There is a *gap* between the inner and outer contexts. Unfortunately, a local exceptional state may be annotated by a raise condition using local variables and functions. Then we may have a problem relating the outer guard with the inner raise condition. We will refer to this problem as *bridging the context gap*.

Of course, if we construct assertions for the exceptional states and expected initial states, runtime checking will go ahead and check them. But the documentation may be hard to follow if we can't see any relationship between various assertions. And we may thereby lack confidence in the overall design of the exceptional behavior of the program.

It is often thought that this problem is compounded by the Ada definition of propagation whereby an exception is propagated to the dynamically (at runtime) closest global handler. But, as we shall see, this is not so.

Let us illustrate the problem using the binary search example once again.

Example: *Incomparable annotations of exception raising and handling.*

```
procedure SEARCH (X : ITEM;
                  A : in out VECTOR;
                  Y : out INTEGER)
is                                  --  No propagation annotations.
...
begin
      ...                  --  Loop manipulating LOW and HIGH.
   if X = A (HIGH) then
      Y := HIGH;
```

```
        else
--|         HIGH ≤ LOW and                                          (1)
--|         X /= A(HIGH);
            raise NOT_FOUND; --   The exception is propagated.
        end if;
        return;
    end SEARCH;

    procedure GO_FISHING(GOT_IT : out INTEGER) is
        KEY : ITEM;
        B : VECTOR;
    begin
        GET(KEY);
        GET(B);
        SEARCH(KEY, B, GOT_IT);
        ...
    exception
        when NOT_FOUND =>
--|         for all I : B'RANGE => KEY /= B(I);                     (2)
            TEXT_IO.PUT("The KEY is not in B");
    end GO_FISHING;
```

Commentary

The expected initial state guard (2) appears to be unrelated to raise condition (1). At the position of (2), local variables HIGH and LOW in the body of SEARCH are not visible. And no subprogram annotations of SEARCH can be used to relate the two annotations. For consistency, (1) should logically imply (2). But the gap between the two annotations is so wide that the steps towards proving consistency are not at all obvious. The best we can do is to check the two assertions at runtime.

The concept of *exceptional state* is now expanded to include states in which a subprogram call terminates by propagating an exception.

- **Guideline: Annotating unhandled exceptions.**

  If a subprogram or block raises an exception and does not handle it locally, then the subprogram or block should have a weak propagation annotation for that exception. The condition of the annotation should formalize the unhandled exceptional states for the exception that are visible at the top level within the scope.

The guideline is aimed at constructing a chain of weak propagation annotations to bridge the gap between an exceptional state in an inner scope and an expected initial state at an outer one. The recipe below is one way to do this.

- **Recipe for annotating exceptional behavior**
  1. **Declare propagation concepts before the exceptions.** Functions used in propagation annotations should be visible where the exceptions are declared. This encourages planning exceptional behavior — an exception is declared together with concepts for specifying the conditions under which it is to be raised.
  2. **Declare exceptions before subprograms that propagate them.** In order to give weak propagation annotations, exceptions must be visible at the declaration of subprograms that may propagate them. This requires a little more planning than Ada enforces: according to Ada rules, an exception need only be visible to the subprogram body in order for the subprogram to propagate it.
  3. **Give exceptional state assertions.** First, each **raise** statement should be given a raise condition. Second, exceptional states arising by propagation from inner blocks should be specified by weak propagation annotations for those blocks.
  4. **Give expected initial state assertions.** Each handler should be given an expected initial state guard.
  5. **Give weak propagation annotations.** For each exception, each subprogram that may propagate the exception should have a weak propagation annotation, constructed according to the guideline above.

Each exceptional state that can arise in a scope will have an annotation.[4] At runtime, such a state will lead either to a local handler in its scope or to another exceptional state that signifies propagation from this scope. In either case, the exceptional state should satisfy the annotation associated with the handler or with propagation from the scope.

We can modify the proof recipe of Section 3.1.1 to check this. At Step 2 we should require:

- In each scope, an exceptional state annotation, which may be either a raise condition before a **raise** or a weak propagation annotation for a called subprogram (or for an inner block), must imply (in the sense of Section 2.5.3) either an expected initial state guard for a local handler or the boolean condition of a weak propagation annotation for the scope.

Consequently, at runtime a chain of annotations, each implying the next one, will always occur between an exceptional state where an exception is raised or propagated, and an expected initial state where that exception is handled.

---

[4]Predefined Ada exceptions could be handled the same way.

Let's see how the recipe applies to the previous example.

Example: *Annotation of exception raising, propagation, and handling.*

```
    NOT_FOUND : exception;

--: function FAILURE(KEY : ITEM; V : VECTOR)
--: return BOOLEAN;
--|     where
--|         return for all I : V'RANGE => KEY /= V(I);

    procedure SEARCH(X : ITEM;
                     A : in out VECTOR;
                     Y : out INTEGER)
--|     where
--|         raise NOT_FOUND => FAILURE(X, A);                    (3)
    is
    ...
    begin
           ...              -- Loop manipulating LOW and HIGH.
        if X = A(HIGH) then
            Y := HIGH;
        else
--|         HIGH ≤ LOW and                                       (1)
--|         X /= A(HIGH);
            raise NOT_FOUND; -- The exception is propagated.
        end if;
        return;
    end;

    procedure GO_FISHING(GOT_IT : out INTEGER) is
        ...                                      -- Body as before.
        SEARCH(KEY, B, GOT_IT);
        ...
    exception
        when NOT_FOUND =>
--|         FAILURE(KEY, B);                                     (2)
            TEXT_IO.PUT("Report Failure of KEY, B");
    end;
```

Commentary

Proving that weak propagation annotation (3) is true when the exceptional state occurs is a matter for local analysis of the body of SEARCH. All the annotations that are true at position (1) should logically imply the condition in (3). This is essentially the same as the proof in Section 3.1.1.

Expected initial state guard (2) must be implied by the exceptional state annotation for the call to SEARCH. This is weak propagation annotation (3) with formal parameters X and A replaced by actual parameters KEY and B.

> The introduction of (3) has afforded us the possibility of proving consistency of our exception annotations with the exceptional behavior of the underlying program. It breaks the proof problem into manageable steps. It should also help us to plan the handling of propagated exceptions as we write the underlying program.

Note that if there are other calls to SEARCH, and more than one possible handler for NOT_FOUND, all the handlers should be within the scope of FAILURE. Presumably, FAILURE would be part of each expected initial state.

The recipe suggests that concepts to be used in propagation annotations should be declared when the exception is declared. This should help in planning the exceptional behavior of the program. The concept definitions should be visible to both a propagating unit and any global handler for the exception. If an exception is reraised and propagated through several levels of nested units, new concepts for annotating propagation may be defined at different levels. The new concepts abstract and hide inner details.

Finally, the recipe can be applied with varying degrees of rigor. For example, some of the suggested assertions might be ommitted. Whatever annotations are supplied can be checked at runtime and used to test and debug the exceptional processing parts of programs.

4

Package Specifications

Topics:

- *annotations and package structure;*
- *application of simple annotations to packages;*
- *package state types;*
- *states, successor states, and their use in specifications;*
- *the hidden state principle;*
- *package axioms.*

The package is the principal construct of Ada for structuring programs. It is intended to be used for specifying programs prior to implementation, as well as for organizing large programs into separately compilable units. The main feature of Ada packages that makes them useful for specifying programs is the separation of the package declaration (or visible part) from the package body (or implementation). Specifying an entire system, hopefully, can be done independently of implementation details, which are hidden in the separate bodies. In general, many different package bodies will satisfy the same specification. Our ability to specify programs using package specifications is greatly improved by formal annotations.

There are three steps in annotating a package.

1. Annotating the package declaration.
2. Annotating the body.
3. Annotating the relationship between the two parts.

The first step is a specification activity as described in Section 2.1. Sufficient annotations in an Ada package declaration should help the user understand how to use the package without having to look at the package body. The process of *specifying a package* henceforth will mean constructing an Ada package declaration together with formal Anna annotations.

Annotations in the specification apply also to the body — they act as constraints on the body. But quite often further details of the way the body implements the specification will be needed. These are supplied by other annotations in the body.

The simple annotations (Chapter 1) and propagation annotations (Chapter 3) are adequate for specifying many kinds of packages and for the formal documentation of their bodies. We begin by describing how to specify packages using these kinds of annotations. However, as we shall see, some new annotation concepts will be needed. These include the concepts of *package state* and *package axiom*, which are also described in this chapter.

4.1 Annotations and Package Structure

The first important point is the scope and visibility of package annotations. Any annotation in a package obeys the Ada scope and visibility rules. Let us see what this means in a little more detail.

Any Anna formal comment can appear in a package declaration or body, including virtual text and the previously described kinds of annotations. These annotations have exactly the same meaning as before. A type annotation, for example, constrains the set of values of the type, and thereby constrains the values of any object of that type wherever it can be declared. Similarly, an **in** annotation of a package subprogram constrains the initial states of calls wherever they can be made. An **out** annotation constrains the subprogram body so that whenever it terminates normally, the final state must satisfy that constraint. The new thing is the region of visibility of these annotations.

• Visible and hidden annotations

Annotations in the visible part of a package declaration are called *visible annotations*; their visibility is the same as an Ada declaration at the same position (see Figure 4.1). Annotations in the private part and body are called *hidden annotations*; their visibility is restricted to the private part and body (see Figures 4.1, 4.2). In fact, the private part should really be viewed as the beginning of the declarative region of the package body.

To specify a package, we construct an Ada package declaration with annotations. Visible annotations constrain the visible package data types and specify the visible subprograms. As an immediate consequence of Ada visibility rules, they can only refer to entities that are visible to a user of the package, so a user can understand the visible annotations without having to know the details in the package body.

In Figure 4.1, we may assume that B expresses constraints on the **in** and **out** parameters of PUBLIC_PROCEDURE. It may also specify exceptions propagated by the procedure and conditions under which they occur. B has exactly the same visibility outside the package as the visible procedure declaration. It is a constraint on all outside calls to the procedure. However, it may also be regarded as a guide to outside callers. Since B can refer only to the formal parameters and visible global objects, it can be understood in the context of the package declaration. If B is "complete" enough, it will explain exactly *what* PUBLIC_PROCEDURE does. The body of PUBLIC_PROCEDURE in the package body tells us *how* the procedure works.

```
      package A_PACKAGE is

          type PRIVATE_TYPE is private;
          type PUBLIC_TYPE is ... ;
--|           where A;   -- A has the same visibility as
                         -- PUBLIC_TYPE.
          procedure PUBLIC_PROCEDURE(... );
--|           where B;   -- B has the same visibility
                         -- as PUBLIC_PROCEDURE and
                         -- applies both to calls and to the
                         -- body of the procedure.
      private
          type PRIVATE_TYPE is ... ;
--|           where C;   -- C is visible where the declaration
                         -- of PRIVATE_TYPE is visible, i.e.,
                         -- in the hidden part of the package.
      end A_PACKAGE;

          -- Outside the package specification, A
      ... -- and B are visible constraints, but C is not.
```

FIGURE 4.1. Visibility of package annotations–1.

Visible annotations not only specify a package independently of its hidden implementation, but they also constrain the package body. In Figure 4.2, the body of PUBLIC_PROCEDURE must satisfy B. Internal calls, that is, calls inside the package body, must also satisfy B.

Hidden annotations are used to document the intended behavior of the package implementation. In Figures 4.1 and 4.2, local data inside the package hidden part is required to satisfy constraints that are hidden from the outside user. These are expressed by hidden type and object constraints C and D.

For example, B expresses constraints on the body of PUBLIC_PROCEDURE, but it can only refer to visible entities such as the formal parameters. So it may be necessary to specify the effects of the procedure on the local data objects declared in the package body. The hidden annotation B$'$ is used to do this. The procedure body must satisfy both B and B$'$, and the two annotations must be consistent (discussed in Chapter 10). The important point is that B$'$ is intended to document local effects of the procedure that are hidden from users. We may regard B$'$ as augmenting B with additional local constraints. Quite often, in practice B$'$ contains a restatement of B in terms of the local entities. So it often happens that the two annotations are

```
package body A_PACKAGE is
    ...           -- A, B, and C are visible constraints.

--|  D;   -- D is an object constraint in the package body
          -- and is not visible outside. It applies from here
          -- to the end of the package body.

    ...

    procedure PUBLIC_PROCEDURE(...)
--|     where B'; -- B' must be consistent with B
                  -- in the Anna definition of consistency,
                  -- which is weaker than Ada
                  -- conformance.  B and B'
                  -- constrain the subprogram body.
    is
        ...

    end PUBLIC_PROCEDURE;
        ...
begin   -- A, B, B', C and D are visible here.
        ...

end A_PACKAGE;
        -- Outside the package body, A and B are
...     -- visible here and constrain values of
        -- the type and calls to the procedure.
```

FIGURE 4.2. Visibility of package annotations–2.

logically related (e. g., parts of B imply parts of B′ and conversely). They must be logically consistent, otherwise it is not possible to implement a body for the procedure.

• Levels of package annotations

Ada packages generally have several *levels* of components. If packages are nested inside other packages, the nesting of levels can be quite complex. Annotations can be used to document relationships between the various levels. Typically, we will use annotations at each of the various levels of a package. In the example in Figure 4.3, there are four levels.

1. *The visible level:* Visible annotations define the behavior of the package in terms of concepts visible outside the package — a user's view

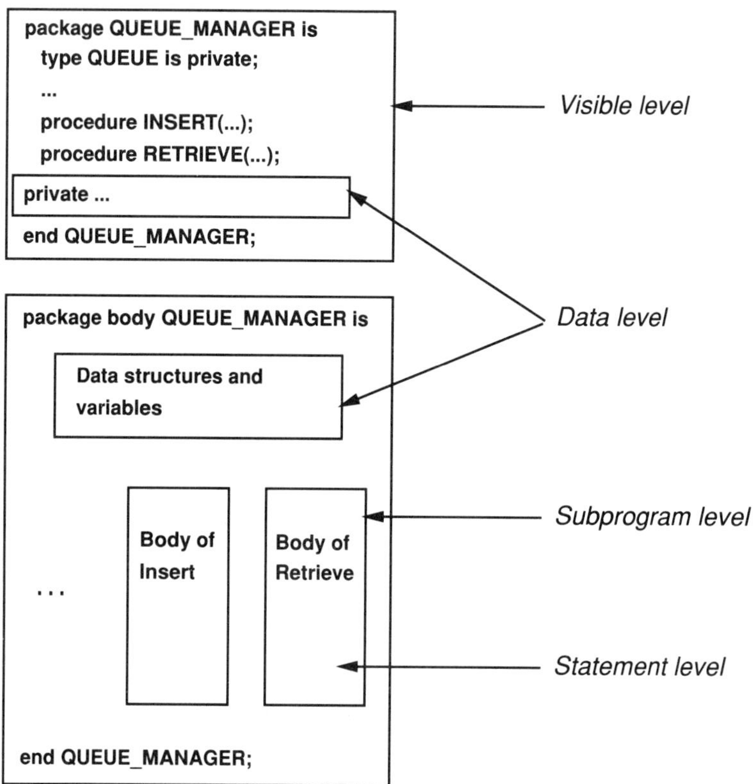

FIGURE 4.3. Levels in an Ada Package.

of its types and operations.

2. *The data level:* Hidden annotations in both the private part and body of the package constrain the types and data objects.
3. *The subprogram level:* Subprogram annotations of the subprogram bodies define the local behavior of subprograms — e. g., their effects on the data in the package body.
4. *The statement level:* Annotations such as assertions and invariants specify how the subprograms work.

In this Chapter and Chapter 5 we describe the use of annotations at the visible level. Hidden levels (levels 2, 3 and 4) are discussed in Chapter 8.

4.2 Simple Annotations in Package Declarations

We begin with an example of a basic library package supplied in a particular commercial Ada environment.[1] The package has a machine-dependent implementation. A user probably will not understand the package body — which is in machine code — even if the manufacturer is willing to make it available. An Ada package declaration without comments or annotations is available in the documentation of the environment.

The problem is to write an Anna specification for the package. In doing so, we illustrate a simple recipe for developing Anna specifications of Ada package declarations. Only simple annotations (Chapter 1) are used.

- **Recipe for specifying Ada packages in Anna**

1. **Document the Ada declaration with informal comments.**
   Gather information about the purpose of the package — there are many sources other than the package itself that often provide details about its intended and actual uses. Make a list of questions a user might ask. Avoid peeping into the package body, if there is one — this will usually result in specifying unnecessary details.
2. **Formalize and test the informal comments.**
   Express the informal comments as annotations. Test them out perhaps by writing small programs that use the package. Make sure you can deduce answers to the list of questions (step 1) if you assume the annotations.
3. **Make the specification as general as possible.**
   This involves adding new annotations, or rewriting existing annotations in logically more general forms. It also involves the opposite activity of deleting unnecessary annotations! — see Chapter 2.

- **Starting with an Ada specification**

Example: Ada specification of a string conversion package.

```
package STRING_CONVERSION is

   type PACKED_STRING is array (INTEGER range <>)
                                        of SHORT_INTEGER;

   procedure PACK_STRING (S : STRING;
                          BUFFER : out PACKED_STRING);
```

[1]Data General Ada Development Environment, circa 1984.

```
    procedure UNPACK_STRING (BUFFER : PACKED_STRING;
                                  S : out STRING);

end STRING_CONVERSION;
```

The names contain a lot of clues.[2] But, quite clearly, this specification does not contain enough information. A potential user must know how many characters are packed into a short integer in order to call the procedures with actual parameters of the correct relative lengths.[3] Otherwise, calls will just result in CONSTRAINT_ERROR. Unfortunately, type SHORT_ INTEGER is dependent on the Ada compiler implementation, and is not defined by Ada. There are other questions a user may ask. Are the two procedures inverse operations? Does the package propagate any exceptions? And so on. How can we use Anna to construct a more informative specification of this package?

• Step 1: Gather information in informal comments

The first step is to gather information. The declaration of package STANDARD or Appendix F of an Ada manual supplied by a manufacturer may tell us the length of a short integer. Or we can try a few tests. The objective is to construct informal documentation that answers the most common questions about what the package does. After some research and experimentation we might arrive at the following.

Example: *Ada specification of a string conversion package with comments.*

```
package STRING_CONVERSION is

    type PACKED_STRING is array (INTEGER range <>)
                                  of SHORT_INTEGER;
--    A short integer is represented as two bytes.

    procedure PACK_STRING (S : STRING;
                           BUFFER : out PACKED_STRING);
--      Pack two consecutive characters of S in each short
--      integer of BUFFER.

    procedure UNPACK_STRING (BUFFER : PACKED_STRING;
                                  S : out STRING);
--      Expand each short integer in BUFFER into two characters
--      and put them in S.
```

[2] I wish there was a theory of using mnemonics in programming notation!

[3] Actual array parameters must be constrained arrays of some definite length.

```
--          PARAMETER_LENGTH_ERROR exception is propagated if
--          parameter lengths do not match.

        end STRING_CONVERSION;
```

• Step 2: Formalize informal comments and test them

The next step is formalization — expressing the informal comments as formal annotations. Since these comments are incomplete and somewhat inaccurate, our understanding of the package is still vague. So, we might first try to construct simple annotations that express behavior on test cases. Annotating properties of some particular parameter values is often a helpful step towards constructing a general specification — one that specifies all intended parameter values. So we can start by annotating what the value of BUFFER must be if we pack "0123" into it. Let's guess that a character in an odd position of the string will pack into the high order byte of a short integer and a character in an even position into the low order byte.

Example: *String conversion package declaration with formal test cases.*

```
        package STRING_CONVERSION is
           type PACKED_STRING is array (INTEGER range <>)
                                                    of SHORT_INTEGER;
--         A short integer is represented as two bytes.

           procedure PACK_STRING (S : STRING;
                                  BUFFER : out PACKED_STRING);
-- Assume S'FIRST = 1 and BUFFER'FIRST = 1 to simplify equations. The
-- following annotations express test cases:

--|           where
--|           out (if S = "0123"
--|                   then
--|                      BUFFER (1) = CHARACTER'POS ('0') *256+
--|                                   CHARACTER'POS ('1')
--|                      and
--|                      BUFFER (2) = CHARACTER'POS ('2') *256+
--|                                   CHARACTER'POS ('3')
--|                      and
--|                      BUFFER'LENGTH = 2
--|                   else
--|                      TRUE
--|                   end if),
```

```
--|          out (if S = "abcde"
--|                 then
--|                    BUFFER(1) = CHARACTER'POS('a')*256+
--|                                CHARACTER'POS('b')
--|                    and
--|                    BUFFER(2) = CHARACTER'POS('c')*256+
--|                                CHARACTER'POS('d')
--|                    and
--|                    BUFFER(3) = CHARACTER'POS('e')*256
--|                    and
--|                    BUFFER'LENGTH = 3
--|                 else
--|                    TRUE
--|                 end if);

        procedure UNPACK_STRING(BUFFER : PACKED_STRING;
                                     S : out STRING);
         ...                         -- Similar annotations of test cases.

--       PARAMETER_LENGTH_ERROR exception is propagated if
--       parameter lengths do not match.

     end STRING_CONVERSION;
```

The annotations express input/output relationships between the parameters of PACK_STRING for small values of the input. They are test cases rather than general specifications for all inputs, but they are expressed as subprogram annotations.

If we want to test our annotations, we can use runtime checking. An Anna runtime checker would transform these "test case annotations" into conditional checks on calls to PACK_STRING. The checks will be executed when the STRING parameter has those values. The runtime checks will compare our annotations against the behavior of the body. If our test annotations are satisfied, we are probably on the right track towards specifying the package.

Runtime checking of specifications against behavior of the package body is probably the best method of analyzing this package. It would not be very likely that we could prove consistency with the body, which is presumed to be in some machine language.

- **Step 3: Construct a general specification**

The final step is to generalize the test cases, thus constructing annotations that specify the subprograms in all cases.

Example: Anna specification of a string conversion package.

```
    package STRING_CONVERSION is

--|    SHORT_INTEGER'SIZE = 16;

       type PACKED_STRING is array (INTEGER range <>)
                                    of SHORT_INTEGER;

       PARAMETER_LENGTH_ERROR : exception;

       procedure PACK_STRING (S : STRING;
                              BUFFER : out PACKED_STRING);
--|       where
--|          in BUFFER'LENGTH = (S'LENGTH/2) +
--|                                 (S'LENGTH mod 2),
--|          in S'FIRST = 1 and in BUFFER'FIRST = 1,
--|          out (if S'LENGTH mod 2 = 0 then
--|                 for all N : BUFFER'FIRST .. BUFFER'LAST =>
--|                 BUFFER (N) = CHARACTER'POS (S (N*2-1)) * 256 +
--|                                 CHARACTER'POS (S (N*2))
--|                 else
--|                 for all N : BUFFER'FIRST .. BUFFER'LAST-1 =>
--|                 BUFFER (N) = CHARACTER'POS (S (N*2-1)) * 256 +
--|                                 CHARACTER'POS (S (N*2))
--|                 and
--|                 BUFFER (BUFFER'LAST) =
--|                          CHARACTER'POS (S (S'LAST)) * 256
--|                 end if),
--|          raise PARAMETER_LENGTH_ERROR;

       procedure UNPACK_STRING (BUFFER : PACKED_STRING;
                                S : out STRING);
--|     where
--|          in S'LENGTH = BUFFER'LENGTH*2,
--|          in S'FIRST = 1 and in BUFFER'FIRST = 1,
--|          for all N in BUFFER'RANGE =>
--|                      0 ≤ BUFFER (N) / 256 ≤ 2**7 - 1 and
--|                       0 ≤ BUFFER (N) rem 256 ≤ 2**7 - 1,
--|          out (for all N : S'RANGE =>
--|                 if N mod 2 = 1 then
--|                    S (N) = CHARACTER'VAL (
--|                            (BUFFER (N/2 + 1) -
--|                             BUFFER (N/2 + 1) rem 256) / 256)
```

```
--|                 else
--|                     S(N) = CHARACTER'VAL(
--|                                           BUFFER(N/2) rem 256)
--|                 end if),
--|             raise PARAMETER_LENGTH_ERROR;

    end STRING_CONVERSION;
```

Commentary

The first annotation specifies that all values of SHORT_INTEGER can be represented in sixteen bits. It is therefore either true or false, independently of the program. If it is false, the package specification is a priori inconsistent. So its role is to specify an assumption on the implementation of SHORT_INTEGER upon which the package specification depends.

The exception declaration has been placed early so that it is visible in the procedure specifications. The **in** annotations of the procedures constrain the parameter lengths. They express precisely the information that experiments would attempt to determine — given only the bare Ada declaration. We can assume the input parameter values satisfy the **in** annotations in making the **out** annotations — which simplifies the **out** annotations.

One interesting point about **in** annotations is worth noting here. PACK_STRING contains an **in** annotation on an **out** parameter:

```
in BUFFER'LENGTH = (S'LENGTH/2) +
                   (S'LENGTH mod 2).
```

This makes sense because BUFFER must be constrained when the call is made. So its length is known when the call is made, even though its value is not.[4]

The **out** annotations define the mappings from **in** parameter values to **out** parameter values for each procedure. We can prove that the previous test cases are logical consequences of these procedure annotations. This increases our confidence that the general annotations express what we intended.

An important aspect of formal specifications is that we can apply proof methods to them. For example, the STRING_CONVERSION specification implies that we cannot pack an odd-length string S into a buffer and then unpack the buffer into the same string variable S. This can be proved from the input annotations together with the Ada conventions about constraining

[4]See the Ada rules about **out** parameters of subprograms, Section 1.9.

array variables.

UNPACK_STRING maps each component of BUFFER into two characters, which are placed in consecutive locations of the string S. A constraint on BUFFER requires its components (16-bit) to be composed of two integers (8–bit) that are in the enumeration range of CHARACTER (0 .. 127). An 8–bit integer N is mapped to the character that is in position N in the enumeration of type CHARACTER.

We have proceeded in three steps: informal documentation, formal test cases, and general specification. The result is a fairly good specification that is understandable independently of any package body.

Of course, specifications can always be improved! This specification can be made more general by eliminating the input assumptions that S'FIRST and BUFFER'FIRST are 1. It can also be made more complete by specifying propagation conditions for the exception — here we have only specified that both procedures may propagate the exception.

• Generalizing the specification

A specification is "more general" than another one if any implementation that satisfies (is consistent with) the latter also satisfies the former. A frequent cause of lack of generality is "early commitment,"[5] which means that unnecessary implementation details creep into the specification. How this happens is not always obvious, but one should be on guard against it. Whether something in a specification is an "early commitment" or not is very subjective, and often a cause for argument — if the "something" is removed, will the specification become too general and allow unintended implementations?

Many people will say that the specification of STRING_CONVERSION above contains an early commitment. Although we did not look at the body of the package, we still let the idea of packing the first character into the high order bits become part of the specification. Others will argue that this detail specifies accurately how the actual package works and that if we remove this detail, the result will be a more general specification that the actual package body won't satisfy. But anyway, to satisfy the "generalists," let's remove the explicit packing algorithm.

[5]See the reference to a paper by Thimbleby at the end of this chapter.

Example: A more general specification of a string conversion package.

```
        package STRING_CONVERSION is

            type PACKED_STRING is private;

--:         function UNSCRAMBLE(P : PACKED_STRING)
--:         return STRING;

          procedure PACK_STRING(S : STRING;
                                BUFFER : out PACKED_STRING);
--|             where out(S = UNSCRAMBLE(BUFFER));

          procedure UNPACK_STRING(BUFFER : PACKED_STRING;
                                       S : out STRING);
--|             where out(S = UNSCRAMBLE(BUFFER));

        end STRING_CONVERSION;
```

Commentary

We have replaced the array type and the explicit packing and unpacking specifications by private type PACKED_STRING and an unspecified UNSCRAMBLE operation. Now the specification is probably too general because we can prove commutativity of packing and unpacking. Suppose variables S1and S2 are strings and B is a packed string.

```
  PACK_STRING(S1, B);
--| S1 = UNSCRAMBLE(B); -- Out value of PACK.
  UNPACK_STRING(B, S2);
--| S2 = UNSCRAMBLE(B); -- Out value of UNPACK.
--| S1 = S2;            -- Follows from the asser-
                        -- tions and the mode of
                        -- B in UNPACK.
```

Certainly, this specification does not commit to any representation of packed strings or to any method of packing. It is too general. But we can develop more details by introducing a virtual SCRAMBLE operation and specifications defining relationships between it and UNSCRAMBLE.[6] SCRAMBLE would be used to specify PACK_STRING. The result will be a less-committed specification than our previous example, but one that logically implies more of the properties of the actual library package than this example does.

[6]We will need *axioms*, which are described later in this chapter.

Note that the package STRING_CONVERSION is just a "bundle" of related facilities — for packing and unpacking strings. It does not contain data. So it can be specified using only the simple annotations.

4.3 Package States

Many packages contain data locally in their bodies. Common examples are stacks, queues, buffers, and symbol tables. Data are stored by performing the visible operations, say the push operation of a stack or the write operation of a buffer. The behavior of a package depends on the data that are stored in it. For example, the value returned by a read operation on a buffer depends on what is in the buffer. The stored data of a package is called the *state* of the package.

Essentially, a package behaves like a composite object. Its state is its value. It gets an initial state when it is elaborated. Its state may change as a result of calling one of its visible subprograms, and only as a result of such a call. The visible operations are the legal operations on its state, just as indexing on arrays and selection on records are legal operations on arrays and records. A package continues to have a state even if a call to a visible subprogram terminates abnormally.

The package state acts as an additional (undeclared) parameter to all the package subprograms. The state consists of local arrays, records, or other objects — perhaps even the states of local packages. The state will be defined at the *data level* as shown in Figure 4.3. This data is global to all of the subprogram bodies. From the outside, at the package declaration, we cannot see any details of the state. It is completely hidden. But, in order to specify a package, we must be able to refer to the package state in the visible part of the declaration. So we must introduce a name for it. The question is how to do this.

• State types

First of all, there is a domain of values that can be states of a package P (say). This domain forms a type, called the *state type* of P.

> *In Anna the state type of a package* P *is a predefined attribute of* P *denoted by* P′TYPE.

This type may be used like any Ada *private type* declared in P except that it can only be used in annotations and virtual text. It is visible wherever the name P is visible. Variables of type P′TYPE can be declared. The equality operator and assignment can be applied to them. Subprograms (virtual ones) can have parameters of a package state type.

In addition, the subprograms of package P are operations of type P′TYPE. They are applied to states using the Ada selection notation. For example, if S is an expression or value of type P′TYPE and F is a subprogram of P, then S.F denotes a call to F when P is in state S.

The meaning of S.F is that the call to F is evaluated when the state of package P is S. The state of a package acts as an additional undeclared parameter to all the visible subprograms of the package.

The syntax of this notation is already included in the Ada syntax for selected components. It is a small extension of the allowable Ada subprogram calls. It is intended mainly for use in annotations. We will give some examples illustrating various uses in a moment.

• Initial and current states

Two particular states occur frequently in package specifications and therefore deserve special notation. The *initial state* of P, denoted by P′INITIAL, is the state of P immediately after the body of P is elaborated. The *current state* of P, denoted by P′STATE, is the state of P at the current observable computation state of the program. It is a dynamic attribute in the sense that its value can change during a computation.

> *The initial and current states of a package* P *are predefined Anna attributes of* P.

These attributes are visible from the beginning of the package declaration.

Examples: *Package states in use.*

1. *Declaring a state variable.*

   --: S : P′TYPE := P′INITIAL;

2. *A function mapping states to states.*

   (*i*) *declared inside the package*:
   --: **function** F **return** P′TYPE;

   (*ii*) *declared outside the package*:
   --: **function** F(X : P′TYPE) **return** P′TYPE;

3. *Annotations on the state.*

   (*i*) *The package remains constant*:
   --| P′STATE = P′INITIAL;

   (*ii*) *The package is returned in its* **in** *state*:
   --| **out** (P′STATE = **in** P′STATE);

   (*iii*) *The* F *component of state variable* S *is current*:
   --| S.F = P′STATE.F;

Note that in the first example of a function mapping states to states, the function is declared in the package. The package state is an implicit parameter of the function. The function can be applied to any state variable S using the Ada selection notation S.F.

• Packages as typed objects

The result of introducing the new Anna attributes is that, within annotations and virtual text, a package P is treated as a typed object. Its type is P'TYPE, its initial value is P'INITIAL, and its current value is P'STATE. Its value at any point in a computation can be saved by assigning P'STATE to a variable of type P'TYPE, or it can be passed as a parameter to a (virtual) subprogram call. The subprograms of P are operations of P'TYPE that can be applied to objects and expressions of the type using selection notation — e.g., P'STATE.F. Finally, we can write quantified expressions such as

```
for all X : P'TYPE => ....
```

With these facilities, we can specify in the package declaration how the visible procedures of the package change its state and depend on its state. We can also annotate how a program using a package changes the state of the package. There is no need to refer to hidden implementation details.[7]

Before we get into too many details, we investigate the usefulness of states. Let us start with a popular example as it appears in the Ada language manual.

Example: TABLE_MANAGER *package from [Ada83], Section 7.5.*

```
package TABLE_MANAGER is

    type ITEM is ...
    procedure INSERT (NEW_ITEM : in ITEM);
    procedure RETRIEVE (FIRST_ITEM : out ITEM);
    TABLE_FULL : exception;  --  Raised by INSERT when
                             --  table is full.
end TABLE_MANAGER;
```

The table manager illustrates an interesting aspect of the use of informal comments to document an Ada package specification. The comment introduces some new informal concepts, "table" and "full," that are not syntactically part of the Ada specification. If they have any meaning at all, it results from our ability to make mnemonic use of these names — i.e., they remind us of previous implementations of similar packages.

The comment is clearly helpful, but it would be nice if we could make its association with the Ada specification more precise. What is the relation

---

[7] A more general view of packages as types is discussed in Section 8.7.

between the table manager and the "table"? Suppose we guess that "table" refers to the state of the table manager, and that "full" is some boolean valued test that can be performed on the state. We can use package states to formalize the comment as follows.

Example: *Specification of the exception propagation in the* TABLE_MANAGER *package.*

```
package TABLE_MANAGER is

        type ITEM is ...
        TABLE_FULL : exception;

--:     function FULL return BOOLEAN;

        procedure INSERT (NEW_ITEM : in ITEM);
--|       where
--|            in TABLE_MANAGER'STATE.FULL =>
--|                                          raise TABLE_FULL,
--|            raise TABLE_FULL =>
--|                 TABLE_MANAGER'STATE =
--|                                  in TABLE_MANAGER'STATE;

        procedure RETRIEVE (FIRST_ITEM : out ITEM);

end TABLE_MANAGER;
```

Commentary

The annotations of INSERT use the current state of table manager. In the first annotation, the expression **in** TABLE_MANAGER'STATE denotes the package state on input. Therefore, **in** TABLE_MANAGER'STATE.FULL denotes evaluation of FULL in the input state. So the first annotation specifies that TABLE_FULL will be propagated by any call if the **in** state has the property that FULL evaluates to true. This captures the intent of the informal comment, although of course FULL is not specified beyond the fact that it is a boolean-valued function. (It will be the responsibility of the implementor to give a sensible virtual interpretation of FULL in the package body — more about this in Chapter 10.)

The second annotation supplies important additional information that is not included in the informal comment: whenever TABLE_FULL is propagated, the state of the package at that moment equals its state when the call started. That is, data already in the package are not lost — the current state at propagation is the input state.

4.4 Using Package States

Now its time to go into a few details about states. The Anna concept of package state applies to a package only if it is constructed so as to control its own state. Such packages must obey the *hidden state principle*, which we discuss first. Then we go into some notational issues. Some abbreviations make expressions with states easier to write (but sometimes a bit overly compact to read, until we get familiar with states). We describe the kinds of expressions that denote states of packages and how to use them in annotations and virtual text.

First of all, an Ada package has an *actual state*. An actual state is the set of objects in the Anna sense of variables, collections, and packages, whose values can affect the result of a call to a visible subprogram of that package. The actual state of a package does not include the generic units and constants that the package may refer to — generics do not have values (they are templates) and constants can't change value, so neither kind of entity can affect the values of subprogram calls to the package. Also, the actual state does not include other packages whose own actual states are constant (e. g., the package STANDARD).

Because of the permissiveness of Ada visibility rules, the actual state of a package may contain objects that are not encapsulated in the body of the package. The package may depend on global variables outside its body. In this case, the Anna concept of package state does not formalize the actual state.

If a package is constructed to satisfy the following principle, then we say that its actual state is hidden.

- **Hidden state principle**

  A package has a hidden state if and only if the result of a call to a visible subprogram depends only on the parameters of the call and the sequence of previous calls to visible subprograms.

The Anna state concept formalizes the actual state of the package if and only if the actual state is hidden.

Packages with hidden states can refer to global constants outside the package or to other outside packages that are generic, or whose states are constant. Reasons for restricting Anna package states to be hidden will become clear later in this section.

Typical examples of packages that satisfy this principle are packages whose states are constant or are encapsulated within the package's hidden part. Constant state packages include abstract data type packages — e. g., rational numbers and package STANDARD. Examples of packages that have nontrivial hidden states are stacks, queues, buffers, and symbol tables.

Generally speaking, packages do not satisfy the hidden state principle if their bodies refer to global variables that are declared outside of the package. Note that our use of "variable" here is the Anna use — it includes other packages whose states are not constant. A special case of nonhidden states occurs when a package body manipulates objects of an access type declared outside the package.

Packages that do not satisfy the hidden principle are really components of larger systems; in this case, the actual state of the complete system is formalized by the Anna state concept.

One can certainly give Anna annotations that express the behavior of a package whose state is not hidden. But one cannot rely on the Anna state concept to formalize the actual state.

4.4.1 Evaluating package functions in a state

For any package P, any function F of P is an operation of P'TYPE. It may be applied to values of P'TYPE, just as Ada operations of any type are applied to values of that type. Anna uses selection notation to apply F. If S is an expression whose type is P'TYPE, then the result of applying F to S is denoted by S.F. The expression S.F denotes the value returned by a call to F when the state of P is S. We say that F *is evaluated in state* S.

Ada has no way of talking about evaluation in some state other than the current state. Using Anna evaluation in states, we can construct annotations that compare the results of function calls in various states of a package. We can also constrain the states of a package in the same way that we constrain the values of an object of any other type.

Here are some examples illustrating uses of package states. They are explained in the text following them.

Examples: *Package states in virtual text and annotations.*

```
--  Declare a variable of a state type with initialization.   (1)

--: T : TABLE_MANAGER'TYPE :=
--:             TABLE_MANAGER'INITIAL;


--  Assign the current state to a variable.                   (2)

--: T := TABLE_MANAGER;


--  Constrain T so that it never has a full state as
--  its value.                                                (3)

--| not T.FULL;
```

```
--    Redefine the equality operator on a state type.                (4)

--: function "=" (X, Y : TABLE_MANAGER'TYPE)
--: return BOOLEAN;
```

• **Abbreviations for current states**

The new notation, when used together with Ada qualified names, can become redundant and cumbersome. So some abbreviations are allowed.

The current state P'STATE may be shortened to the package name P. Conversely, P, when used to qualify a name, as in the call P.F, is interpreted as meaning P'STATE.F. F by itself in an expression always means P'STATE.F.

Example (2) shows an abbreviation in which the name of the package TABLE_MANAGER, is used in place of the current state, TABLE_MANAGER'STATE.

• **Evaluation in arbitrary states**

Example (3) might raise some eyebrows! It is an example of applying an operation of type TABLE_MANAGER'TYPE to a variable of that type, using selection notation. T is a variable and FULL is a function of TABLE_MANAGER.
T.FULL denotes the result of calling FULL when the TABLE_MANAGER package is in state T. But why don't we write

not TABLE_MANAGER.FULL(T);?

This would be more in line with Ada notation because TABLE_MANAGER.FULL is the Ada name of the function. But we would actually be calling a different function from the FULL declared in the package — one that has the state parameter explicitly declared.

So, instead of introducing extra functions with explicit state parameters, Anna allows us to write a state type variable in the position of the package name in calls. When we write T.FULL, the T performs double duty. Its type, TABLE_MANAGER'TYPE, tells us which package the FULL subprogram belongs to, and its value tells us which state of the package is to be used in evaluating the call.

• **Eliminating qualifiers**

The idea that the package state prefix can also act as a name qualifier allows us to eliminate the Ada use of a package name as a qualifier in some cases. Consider again the call S.F, where S is a state of the package P — i. e., a variable or expression of the state type. All the information we need about F is already contained in the type of S. So we do not have to write

S.P.F, although it is legal.

• Modifiers and states

Modifiers can be applied to state attributes in expressions. **in** P.F means (**in** P).F — **in** modifies only P, so the expression denotes the value of F in the state upon entry to the scope of the annotation. **in** (P.F) denotes the value of P.F when all variables of the expression have their **in** values on entry to the scope of the annotation. **out** (P.F) denotes the value of P.F upon normal termination of the scope of the annotation.

The next example illustrates some uses of expressions in which package functions are evaluated in various states of a package.

Example: State expressions in annotations.

```
      package TABLE_MANAGER is ... end;

      package body TABLE_MANAGER is ... end;
      ...
      use TABLE_MANAGER;
      declare

--:      type HISTORY is array (INTEGER range <>)
--:                                     of TABLE_MANAGER'TYPE;
--|         where S : HISTORY => for all I : S'RANGE =>
--|                                              not S(I).FULL;

--:      H : HISTORY(1 .. N);

      begin

         for I in 1 .. N loop
            ...                        -- Operations on table manager,

--:         H(I) := TABLE_MANAGER;         -- Save current state.
--|         for all J : 1 .. I-1 =>
--|            TABLE_MANAGER.RETRIEVE'OUT.FIRST_ITEM /=
--|                              H(J).RETRIEVE'OUT.FIRST_ITEM;
         end loop;

      end;
```

Commentary

Type HISTORY is an array of states of TABLE_MANAGER. It is constrained so that no state that is a component of a history value is full. The constraint **not** S(I).FULL evaluates the function FULL in state S(I), and I ranges over S'RANGE. History variable H is used to keep track of states that result from operations on the TABLE_MANAGER in the loop. Because of the type constraint on histories, none of those tables can be full.

The assertion inside the loop requires that the first item retrieved from the current state is not the first item that would be retrieved from any of the previous states.
Looking at this assertion, one may wonder if it contradicts the Anna principle that there must be no side effect on a program variable — package states being variables. The expression

```
H(J).RETRIEVE'OUT.FIRST_ITEM
```

denotes the FIRST_ITEM parameter value returned by calling RETRIEVE in state H(J). RETRIEVE'OUT is a *function* and does not have a side effect on the package state; it simply tells us what parameter values would result if procedure RETRIEVE was called.[8]

Finally, a word of caution about expressions having side effects on package states. Remember that annotations are not allowed to have any effect on actual or virtual program variables. In particular, calls to functions that have a side effect on a package state are not allowed in annotations. This does not mean that we can't annotate functions that have side effects, but that we can't call such functions in annotations.

4.4.2 Successor states

A package starts life in its initial state. Its state changes as a result of performing calls to subprograms of the package. These new states are called *successor states*.

Example: *Need for a notation for successor states.*

```
--:      S0 : TABLE_MANAGER'TYPE;
     begin
--:      S0 := TABLE_MANAGER;              --  Save the current state.
         TABLE_MANAGER.INSERT(A);
         TABLE_MANAGER.INSERT(B);
--|      TABLE_MANAGER = ...
--   The current state is now what?
```

To complete the assertion, we need an expression on the right side that denotes a successor state resulting from initial value S0 by performing two INSERT operations. We might think of writing S0.INSERT(A).INSERT(B) but we can't because INSERT is a procedure.

The solution is this.

> *In Anna every visible subprogram of a package has a predefined function attribute called the* 'NEW_STATE *attribute.*

---

[8]See Section 1.9.1 for the 'OUT attribute.

In the case of INSERT, it is INSERT'NEW_STATE. It returns the state resulting from performing an INSERT. Essentially, INSERT has a procedure declaration

```
procedure INSERT (NEW_ITEM : ITEM);
```

and INSERT'NEW_STATE is an attribute that behaves as if it were declared as

```
--:  function INSERT'NEW_STATE (NEW_ITEM : ITEM)
--:  return TABLE_MANAGER'TYPE;
--|     where return in TABLE_MANAGER.INSERT (NEW_ITEM);
```

It defines the mapping from states to states associated with the INSERT procedure. Note that INSERT'NEW_STATE does not change the state of the package; it simply tells us how the state is changed if INSERT is called.

We can write S.INSERT'NEW_STATE (I) to denote the next state after the call INSERT (I) when the package is in state S. In the example above, we can complete the assertion by writing,

```
S0.INSERT'NEW_STATE (A).INSERT'NEW_STATE (B).
```

A small detail:

Attribute 'NEW_STATE is similar to the attribute 'OUT. It provides us with the final value of a package state, whereas 'OUT gives the final values of **in out** and **out** parameters. The modes of the formal parameters are treated the same way in both of these function attributes (see Section 1.9.1).

Next, we come to the major consequence of requiring a package state to be completely hidden.

- **Hidden state lemma**:

  If a package satisfies the hidden state principle, then any possible state can be expressed as a sequence of calls to NEW_STATE *attributes that begins with the initial state.*

Since these attributes are visible in the package declaration, any possible state of the package is the value of an expression that can be written in the Ada visible part of the package.

On the other hand, if the actual package state is not hidden, the lemma is no longer true. The state of a package, and the result of a package operation, may depend on whether or not some operation outside the package (which changes its actual state) has been performed. This kind of behavior is not possible to specify in the package visible part — e.g., if the outside operation is not visible to the package.

• Square bracket notation

Anna provides a shorthand notation for writing successor states. Instead of writing

```
TABLE_MANAGER.INSERT'NEW_STATE(A)
             .INSERT'NEW_STATE(B)
```

we can use a special square bracket notation for successor states:

```
TABLE_MANAGER[INSERT(A); INSERT(B)].
```

Both expressions denote the state of the table manager after A and B have been inserted in succession, starting in its current state. The expression before the square brackets must denote a state; within the brackets is a sequence of calls to visible subprograms of the package. Any procedure call in the sequence is understood to be a shorthand for the corresponding call to a 'NEW_STATE function.

Example: Successor states in assertions.

```
--| for all TM : TABLE_MANAGER'TYPE; X : ITEM =>
--|                                   not TM[RETRIEVE(X)].FULL;

--| for all S : TABLE_MANAGER'TYPE; A, X : ITEM =>
--|     S[INSERT(A); RETRIEVE(X)] =
--|                                   S[RETRIEVE(X); INSERT(A)];
```

Commentary

The first assertion expresses formally that "any state resulting from a RETRIEVE operation is not full." It is an assertion about all successor states in which RETRIEVE is the last operation performed.

The second assertion expresses that equal successor states result when INSERT and RETRIEVE operations are performed in either order and terminate normally. Essentially, the operations commute whenever they both terminate normally when performed in either order. (This assertion uses the "=" operation on the state type.)

There is one final point about package state expressions — definedness. The normal rules for evaluation of expressions apply. So if any subexpression is undefined, perhaps because a call terminates abnormally or does not terminate at all, the whole expression is undefined. For example, if one of the calls to INSERT propagates an exception, the expression

```
TABLE_MANAGER[INSERT(A); INSERT(B)]
```

is undefined. The table manager will have a state of course, but this expression simply does not denote it if the calls do not terminate normally. (Exactly the same situation arises when evaluation of an expression yields a NUMERIC_ERROR exception. The numerical value exists but the expression does not give it to us.)

Now perhaps we can give a more detailed specification of the table manager, formalizing some of the English description in Ada83, 7.5. (Our data types differ slightly, but nothing of importance is changed.)

Example: *Informal specification of the* TABLE_MANAGER *package.*

```
   package TABLE_MANAGER is

      subtype DATA is STRING(1 .. 10);
      type PRIORITY is range 0 .. 255;

      type ITEM is
         record
            D : DATA;
            P : PRIORITY;
         end record;

      TABLE_FULL : exception;

--:   function FULL return BOOLEAN;

      procedure INSERT(NEW_ITEM : in ITEM);
--|      where
--|         in TABLE_MANAGER.FULL => TABLE_FULL,
--|         raise TABLE_FULL =>
--|                  TABLE_MANAGER = in TABLE_MANAGER;
--     Each inserted NEW_ITEM has a priority.
--     If NEW_ITEM is not in table then add it to table.
--     If NEW_ITEM is in table then INSERT has no effect.

      procedure RETRIEVE(FIRST_ITEM : out ITEM);

-- When RETRIEVE returns an item from table, it is no longer in the table.
-- RETRIEVE always returns an item from table with lowest priority value –
-- just like standing in line, the lowest priority value means highest priority.

   end TABLE_MANAGER;
```

In formalizing these requirements, we will again identify "table" with the table manager state. The concept of an item being *in* the table is formalized by the virtual concept MEMBER.

Example: *Specification of the* TABLE_MANAGER *package.*

```
   package TABLE_MANAGER is

      subtype DATA is STRING(1 .. 10);
      type PRIORITY is range 0 .. 255;
```

```
      type ITEM is
          record
              D : DATA;
              P : PRIORITY;
          end record;

      TABLE_FULL : exception;

--:   function FULL return BOOLEAN;
--:   function MEMBER(X : ITEM) return BOOLEAN;

      procedure INSERT(NEW_ITEM : in ITEM);
--|     where
--|         in TABLE_MANAGER.FULL => raise TABLE_FULL,
--|         raise TABLE_FULL =>
--|                   TABLE_MANAGER = in TABLE_MANAGER,
--|         in NEW_ITEM.PRIORITY'DEFINED,
--|         out(TABLE_MANAGER.MEMBER(NEW_ITEM)),
--|         out (in TABLE_MANAGER.MEMBER(NEW_ITEM)→
--|               TABLE_MANAGER = in TABLE_MANAGER);

      procedure RETRIEVE(FIRST_ITEM : out ITEM);
--|     where
--|         out (in TABLE_MANAGER.MEMBER(FIRST_ITEM)),
--|         out (not TABLE_MANAGER.MEMBER(FIRST_ITEM)),
--|         out (for all X : ITEM =>
--|                TABLE_MANAGER.MEMBER(X) →
--|                   X.PRIORITY >= FIRST_ITEM.PRIORITY);

   end TABLE_MANAGER;
```

Commentary

The annotations of INSERT and RETRIEVE use the current state. This attribute gives us a powerful way of expressing invariant properties, for example, that "INSERT has no effect" if the item is already in the table. We simply express that "the state doesn't change" if the item is already in the table. It is also useful in expressing relationships between an item and all other items in the table, e.g., that RETRIEVE returns "an item of lowest priority value." This property is expressed as "all items remaining in the output state have greater or equal priority value."

Note the use of the state attribute in the first annotation of RETRIEVE:

```
out (in TABLE_MANAGER.MEMBER(FIRST_ITEM)).
```

This annotation expresses that "the **out** value of FIRST_ITEM is a member of the **in** state of TABLE_MANAGER."

This example illustrates a certain style in writing annotations with package states. It is legal to omit the current state attribute — remember a call F always means P'STATE . F. When there are modifiers that apply to states, an annotation is clearer if the states are explicit. Suppose we omit the current states in the annotations. Since functions MEMBER and FULL are directly visible, no Ada name qualification is necessary. So we could write the fourth annotation of INSERT compactly as

```
out (not in MEMBER (NEW_ITEM) →
                        MEMBER (NEW_ITEM)) .
```

The **in** modifier on the left side of the implication applies to the implicit current state of the call to MEMBER — MEMBER is evaluated in the **in** state when INSERT is called. The **out** modifier applies to the implicit current state on the right side. (Since NEW_ITEM is a parameter of INSERT with mode **in** the current state on the right side is the only unmodified program variable or dynamic attribute in the annotation to which **out** can apply.) The expanded form of this annotation contains all the state parameters and their modifiers explicitly:

```
out (not in TABLE_MANAGER . MEMBER (NEW_ITEM) →
            TABLE_MANAGER . MEMBER (NEW_ITEM)) .
```

But when we get used to states, we may prefer the compact form that omits them!

Finally, this specification of the table manager certainly leaves some important properties unspecified. The reader may try to fill some of the "holes," perhaps by invoking the initial state attribute.

4.4.3 Equality on state types

The previous table manager example illustrates the importance of the standard operation of "=" on the state type. Equality and assignment are standard, predefined operations on package state types, analogous to the Ada operations on private types. Intuitively, the predefined equality between two states means that the states are component-wise identical — i. e., each object in the package hidden part has the same value in the two states. We give an explicit definition when we discuss package bodies in Chapter 8.

One important point is immediately clear. To specify abstract objects such as stacks, symbol tables, and table managers, the predefined equality will often be too restrictive. We may need to specify that two states, viewed from the "outside," are equal without being identical "inside" (e. g., equal states may not be identical because one of them contains garbage). In such

Concept	Notation	Meaning
Type of states of P	P′TYPE	**Attribute**: treated as a private type declared at beginning of P.
Initial state of P	P′INITIAL	**Attribute**: treated as a deferred constant of type P′TYPE.
Current state of P	P′STATE *or* P	**Attribute**: treated as a function of P returning a value of type P′TYPE.
Successor state of P	S[f; g; h]	Expression denoting state of P after calls f, g, h to subprograms of P are executed starting in state S.
New state functions	Q′NEW_STATE(...)	**Attribute**: a function attribute of subprogram Q (...) returning the state of P resulting from a call P.Q (...).

FIGURE 4.4. Anna predefined attributes for package states

cases, we must be able to redefine "=". Therefore, Anna permits redefinition of "=" on state types. This deviates from the Ada treatment of private types, where "=" cannot be redefined. But since the package state types are "new" types not in Ada, this changes only the Ada philosophy and not the language. (Again, see Chapter 10 for examples.)

Some restrictions on the use of package state attributes are discussed in Section 4.6.

4.5 Package Axioms

A package is a grouping of data types and operations. Usually this grouping is more than just a boundary. The operations are interrelated. Relationships between the operations should be part of the package specification. For example, the operations on type INTEGER in package STANDARD obey rules such as

```
for all A, B, N : INTEGER =>
    A mod B = (A+N*B) mod B.
```

Operations PUSH and POP of a stack package obey a cancellation rule:

```
for all S : STACK'TYPE; X, Y : ELEM =>
                               S[PUSH(X); POP(Y)] = S.
```

A subprogram annotation is inappropriate for expressing such relationships between two or more subprograms, not only because it is often difficult but because a relation is a property of all the subprograms. So a new kind of annotation, *axiom*, is used in package visible parts for this purpose.

We must explain two things about axioms: (1) how to write them (the syntax) and (2) what they mean (the semantics).

First, the syntax. An axiomatic annotation may appear as a virtual declaration anywhere in the visible part of a package. It consists of the reserved word **axiom** followed by one or more boolean expressions. Each individual boolean expression is called *an axiom* of the package. Here's a schematic outline:

```
    package P is
        ...                                 -- Types and subprograms.
--|     axiom
--|         for all X, Y : T; ... =>
--|             A(X, Y, ...),
--|             B(X, Y, ...),
--|             C(X, Y, ...);

    end P;
```

In the outline, A, B, C are Anna boolean expressions (axioms).

Note a few things about this notation. A list of boolean expressions may follow a single quantifier prefix; they are separated by commas. Axioms are the only annotations where a list of expressions is allowed *inside* a quantifier. The notation

```
quantifier domain => A, B;
```

means

```
(quantifier domain => A) and (quantifier domain => B);      (1)
```

This allows several axioms to be stated within one quantifier prefix without repeating the prefix for each individual axiom. The most common kind of prefix is the **for all** quantifier over a number of different type domains. Although A and B may also contain quantifiers, it is usually the case that a package specification contains a list of axioms all governed by the same quantifiers.

Note also that when **for all** quantifiers are present, the above axiomatic annotation is not logically equivalent to

```
(quantifier domain => A and B);                                    (2)
```

unless A and B are always defined (see Section 1.4). That is, when the quantifier prefix is distributed throughout the list of axioms, as in (1), each constituent axiom must then be true for the axiomatic annotation to be true. On the other hand, if we replaced commas by **and** as in (2), the resulting conjunction of the list is undefined when one of the constituent conjuncts is undefined, even if other conjuncts are false. So the quantified conjunction (2) can be true in cases when a constituent axiom is false.

Examples: Axioms.

1. *The initial state of* TABLE_MANAGER *is not full.*

```
--| axiom
--|     not TABLE_MANAGER'INITIAL.FULL;
```

2. *Stack operations* PUSH *and* POP *commute, and* POP *is an inverse of* PUSH.

```
--| axiom
--|     for all S : STACK'TYPE; X, Y : ITEM =>
--|         S[PUSH(X); POP(Y)] = S[POP(Y); PUSH(X)],
--|         S[PUSH(X); POP(Y)] = S;
```

3. *There are integer values* 0 *and* 1.

```
--| axiom
--|     exist X : INTEGER => X = 0, X = 1;
```

Now we come to the meaning of an axiom as part of the specification of a package. Its meaning follows naturally from its intended purpose — to present the user with a specification that can be depended upon and to require the implementor of the package body to satisfy the specification.

Here are the main points:

1. The visibility of an axiom is exactly that of a declaration in the package declaration (see Section 4.1).
2. An axiom expresses a *promise* to users that a boolean expression will be satisfied by all states of the package. A *promise* is an annotation that may be assumed to be true in a particular region of text. So a package axiom may be assumed to be true after any call to a package subprogram. This can be viewed as a more general form of an **out** annotation on a subprogram.

3. An axiom expresses a *constraint* on the implementation of the package in its hidden (private and body) parts. When we deal with interpretation of axioms in Chapter 9, we will see how axioms constrain the package body so that the "promised" relationships are true of all states.
4. Axioms are elaborated when the package declaration is elaborated. At this point, all program variables are replaced by their values. Deferred constants (of a private type, such as the initial state attribute) are not replaced by their values (which may not be known until the package body is elaborated). Expressions that do not contain logical variables or deferred constants are evaluated. The elaborated axiom does not have any program variables. It is a fully quantified expression. This means that an axiom describes a property that is true of all states of the package (i. e., values of the state type), just as a type annotation describes all values of a type.

If an axiom contains a generic parameter, it is a template for instances, i. e., for axioms resulting from applying the Ada generic instantiation rules.

Now for some examples. Suppose we try to specify the predefined package STANDARD. This is really several packages enveloped together, one for each of the Ada predefined types BOOLEAN, INTEGER, FLOAT, and so on. Each of these types is implemented by the Ada compiler and/or accompanying environment. The official declaration of package STANDARD in Ada83 (Appendix C) gives no formal specification for the implementation to live up to. Ada programmers probably expect the arithmetic operators to obey the classical rules, at least when their computations terminate normally. A specification for the predefined integers might be given axiomatically as follows.

Example: *An axiomatic annotation for an integer package.*

```
    package INTEGERS is

        type INTEGER is private;

--  The predefined operators:
        function "=" (LEFT, RIGHT : INTEGER)
            return BOOLEAN;
        function "+" (LEFT, RIGHT : INTEGER)
            return INTEGER;
        function "-" (LEFT, RIGHT : INTEGER)
            return INTEGER;
        function "*" (LEFT, RIGHT : INTEGER)
            return INTEGER;
        ...                                    -- Other operations.
```

```
--|     axiom
--|        for all A, B, N : INTEGER =>
--|           A mod B  = (A + N*B) mod B,
--|           A = (A/B)*B + (A rem B),
--|           (-A)/B = -(A/B),
--|           A/(-B) = -(A/B),
--|           A rem (-B) = A rem B,
--|           (-A) rem B = -(A rem B),
--|           ...;                      -- Other arithmetic axioms.

   end INTEGERS;
```

Commentary

Axiomatic annotations allow us to write the classical axioms of arithmetic just as they have been written in the mathematical texts. This is the most natural way to express that the package operations satisfy the classical axioms. It would not be suitable to specify the axioms as subprogram annotations on the operators, even if we could, because each axiom is a relationship between all the operators in it.

The meaning of the Anna axioms is as follows. First, the user's view from outside of the package: the axioms promise to be true always. Now, the universal quantifiers imply that whenever the equality tests in their scope are defined, those tests are true. So whenever A, B, N are such that the simple expressions in an axiom are defined (i. e., their evaluation terminates normally), then the equality test evaluates to true. For example, in the axiom

```
for all A, B, N : INTEGER =>
                        A mod B = (A+N*B) mod B,
```

A, B, N have values so that A **mod** B evaluates to U and (A+N*B) **mod** B evaluates to V. Then the axiom promises that U = V. On the other hand, if the evaluation of either simple expression is abnormal (e. g., by propagating the numeric error exception), the axiom is true for these particular values of A, B, N by definition, and promises nothing for these values.

The implementor's view, from the hidden part of the package, is that the axioms are constraints that must be satisfied by that hidden part. Thus, referring to the previous paragraph, type INTEGER and the operations "+", "*", **mod**, "=" must be implemented so that U = V. The implementation is forced to honor what the specification promises.

- **Implicit state quantifier in axioms**

A notational simplification for axioms is used in the previous example. Axioms specify properties that are true of all states of a package. An axiomatic formalization of such properties contains a universal quantifier over the package state type. In many examples, as here, the properties of the package operations are independent of the package state. In order to allow properties that are independent of the package state to be expressed conveniently, the universal quantifier over states may be omitted. An outermost quantifier **for all** over the state type is assumed wherever a package subprogram appears unqualified in an axiom. Thus,

```
axiom
   for all A, B, N : INTEGER =>
      A mod B = (A+N*B) mod B,
         ...
```

is interpreted as

```
axiom
   for all S : INTEGERS'TYPE; A, B, N : INTEGER =>
      S."=" (S.mod (A, B), S.mod (S."+"(A, S."*"(N, B))), B),
         ...
```

That is, the first version is interpreted as true of all states.

In the previous example we made the point that the Anna semantics of universal quantification implies that universally quantified axioms are trivially true for those parameter values where the computations of subexpressions do not complete normally. This allows us to write axioms describing properties of terminating computations — which is what we want to do — without having to clutter them up with input conditions as premises. The input conditions necessary to ensure normal termination can be associated with the subprogram declarations.

Now let's use axioms to give a more complete specification of our previous table manager example. Here we may need to choose between using a subprogram annotation or an axiom to express certain properties — often a property can be expressed either way.

- **Guideline: Choosing between subprogram annotations and axioms.**

  Generally, algebraic relationships between subprograms, such as conditions under which they commute, should be expressed as axioms. Conditions governing the parameters of an individual subprogram, such as input conditions, propagation conditions, and output conditions, should be expressed by subprogram annotations.

However, there are no rigid rules about when to use which kind of annotation.

Example: *Specification of the table manager package using axioms.*

```
     package TABLE_MANAGER is

          subtype DATA is STRING(1 .. 10);
          type PRIORITY is range 0 .. 255;

          type ITEM is
               record
                    D : DATA;
                    P : PRIORITY;
               end record;

          TABLE_FULL : exception;

--:       function FULL return BOOLEAN;
--:       function MEMBER(X : ITEM) return BOOLEAN;
--:       function "=" (S, T : TABLE_MANAGER'TYPE)
--:       return BOOLEAN;

--:       function LEAST_PRIORITY(I : ITEM) return BOOLEAN;
--|            where return (for all X : ITEM =>
--|                 MEMBER(X) → X.PRIORITY >= I.PRIORITY);

          procedure INSERT(NEW_ITEM : in ITEM);
--|            where
--|                 in TABLE_MANAGER.FULL => TABLE_FULL,
--|                 raise TABLE_FULL =>
--|                      TABLE_MANAGER = in TABLE_MANAGER,
--|                 in NEW_ITEM.PRIORITY'DEFINED,
--|                 out(in TABLE_MANAGER.MEMBER(NEW_ITEM) →
--|                        TABLE_MANAGER = in TABLE_MANAGER);

          procedure RETRIEVE(FIRST_ITEM : out ITEM);
--|            where
--|                 out(in TABLE_MANAGER.MEMBER(FIRST_ITEM)),
--|                 out(not TABLE_MANAGER.MEMBER(FIRST_ITEM)),
--|                 out (not TABLE_MANAGER.FULL),
--|                 out LEAST_PRIORITY(FIRST_ITEM);

--|       axiom
--|            for all TM : TABLE_MANAGER'TYPE;
--|                 X, I, J : ITEM =>
--|                 not TABLE_MANAGER'INITIAL.MEMBER(X), --(1)
--|                 not TABLE_MANAGER'INITIAL.FULL,

--|                 TM[INSERT(I)].MEMBER(J) = if I = J then -- (2)
--|                                                   TRUE
--|                                               else
--|                                                   TM.MEMBER(J)
--|                                               end if,
```

```
--|            TM[INSERT(I); RETRIEVE(J)] =
--|               if not TM.LEAST_PRIORITY(I) then      -- (3)
--|                  TM[RETRIEVE(J); INSERT(I)]
--|               elsif not TM.MEMBER(I) then
--|                  TM
--|               else
--|                  TM[RETRIEVE(J)]
--|               end if;

   end TABLE_MANAGER;
```

Commentary

Compare this version of the TABLE_MANAGER specification with the previous one in Section 4.4.2. There are two new virtual concepts. LEAST_PRIORITY is introduced to name its return annotation; it is used to shorten annotations. The declaration of the equality operator on the state type permits equality of states to be redefined in the TABLE_MANAGER body (more about this in Chapter 8) — why this may be necessary will become clear in a moment.

Some of the previous **out** annotations of INSERT and RETRIEVE have been replaced by axioms that logically imply them. The axioms also specify some new properties of the package. Axiom (1) expresses that initially the TABLE_MANAGER has no members and is not full. Axiom (2) deals with the relationship between INSERT and MEMBER. It implies one of the old **out** annotations of INSERT, that inserted items become members. But it also implies that inserting an item does not alter the existing membership. That is, from axiom (2) the following assertion can be proved:

```
for all TM : TABLE_MANAGER'TYPE; X : ITEM =>
      TM.MEMBER(X) → TM[INSERT(I)].MEMBER(X);
```

The previous specification did not imply this.

Axiom (3) deals with the relationship between INSERT and RETRIEVE. It is a conditional equation between states. It expresses when the two operations commute without affecting the state. It also expresses when the two operations cancel each other.

Axiom (3) appears tricky because RETRIEVE is underspecified — if there is more than one item having the lowest priority, any one of them can be returned.

In order to satisfy axiom (3) an implementor may want to define "=" between states more generally than the predefined Anna operator on the state type. The predefined "=" is the identity on the hidden structure of the states — just like the predefined Ada equality operator on private types. For example, one may want to define two states to be equal if they contain the same items, regardless of any other internal details. The virtual declaration of the equality operator allows a redefinition in the body.

4.5.1 AXIOMS FOR EQUALITY

The equality operator on an Ada limited private type or on an Anna state type may be defined explicitly. To do this, a visible declaration

```
function "=" (X, Y : T) return BOOLEAN;
```

is included in the package specification containing the limited private type. A function body for "=" on type T will be declared in the package body. This function body defines a new equality operator on T.

Ada does not require a user-defined equality operator to possess the normal properties of equality. However, if our software is to behave as expected, an operator with the name "=" should behave as that name implies.[9]

In Anna a predefined set of axioms for equality must be satisfied by each explicitly defined equality operator "=" on a limited private type or on the state type of a package. This applies to the new "=", whether it is actual or virtual. These axioms are automatically added to the set of package axioms whenever an explicit declaration of "=" appears in the package.

As an example, consider the previous TABLE_MANAGER, in which an equality on the state type is explicitly declared. The implicit predefined axioms are shown below.

Example: Implicit equality axioms for the TABLE_MANAGER.

```
    package TABLE_MANAGER is

       ...

--:    function FULL return BOOLEAN;
--:    function MEMBER(X : ITEM) return BOOLEAN;
--:    function "=" (S, T : TABLE_MANAGER'TYPE)
--:    return BOOLEAN;

--:    function LEAST_PRIORITY(I : ITEM) return BOOLEAN;
       procedure INSERT(NEW_ITEM : in ITEM);
       procedure RETRIEVE(FIRST_ITEM : out ITEM);
```

[9] Otherwise we should give the operator another name.

```
        ...
--| axiom
--    Axioms of equivalence:
--|       for all U, V, W : TABLE_MANAGER'TYPE; I : ITEM =>
--|           U = U,                                  --  Reflexivity.
--|           U = V → V = U,                          --  Symmetry.
--|           U = V and V = W → U = W,                --  Transitivity.

--    Substitution axioms for each function:
--|           U = V → U.MEMBER(I) = V.MEMBER(I),
                ...

--    Substitution axioms for each procedure:
--|           U = V → U[INSERT(I)] = V[INSERT(I)],
--|           U = V → U[RETRIEVE(I)] = V[RETRIEVE(I)],
--|           U = V → U.RETRIEVE'OUT(I).FIRST_ITEM =
--|                          V.RETRIEVE'OUT(I).FIRST_ITEM,

--    Independence of the package state:
--|           for all ST1, ST2 : TABLE_MANAGER'TYPE =>
--|                          ST1."=" (U,V) = ST2."=" (U,V);

                  ...
    end TABLE_MANAGER;
```

Commentary

The axioms include the axioms of equivalence relations and the axioms of substitution of equal values for each subprogram of the package. For example, one of the substitution axioms tells us that calling RETRIEVE in two equal states of TABLE_MANAGER will result in the same value for **out** parameter FIRST_ITEM.

These standard axioms of the mathematical theory of equality are assumed to be satisfied by any implementation of "=".

The "=" on TABLE_MANAGER'TYPE may be redefined by a virtual subprogram of the TABLE_MANAGER package. The current state could be a global parameter of this function. If the new equality relation depends on the current state, calls such as TABLE_MANAGER. "=" (U, V) where U, V are fixed values, could have different results at different times. This would mean that U and V would sometimes be equal and sometimes not, depending on the state in which the tests are made. The last equality axiom disallows this possibility (note that ST1, ST2 are any two states).

There is an example of a function body for "=" in Section 8.6.

4.6 Restrictions on Package States *

In this section we discuss some restrictions on the use of Anna package state attributes. The main restrictions follow from the fact that a state type is a predefined Anna attribute that is a virtual Ada private type of a package. Ada restricts the use of private types to ensure implementability. Similar restrictions are adopted for the use of states in annotations and virtual text. Here, we deal with restrictions in the visible part of a package and outside the package. Restrictions in the hidden part are discussed in Chapter 8.

We also discuss briefly restrictions on using states of generic packages. This could be dealt with in Chapter 6, but many readers may already have questions about generic states by now.

4.6.1 Restrictions on use of state attributes *

A state type is treated like an Ada private type declared at the beginning of the package specification. This semantics implies certain restrictions on the use of state type attributes. In most cases, Anna follows the Ada rules restricting the use of private types. That is, a rule is adopted that would apply by analogy with an Ada rule if the state type was actually declared as a private type.[10]

It is helpful to imagine that a package has implicit virtual declarations for its state attributes, as follows:

```
        package P is
--:         type P'TYPE is private;
--:         function P'STATE return P'TYPE;
--:         P'INITIAL : constant P'TYPE;
            ...                          -- Actual and virtual text of P.
        end P;
```

(In fact, if Anna did not provide 'TYPE and 'STATE, and we needed to use the state concepts, this is how they could be defined.)

We can then apply the Ada rules for using private types to see if a particular usage of state attributes is consistent with the restrictions of Ada. The main Ada rule that we worry about is the general rule that an entity (package, subprogram, type, or whatever) must be elaborated *before* it can be used in a computation.

The use of 'TYPE as a type name in annotations is not restricted. The use of 'TYPE in virtual text follows the Ada rules for using private types, except that the predefined equality operator may be redefined. But in addition, the Anna rules are more restrictive in the hidden part of the package. The

[10] In a few cases, however, the Ada rule is not adopted.

purpose of these restrictions is to prevent circular state type definitions. How they do this is discussed in Chapter 8 where the full declaration of 'TYPE in the hidden part is defined.

Outside the package, the main change from the analogous Ada rules is the position of declarations of variables of the state type. Such declarations should be placed so that they are elaborated after the package body. This is because the full declaration of 'TYPE is usually placed in the package body, and cannot be assumed to be in the private part.

Attribute 'INITIAL behaves as a deferred constant of type 'TYPE. It is initialized when the package body is elaborated. Therefore, it should not be used in annotations that require using its value to check constraints before the package body is elaborated.

The current state attribute, 'STATE, behaves as a visible virtual function of the package having the package state as its parameter. Each time it is called it returns the current state.

This view of 'STATE enables us to determine where it can be used in annotations and virtual text. Recall that in Ada a package subprogram cannot be called in a computation (including an elaboration of a declaration) until the package body has been elaborated. The same rule applies to 'STATE. If 'STATE must be computed, either in the elaboration or checking of an annotation or in virtual text, the package body must have been elaborated when such a point is reached.

Now let's see how the Ada rules determine where we can use the package state attributes.

1. A package subprogram cannot be called (and its annotation checked) before the package body is elaborated (Ada rule). Therefore the use of 'STATE and 'INITIAL in annotations of the visible subprograms is okay (as in the last example of Section 4.5). Such use specifies an effect on a parameter of a package subprogram — the state.
2. Package axioms (Section 4.5) are elaborated when the package specification is elaborated (Anna rule). Expressions that do not contain logical variables are evaluated and replaced by their values; deferred constants are deferred — i.e., their names are *not* replaced by their values until the package body is elaborated. Consequently, P'STATE may not be used in an axiom of P since it would have to be computed prior to elaboration of the package body. But deferred constants such as attribute 'INITIAL can be used in axioms.

The rationale for these Anna rules is to allow runtime checking of annotations on package states. The treatment of axioms is analogous to the treatment of Anna type constraints — axioms are intended to constrain all values of the package state type.

Here is a schematic view of legal and illegal uses.

Example: *Legal and illegal uses of package state attributes.*

```
     package P is
        procedure Q;
--|        where C(P'INITIAL, P'STATE);
--         Legal; Q cannot be called before body of P is elaborated.

--:     X : P'TYPE;          -- Illegal by Ada rules for private types.

--|     axiom for all X : P'TYPE => --  Legal; X is a logical
--|                                  --  variable.
--|        D(P'INITIAL),            -- Legal use of a deferred constant.
--|        E(P'STATE),               --  Illegal use of the current state
--|                                  --  attribute; it is undefined
--|                                  --  when the axioms are
--|                                  --  elaborated.
                    ...
     end P;

--: X : P'TYPE;              -- Illegal; body of P is not yet elaborated.

     package body P is       -- Restrictions on the use of P'TYPE,
                             -- P'INITIAL, and P'STATE in the body
                             -- are described in Section 8.7.
        ...
     end P;
     ...                                     -- All uses are legal here.
```

4.6.2 State attributes of generic packages

A generic package P, say, is a template for other packages defined from it by instantiation. Consequently, the state of a generic package is also a template for states of its instances. Its state attributes are treated as generic. That is, P'TYPE, P'INITIAL, and P'STATE are templates for the corresponding attributes of instances of P. Generic specifications may be written using expressions for states of P. At instantiation, they become actual specifications of the instances of P. The name P is treated as a generic parameter of the specifications and is replaced by the name of an instance.[11]

In general, the Ada rules restricting the use of generics apply to attributes of generic units — i. e., generics can only be instantiated. So if P is a generic package, one can't declare virtual variables of P'TYPE or call P'STATE in an annotation outside of P.

[11] Further details about generic packages are given in Chapter 6.

Summary

Package specifications are constructed using simple annotations and package axioms. The Anna abstract package state attribute provides a visible name for the state of a package. It allows us to specify how the behavior of the package subprograms depends on the history of prior calls to the package, and how subprograms of the package are related. Properties of the state are specified by visible annotations referring to it. These features give us many different options in specifying any particular package. Our next step is to experiment with methods of building package specifications. Chapter 5 introduces some methods of building package specifications and gives more examples of the uses of states and axioms.

Further Reading

There is an extensive literature on algebraic methods of specifying data structures. Application of these methods to Ada requires Anna package axioms. Many of the papers illustrate how to express properties algebraically. The papers by Hoare and by Guttag are classics in this field.

A general discussion of commitment in specifications may be found in the paper by Thimbleby.

1. C. A. R. Hoare. Proof of correctness of data representations. *Acta Informatica*, Vol. 1, pp. 271–281, 1972.
2. J. V. Guttag. Abstract data types and the development of data structures. *Communications of the ACM*, Vol. 20, No. 6, pp. 396–404, 1977.
3. H. Thimbleby. Delaying commitment, *Software*, pp. 78–86, 1988.

5

The Process of Specifying Packages

Topics:

- *getting started building a specification;*
- *theory packages;*
- *dependent specification;*
- *relative specification by extension and association;*
- *modeling types by association with other types;*
- *symbolic execution of specifications;*
- *generators and iterators.*

This chapter is about building package specifications and understanding them. Given an English description, how should we tackle the problem of specifying a package to fit the description? How do we begin? What are the steps in the process — can we build upon (or "reuse") previous specifications? How can we figure out the consequences of a specification? When are we finished?

There is no unique process for constructing a package specification, nor a unique specification expressing a given requirement. In fact, Anna intentionally does not impose a style of specification. However, there are some useful guidelines and techniques, which are best illustrated by examples.

We have set ourselves three goals in this chapter. First, to describe some simple techniques for constructing package specifications, in particular for using previous specifications to construct new ones. Second, to give specifications for some substantial packages that illustrate the use of different kinds of annotations. And third, to describe a method of symbolic execution and its use to analyze specifications.

Throughout, we emphasize the process of recognizing informal concepts and defining them formally — *formalization* (see Section 2.2.1). This is a fundamental part of constructing specifications. It is this step that is a crucial difference between programming with specifications and programming without them in the traditional way.

Finally, we point out that informal comments are still needed to help explain formal specifications. This may indicate directions in which we should try to improve our current annotation languages. The reader should be aware, for example, of our continued reliance on suitable mnemonics in packages with formal specifications. Ordering and grouping of the declarations within a package specification is also an important form of informal documentation.

Terminology

The *types of a package* are the types declared explicitly in the visible part of the package, as well as its Anna state type. Recall also that *concepts* refers to the functions used in annotations and include the operations of types used in annotations.

5.1 Getting Started

Consider building a specification for a new package. This section presents one approach to getting started — certainly not the only approach — that involves choosing a set of concepts sufficient to specify the package. We start with two questions:

1. What are the types and operations of the package?
2. What are the types and functions needed to specify them?

Assume we have decided on the types and operations of a package P — more on how we do that later. What concepts can we use to specify the package? The answer is that we may use any set of *concepts* chosen from the available (virtual and actual) concepts of the environment in which we are defining the package. Annotation concepts can also be declared in the package itself — they can be either Ada or Anna types and functions.

Possible annotation concepts

1. All Ada and Anna predefined types and operations, especially Anna attributes associated with package P
2. All Ada and Anna types and functions in separate library packages,
3. The generic type and function parameters of P,
4. A set of Ada and Anna functions of P, (including operations defined on its state type).

We may choose a set of concepts from among these possibilities. In fact (category 4) we can declare additional virtual functions in P for use in its specification.

Consider the set of concepts in the above four categories that finally end up being used in specifying package P.

- **Basic concepts**

  Those concepts that fall in categories 1–3, together with all functions in category 4 that have no result annotations, are called the *basic concepts* for that specification of P.

The basic concepts are those concepts needed to understand the specification of P.

Basic concepts in category 1 are types and functions that are predefined in Ada and Anna. Remember that Anna provides a set of predefined concepts with each package: its state type, operations of the state type, and the 'OUT and 'NEW_STATE function attributes of procedures declared in the package.

Basic concepts in category 2 are those specified in packages that P depends upon as a consequence of its **with** clauses (actual and virtual).[1] They are said to be *imported* into P.

The generic parameters of P (category 3) also introduce basic concepts that can be used in specifying P. For example, if P has a generic type parameter that is an array type, then P may assume all the standard array operations on that type. Annotations of generic parameters (Chapter 6) are used to specify assumptions about these basic concepts of P — e. g., type, object, and function generic parameters may together form an algebraic structure such as a group.

The basic concepts that are declared in P itself are those (actual and virtual) functions of P that are used in annotations, but whose values are not defined by **return** annotations. If a function in P has a **return** annotation, then it is specified using other concepts. Such functions are not included in the set of basic concepts because they can be understood in terms of other concepts. For example, functions that are introduced for notational reasons, such as to define and parameterize complicated expressions in order to shorten annotations, are not considered basic.

In the TABLE_MANAGER specification in Section 4.5, functions FULL, MEMBER, "=", and LEAST_PRIORITY all appear in subsequent annotations of INSERT and RETRIEVE and the axioms. In this specification, FULL, MEMBER, and "=" are basic functions. LEAST_PRIORITY is not a basic function; it names and parameterizes a concept that is defined by a result annotation using MEMBER.

Example: *Possible basic concepts for specifying package* P.

```
package STANDARD is
   ...      -- Predefined concepts in STANDARD.

   package Q is ... end Q;
   ...      -- Types and subprograms of Q.

   package R is ... end R;
   ...
```

[1]The use of concepts from other units in annotations of a new unit follows the normal Ada rules for declaring dependency between the units.

```
    with Q;
    generic
        type S is private;
        with function F return ... ;
    package P is           -- S and F.
        ...                -- Anna attributes of P
        ...                -- and private types of P.
    end P;
  ...
end STANDARD;
```

Commentary

The example shows the Ada view of things, whereby every unit is considered as declared within package STANDARD, after all the Ada predefined types.

In constructing a new specification for a package P, the predefined Ada concepts in STANDARD may be assumed in specifying P. The ones we actually use in P are basic to P. To use concepts from another package Q, we must import Q by a **with** clause to make it visible in P. If we use Q only in annotations, we can use a virtual **with** clause.

The generics and private types of P can be basic. Similarly, Anna predefined attributes of P such as its state type are basic concepts.

A library unit that is not visible to P, such as R, cannot be used in the specification of P.

• Recipe for building a new package specification

This recipe consists of iterating some general steps.

1. **Identify the types and operations of the package.**
   The types and operations will be extracted from the informal description of the purpose of the package and the background knowledge concerning its domain of application.
2. **Choose a set of informal basic concepts.**
   A set of concepts should be identified that is sufficient to define and explain the types and operations that result from the first step.
3. **Define the actual types and subprograms of the package visible part.**
   Definitions are given by Ada type and subprogram declarations. Informal comments explaining the types and subprograms should be given where possible using only the chosen basic concepts. Informal comments describing algebraic relationships between subprograms should be written as informal axioms. Informal comments defining values of

subprogram parameters explicitly as transformations from input values to output values should be written as subprogram annotations. Exceptional behavior and constraints on input values should be written as subprogram annotations.

4. **Define all informal concepts.**
   All informal concepts used in describing the actual types and operations at Step 3 that are not actual operations must be defined by virtual Ada declarations. This should involve, as much as possible, importing by **with** clauses concepts that were previously defined in other packages. The virtual concepts that are not imported are defined as virtual basic functions of the package. Steps 1–4 are iterated until no new concepts appear.
5. **Express all informal comments as formal package annotations.**
   At this final step, we have declared all the necessary basic concepts, and now we can express our informal comments as formal annotations.

This recipe is an extension of the one given in Section 4.2. Here we are faced with the situation where the Ada package declaration is not given. The recipe in Section 4.2 deals mainly with Step 5 in this recipe.

As we get better at programming with specifications, the writing of informal comments will often be short-circuited or omitted altogether. We will be able to rely on library packages for formal definitions of most of our basic concepts.

- **Guideline: Minimality of basic concepts.**

  A set of basic concepts should be as small as possible without complicating the package specification.

The guideline is rather vague, but it has a point. Try to keep the number of basic concepts small. For example, in specifying a sets package, as we will do later, we might be faced with choosing one or both of IS_MEMBER and "=" as basic functions. If we leave both unspecified, they will both be basic; if we define "=" using IS_MEMBER, then only IS_MEMBER will be basic.

The guideline does not mean, however, that the concepts have to be independent in the sense that no concept could possibly be defined in terms of the others. An independent set of concepts sometimes leads to complicated and lengthy specifications. Remember, the idea of trying to identify a set of basic concepts is a technique for getting started. Generally, a given specification need not have a unique minimal set of basic concepts.

Here's how the recipe might be followed to specify a stack package.

Step 1: Informal operations and concepts

Starting with our informal knowledge about stacks, we list the following operations and concepts:

1. *Push, pop* — stack operations to be implemented as procedures.
2. *Top, length, membership* — concepts for talking about stacks, and perhaps for use as Ada operations too.
3. *Generic parameters* — type of the stack items and its maximum size.

Step 2: Informal basic concepts

We choose the following basic concepts:

1. *Top, length, membership.* We might be tempted to choose *push* and *pop* until we decide they should be procedures, or until we try writing a few specifications.
2. *Predefined concepts* — natural numbers (for length) and boolean (for membership test).
3. *The generic parameters.*

Maybe we've forgotten a concept needed for specification?

Steps 3 and 4: Outline the package declaration

Here we combine steps 3 and 4 of the recipe. At some point the stack specification might look like this:

Example: *Informal outline of a stack specification.*

```
      generic
         type ITEM is private;
         MAX : POSITIVE;
      package STACK is

         -- Basic functions.
--:      function MEMBER(X : ITEM) return BOOLEAN;
--:      function LENGTH return NATURAL;
--:      function TOP return ITEM;
         -- End basic functions.

         OVERFLOW, UNDERFLOW : exception;

         -- Actual operations.
         procedure PUSH(X : in ITEM);
--|         where
         -- If the stack length is MAX then propagate OVERFLOW,
         -- otherwise increment the stack length, put the item on top.
```

```
           procedure POP(Y : out ITEM);
--|            where
           -- If the stack is empty then propagate UNDERFLOW, delete
           -- its top item, and store it in Y.

--|        axiom
           -- All stacks are initially empty, push adds an item and does
           -- not delete items, and push and pop have inverse effects on
           -- the STACK.

      end STACK;
```

Step 5: Formalize the informal annotations

In this step, missing concepts are likely to be discovered. We will find that we need equality on stacks to write the annotations formally. Also, the "inverses" axiom may cause us to think. What are the basic concepts needed to express this axiom? They are the Anna predefined 'NEW_STATE function attributes of PUSH and POP (see Section 4.4.2).

Example: *A formal stack specification.*

```
      generic
           type ITEM is private;
           MAX : POSITIVE;
      package STACK is

           -- Basic functions.
--:        function MEMBER(X : ITEM) return BOOLEAN;
--:        function LENGTH return NATURAL;
--:        function TOP return ITEM;
--:        function "=" (S, T : STACK'TYPE) return BOOLEAN;
           -- End basic functions.

           OVERFLOW, UNDERFLOW : exception;

           -- Actual operations.
           procedure PUSH(X : in ITEM);
--|            where in STACK.LENGTH = MAX => raise OVERFLOW,
--|                out (STACK.LENGTH = in STACK.LENGTH+1),
--|                out (STACK.TOP = X);

           procedure POP(Y : out ITEM);
--|            where in STACK.LENGTH = 0 => raise UNDERFLOW,
--|                out (STACK.LENGTH = in STACK.LENGTH-1),
--|                out (Y = in STACK.TOP);
```

```
--|     axiom
--|     for all S : STACK'TYPE; U, V : ITEM =>
--|         STACK'INITIAL.LENGTH = 0,
--|         not STACK'INITIAL.MEMBER(U),
--|         S[PUSH(V)].MEMBER(U) = S.MEMBER(U) or U=V,
--|         S[PUSH(U); POP(V)] = S;

    end STACK;
```

Commentary

The basic concepts are: (1) the Ada predefined types INTEGER and BOOLEAN and their operations, and the generic parameters ITEM and MAX; (2) the Anna predefined package attributes STACK'TYPE and its operations, which include attributes 'NEW_STATE and "="; and (3) functions MEMBER, LENGTH, and TOP, which are user-defined basic functions on STACK'TYPE.

The explicit declaration of "=" means that it need not be understood as the identity relation on stack states; it may be redefined to be any equality relation.

These concepts form a sufficient set of types and functions to specify package STACK. The subprogram annotations on the procedures express propagation conditions and transformations of the package state. The axioms express algebraic relationships between the basic concepts, particularly between the 'NEW_STATE attributes of procedures PUSH and POP and the user-defined basic functions.

If we want actual Ada operations LENGTH and TOP, we can do one of two things. The simplest is to make our virtual basic functions into actual ones — just delete the virtual code symbols. A more rigorous approach is to keep specification concepts separate from Ada operations, even when they are identical, since they may then be implemented in different ways. So, the Ada operations would be declared as actual functions[2] specified as returning values identical to the corresponding Anna basic functions on STACK'TYPE.

Digression

At this point, we digress briefly to review the Anna successor state notation. This is defined in Section 4.4.2. If the reader has forgotten the notation, the axiom,

[2]We would change the names of the Anna LENGTH and TOP.

```
--| for all S : STACK'TYPE; U, V : ITEM =>
--|     S[PUSH(U); POP(V)] = S;
```

may be puzzling. It seems to contain a quantifier over V that appears as an **out** parameter of POP. This is not so.

Recall that the square bracket notation denotes the application of 'NEW_STATE functions. The axiom is a shorthand version of

```
--| for all S : STACK'TYPE; U, V : ITEM =>
--|     S.PUSH'NEW_STATE(U).POP'NEW_STATE(V) = S;
```

where PUSH'NEW_STATE, POP'NEW_STATE are function attributes of procedures PUSH and POP. These attributes denote the mapping between package states that results from the procedures. In particular, POP'NEW_STATE is the mapping from states to states that results from executing POP. It has an **in** mode parameter corresponding to the **out** mode parameter of POP, which is included to complete its Ada parameter profile.

The axiom expresses "for all states S and all parameter values, the state resulting from executing PUSH followed by POP equals S". This ends the digression.

end digression

The purpose of the recipe is to give us some methodology towards arriving at a first specification. The basic concepts are, so to speak, the foundation for the specification. The concepts from outside the package are already defined and implemented (even if they are virtual, we can assume we know how to implement them). So we can assume that we already understand outside concepts and can thereby understand package specifications that refer to them.

Sometimes, however, the specification is not definable entirely in terms of the existing environment. In this case, the basic functions in the package divide understanding the specification into steps: first understand the basic functions; then use the specification to understand the other (nonbasic) operations. (Here, "understand" can have different meanings, e. g., predict behavior from specifications or conceptualize an implementation — usually a naive, incomplete, and inefficient one.)

All operations of some package specifications are basic functions, as we shall see. This happens, for example, in algebraic specifications of abstract types, such as type INTEGER in package STANDARD.

The set of basic concepts is seldom unique, and equivalent specifications [3] can usually be built using different basic concepts. The same is true of the

[3]Informally speaking, package specifications are *equivalent* if the same set of implementations (package bodies) are consistent with them.

set of basic functions within a particular specification: one can often choose either of two functions as basic and define the other by a result annotation using the first one.

5.2 Theory Packages

Normally, people do not object to basic concepts imported from outside the package specification because there is an implicit assumption of their prior specification and implementation. So it may seem reasonable to say that they are understood before the new package is specified. Basic concepts within the package specification, however, may raise criticism. Some people may object to the previous example, saying that basic functions MEMBER, LENGTH, and TOP are no easier to understand than the Ada operations PUSH and POP. In that case, they may prefer a different style of building specifications.

Another style of specification is to specify all basic functions separately in virtual *theory* packages, such as we discussed in Section 2.8.2. Basic functions are not allowed in the specification of an actual package.

This style, taken to the limit, requires all theory packages to be *algebraic*. That is, all operations in a theory are declared as mathematical functions that are defined for all parameter values — no EXCEPTIONS. And, all specifications are algebraic — only axioms, no subprogram annotations. And, the state of a theory package must be trivial (constant). Of course, we do not have to accept all these restrictions. We can use theory packages without going to the extreme of mandating trivial states and only using algebraic specifications. Here is an example of an algebraic theory package.

Example: A theory of stacks.

```
--: generic
--:     type ELEMENT is private;
--:     type STACK_TYPE is private;
--:     INITIAL_STACK : STACK_TYPE;
--: package STACK_THEORY is

--:     function MEMBER(X : ELEMENT; S : STACK_TYPE)
--:     return BOOLEAN;
--:     function LENGTH(S : STACK_TYPE) return NATURAL;
--:     function TOP(S : STACK_TYPE) return ELEMENT;
--:     function PUSH_STATE(X : ELEMENT; S : STACK_TYPE)
--:     return STACK_TYPE;
--:     function POP_STATE(S : STACK_TYPE)
--:     return STACK_TYPE;
```

```
--|      axiom
--|      for all S : STACK_TYPE; U, V : ELEMENT =>
--|           LENGTH (INITIAL_STACK) = 0;
--|           not MEMBER (U, INITIAL_STACK),
--|           MEMBER (U, PUSH_STATE (V, S)) =
--|                                      MEMBER (U, S) or U = V,
--|           LENGTH (PUSH_STATE (U, S)) = LENGTH (S)+1,
--|           LENGTH (POP_STATE (S)) =
--|                            if S /= INITIAL_STACK then
--|                               LENGTH (S)-1,
--|                            else
--|                               0
--|                            end if,
--|           TOP (PUSH_STATE (U, S)) = U,
--|           POP_STATE (PUSH_STATE (U, S)) = S;

--: end STACK_THEORY;
```

Commentary

This is a generic theory of stacks. It is specified by algebraic axioms. The functions map the two generic type domains ELEMENT and STACK_TYPE into the domain of one of these types, or into INTEGER or BOOLEAN. No exceptional behavior is specified. For example, the value of TOP on INITIAL_STACK is not specified. We can therefore understand these functions as being well-defined for all values of their arguments, which include arbitrarily long stacks.

Notice that this theory imports basic concepts from types INTEGER and BOOLEAN. Also, the generic types and their operations, which include "=" on the STACK_TYPE generic parameter, are basic concepts. All of functions of the theory are also basic concepts since none of them has a return annotation.

Notice one other thing. It makes no sense to attempt to build a body for this particular theory package, even though it is a legal Ada package declaration! The operations of the theory manipulate values of the generic formal private type STACK_TYPE. Implementing them would require knowing other operations of the generic type parameter. In fact, we do not know enough about STACK_TYPE. This example is constructed this way because it will be used to specify other packages by means of Ada generic instantiation, as we shall see later. In general, theory packages are implementable.

To understand the theory, we must reason about its axioms. Are they consistent? If the generic parameters satisfy certain properties,[4] then do the axioms define the values of the package functions uniquely? What kinds of Ada packages satisfy similar axioms?

Writing theory packages should be supported by at least the same facilities provided for writing Ada packages. Otherwise, no one will bother to write theories. We can import other virtual theory packages to support the construction of a new theory by virtual context clauses. And we may take the standard Ada types and operations as basic. But we should not use actual packages in specifying a new theory—to maintain the independence of theories from actual packages.[5] Following Anna rules for virtual packages, we do not have to implement a body for a theory package.

- **Guideline: Defining theory packages.**

  A theory package should be a parameterized (by its generic parameters) declaration of concepts basic to a class of programs, together with axioms implying the properties of the concepts.

The idea of this style of specification is that basic concepts are defined separately from any actual package. A theory package defines the concepts that are common to many packages — say, all stack packages. It encapsulates a theory of a class of programs. The properties of the common concepts must be logical consequences of the axioms of the theory package.

To use STACK_THEORY to specify an actual stack package, the theory is imported into the actual package by a virtual **with** clause. It is instantiated to the generic types and state type of the actual package. The types and operations of the actual package are specified by type and subprogram annotations using the theory concepts. Essentially, STACK_THEORY is used as a macro definition of basic concepts.

Example: *A stack specification using stack theory.*

```
--: with STACK_THEORY;
    generic
        type ITEM is private;
        MAX : POSITIVE;
    package STACK is

--:     package IMPORT_THEORY is new STACK_THEORY(ITEM,
--:                                              STACK'TYPE,
--:                                              STACK'INITIAL);
--:     use IMPORT_THEORY;

        OVERFLOW, UNDERFLOW : exception;
```

[4]Chapter 6 deals with using annotations of generic parameters to ensure that they have required properties.

[5]This is a methodology rule; it is not enforced by Anna since it implies duplication of effort.

```
      procedure PUSH(X : in ITEM);
--|      where LENGTH(in STACK) = MAX =>
--|                                         raise OVERFLOW,
--|         out (STACK = PUSH_STATE(X, in STACK)),
--|         out (TOP(STACK) = X);

      procedure POP(Y : out ITEM);
--|      where LENGTH(in STACK) = 0 =>
--|                                         raise UNDERFLOW,
--|         out (STACK = POP_STATE(X, in STACK)),
--|         out (Y = TOP(in STACK));

   end STACK;
```

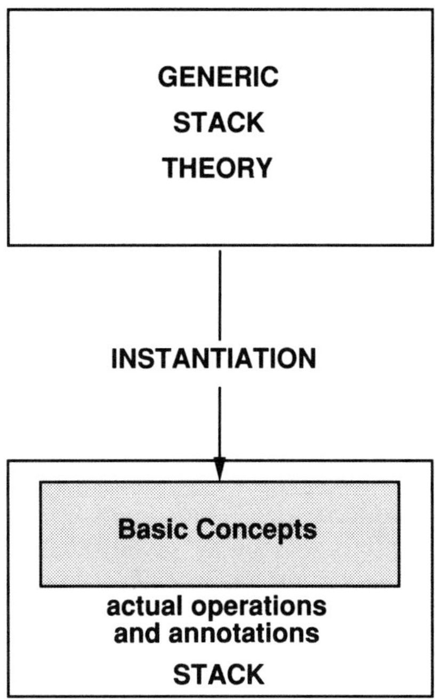

FIGURE 5.1. Using stack theory to specify a stack package.

Commentary

A virtual instance of STACK_THEORY is introduced into STACK. This instance is constructed by binding its generic parameters to ITEM, STACK'TYPE and STACK'INITIAL. It is called IMPORT_THEORY.

The effect of the theory instance is that STACK inherits the concepts of STACK_THEORY — that is, package STACK includes all the virtual functions of STACK_THEORY instantiated so that they apply to its types and generic parameters. These concepts are used to specify its other operations. The actual operations of STACK, namely PUSH and POP, are specified explicitly by subprogram annotations. They return states and values defined by the functions of IMPORT_THEORY. Exceptional behavior is also specified.

The basic concepts of STACK are included in the functions of IMPORT_THEORY and the predefined concepts of package STANDARD. Thus, all basic concepts are either predefined or declared outside of the actual STACK package.

Is this specification equivalent to the first example of a stack (Section 5.1)? To check this, we can textually replace the generic instantiation IMPORT_THEORY by the instantiation of the STACK_THEORY package declaration. This will give us the complete text of this STACK specification containing the basic concepts and the axioms. Then we can analyze the specifications of the two actual packages to see if they have the same consequences. Do both specifications allow insertion of duplicate items?

We must emphasize that theory packages usually are implementable — an example is given in Section 5.4. Implementability depends on the choice of generic parameters.

The development of theory packages may be a natural outcome of the process of specifying many different application packages in a given problem domain. It represents a maturing of programming with specifications. Each new problem area will probably start with specifications in which basic functions are declared in the actual application packages. This is because it is never clear at the start what are the best basic concepts and because of the need to finish applications in a reasonable amount of time.

The separation of basic concepts is enforced by the Larch language as the only way to develop specifications in Larch.[6]

5.3 A PL/1 String Manipulation Package

Our next example is one where it is natural to choose all the basic concepts from the set of predefined Ada concepts. We specify a package that provides operations on strings similar to the PL/1 facilities for manipulating variable-length strings. These operations can be easily described using the standard Ada string operations and attributes. There are no basic concepts outside the Ada domain of strings and natural numbers, so the package

[6]See the reference to Larch at the end of this chapter.

should be easily understood from a quick reading of its specification.

Two virtual functions are used to define expressions that occur frequently in the annotations. These virtual definitions are a notational convenience to shorten the annotations. In fact, one of them, SLENGTH, duplicates actual function LENGTH. It is introduced to illustrate the technique of defining annotation concepts prior to specification of the Ada units. The package has a trivial state, i. e., its state is constant. This example was suggested by Paul Reilly.[7]

Example: A PL/1 string manipulation package.

```
package PL1_STRINGS is

      subtype PL1_STRING is STRING;
--|       where S : PL1_STRING => S'LENGTH > 0 and
--|             exist I : S'RANGE => S(I) = ASCII.NUL;

--       Virtual functions naming commonly used expressions.

--:   function SLENGTH(STR : PL1_STRING)
--:   return NATURAL;
--       Maximum initial slice of non-null characters.
--|       where return LEN : NATURAL =>
--|          (for all I : NATURAL =>
--|              (I in STR'FIRST .. STR'FIRST+LEN-1
--|                → STR(I) /= ASCII.NUL))
--|          and
--|          STR(STR'FIRST+LEN) = ASCII.NUL;

--:   function SLAST(STR : PL1_STRING)
--:   return NATURAL;
--|       where return STR'FIRST+SLENGTH(STR)-1;


--      Actual subprograms.

      procedure NUL(STR : out PL1_STRING);
--      Create an empty PL/1 string.
--|       where out (for all I : STR'RANGE =>
--|                     STR(I)'DEFINED and STR(I) = ASCII.NUL);

      function IS_EMPTY(STR : in PL1_STRING)
      return BOOLEAN;
-- Indicate whether or not a string is empty.
--|       where return STR(STR'FIRST) = ASCII.NUL;

      function LENGTH(STR : in PL1_STRING) return NATURAL;
--      Return the length of a string.
--|       where return SLENGTH(STR);
```

[7]Reilly, P., Data General Corporation, private correspondence, 1984.

```
    procedure ASSIGN (TARGET : out PL1_STRING;
                      SOURCE : in PL1_STRING);
--    Assign source to target; differs from PL/1 ASSIGN.
--|     where
--|         SLENGTH (SOURCE) >= TARGET'LENGTH =>
--|                                    raise CONSTRAINT_ERROR,
--|         out (TARGET (TARGET'FIRST..TARGET'FIRST+
--|                                    SLENGTH (SOURCE)-1) =
--|              in SOURCE (SOURCE'FIRST .. SLAST (SOURCE))),
--|         out (TARGET (TARGET'FIRST+SLENGTH (SOURCE)) =
--|                                                ASCII.NUL);

    function CATENATE (LEFT, RIGHT : PL1_STRING)
    return PL1_STRING;
--    Return the catenation of LEFT followed by RIGHT.
--|     where return STR : PL1_STRING =>
--|         STR (STR'FIRST .. STR'FIRST+SLENGTH (LEFT)-1) =
--|                           LEFT (LEFT'FIRST .. SLAST (LEFT))
--|         and
--|         STR (STR'FIRST+SLENGTH (LEFT) ..
--|         STR'FIRST+SLENGTH (LEFT)+SLENGTH (RIGHT)-1) =
--|                        RIGHT (RIGHT'FIRST .. SLAST (RIGHT))
--|         and
--|         STR (STR'FIRST+SLENGTH (LEFT) +
--|                           SLENGTH (RIGHT) = ASCII.NUL;

    function EQUAL (LEFT, RIGHT : PL1_STRING)
    return BOOLEAN;
--    Indicate if string LEFT matches string RIGHT.
--|     where return
--|         SLENGTH (LEFT) = SLENGTH (RIGHT)
--|             and then
--|         LEFT (LEFT'FIRST .. SLAST (LEFT)) =
--|             RIGHT (RIGHT'FIRST .. SLAST (RIGHT));

    function INDEX (BASE_STRING, FRAGMENT : PL1_STRING)
    return NATURAL;
-- Return the starting position in BASE_STRING where a copy of FRAG-
-- MENT is found; return 0 otherwise. This differs from PL/1 INDEX.
--
--|     where return I : NATURAL =>
--|         (I /= 0 and
--|          BASE_STRING (I .. I+SLENGTH (FRAGMENT)-1) =
--|          FRAGMENT (FRAGMENT'FIRST..SLAST (FRAGMENT)))
```

```
--|          or
--|          (I = 0 and (for all J : BASE_STRING'FIRST ..
--|           SLAST(BASE_STRING)-SLENGTH(FRAGMENT)+1 =>
--|           BASE_STRING(J .. J+SLENGTH(FRAGMENT)-1) /=
--|           FRAGMENT(FRAGMENT'FIRST .. SLAST
--|                                            (FRAGMENT))));

   end PL1_STRINGS;
```

Commentary

This specification depends only on Ada string concepts.

These are the basic concepts required to understand this specification.

A PL/1 string is represented as the initial part of an Ada string up to the first NUL character. This representation can be deduced from the subtype constraint and the annotation of SLENGTH and the other operations. For example, the Ada string <H, I, !, NUL, T, H, E, R, E> represents the PL/1 string "Hi!".

Two virtual functions, SLENGTH and SLAST, are used in the annotations. SLENGTH is exactly the same function as LENGTH and could be deleted. It is used here to separate concepts used in annotations from actual functions being specified; this is a matter of style. SLAST names an expression that occurs often in the annotations and is used to shorten them. Note that SLENGTH is not in general equal to the Ada attribute 'LENGTH.

This example specification may have some unsatisfactory features, among which we mention the following. Function INDEX does not have to return the first occurrence of the FRAGMENT. Indeed, one of the first things we may want to do with a package specification is to explore its consequences on simple examples of input data.

One way to do this is to deduce logically the consequences of the specifications on short sequences of operations with different parameter values. Consider the following formulation of the expected result of a call to ASSIGN for a pair of actual parameter values:

```
declare
   A : STRING(1 .. 3) :=
       (1 => "A", 2 => "B", 3 => ASCII.NUL);
   B : STRING(1 .. 5) :=
       (1 .. 4 => "F", 5 => ASCII.NUL);
```

```
    begin PL1_STRINGS.ASSIGN (B, A);
--|       B (1 .. 2) = A (1 .. 2),
                     -- Is this assertion true?
--|       B (3) = ASCII.NUL,
                     -- How about this assertion?
--|       B (4) = "F";
                     -- And, how about this?
    end;
```

We have formalized a small experiment on PL1_STRINGS. It consists of input data, one procedure call, and some assertions about the expected results. The assertions specify how we expect the components of B to be overwritten after the call.

To deduce the result of the call, we must substitute the actual parameter values for the formal parameters TARGET and SOURCE in the annotations of ASSIGN and then evaluate the annotations.

The propagation annotation must be evaluated first. We can deduce that at the **begin**, SLENGTH (A) = 2 and B'LENGTH = 5. The computation of SLENGTH (A) should be done carefully. Substitute the initial value of A for STR in the specification of SLENGTH; then find a value of LEN in the **return** annotation that satisfies the quantified expression, perhaps by trying each possible value, 0, 1, 2, ... until the first time the expression is true. These values imply that the call ASSIGN (B, A) should not raise the exception since the condition of the propagation annotation of ASSIGN is not satisfied.

Now, the **out** annotation of ASSIGN can be used to compute the value of B after the call. New components are substituted in B so that the **out** annotation is satisfied for A and the new B. The result should satisfy the first two assertions.

The third assertion cannot be deduced from the specification of ASSIGN. Only the slice of TARGET from the index value TARGET'FIRST up to TARGET'FIRST+SLENGTH (SOURCE) is specified, in this case B (1 .. 3). So there is no requirement on the implementation of ASSIGN for B (4). Since it is unspecified, an implementation has the freedom to fill in such components with characters (e. g., ASCII.NUL) or to leave them untouched. The **out** value of B (4) is unknown.

- **Steps towards reasoning about package specifications**

Reasoning about a package specification on small test cases is a powerful method of determining consequences of the specification before a package body is implemented. In so doing, we will need to use properties (often called lemmas or theorems) of the basic concepts, so it is important to specify basic concepts.

Sometimes, such experiments can reveal effects that were not intended or intended effects that were omitted (incompleteness). This allows us to change the specification before implementation begins. We shall describe a more general method of *symbolic execution* in later examples.

- **Guideline: Understanding package specifications.**

  Express tests formally as small test programs with input data, package operations, and assertions about the output data. Then try to prove the output assertions are logical consequences of the package specifications. Or else prove that they are not.

Subprogram specifications and package axioms can interact in ways that have unforeseen consequences. The guideline may be thought of as suggesting a kind of "formal testing." PL1_STRINGS has a simple specification. There are no axioms. The individual subprograms are independent (i. e., no actual subprogram is used to specify another), and no relationships between them are specified by axioms. Therefore, any surprise must be a consequence of an individual subprogram specification. We might wish to extend the specification to include an axiom such as

```
PL1_STRINGS [ASSIGN (B, A)] . EQUAL (A, B)
```

for all pairs of PL1_STRINGs A and B. Is this property already a consequence of the existing specifications?

5.4 A Simple Sets Package

The following is a specification of a package that provides some of the standard operations of set theory. It is a typical *abstract data type* package. It defines data type SET by specifying its operations, but hides details of the structure of SET. We will use this example frequently in subsequent examples.

Example: A sets package.

```
generic
    type ELEM is private;
package SETS is
    type SET is limited private;

--      Basic functions.
    function IS_MEMBER (E : ELEM; S : SET)
    return BOOLEAN;
    function IS_FULL (S : SET)
    return BOOLEAN;
    function CARDINALITY (S : SET)
    return NATURAL;
--      End basic functions.
```

```
--      Exceptions and constants.
        SET_FULL : exception;
        NULL_SET : constant SET;

--|     axiom
--|        for all E : ELEM =>
--|           not IS_MEMBER(E, NULL_SET),
--|           not IS_FULL(NULL_SET);

--      Relations on SETs
        function "=" (S, T : SET) return BOOLEAN;
--|        where return (for all E : ELEM =>
--|                        IS_MEMBER(E,S) ↔ IS_MEMBER(E,T));

        function IS_EMPTY(X : SET) return BOOLEAN;
--|        where return X = NULL_SET;

--      Subprograms for constructing SETs.
        function "+" (X, Y : SET) return SET;
--|       where
--|          raise SET_FULL,
--|          return Z : SET =>
--|             (for all U : ELEM => IS_MEMBER(U, Z) ↔
--|                 IS_MEMBER(U, X) or IS_MEMBER(U, Y));

        function "–" (X, Y : SET) return SET;
--|       where
--|          return Z : SET =>
--|             (for all U : ELEM => IS_MEMBER(U, Z) ↔
--|             IS_MEMBER(U, X) and not IS_MEMBER(U, Y));

        procedure ADD(E : in ELEM; S : in out SET);
--|       where
--|          IS_FULL(S) => raise SET_FULL,
--|          out (for all U : ELEM => IS_MEMBER(U, S) ↔
--|                            U = E or IS_MEMBER(U, in S));

        procedure REMOVE(E : in ELEM; S : in out SET);
--|       where
--|          out (for all U : ELEM => IS_MEMBER(U, S) ↔
--|                         IS_MEMBER(U, in S) and U /= E);

        procedure COPY(S : in SET; S1 : out SET);
--|        where out (S1 = S);

--|     axiom
--|        SET'INITIAL = NULL_SET;
```

```
--|     axiom
--|         for all A, B : SET; E : ELEM =>
--|             CARDINALITY(NULL_SET) = 0,
--|             CARDINALITY(ADD'OUT(E, A).S) =
--|                         if IS_MEMBER(E, A) then
--|                             CARDINALITY(A)
--|                         else
--|                             CARDINALITY(A)+1
--|                         end if,
--|             CARDINALITY(REMOVE'OUT(E, A).S) =
--|                         if IS_MEMBER(E, A) then
--|                             CARDINALITY(A)-1
--|                         else
--|                             CARDINALITY(A)
--|                         end if;

    private
        ...

    end SETS;
```

Commentary

Package SETS raises some points about package specifications which we note briefly.

Type SET is specified as a limited type, so the only way to make a copy of a set is by using operation COPY. Relation "=" is specified so that two sets are "=" if and only if they have the same elements. This defines the equality operator on the abstract SET type as viewed by a user of the package. If SET is implemented as an access type in the private part, then "=" on sets will have to be a different function from the Ada "=" on access values. (For more about this, see Chapter 8.)

The NULL_SET is declared to be a constant. This constrains only its Ada value. If that value happens to be an access value, no constraint at all is placed on the designated structure. A much stronger abstract property is specified by an axiom that says that NULL_SET has no member.

The Anna attribute 'INITIAL, an attribute of any private type, denotes the default initial value of objects of the type. SET'INITIAL denotes the initial value of any set object upon declaration. This is specified axiomatically to equal the NULL_SET.

The basic concepts for this specification include (category 1, Section 5.1) the predefined Anna attributes ADD'OUT and REMOVE'OUT since these functions occur in axioms. But these axioms can be replaced by equivalent subprogram **out** annotations of the SET parameters of ADD and REMOVE in which the

'OUT functions do not appear.

The choice to specify ADD and REMOVE as procedures is motivated by considering efficiency of implementation — we want to add an element to a set without having to copy the set. If we want to reuse this specification in other specifications, following the ideas in Section 5.2, we could define an equivalent theory package with functions and a purely algebraic specification.

• Incompleteness of package specifications

It is common for a package specification to be *incomplete*. This means that it is satisfied by implementations that *contradict each other* in the following sense. One implementation satisfies some additional property and the other one satisfies the negation of that property. That is a strong way for implementations to differ — especially if the additional property is one that ought to have been specified!

Usually, an axiom has been forgotten. Consequently, one possible implementation will satisfy an additional axiom A (not in the specification), while another possible implementation will satisfy **not** A. The specification is not logically strong enough to imply either A or **not** A.

In this example, basic function IS_FULL has different implementations, each of which satisfies the package specification, but differs on a property that is not implied by the package axioms. Remember, IS_FULL has two parameters: an explicit set parameter and, implicitly, the state of package SETS. Two possible implementations are: (1) as a function of set values, expressing that a set is full; and (2) as a function of the state of the package, expressing that the state is full — i. e., no more elements can be added to any set.

If we wish to complete the specification so that one of these possibly contradictory implementation decisions must be used, we can add new axioms to the package specification.

For example, to disallow implementation (2), we can add,

for all P, Q : SETS'TYPE; A : SET =>
P.IS_FULL(A) = Q.IS_FULL(A),

which expresses that IS_FULL does not depend on the package state. This is not a consequence of the axioms for "=" on type SET, which are implicit Anna axioms of the package (Section 4.5.1). But the substitution axiom

for all A, B : SET; P : SETS'TYPE => A = B →
P.IS_FULL(A) = P.IS_FULL(B),

together with the new independence axiom, implies

```
for all A, B : SET; P, Q : SETS'TYPE => A = B →
                         P.IS_FULL(A) = Q.IS_FULL(B).
```

This is a property that is satisfied if IS_FULL is a function of its set parameter, i. e., it means that a set is full.

To force implementation (2), we would first delete the axiom for NULL_SET; otherwise, a state can never be full. Then we can add a new axiom such as

```
for all P : SETS'TYPE; A, B : SET =>
                         P.IS_FULL(A) = P.IS_FULL(B),
```

which expresses that IS_FULL does not depend on its set parameter. This property is satisfied if IS_FULL is a function only of the package state.

5.5 Dependent Specification

When we specify a new package, we want to make use of previous specifications as much as possible to reduce the work involved. Here, we discuss some ways to reuse specifications in building new ones. There are other ways to reuse specifications, which are not discussed here.

A new package is specified using actual and virtual packages from a library of package specifications, called *library packages*. Anna uses only the Ada textual facilities for expressing context and dependency. Dependency of one specification upon another is expressed using Ada **with** clauses. A virtual **with** clause is used whenever the features of P are used only in annotations of T, and must be used if P is virtual:

```
--: with P;
    package T is ... end T;
```

Virtual library packages may consist of both virtual copies (possibly renamed) of actual "reusable software" packages and "theory" packages that encapsulate the concepts of various mathematical theories, like STACK_THEORY (Section 5.1) and SORTING_CONCEPTS (Section 2.5.3).

Figure 5.2 shows a tree of dependent package specifications. The complete tree includes all the dependencies between the actual and virtual library package specifications. Such a tree looks like an Ada compilation tree, except that some packages (nodes) and dependencies (arcs) are virtual. In Figure 5.2, the virtual nodes are shaded and the virtual arcs are broken lines. A change to a virtual node does not affect the Ada compilation at all. However, it may affect the specifications of *all* dependent packages below it in the tree — a sweeping change to a system specification. This in turn

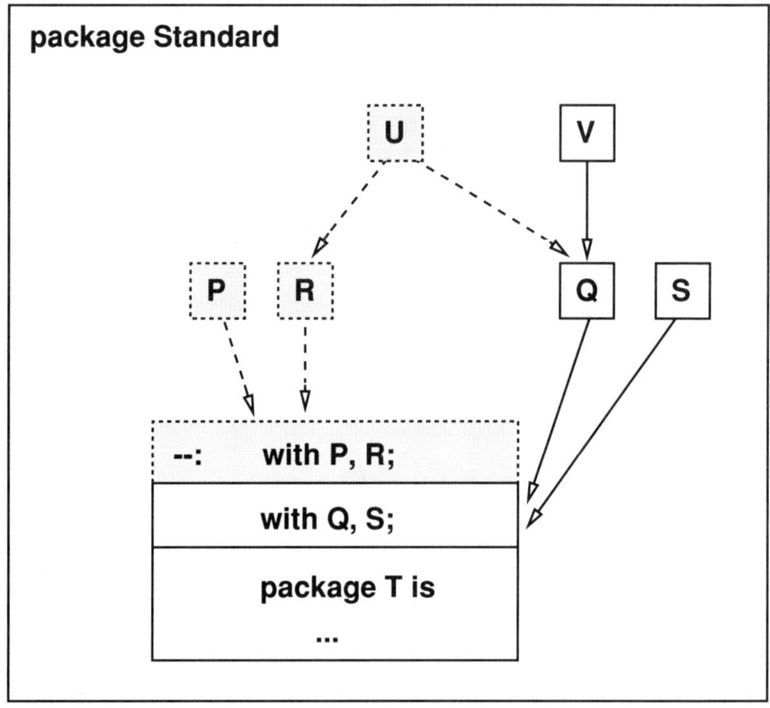

FIGURE 5.2. A dependency tree for Anna specifications.

can result in changing the set of implementations (actual package bodies that are consistent with the changed specification). For example, to change a system specification from requiring stack-like properties to queue-like properties, we might simply change a few axioms in STACK_THEORY.

A specification is considered to be nested in package STANDARD after all the standard Ada declarations, as shown in Figure 5.2.[8] Therefore, a specification may refer to, and thus depend on, the Ada predefined types even though there is no formal specification of those types. We are allowed to accept the Ada declaration of STANDARD in constructing annotations, just as the Ada programmer uses it in programs. In building specification libraries in the future, we should certainly try to formally specify the types that are encapsulated in STANDARD. And in the following discussion, when we talk about deducing properties of other packages from STANDARD, we are assuming that there is a set of axioms that the types and operations of STANDARD satisfy.

[8] Anna follows the Ada visibility rules.

Next we describe some ways of building new specifications that result in a strong relationship between the new and old specifications.

5.6 Relative Specification

The Ada notion of dependency is too broad to distinguish accurately the various relationships that can exist between Anna package specifications. In this section, we describe two methods of building a new specification by using, or "reusing," an existing specification. Both methods lead to a new specification that not only depends, in the Ada sense, upon the previous one, but is related to it in a stronger way, which we call *relative specification*.

The terminology *relative specification* is used to describe dependency, where all the basic concepts of a new package specification are basic concepts of the package specifications that it depends upon or generic instances of those packages. Relative specification is a relationship that implies that the new specification has been completely defined using the existing ones.

We have already seen some examples of relative specification. The PL/1 string package (Section 5.3) is specified relative to the standard operations and attributes of Ada types STRING, INTEGER, BOOLEAN. All the basic concepts of the PL/1 string package are predefined Ada operations, so we can deduce the properties of the new operations using only the predefined ones.

The STACK in Section 5.2 is also a relative specification. It is specified relative to STACK_THEORY. All its basic concepts are basic concepts of the instance of the theory IMPORTED_THEORY. (Note that the use of the state type as an actual generic parameter means that it becomes a basic concept of the instance.) The properties of the actual operations PUSH and POP can be deduced from properties of STACK_THEORY.
STACK_THEORY itself, however, is not a relative specification. Although it depends on NATURAL and BOOLEAN from package STANDARD, all its own functions are basic concepts. Its properties can only be determined by analysis of its own specification.

The TABLE_MANAGER example in Section 4.5 is not a relative specification. The basic concepts are the package state type and its operations, the predefined types STRING, BOOLEAN and INTEGER and their operations, and the virtual functions FULL and MEMBER. Since FULL and MEMBER are basic functions declared in the package itself, we cannot deduce many properties of TABLE_MANAGER from STANDARD (which is the only library package it refers to). We have to reason about its own specification — its subprogram annotations and axioms. Similarly, package SETS of Section 5.4 is not a relative specification.

Below we describe two simple techniques of relative specification.

5.6.1 Extension

- **Specification by extension**

  A subprogram is an extension *of an existing package if it is specified by subprogram annotations using only types and functions of that package or of a generic instance of that package. A package is an* extension *of an existing package if all of its subprograms are extensions of the package, or a single generic instance of the package.*

Extension is the simplest kind of relative specification. Note that specification by extension does not permit the use of axioms in the package being specified. New types and exceptions are allowed, but their use is limited by the following restriction. The operations of the new package are specified solely by subprogram annotations using the functions of an instance of the library package.

Specification by extension applies in common situations where a generic library package is "customized" for a particular application.[9] Typically, the library package is instantiated to the parameters of the application and some new operations that combine previous operations are defined.

As an example, we extend package SETS in Section 5.4. Let us specify a new set operation that computes the symmetric difference of two sets. This operation can be specified entirely using types, operations, and exceptions of the existing SETS package. Indeed, it can be viewed as an addition to the already existing operations, thus defining a larger, special-purpose set operations package.

Example: *Extending the sets package—symmetric difference of two sets.*

```
with SETS;
generic
    type NEW_ELEM is private;
package SPECIAL_SETS is

    package NEW_SETS is new SETS(ELEM => NEW_ELEM);

    use NEW_SETS;

    function SYMMETRIC_DIFFERENCE(A, B : SET)
```

---

[9] A survey of Ada software projects has found that 87% of changes to Ada package declarations are extensions.

```
        return SET;
--|         where
--|             raise SET_FULL,
--|             return (A-B)+(B-A);

    end SPECIAL_SETS;
```

Commentary

In this example a new package, SPECIAL_SETS, inherits all the operations of SETS from the instance NEW_SETS.[10] The new operation is then declared and specified by subprogram annotations that use the operations of NEW_SETS.

The set of basic concepts for this specification of SPECIAL_SETS is the set of basic concepts for SETS plus the functions "+" and "−". However, the **return** annotation of SYMMETRIC_DIFFERENCE can be replaced by an equivalent annotation using only IS_MEMBER. So the same basic concepts suffice to specify the extension.

Other examples of specification by extension have been given previously. In Section 2.5.3, sorting procedure SORT is specified using only operations and types from package SORTING_CONCEPTS. It can be viewed as an operation that extends those of the concepts package. In package PL1_STRINGS (Section 5.3), each of its operations is specified relative to the Ada package STANDARD by subprogram annotations. It is therefore an extension of package STANDARD (see note below) — it adds some new string operations to the existing Ada ones. In Section 5.2, a STACK package is specified as an extension of the STACK_THEORY package.

Notes

Finally, a few notes about our definition of extension. First, a package that extends a previous one does not have to include all the operations of its parent. Second, any set of basic concepts used to specify a package will suffice to specify an extension of it. Third, *extension* describes a technique of building specifications that uses another specification in a particularly simple way. There can be equivalent but different specifications of a package, one being an extension of a given package and the other not.

5.6.2 Association—Modeling types with other types

To allow specification of new abstract types that are similar to existing ones, but are not merely extensions, we broaden our classification of relative

---

[10]This example of extension is equivalent to the SmallTalk notion of inheritance.

specification a little. The new package is specified relative to existing ones by *association* if the only new basic functions (i. e., basic functions in the new package) are mappings between the new types and the old types.

Let P be a new package with private type S. Virtual functions are defined in P that return values of types declared in library packages. They map values of a private type S of P into values of types in the library packages. These functions are called *association functions*. Association functions are required to be mathematical functions in the sense that their values depend only on their parameters.

- **Specification by Association**

  P *is* specified by association *with library packages if the only new basic functions (i e., functions that are not declared in the library packages) in the specification of* P *are association functions that map its private types to types in the library packages.*

Specification by association is a technique for defining new abstract types by relating them with existing types. In many examples, the association functions suffice to reduce questions about the specification of P, such as whether or not it implies a property, to similar questions about the specifications of the library packages.

Example: *Outline of specification by association.*

```
--: package LIBRARY_PACKAGE is
--:     type T is private;
--:     function OP1 (X : T) return T;
        ...
--: end LIBRARY_PACKAGE;


--: with LIBRARY_PACKAGE;
    package NEW_PACKAGE is

--:     use LIBRARY_PACKAGE;
        type S is private;
--:     function ASSOCIATE (Y : S) return T;

        procedure NEW_OP (A : in out S);
--|     where out (ASSOCIATE (A) = OP1 (ASSOCIATE (in A)));
        ...
--| axiom
--|     for all E, F : S =>
--|         R (ASSOCIATE (E), ASSOCIATE (F)),
--          Equality axiom: one -one mapping
--|         E ≠ F → ASSOCIATE (E) ≠ ASSOCIATE (F);
    ...

    end NEW_PACKAGE;
```

Commentary

In this outline, function ASSOCIATE maps values of the new type S into values of library package type T. New operation NEW_OP is specified by mapping the **in** and **out** values of its parameter of type S into the associated values of type T and using OP1 on those values to express a relationship.

Intuitively, the association function can be viewed as a virtual declaration "let S have an attribute of type T." The operations on S are specified using only its "T attribute."

Except for the axioms for "=" on type S, all the axioms of NEW_PACKAGE are expressed as relationships between associated values of type T. Conceptually, we can reason about the new specification by reasoning about the old specification, perhaps with some additions to its axioms.

This technique allows us to specify some aspects of S using T as a model. S may be more complex than T. For example, it could have another association function that defines a different attribute of type T′.

The first STACK example in Section 5.1 is *not* specified by association with STANDARD. Although LENGTH is an association function that maps private type STACK′TYPE into INTEGER, values of STACK′TYPE appear in some of the axioms without being mapped into integers. It is simply a specification of STACK that depends on STANDARD.

Next we show that association allows us to apply runtime checking in situations where we previously could not.

• Specification by association with implementable theories

Recall that the STACK_THEORY in Section 5.2 is really an axiom macro. It cannot be implemented because there is not enough information about its generic parameters. It has a generic STACK_TYPE parameter so that it can be used in another specification by generic instantiation. It is instantiated so that the state type (or private type) of an Ada package replaces the STACK_TYPE generic formal parameter.

If association mappings are used instead of instantiation to map the types of the new package to types of the theory package, the generic state type formal parameter can be omitted and replaced by a private type. Then the theory is implementable. We review briefly how the example in Section 5.2 can be rewritten using association mapping.

Example: Specification relative to a theory by association.

```
--   Generic theory package that can be implemented.
--:  generic
--:      type ELEMENT is private;
--:  package STACK_THEORY is
```

```
--:      type STACK is private;

--:      function MEMBER (X : ELEMENT; S : STACK)
--:      return BOOLEAN;
--:      function LENGTH (S : STACK) return NATURAL;
--:      function TOP (S : STACK) return ELEMENT;
--:      function PUSH_STATE (X : ELEMENT; S : STACK)
--:      return STACK;
--:      function POP_STATE (S : STACK)
--:      return STACK;

--|      axiom
--|      for all S : STACK; U, V : ELEMENT =>
--|          LENGTH (STACK'INITIAL) = 0,
--|          not MEMBER (U, STACK'INITIAL),
--|          MEMBER (U, PUSH_STATE (V, S)) =
--|              MEMBER (U, S) or U = V,
--|          ...
--|          POP_STATE (PUSH_STATE (U, S)) = S;

--:  end STACK_THEORY;

--   Actual stack package.
--:   with STACK_THEORY;
     generic
         type ITEM is private;
         MAX : POSITIVE;
     package MY_STACKS is

--:      package MY_THEORY is new STACK_THEORY (ITEM);
--:      use MY_THEORY;

         type STACK is private;
         OVERFLOW, UNDERFLOW : exception;

--   Function mapping actual stacks to theory stacks.
--:      function MAP (S:STACK) return MY_THEORY.STACK;

         procedure PUSH (X : in ITEM; S : in out STACK);
--|        where LENGTH (MAP (in S)) = MAX =>
--|                                               raise OVERFLOW,
--|            out (MAP (S) = PUSH_STATE (X, MAP (in S))),
--|            out (TOP (MAP (S)) = X);

         procedure POP(Y : out ITEM; S : in out STACK);
--|          where LENGTH (MAP (in S)) = 0 =>
--|                                             raise UNDERFLOW,
--|              out (MAP (S) = POP_STATE (X, MAP (in S))),
--|              out (Y = TOP (MAP (in S)));

     end MY_STACKS;
```

Commentary

STACK_THEORY differs from the previous theory of the example in Section 5.2 in that the generic formal type parameter STACK_TYPE of the previous theory is replaced by a private type STACK in the new theory. There is no problem implementing a body for this theory. Now we have an executable theory. Association function MAP maps the actual stack type to the theory stack type. All annotations of MY_STACKS are given in terms of theory stack values. If MAP is implemented (by a virtual function body in the body of MY_STACKS), then values of annotations such as

out (MAP (S) = POP_STATE (X, MAP (**in** S)))

can be computed. We can then check the behavior of package MY_STACKS with the theory.

The effect of the instantiation MY_THEORY is to copy all of STACK_THEORY into the specification of MY_STACKS. This is really overkill, given the MAP function. Unfortunately, at present there is no other operation for relating generic packages in Ada and Anna. We need the instantiation MY_THEORY only to identify the generic component types ELEMENT and ITEM and to follow Ada rules for using generic units in the declaration of MAP.

5.6.3 An example of relative specification by association — Small Library

In practice, we may associate more than one library type with a new type. This is equivalent to modeling the new type S as having more than one attribute, each of an existing type T_1, T_2, ... Also, more than one private type of a package may be specified by association with library types. To illustrate specification by *association*, consider the following problem.[11]

Problem:

Consider a small library database with the following transactions:

1. Check out a copy of a book/Return a copy of a book.
2. Add a copy of a book to/Remove a copy of a book from the library.
3. Get the list of books by a particular author or in a particular subject area.

---

[11]Due to R. A. Kemmerer, adopted as a benchmark example for the 4th International Workshop on Software Specification and Design (April 1987).

4. Find out the list of books currently checked out by a particular borrower.
5. Find out what borrower last checked out a particular copy of a book.

There are two types of users: staff users and ordinary borrowers. Transactions 1, 2, 4, and 5 are restricted to staff users, except that ordinary borrowers can perform transaction 4 to find out books currently borrowed by themselves. The database must also satisfy the following constraints:

1. All copies in the library must either be available for checkout or be checked out.
2. No copy of a book may be both available and checked out at the same time.
3. A borrower may not have more than a predefined number of books checked out at one time.

We begin by constructing an Ada package specification for the library, following the recipe in Section 5.1 rather loosely. Names of entities will refer to corresponding elements of the problem description. The package presents the "user" with a view of the library, essentially a menu of facilities. "Use" of facilities is "subprogram call." Dependency on time, as indicated by "currently checked out" or "at one time" is represented by the current state of the library. Resolution of simultaneous access is an implementation detail; at the library interface, each user may assume he has his own library, and the actions of other users cannot be seen.

Example: *Ada package specification of the small library.*

```
package LIBRARY is

    type BOOK is private;
    type BOOK_LIST is private;
    type PASSWORD is limited private;

    type USER_KINDS is (STAFF, BORROWER);
    type STATUS is (AVAILABLE, CHECKED_OUT);

    subtype USER is STRING;
    subtype AUTHOR is STRING;
    subtype SUBJECT is STRING;

    BOOK_LIMIT : constant POSITIVE := MAX;

    NOT_AVAILABLE, STAFF_PASSWORD_REQUIRED :
                                                exception;
```

```
--   Actual operations.
--        Check out a copy of a book.
          procedure CHECK_OUT (B : BOOK;
                               U : USER;
                               P : PASSWORD);

--        Return a copy of a book.
          procedure RETURN_BOOK (B : BOOK;
                                 U : USER;
                                 P : PASSWORD);

--        Add a copy of a book to the library.
          procedure ADD (B : BOOK; P : PASSWORD);

--        Remove a copy of a book from the library.
          procedure REMOVE (B : BOOK; P : PASSWORD);

--        Find the list of books in a particular subject area.
          function RETRIEVE (S : SUBJECT)
          return BOOK_LIST;

--        Find the list of books by a particular author.
          function RETRIEVE (S : AUTHOR)
          return BOOK_LIST;

--        Find the list of books currently checked out by a borrower.
          function RETRIEVE (S : USER; P : PASSWORD)
          return BOOK_LIST;

--        Find who last checked out a particular copy of a book.
          function RETRIEVE (B : BOOK; P : PASSWORD)
          return USER;

-- Virtual concepts needed to specify the actual operations will include set of
-- books, library books, set operations, attributes of books (author, subject,
-- borrower, last borrower, status), attributes of passwords (user kind, user).

--| axiom
-- 1. All copies in the library must be available for checkout or be checked out.
-- 2. No copy of the book may be both available and checked out at the same
--    time.
-- 3. A borrower may not have more than a predefined number of books checked
--    out at one time.

     end LIBRARY;
```

Commentary

The Ada types and subprograms required by the problem statement are declared in the Ada package specification. We can think of this specification as a "preliminary design." It is lacking semantic content, even though some design decisions are implied by the choice of types, exceptions, and subprograms. Annotations of these actual units are needed in order to make the implied design decisions explicit. Only then are we able to discuss whether this is a good design.

Attempts to specify this preliminary design may lead to changes. Additional elements may be needed. Some elements, such as "password," which does not occur in the problem description, may turn out to be unnecessary.

Our next step is to give an Anna specification for this preliminary design. The library operations work on a private type BOOK_LIST. The informal comments suggest that the operations on BOOK_LIST can be defined in terms of SET operations. To do this, we model BOOK_LISTs as SETs.

A virtual SETS_OF_BOOKS package will be declared. This allows us to refer to sets of books and to use set operations in specifying the library. For example, the set of books that constitutes the library can now be declared as a virtual object. Next, a virtual function, BOOKS that maps a BOOK_LIST into a set of books will be declared. This function can be viewed as a user-defined attribute of type BOOK_LIST. Its role is to associate *virtual sets* of books with actual *lists* of books. As a result, properties of the Ada operations of the library (which compute on book lists) can be specified in terms of the associated sets of books. The library body will be required to be consistent with the specifications that use set operations on associated sets of books, but it is not required to implement the set operations.

We note here that our choice of *association* with sets to specify the small library gives us flexibility to introduce other attributes of BOOK_LIST as we build the specification. It is too early for us to say that BOOK_LISTs *are* SETs of books.

The state of the library package plays an important role in the specification. The state contains the books that are in the library, the users and their passwords, and the status of books. Throughout the specification, explicit reference to the current state has been omitted in order to shorten annotations. Any call to a package function that is written as F means LIBRARY . F — i. e., the call is evaluated in the current state. This is particularly important in interpreting the use of modifiers **in** and **out**. An annotation of CHECK_OUT in the following example

```
out (BORROWED (U) = PLUS (B, in BORROWED (U)))
```

is a shorthand form of

```
out (LIBRARY . BORROWED (U) =
                    PLUS (B, in LIBRARY . BORROWED (U)))
```

The **out** modifier applies to the program variables that can change value, in this case the (omitted) state. The calls to BORROWED are evaluated in different states of the library — when the scope of the annotation is entered and when it is exited normally.

Example: Anna specification of the small library.

```
--:  with SETS;
     package LIBRARY is

         type BOOK is private;
         type BOOK_LIST is private;
         type PASSWORD is limited private;

         type USER_KINDS is (STAFF, BORROWER);
         type STATUS
            is (AVAILABLE, CHECKED_OUT, NOT_AVAILABLE);

         subtype USER is STRING;
         subtype AUTHOR is STRING;
         subtype SUBJECT is STRING;

         BOOK_LIMIT : constant POSITIVE := MAX;
         NULL_USER  : constant USER := "";
         UN_AVAILABLE : exception;
         BOOK_AVAILABLE : exception;
         STAFF_PASSWORD_REQUIRED : exception;
         INCORRECT_PASSWORD : exception;
         LIMIT_EXCEEDED : exception;

--   Basic concepts used in the specifications.
--       Sets of books.
--:      package SETS_OF_BOOKS is new SETS (BOOK);
--:      subtype BOOK_SET is SETS_OF_BOOKS . SET;

--       Attribute of book lists (association function).
--:      function BOOKS (X : BOOK_LIST)
--:      return BOOK_SET;

--       Sets of authors.
--:      package SETS_OF_AUTHORS is new SETS (AUTHOR);
--:      subtype AUTHOR_SET is SETS_OF_AUTHORS . SET;

--       The books in the library.
--:      function LIBRARY_BOOKS return BOOK_SET;

--       Attributes of books.
--       (author, aubject, borrower, last borrower, status)
--:      function AUTHOR_OF (B : BOOK)
--:      return AUTHOR_SET;
--:      function SUBJECT_OF (B : BOOK) return SUBJECT;
--:      function LAST_BORROWER (B : BOOK) return USER;
--:      function STATUS_OF (B : BOOK) return STATUS;
--:      function BORROWER (B : BOOK) return USER;
--|          where STATUS_OF (B) = AVAILABLE =>
--|                                           raise BOOK_AVAILABLE;
```

```
--        Attributes of passwords (user kind, user).
--:       function USER_KIND (P : PASSWORD)
--:       return USER_KINDS;
--:       function USER_OF (P : PASSWORD) return USER;
--    End of basic concepts.

--        Attribute of user.
--:       function BORROWED (U : USER) return BOOK_SET;
--|           where
--|           return S : BOOK_SET => for all B : BOOK =>
--|               MEMBER (B, S) ↔
--|                   (STATUS_OF (B) = CHECKED_OUT
--|                        and
--|                    BORROWER (B) = U);

-- Simplifying notation — ADD and REMOVE are procedures in the SETS
-- package.
--:       function PLUS (B : BOOK; T : BOOK_SET)
--:       return BOOK_SET;
--|           where
--|               return SETS_OF_BOOKS.ADD'OUT (B, T).S;

--:       function MINUS (B : BOOK; T : BOOK_SET)
--:       return BOOK_SET;
--|           where
--|               return SETS_OF_BOOKS.REMOVE'OUT (B, T).S;

-- Actual operations.
          procedure CHECK_OUT (B : BOOK;
                               U : USER;
                               P : PASSWORD);
--|          where
--|              USER_KIND (P) /= STAFF =>
--|                            raise STAFF_PASSWORD_REQUIRED,
--|              STATUS_OF (B) /= AVAILABLE
--|                                        raise UN_AVAILABLE,
--|              CARDINALITY (BORROWED (U)) = BOOK_LIMIT =>
--|                                      raise LIMIT_EXCEEDED,
--|              out (STATUS_OF (B) = CHECKED_OUT),
--|              out (BORROWER (B) = U),
--|              out (BORROWED (U) =
--|                                PLUS (B, in BORROWED(U));

          procedure RETURN_BOOK (B : BOOK;
                                 U : USER;
                                 P : PASSWORD);
--|           where
--|               USER_KIND (P) /= STAFF =>
--|                            raise STAFF_PASSWORD_REQUIRED,
--|               out (STATUS_OF (B) = AVAILABLE),
--|               out (BORROWER (B) = NULL_USER),
--|               out (BORROWED (U) =
--|                              MINUS (B, in BORROWED(U));
```

```
    procedure ADD (B : BOOK; P : PASSWORD),
--|     where
--|        USER_KIND (P) /= STAFF =>
--|                        raise STAFF_PASSWORD_REQURIRED,
--|        out (STATUS_OF (B) = AVAILABLE),
--|        out (LIBRARY_BOOKS =
--|                             PLUS (B, in LIBRARY_BOOKS));

    procedure REMOVE (B : BOOK; P : PASSWORD);
--|     where
--|        USER_KIND (P) /= STAFF =>
--|                        raise STAFF_PASSWORD_REQURIRED,
--|        in STATUS_OF (B) = AVAILABLE,
--|        out (STATUS_OF (B) = NOT_AVAILABLE),
--|        out (LIBRARY_BOOKS =
--|                           MINUS (B, in LIBRARY_BOOKS));

  function RETRIEVE (S : SUBJECT) return BOOK_LIST;
--|   where return L : BOOK_LIST =>
--|      for all X : BOOK => MEMBER (X, BOOKS (L)) ↔
--|                                  SUBJECT_OF (X) = S;

  function RETRIEVE (A : AUTHOR) return BOOK_LIST;
--|   where return L : BOOK_LIST =>
--|      (for all X : BOOK => MEMBER (X, BOOKS (L)) ↔
--|                           MEMBER (A, AUTHOR_OF (X)));

  function RETRIEVE (U : USER; P : PASSWORD)
  return BOOK_LIST;
--|   where
--|      USER_KIND (P) /= STAFF or USER_OF (P) /= U =>
--|                           raise INCORRECT_PASSWORD,
--|      return L : BOOK_LIST =>
--|                           BOOKS (L) = BORROWED (U);

  function RETRIEVE (B : BOOK; P : PASSWORD)
  return USER;
--|   where
--|      USER_KIND (P) /= STAFF =>
--|                      raise STAFF_PASSWORD_REQUIRED,
--|      return LAST_BORROWER (B);

--| axiom
--| for all ST : LIBRARY'TYPE; B : BOOK; U : USER =>
--|    MEMBER (B, ST.LIBRARY_BOOKS) →
--|              (ST.STATUS_OF (B) = AVAILABLE
--|                   or
--|               ST.STATUS_OF (B) = CHECKED_OUT),
```

```
--|       MEMBER (B, ST . LIBRARY_BOOKS) →
--|                  (ST . STATUS_OF (B) = AVAILABLE ↔
--|                   not exist U : USER =>
--|                                    MEMBER (B, BORROWED (U))),
--|       CARDINALITY (ST . BORROWED (U)) ≤ BOOK_LIMIT;

    end LIBRARY;
```

Commentary

This specification is relative to SETS by *association*. All new basic functions are association functions mapping private types to predefined types or set types. Virtual function, BOOKS *associates* BOOK_SETs with BOOK_LISTs. This allows the operations on BOOK_LISTS to be specified by set operations.

The *basic concepts* upon which this specification depends are the virtual set operations imported by generic instantiation of SETS, and the virtual attributes (association functions) in the specification. The virtual attributes express properties of books such as the subject of a book or the borrower of a book, that are used in the problem description without definition.

Note that values of type BOOK_LIST are always mapped to their associated sets in the annotations. For example, in the annotations of the RETRIEVE functions, the BOOK_LIST value returned is defined by a property of the associated BOOK_SET. In effect, the declaration of BOOKS is making an informal statement, "*let BookLists have an attribute whose value is a set of books.*" As a result of this declaration, all the usual set operations can be applied to the set of books associated with a booklist. There is also the implication that set operations are sufficient and that other properties of *lists*, such as order or repetition of elements, are not important in this specification. This means that different copies of the same book have to have unique identifiers.

We can model BOOK_LISTs by BOOK_SETs that are never full by using a type constraint:[12]

```
--:    subtype BOOK_SET is SETS_OF_BOOKS . SET;
--|       where S : BOOK_SET =>
--|       for all  P : SETS_OF_BOOKS'TYPE =>
--|                                  not P . IS_FULL (S);
```

This LIBRARY specification can be improved or extended in several ways. For example, the initial state of the library is

[12]We could omit the quantifier over the state type since SETS has a constant state.

not specified. We do not know how many books we have at the beginning. Also, there is no way to manipulate the set of library users, either staff or borrowers. Such features were not required in the problem description. We may therefore expect to use the method of extension on this small library specification to add new facilities in specifying more realistic libraries.

Why not delete the private type BOOK_LIST together with the mapping function and simply use BOOK_SETs, thus shortening the specification? The advantage of keeping the mapping function is to allow the addition of new mapping functions that express ordering and multiplicity of components of lists.[13]

Another approach to improving this specification is to change the theory that it depends on. We may be able to model required new properties by replacing SETS by ORDERED_ MULTI_SETS in which elements of a set are ordered and repetitions of elements are allowed. The association function declarations would be updated to reflect new type names. New properties would be expressed by additional annotations using operations of the new theory for multiplicity and ordering of members in a multiset.

Summary

Specification by extension and by association are two common techniques of relative specification. They are not the only ones. Following Ada visibility rules, the package STANDARD is always visible, which allows for a good deal of cleverness in constructing new specifications. It is often possible to show that a specification constructed by one technique, say association, is equivalent to a specification constructed relative to the same set of library packages using another technique, say extension.

We are not restricted to using any one technique. Given a problem, we should choose a technique that makes it easy to build upon previous specifications. We should try to keep the basic concepts to a minimum without making the specification difficult.

5.7 The DIRECT_IO Package

The predefined Ada generic package DIRECT_IO specifies a standard input/output facility. It is described in Chapter 14 of Ada83 (specifically Sections 14.1, 14.2, and 14.4). Every implementor of Ada must provide an implementation that satisfies this description. The description of DIRECT_IO consists of: (1) an English description of rather sophisticated concepts associated with file management (such as direct access); (2) a description of

---

[13] See also commentary on the last example in Section 5.6.2.

each visible subprogram, which consists of an Ada subprogram declaration followed by paragraphs in English saying what the subprogram does (using the file management concepts); and (3) an Ada package declaration.

In this section we discuss an Anna specification of DIRECT_IO. This is an interesting example since the English description has been the subject of ongoing questions and requests for clarification in various Ada language committees. Our objective is to illustrate techniques for formalizing such descriptions in Anna.

The Anna specification given here is incomplete in the sense that answers to some questions cannot be logically deduced from it. But it does allow us to apply logical rules to deduce consequences of various interpretations of the English requirements. This allows us to predict what an implementation will do in some cases. As a result, the Anna specification can serve several different roles. It can be used as a basis for negotiation as part of the design process described by Parnas.[14] When it is finally completed, it can serve as a standard specification for all implementations. It also can be used for testing implementations.

The reader may approach this example in two ways. Jump right into the Anna specification and see how much of it is intuitively understandable, say from the point of view of a user about to write an I/O routine using DIRECT_IO. Or read the relevant sections of [Ada83] along with the Anna specification, checking that each section has been correctly expressed.

One small note: in Anna the equality operator is predefined for all types including limited types.

Example: *Specification of the* DIRECT_IO package.

```
with IO_EXCEPTIONS;
generic
    MAX_COUNT : POSITIVE;
    type ELEMENT_TYPE is private;
package DIRECT_IO is

    type FILE_TYPE is limited private;
    type FILE_MODE is (IN_FILE, INOUT_FILE, OUT_FILE);
    type COUNT is range 0 .. MAX_COUNT;
    subtype POSITIVE_COUNT is COUNT
        range 1 .. COUNT'LAST;
```

[14]See the paper cited at the end of Chapter 0.

```
-- Basic concepts.
--:         package EXTERNAL_SYSTEM is
--:
--:             type EXTERNAL_FILE is limited private;
--:             NO_FILE : constant EXTERNAL_FILE;
--:
--:             function PROPER_NAME (NAME : STRING)
--:             return BOOLEAN;
--:             function FILE_MAP (F : FILE_TYPE)
--:             return EXTERNAL_FILE;
--:             function NAME_MAP (NAME : STRING)
--:             return EXTERNAL_FILE;
--|                 where in PROPER_NAME (NAME);

--:             function
--:                 CAPACITY_EXCEEDED (E : EXTERNAL_FILE)
--:             return BOOLEAN;
--:             function
--:                 DELETION_SUPPORTED (E : EXTERNAL_FILE)
--:             return BOOLEAN;
--:             function RESET_SUPPORTED (E : EXTERNAL_FILE;
--:                                       M : FILE_MODE)
--:             return BOOLEAN;
-- End of basic concepts.

--:             function INACCESSIBLE (E : EXTERNAL_FILE)
--:             return BOOLEAN;
--|                 where return (for all X : FILE_TYPE =>
--|                                    E /= FILE_MAP (X))
--|                                  and
--|                              (for all S : STRING =>
--|                                    E /= NAME_MAP (S));

--:             function DISTINCT (F, F1 : FILE_TYPE)
--:             return BOOLEAN;
--|                 where return FILE_MAP (F) /= FILE_MAP (F1);
--:
--:         end EXTERNAL_SYSTEM;

--:         use EXTERNAL_SYSTEM;

-- Exceptions.
-- [Exceptions have been positioned so that they are visible in the annotations.]

            STATUS_ERROR : exception
                renames IO_EXCEPTIONS.STATUS_ERROR;
            MODE_ERROR : exception
                renames IO_EXCEPTIONS.MODE_ERROR;
```

```
          NAME_ERROR : exception
              renames IO_EXCEPTIONS.NAME_ERROR;
          USE_ERROR : exception
              renames IO_EXCEPTIONS.USE_ERROR;
          DEVICE_ERROR : exception
              renames IO_EXCEPTIONS.DEVICE_ERROR;
          END_ERROR : exception
              renames IO_EXCEPTIONS.END_ERROR;
          DATA_ERROR : exception
              renames IO_EXCEPTIONS.DATA_ERROR;

-- [The following function declarations have been positioned and reordered to
-- make them visible in the annotations.]

          function IS_OPEN (FILE : in FILE_TYPE)
          return BOOLEAN;
--|           where return FILE_MAP (FILE) /= NO_FILE;

          function MODE (FILE : in FILE_TYPE)
          return FILE_MODE;
--|           where
--|               not IS_OPEN (FILE) => raise STATUS_ERROR;

          function NAME (FILE : in FILE_TYPE)
          return STRING;
--|           where
--|               not IS_OPEN (FILE) => raise STATUS_ERROR;

          function FORM (FILE : in FILE_TYPE)
          return STRING;
--|           where
--|               not IS_OPEN (FILE) => raise STATUS_ERROR;

          function INDEX (FILE : in FILE_TYPE)
          return POSITIVE_COUNT;
--|           where
--|               not IS_OPEN (FILE) => raise STATUS_ERROR;

          function SIZE (FILE : in FILE_TYPE)
          return COUNT;
--|           where
--|               not IS_OPEN (FILE) => raise STATUS_ERROR;

          function END_OF_FILE (FILE : in FILE_TYPE)
          return BOOLEAN;
--|           where
--|               not IS_OPEN (FILE) => raise STATUS_ERROR,
--|               MODE (FILE) = OUT_FILE =>
--|                                            raise MODE_ERROR,
--|               return (INDEX (FILE) > SIZE (FILE));
```

```
-- File management.
        procedure CREATE(FILE : in out FILE_TYPE;
                         MODE : in FILE_MODE :=
                                          INOUT_FILE;
                         NAME : in STRING := "";
                         FORM : in STRING := "");
--|       where
--|         is OPEN(in FILE) => raise STATUS_ERROR,
--|         not PROPER_NAME(NAME) =>
--|                               raise NAME_ERROR,
--|         raise USE_ERROR,
--|         out IS_OPEN(FILE),
--|         out (INDEX(FILE) = 1),
--|         out (MODE(FILE) = MODE),
--|         out (in EXTERNAL_SYSTEM.INACCESSIBLE
--|                               (FILE_MAP(FILE))),
--|         out (FILE_MAP(FILE) /= NO_FILE),
--|         out (FILE_MAP(FILE)=NAME_MAP(NAME));

        procedure OPEN(FILE : in out FILE_TYPE;
                       MODE : in FILE_MODE;
                       NAME : in STRING;
                       FORM : in STRING);
--|       where
--|         IS_OPEN(in FILE) => raise STATUS_ERROR,
--|         not PROPER_NAME(NAME)
--|             or NAME_MAP(NAME) = NO_FILE =>
--|                               raise NAME_ERROR,
--|         raise USE_ERROR,
--|         out IS_OPEN(FILE),
--|         out (INDEX(FILE) = 1),
--|         out (MODE(FILE) = MODE),
--|         out (FILE_MAP(FILE) =
--|                          in NAME_MAP(NAME));

        procedure CLOSE(FILE : in out FILE_TYPE);
--|       where
--|         not IS_OPEN(in FILE) => raise STATUS_ERROR,
--|         out (not IS_OPEN(FILE)),
--|         out (FILE_MAP(FILE) = NO_FILE);

        procedure DELETE(FILE : in out FILE_TYPE);
--|       where
--|         not IS_OPEN(in FILE) => raise STATUS_ERROR,
--|         not in
--|             DELETION_SUPPORTED(FILE_MAP(FILE))=>
--|                                 raise USE_ERROR,
--|         out (not IS_OPEN(FILE)),
--|         out (FILE_MAP(FILE) = NO_FILE),
--|         out INACCESSIBLE
--|               (in EXTERNAL_SYSTEM.FILE_MAP
--|                                    (in FILE));
```

```
         procedure RESET (FILE : in out FILE_TYPE;
                          MODE : in FILE_MODE);
--|         where
--|            not IS_OPEN (FILE) =>
--|                                         raise STATUS_ERROR,
--|            not in RESET_SUPPORTED (FILE_MAP (FILE),
--|                                   MODE) => raise USE_ERROR,
--|            out (INDEX (FILE) = 1),
--|            out (MODE (FILE) = MODE);

         procedure RESET (FILE : in out FILE_TYPE);
--|         where
--|            not IS_OPEN (FILE) =>
--|                                         raise STATUS_ERROR,
--|            not in RESET_SUPPORTED (FILE_MAP (FILE),
--|                                   MODE) => raise USE_ERROR,
--|            out (INDEX (FILE) = 1);

-- Input and output operations.
         procedure READ (FILE : in FILE_TYPE;
                         ITEM : out ELEMENT_TYPE;
                         FROM : POSITIVE_COUNT);
--|         where
--|            not IS_OPEN (FILE) =>
--|            raise STATUS_ERROR,
--|            MODE (FILE) = OUT_FILE =>
--|                                         raise MODE_ERROR,
--|            FROM > SIZE (FILE) => raise END_ERROR,
--|            raise DATA_ERROR,
--|            out (INDEX (FILE) = FROM+1);

         procedure READ (FILE : in FILE_TYPE;
                         ITEM : out ELEMENT_TYPE);
--|         where
--|            not IS_OPEN (FILE) => raise STATUS_ERROR,
--|            MODE (FILE) = OUT_FILE =>
--|                                         raise MODE_ERROR,
--|            END OF_FILE (FILE) => raise END_ERROR,
--|            raise DATA_ERROR,
--|            out (INDEX (FILE) = in INDEX (FILE)+1);

         procedure WRITE (FILE : in FILE_TYPE;
                          ITEM : in ELEMENT_TYPE;
                          TO_COUNT : POSITIVE_COUNT);
--|         where
--|            CAPACITY_EXCEEDED (FILE_MAP (FILE)) =>
--|                                         raise USE_ERROR,
--|            not IS_OPEN (FILE) =>
--|                                         raise STATUS_ERROR,
--|            MODE (FILE) = IN_FILE =>
--|                                         raise MODE_ERROR,
--|            out (INDEX (FILE) = TO_COUNT+1);
```

```
    procedure WRITE (FILE : in FILE_TYPE;
                     ITEM : in ELEMENT_TYPE);
--|     where
--|         CAPACITY_EXCEEDED (FILE_MAP (FILE)) =>
--|                                     raise USE_ERROR,
--|         not IS_OPEN (FILE) =>
--|                                     raise STATUS_ERROR,
--|         MODE (FILE) = IN_FILE =>
--|                                     raise MODE_ERROR,
--|         out (INDEX (FILE) = in INDEX (FILE)+1);

    procedure SET_INDEX (FILE : in FILE_TYPE;
                         TO_COUNT : in POSITIVE)
--|     where
--|         not IS_OPEN (FILE) =>
--|                                     raise STATUS_ERROR,
--|         out (INDEX (FILE) = TO_COUNT);

--|     axiom for all S : DIRECT_IO'TYPE;
--|                   F, F1 : FILE_TYPE;
--|                   INDEX, I, J : POSITIVE_COUNT;
--|                   ITEM, X, Y : ELEMENT_TYPE;
--|                   NAME, FORM : STRING;
--|                   MODE : FILE_MODE
--|         =>
-- (1) Relation between overloaded forms of READ and of WRITE.
--|         S [READ (F, ITEM, INDEX)] =
--|                    S [SET_INDEX (F, INDEX); READ (F, ITEM)],
--|         S [WRITE (F, ITEM, INDEX)] =
--|                    S [SET_INDEX (F, INDEX); WRITE (F, ITEM)],
-- (2) Relations between READ and WRITE; see commentary.
--|         S [WRITE (F1, X, I)].READ'OUT (FILE => F,
--|                                        ITEM => Y,
--|                                        FROM => J).ITEM=
--|             if not DISTINCT (F, F1) and then I = J then X
--|             else S.READ'OUT (FILE => F,
--|                              ITEM => Y,
--|                              FROM => J).ITEM
--|             end if,

--|         S [WRITE (F, X, I); READ (F1, Y, J)] =
--|                        S [READ (F1, Y, J); WRITE (F, X, I)],
-- (3) WRITE overwrites WRITE; see commentary.
--|         S [WRITE (F, X, I); WRITE (F, Y, I)] =
--|                                     S [WRITE (F, Y, I)],
-- (4) READ is nondestructive; see commentary.
--|         S [READ (F, X, I)].READ'OUT (FILE => F,
--|                                      ITEM => X,
--|                                      INDEX => I).ITEM =
--|                 S.READ'OUT (FILE => F,
--|                             ITEM => X,
--|                             INDEX => I).ITEM,
```

```
-- (5) Conditions under which successive operations are independent.
--|          S [DELETE (F) ; WRITE (F1, X, I)] =
--|              if DISTINCT (F, F1) then
--|                  S [WRITE (F1, X, I) ; DELETE (F)]
--|              else
--|                  S [DELETE (F)]
--|              end if,
--|          ... ; -- Independence axioms for other pairs of procedures.

    end DIRECT_IO;
```

In the following we discuss the derivation of this Anna specification from Ada83, Chapter 14.

DIRECT_IO clearly has a nontrivial state, since it must contain information such as which files are open and which external file is associated with a given file. The effects of its subprograms are described in Ada83 using concepts such as "external file," "establishing an external file," "a new file," "associating an external file with a visible file," "severing an association between files," and "an external file ceasing to exist." It is assumed that these concepts do not require explanation. An external file is described as an indexed linear sequence of elements with a current size. Any open visible file has an index, which is used by "the next" read or write operation. Much of the specification of DIRECT_IO has to be deduced by considering the consequences of the informal description. For example, when do read and write operations commute?

Our approach to constructing an Anna specification is in three steps.[15] First, the basic concepts are encapsulated in package EXTERNAL_SYSTEM. These concepts express some of the concepts used in the English description. The second step is to specify each subprogram of DIRECT_IO by expressing the transformations of its parameter values from input to output and by expressing its exception propagation conditions. These specifications express the English paragraphs in Ada83(14) that describe each subprogram. They are incomplete, since some parts of the English rely on the set theory description of external files; these parts are best expressed as relationships between the subprograms. The third step is to specify relationships between the subprograms by algebraic equations stated as axioms. Essentially, these relationships are the important consequences of the informal English description of direct access files, which was couched in terms of set theoretic concepts.

Basic concepts

The basic concepts are encapsulated in the virtual package EXTERNAL_SYSTEM. It specifies a set of virtual attributes of some of the machine-dependent parts of DIRECT_IO.

---

[15] Some of the recipe steps of Section 5.1 are already taken by Ada83, 14.

The fundamental concepts are the two functions FILE_MAP and NAME_MAP, which express the *association* of visible files and names with external files. The important thing is that these operations are *functions*, i. e. many-one mappings from visible files and names to external files. This expresses the principle that no visible file or name has more than one external file associated with it simultaneously. Some concepts name implementation dependent features such as a file name being proper. Finally, some concepts are defined in terms of the basic mappings. An external file is INACCESSIBLE if no visible file or name is associated with it. Two visible file objects are DISTINCT if they are mapped to different external files. These basic concepts allow different visible files to be mapped to the same external file.

The informal English concepts used to describe DIRECT_IO operations are expressed formally by our basic concepts. For example, the concept of a "*new* external file E" is expressed formally by INACCESSIBLE (E). Boolean-valued function INACCESSIBLE is always evaluated relative to a state of EXTERNAL_SYSTEM. *New* means new relative to the current state of SYSTEM. That is, an external file is *new* if there is no way of reaching it (i. e., constructing its value), either by a name or by a visible file, in the current state of EXTERNAL_SYSTEM. It does not mean that the external file has never been used before in some previous state of SYSTEM.

Here, EXTERNAL_SYSTEM is presented as a package nested within DIRECT_IO. Its (virtual) state is a component of the state of DIRECT_IO and is a nontrivial implicit parameter of its functions. Alternatively, we could have specified EXTERNAL_SYSTEM as a separate generic package with a formal generic type parameter. Its functions would then have an explicit parameter of this type. The package would then be instantiated to the state type of DIRECT_IO. This would show explicitly that the basic concepts are function attributes of the state of DIRECT_IO.

Subprogram specifications

Most of the subprogram specifications are straightforward translations of the English paragraphs that describe each subprogram. Some concepts, however, are replaced by new concepts that involve the virtual mappings of package EXTERNAL_SYSTEM. We use inaccessibility to express both "new external file" and "deleted external file."

For example, Ada83 says that CREATE "establishes a new external file." This is formalized by an annotation expressing that the new external file on output from CREATE is inaccessible on input:

out (**in** EXTERNAL_SYSTEM . INACCESSIBLE (FILE_MAP (FILE))) .

Here, **in** modifies the state of EXTERNAL_SYSTEM in which INACCESSIBLE is evaluated, and **out** modifies all the program variables in the argument to INACCESSIBLE, namely the value of FILE and the state of EXTERNAL_SYSTEM in which FILE_MAP is evaluated (omitted by default). So the annotation refers to the **out** value of FILE returned by CREATE and to the external file to which it is mapped when CREATE terminates.

Similarly, the description of DELETE says that "the external file ceases to exist." This is formalized by

out INACCESSIBLE (**in** EXTERNAL_SYSTEM . FILE_MAP (**in** FILE)) ;

which expresses that the old external file returned by FILE_MAP in the **in** state of EXTERNAL_SYSTEM is inaccessible in the new state on output. Thus, new external files must have been inaccessible before they were created, and deleted files thereby become inaccessible again. These two specifications together imply that deleted files can be reused.

Note that the current state of EXTERNAL_SYSTEM is frequently omitted from calls to functions of the package such as INACCESSIBLE and FILE_MAP. Anna notation permits shortening by omitting package state prefixes. The default is always the current state of the package. For clarity, it is sometimes a good idea to include all states when modifiers are present. For example, the annotation of CREATE above is a short form of

out (**in** EXTERNAL_SYSTEM . INACCESSIBLE
(EXTERNAL_SYSTEM . FILE_MAP (FILE))) .

Now it is clear that **in** modifies the state in which INACCESSIBLE is evaluated, whereas **out** modifies the state in which FILE_MAP is evaluated.

In the DIRECT_IO specification, it is possible for two or more strong propagation conditions in a single subprogram specification to be satisfied at the same time. The propagation conditions are not mutually exclusive (see Section 3.2). It is a simple matter to modify the conditions so that exception propagation is specified in the priority order given in Ada83 (14.5).

Axioms

The axioms express relationships between the subprograms. The most important ones express when the order of READ and WRITE operations is significant (2). The first axiom in (2) expresses that the result of a READ depends on the last WRITE if the two operations are on files that are not distinct and the indices are equal. We will say more about distinctness later. The second axiom in (2) expresses that the package state is not affected by the order of READ and WRITE operations. Axiom (3) relates successive WRITE operations: essentially it says "WRITE overwrites WRITE," which is a consequence of the set-theoretic model of external files in Ada83. However, some may feel that this axiom is an overly strong interpretation of the English because it constrains the implementation to return the package state to its previous value, and therefore might preclude temporary buffering. It can be deleted without changing the overall specification much. A similar axiom, (4), says that READ is not destructive; note here that we would like to be able to say

```
S[READ(F, Y, J)] = S;
```

but this is not quite true because READ is specified to change the file index. Other axioms specify situations in which pairs of operations are independent. The first one gives conditions under which DELETE and WRITE are independent. Interestingly, some validated Ada compilers/environments do not satisfy this axiom (see Section 5.8.2).

The initial state

It is stated in Ada83(14.1) that "the language does not define what happens to external files after the completion of the main program." Neither does our Anna specification! The semantics of Anna implies that the state of DIRECT_IO on elaboration will be DIRECT_IO'INITIAL. Specification of some kind of permanent memory between elaborations would be expressed by giving properties of the initial state. Since no properties are specified, an implementation that always starts with an empty initial state is consistent with our specification.

5.8 Symbolic Execution of Specifications *

The DIRECT_IO specification has many logical consequences that are not stated explicitly. Sometimes these implications are quite surprising, maybe even unforeseen. Discovery of such implications may motivate changes. In trying to understand the specification we must be able to reason about it and answer questions about its consequences.

An important kind of question is: "What are the properties of the state of a package after performing a given sequence of operations?" A package specification can be used to answer such questions *before* the package is implemented by *symbolic execution* of subprograms.

In symbolic execution, the names of objects are taken to represent their values, so no special assumptions (that might apply to a literal value) are made. These names are called *symbolic values*.

A *symbolic state* is a set (conjunction) of boolean assertions containing symbolic values, e. g.

```
IS_OPEN(F), MODE(F) = IN_FILE, INDEX(F) = E+1, ...
```

The assertions belonging to a symbolic state are the assertions that are true in (or satisfied by) that state.

A *symbolic state* represents what is known about the values of objects in a program. An actual computation state, which is a mapping from objects to values,[16] may satisfy the same set of assertions. In this case, we say that the symbolic state represents the actual state. If a symbolic state is consistent, there will generally be many computation states that satisfy its boolean assertions. Thus, a symbolic state is an abstraction representing a set of actual computation states.

Whenever a subprogram is called there is a change in the state of the package. The change in a symbolic state is represented by changing its assertions — some assertions change value from true to false, and some new assertions become true, and are added. The changes to a state resulting from a subprogram call are deduced from the subprogram annotations. For example, starting in a symbolic state

```
X = A, ...
```

execution of a procedure call, P (Y => X), where P has an **in out** formal parameter Y and an annotation

```
--|      out (Y = in Y+1);
```

changes the state to

```
X = A+1, X_in = A, ...
```

where X is the current symbolic value and X_*in* is the previous (input) value of X. Of course, other assertions of the symbolic state, hiding in our "...", may change value also, as a result of the specified change to X. These secondary changes must be inferred logically from the axioms for predefined data types such as INTEGER and the axioms of the package being analyzed.

Here is an example of symbolic execution of DIRECT_IO. We present it first, and explain it afterwards.

Example: *Symbolic execution of a call to the* CREATE *procedure in* DIRECT_IO.

Initial State S0:
    PROPER_NAME (N), **not** IS_OPEN (F), **not** IS_OPEN (G);

Procedure call:
    CREATE (FILE => F, NAME => N);

New assertions (*from* **out** *annotations of* CREATE):
    IS_OPEN (F), FILE_MAP (F) = NAME_MAP (N) = E,
    E /= NO_FILE, MODE (F) = INOUT_FILE,
    INDEX (F) = 1, S0 . INACCESSIBLE (E);

[16] See Section1.2 for computation states, etc.

Final State S1:

```
IS_OPEN (F), FILE_MAP (F) = NAME_MAP (N) = E,
E /= NO_FILE, MODE (F) = INOUT_FILE,
INDEX (F) = 1, S0 . INACCESSIBLE (E),
PROPER_NAME (N), not IS_OPEN (G),
not S0 . IS_OPEN (F_0);
```

In the new assertions, a fresh identifier E has been introduced for the value of the mapping functions — just to shorten the notation.

First, a word about computation states and notation. A symbolic execution results in successive symbolic computation states, which we denote by S0, S1, ..., assuming these names do not occur in the program. If X is a program variable in the symbolic execution, then X_0, X_1, ... denote its symbolic values in each of the previous states, and X is its value in the current state.

S0 and S1 each contain a package state of DIRECT_IO and a (virtual) package state of EXTERNAL_SYSTEM, which is nested inside DIRECT_IO. The package states can be referred to by their symbolic names, treating them as part of the computation states, just as any other program variable. For example, DIRECT_IO_0 and EXTERNAL_SYSTEM_0 are the states of the two packages in S0, and

```
not DIRECT_IO_0 . IS_OPEN (F_0),
EXTERNAL_SYSTEM_0 . INACCESSIBLE (E)
```

are assertions about them. To shorten our notation in the following examples, we write instead,

```
not S0 . IS_OPEN (F_0),
S0 . INACCESSIBLE (E)
```

to denote the value of the calls to IS_OPEN and INACCESSIBLE (E) in the state, S0.

If we omit the package name in a call to a package function, then the call takes place in the current symbolic state.

Next, some comments about the example.

In S0, the objects F and G are of type FILE and N is a string. These names perform double duty: they are the names of objects and they denote the values of those objects.

S0 has three facts asserted about it, namely, F and G are not open and N is a proper name. The assertions use concepts defined in the specification of DIRECT_IO. Here, conjunctions are written as lists for brevity. Only atomic assertions appear in this example, but in general any Anna assertion may be a conjunct in a symbolic state.

We may ask if a call to CREATE will be executed successfully in any state that satisfies the three assertions of S0. And if so, what can we assert about the resulting state?

The answers to our questions can be found by symbolic execution of a call to CREATE in state S0 carried out according the recipe below.

5.8.1 A RECIPE FOR SYMBOLIC EXECUTION *

Our recipe for symbolic execution of subprograms uses the example above as an illustration. It is really an outline allowing many different variations. We then give an example that applies the recipe to analyze a tricky question about DIRECT_IO. A general formal treatment of methods of symbolic execution is beyond the scope of our book.

Consider the procedure call

```
CREATE(FILE => F, NAME => N)
```

in symbolic state S0.

- **A recipe for symbolic execution of subprogram calls**

  1. Ensure the preconditions of the call are satisfied by **S0**.
     To determine this, the formal parameters in the specification of CREATE are replaced by the actual parameters of the call. This yields a specification for that particular call. Refer to this as the *instantiated specification.*

     All **in** conditions, as well as the negations of all strong propagation conditions, in the instantiated specification of CREATE must be logically implied by S0. If so, the call is assumed to terminate normally [17] when executed in S0. (By replacing FILE by F and NAME by N in the specification of CREATE, we see that the preconditions for the symbolic call are satisfied in S0; other parameters are given their default values.)

  2. Archive the old state **S0**.
     S0 denotes true statements about **in** values of program variables before the call. We want to keep these assertions as part of the new state, but they may no longer be true as a result of changes of values of **in out** parameters and global variables of the subprogram call. So we need two sets of symbolic names in the new state, one for the **in** values (values in the old state) and one for the new **out** values. (Note that in our example the package state DIRECT_IO is an **in out** parameter of the procedure CREATE, although it has been omitted from the **out** conditions as a notational shorthand.)

[17] We assume the strong exception propagation annotations are complete.

First we determine which variables of S0 might change value, and then which assertions of S0 might change value.

A program variable in S0 is *changeable* if it appears in an instantiated **out** condition without an **in** modifier and is not an **in** parameter of the call. For each changeable program variable, X, we introduce a fresh symbolic name, X_0 for its **in** value. (A fresh identifier is an identifier that has never occurred previously in the program nor in any symbolic state. If the input state is S*i* the fresh symbolic name is X_*i*.)

X is replaced everywhere it occurs in assertions of S0 by X_0. Call the resulting state, S0′. It is a temporary state used to construct the new state.

The *new assertions* are the instantiated **out** conditions in which those occurrences of X that are modified by **in** have been replaced by X_0.

At this point the fresh identifiers such as X_0 denote symbolically the **in** values of changeable variables in both S0′ and the new assertions. The program variables themselves, such as X, denote the new values of changeable variables and the values of unchangeable variables.

An assertion in S0 is *changeable* if it is contradicted by the new assertions together with the assertions of S0′ — i. e., if its negation can be proved using the new assertions, old assertions about old values, package axioms, subprogram specifications of concepts in the assertions, and lemmas about those concepts.

The *archived state*, S0′, is obtained by replacing changeable variables X by the names for their old values X_0 everywhere in the *changeable assertions* of the old state S0.

In our example, F and DIRECT_IO are changeable parameters of the call. F_0 is the fresh identifier for the symbolic **in** value of F. DIRECT_IO_0 is the fresh identifier for the **in** value of the package state; as a notational shorthand we replace it by S0 in our examples.

3. Compute the state **S1** when the call terminates.

   (a) The new assertions are added to S0′ to form S1.

   (b) Logical consequences of S1 and any set of lemmas (including the axioms of the package in question) are added to S1.

end recipe

In the CREATE example above, we have already seen that the call is executable at Step 1.

The new assertions are the **out** conditions of the instantiated specification of CREATE with S0 replacing **in** EXTERNAL_SYSTEM.

In constructing the archived state S0′, the file parameter F and the package state DIRECT_IO are both changeable variables, and are replaced by fresh identifiers in the assertion,

not S0 . IS_OPEN (F_0)

since **not** DIRECT_IO . IS_OPEN (F) is clearly changeable.

The other symbolic program variables in S0 are N and G. N is an **in** parameter of the call to CREATE, and G is not a parameter and does not appear in the new assertions. Their values are therefore assumed to be unchanged — i. e., they have the same values in S1 as in S0, so no new names are introduced for their **in** values in S0′.

The other assertions of S0, written in full:

DIRECT_IO . PROPER_NAME (N) ,
not DIRECT_IO . IS_OPEN (G) ,

are not changeable and therefore remain the same in S0′ as in S0.

The new assertions are added to S0′ to form S1. This forms the final output state since we can deduce nothing further about these symbolic values from the package axioms.

Here is another simple example of the recipe:

Example: *Symbolic execution of a call to the* ADD1.

Initial State S0: −1 ≤ X, X ≤ 1

Procedure call: ADD1 (X);

out *annotations of* **ADD1** : X = **in** X + 1;

State S0′: −1 ≤ X_0, X_0 ≤ 1

New assertion: X = X_0 + 1 ;

Changeable assertion: X ≤ 1 ;

Final State S1: X = X_0 + 1 , −1 ≤ X , X_0 ≤ 1 ;

Commentary

There are two critical assumptions about the semantics of subprogram annotations that are made in this recipe:

1. What assertions must be true in the new state.
2. *Frame Axiom:* How much of the old state remains true.

The general idea is that subprogram **out** annotations express what must be true, but generally do not express what does not change (the frame problem). However other information about invariance may be expressed in package axioms.

In this recipe a subprogram call is treated as if it may change the value of any variable in its **out** conditions that is not a mode **in** parameter or else modified by **in** in the new assertions. This includes **in out** parameters, **out** parameters, and global variables of the subprogram. But it is not expected to change the values of variables that are not mentioned in its **out** conditions.

The recipe also assumes a strong "frame" axiom: Assertions of the input state that are not contradicted by the new assertions, together with the input assertions about the input values of changeable variables, are assumed to remain true in the new state. Keeping as much as possible of the previous state (archiving) improves our chances of detecting inconsistent states and of finding inadequacies in the specification.

Note that the general recipe is not fully implementable. The final state resulting from a subprogram call is a set of assertions that is inferred by reasoning about the new assertions, the archived **in** state, package axioms, and any relevant lemmas.

Symbolic execution is a useful analysis technique provided the logical consequences of specifications are not too complex. It applies best to package specifications that depend mainly on subprogram annotations (*transformational* style sepecifications) and not so well to package specifications involving a lot of axioms (*algebraic* style specifications).

Many real–life systems packages have specifications that rely heavily on subprogram annotations, and it turns out that the logical reasoning needed to carry out our recipe is not lengthy. Experiments show that the reasoning needed to check if the **in** conditions for a symbolic procedure call are satisfied, or to determine if an assertion is changeable, or to answer a question about a particular state, can usually be decided (true or false) quickly.

A specification analysis tool based on symbolic execution methods similar to this recipe is described in Appendix B.

When an implementation of this recipe is used on a sequence of subprogram calls, a history of symbolic states results. In the course of constructing this history and querying it, there are three common results:

1. Inability to prove or disprove an assertion about a state — a "don't know" answer,
2. An inconsistent state,
3. A surprising assertion about a state.

All three results usually indicate a weakness in the package specification, or in the requirements that they formalize. For example, an inconsistent state often indicates that a property of a package specification is buried in the logical implications (or else has been forgotten) and should be stated explicitly as an annotation or axiom.

5.8.2 AN EXAMPLE OF SYMBOLIC EXECUTION *

We illustrate symbolic execution to determine the consequence of a sequence of operations using DIRECT_IO. To shorten the number of assertions in each state in this example, we omit archiving the input state at each subprogram call. Instead we delete old assertions about fresh identifiers like X_0. All that remains of an input state, therefore, are the unchangeable assertions. This is a notational short cut. In general, it is an unsafe thing to do and can lead to inconsistent states.

Example: Symbolic execution of DIRECT_IO.

```
State S0:
    PROPER_NAME(N), not IS_OPEN(F), not IS_OPEN(G);

Operation sequence:
    CREATE(FILE => F, NAME => N);
    CREATE(FILE => G, NAME => N);
    CLOSE(F);
    OPEN(FILE => F, NAME => N, MODE => INOUT_FILE);
    DELETE(G);
    READ(F);

-- State S0 is assumed as the initial state.

Procedure call:
    CREATE(FILE => F, NAME => N);

New assertions:
    IS_OPEN(F), FILE_MAP(F) = NAME_MAP(N) = E,
    E /= NO_FILE, MODE(F) = INOUT_FILE,
    INDEX(F) = 1, S0.INACCESSIBLE(E);

State S1:
    PROPER_NAME(N), not IS_OPEN(G), IS_OPEN(F),
    FILE_MAP(F) = NAME_MAP(N) = E, E /= NO_FILE,
    MODE(F) = INOUT_FILE, INDEX(F) = 1,
    S0.INACCESSIBLE(E);

Procedure call:
    CREATE(FILE => G, NAME => N);

New assertions:
    IS_OPEN(G), FILE_MAP(G) = NAME_MAP(N) = E1,
    E1 /= NO_FILE, MODE(G) = INOUT_FILE, INDEX(G) = 1,
    S1.INACCESSIBLE(E1);
Consequences of S1.INACCESSIBLE(E1) : E1 /= E;
```

State S2:
```
PROPER_NAME (N) , IS_OPEN (F) , IS_OPEN (G) ,
FILE_MAP (F) = E, E /= NO_FILE,
FILE_MAP (G) = NAME_MAP (N) = E1, E1 /= NO_FILE,
MODE (F) = INOUT_FILE, INDEX (F) = 1,
S0 . INACCESSIBLE (E) ,
MODE (G) = INOUT_FILE, INDEX (G) = 1,
S1 . INACCESSIBLE (E1) , E1 /= E;
```

Procedure call:
```
CLOSE (F) ;
```

New assertions:
```
not IS_OPEN (F) , FILE_MAP (F) = NO_FILE;
```

State S3:
```
PROPER_NAME (N) , not IS_OPEN (F) , IS_OPEN (G) ,
FILE_MAP (F) = NO_FILE, E /= NO_FILE,
FILE_MAP (G) = NAME_MAP (N) = E1, E1 /= NO_FILE,
MODE (G) = INOUT_FILE, INDEX (G) = 1,
E1 /= E, S0 . INACCESSIBLE (E) , S1 . INACCESSIBLE (E1) ;
```
Consequence: S3 . INACCESSIBLE (E) .

Procedure call:
```
OPEN (FILE => F, NAME => N, MODE => INOUT_FILE) ;
```

New assertions:
```
IS_OPEN (F) , FILE_MAP (F) = NAME_MAP (N) = E1,
MODE (F) = INOUT_FILE, INDEX (F) = 1;
```

State S4:
```
PROPER_NAME (N) , IS_OPEN (F) , IS_OPEN (G) ,
FILE_MAP (F) = FILE_MAP (G) = NAME_MAP (N) = E1,
MODE (F) = INOUT_FILE, INDEX (F) = 1,
MODE (G) = INOUT_FILE, INDEX (G) = 1,
E1 /= NO_FILE, E /= NO_FILE, E1 /= E,
S0 . INACCESSIBLE (E) , S3 . INACCESSIBLE (E) ,
S1 . INACCESSIBLE (E1) ;
```

Commentary

In this example initial state S0 implies that the first call to CREATE will not raise an exception. The new assertions are instantiations of the **out** annotations of CREATE obtained by replacing the formal parameters by the actuals. Fresh identifier E denotes the new external file that is created.

State S1 is the input state for the second call to CREATE. In computing S2 an important consequence of the new assertions is added: E1 /= E. This inequality follows because E1 must be inaccessible in S1 at the second call to CREATE, whereas E is accessible in S1, since it is associated with F by FILE_MAP in

S1.

Similarly, S2 is the input state to operation CLOSE. The resulting state, S3, is the input state for the OPEN operation.

The states contain important consequences of the DIRECT_IO specification. First, S2 shows that an external file can be left without a name as a result of a CREATE. Second, S3 shows that an external file can become inaccessible as a result of a CLOSE operation. Finally, S4 shows that it is possible to have two visible file objects associated with one external file and name. When this happens, the specification does not imply that the two visible files must have the same value. This is why we use concept DISTINCT in specifying when READ and WRITE are independent.

Symbolic evaluation can be continued from state S4 as the input state. Since S4 represents a somewhat anomalous situation, it may be interesting to continue the search for consequences.

Let us assume that deletion is supported for external files so that the **in** conditions for DELETE are satisfied in S4.

Example: More symbolic execution of DIRECT_IO.

Initial state : S4

Procedure call: DELETE (G) ;

New assertions:
  not IS_OPEN (G) , FILE_MAP (G) = NO_FILE,
  S5 . INACCESSIBLE (E1) ;
Consequences of S5 . INACCESSIBLE (E1) :
  NAME_MAP (N) = NO_FILE, FILE_MAP (F) = NO_FILE,
  not IS_OPEN (F) .

State S5: New assertions **and** archived **S4**

Procedure call:
  READ (F) ;
-- *This should propagate* STATUS_ERROR, *since* F *is no longer open.*

Commentary

The consequences of calling DELETE (G) in state S4 results from our strong formalization of the English "the external file *ceases to exist*," which is used in Ada83 (14.2.1) to describe DELETE. Here, "ceases to exist" has been formalized as INACCESSIBLE. So, when E1 becomes inaccessible in S5, the values of FILE_MAP (F) and NAME_MAP (N) must change from E1 to something else. If we choose NO_FILE as the default value when none is specified, then **not** IS_OPEN (F) is also true.

Our interpretation of "ceases to exist" is open to discussion. Some Ada implementations do not close F and permit READ (F) in state S5; in such cases we would argue that E1 does not cease to exist.
Note also that the only **out** parameters of DELETE (G) are G and the state of DIRECT_IO. Changes in assertions about F, such as

FILE_MAP (F) = E1,

which is a shortened notation form of the assertion,

DIRECT_IO . FILE_MAP (F) = E1,

happen as a result of the change to the package state, DIRECT_IO.

The results of this symbolic execution provide logical consequences that cannot be ignored. We will be forced to revise our specification of DIRECT_IO in Section 5.7. There are several options. One is to change the formalization of the English description of DELETE in Ada83, perhaps weakening our formalization of "ceases to exist." Another is to constrain CREATE and OPEN so that state S4 cannot happen. This will disallow some current implementations of Ada.

To maintain our formalization of "ceases to exist," one may express the effects of DELETE explicitly in its subprogram annotations. It must change the current state of the DIRECT_IO package so that no file is mapped to the same external file as the one being deleted. We might add an **out** annotation to DELETE (written with the state explicitly mentioned), such as:

```
out (for all X : FILE =>
in DIRECT_IO . FILE_MAP (X) = in DIRECT_IO . FILE_MAP (G)
                         →    not DIRECT_IO . IS_OPEN (X) );
```

which is a constraint on the **out** state of DIRECT_IO resulting from performing a DELETE operation.

An effect of studying the consequences of a formal specification of DIRECT_IO may be to tighten the informal English requirements, making them more precise, and eventually to replace them by a formal specification.

5.9 Iterators and Generators

Some of the functions that we meet in everyday programming are really small packages in disguise. A Random Number Generator is an example. The generator remembers the history of previous values it has generated, or part of the history, starting with an initial seed value. Its next value depends on its seed or previous values. It behaves like a small package that contains one function, which uses the package state to maintain its previous history.

Another example is an iterator function, or group of functions, in an abstract type package. Suppose a package P exports a private type T with functions that relate values of T with values of some component type. Essentially, T is an abstract type that has components — like type SET. An application using P may rely on the ability to enumerate the components of objects of type T, e. g., in order to perform an operation on each component. To support such appications, a package P provides enumeration functions for objects of type T. Each time the enumeration function is called, it returns "the next" component. Obviously such functions, called *iterators*, must remember which components they have already returned. They use the state of P to do this.

There are several different versions of iterators in the literature on reusable software — Booch describes both "active" and "passive" iterators in his book. [18] All these forms are easily specifiable abstractly in Anna as subprograms that depend on the package state.

Consider adding an iterator to package SETS in Section 5.4.

Example: An Ada sets package with iteration.

```
     generic
         type ELEM is private;
     package SETS is
         type SET is limited private;

-- Basic concepts.
         function IS_MEMBER(E : ELEM; S : SET)
         return BOOLEAN;
         function IS_FULL(S : SET) return BOOLEAN;
         function CARDINALITY(S : SET) return NATURAL;
-- End basic concepts .

-- Exceptions and constants.
         SET_FULL : exception;
         NULL_SET : constant SET;
```

[18] See the reading list at end of this Chapter.

```
-- Relations on sets.
      function "=" (S, T : SET) return BOOLEAN;
      function IS_EMPTY(X : SET) return BOOLEAN;

-- Subprograms for constructing SETs.
      function "+" (X, Y : SET) return SET;
      function "-" (X, Y : SET) return SET;
      procedure ADD(E : in ELEM; S : in out SET);
      procedure REMOVE(E : in ELEM; S : in out SET);
      procedure COPY(S : in SET; S1 : out SET);

-- Iterators.
      NOT_INITIALIZED, NO_MORE : exception;
      procedure INITIALIZE(S : in SET);
      procedure ITERATE(ITEM ; out ELEM);
      function FINISHED return BOOLEAN;

   end SETS;
```

Iteration works as follows. Suppose we want to enumerate the elements of some set S. First we initialize the iteration to S. Then we call ITERATE repeatedly, getting a new member at each call, until FINISHED is true. Exception NO_MORE is propagated by ITERATE if all the elements of S have been listed. Here is a typical loop over a set.

```
-- Suppose MY_SETS is an instantiation of SETS and V is a variable of type
-- ELEM.
      MY_SETS.INITIALIZE(S);
      loop
      -- Get the next element of S.
         MY_SETS.ITERATE(V);
--|      MY_SETS.IS_MEMBER(V, S);
         ...                                     -- Compute on V.
         exit when MY_SETS.FINISHED;
      end loop;
```

This iterator facility may be specified within the sets package as follows.

Example: An Anna sets package that specifies iteration.

```
   generic
      type ELEM is private;
   package SETS is
      type SET is limited private;

--    Basic concepts.
      function IS_MEMBER(E : ELEM; S : SET)
      return BOOLEAN;
```

```
        function IS_FULL (S : SET) return BOOLEAN;
--:     function GENERATED (ITEM : ELEM)
--:     return BOOLEAN;
--:     function IS_INITIALIZED (S : SET ) return BOOLEAN;
        function CARDINALITY (S : SET) return NATURAL;
--      End basic concepts .

--      Exceptions and constants.
        SET_FULL : exception;
        NOT_INITIALIZED, NO_MORE : exception;
        NULL_SET : constant SET;

--      Relations on sets.
        function "=" (S, T : SET) return BOOLEAN;
        function IS_EMPTY (X : SET) return BOOLEAN;

--      Subprograms for constructing SETs.
        function "+" (X, Y : SET) return SET;
        function "-" (X, Y : SET) return SET;
        procedure ADD (E : in ELEM; S : in out SET);
        procedure REMOVE (E : in ELEM; S : in out SET);
        procedure COPY (S : in SET; S1 : out SET);

--      Iterators.
        procedure INITIALIZE (S : in SET);
        procedure ITERATE (ITEM : out ELEM);
--|       where out (not in SETS . GENERATED (ITEM));
        function FINISHED return BOOLEAN;

--|       axiom
--|           for all ST : SETS'TYPE;
--|                   S : SET;
--|                   X : ELEM =>
--|           not ST [INITIALIZE (S) ] . GENERATED (X) ,
--|           ST [INITIALIZE (S) ] . IS_INITIALIZED (S) ,
--          Invariance of IS_INITIALIZED under all other set operations.
--|           ST . IS_INITIALIZED (S) →
--|                                 ST [ADD (X, S) ] . IS_INITIALIZED (S) ,
                   . . .

--|           ST . IS_INITIALIZED (S) →
--|                         IS_MEMBER (ST . ITERATE'OUT.ITEM, S) ,
--|               ST [ITERATE (ITEM) ] . GENERATED (X) =
--|                     if ST . ITERATE'OUT.ITEM = X then
--|                         TRUE
--|                     else
--|                         ST . GENERATED (X)
--|                     end if,
--|               IS_MEMBER (X, S) →
--|                   exist ST : SETS'TYPE =>
--|                                                ST . GENERATED (X) ,
```

```
--|                  ST.FINISHED = ST.IS_INITIALIZED(S) and
--|                         IS_MEMBER(X, S) → ST.GENERATED(X);

        ...                                  -- Rest of sets specification.

    end SETS;
```

Commentary

Two new basic functions, GENERATED and IS_INITIALIZED, have been introduced to specify the iteration operations. The main iteration operations INITIALIZE and ITERATE are procedures since they change the state of package SETS — the state is an implicit **in out** parameter.

The axioms fall into two groups, initialization and enumeration. When a state is initialized to a set, calls to ITERATE will return elements of that set. The basic function IS_INITIALIZED (S) formalizes the intuitive idea of a state being set up for iteration over S. The axioms involving IS_INITIALIZED express that whenever a call ST.INITIALIZE (S) is made, all subsequent successor states are initialized to the same set S, no matter what other set operations may be performed, until the next initialization. Also, iteration operations output only members of a set to which a state has been initialized.

The basic function GENERATED formalizes the concept of a membership test for the set of items that have been output by calls to ITERATE. It maps states of package SETS into subsets of sets to which states are initialized.

The enumeration axioms involve GENERATED. They express that calls to ITERATE generate members of set S to which the package state is initialized. An existential axiom implies that each member will be generated eventually by performing sufficiently many calls to ITERATE, and a subprogram annotation implies that each member will be generated only once.

Note that this sets package specification with the iterator subprograms is not an extension of the original sets package in the sense of Section 5.6.1. The iterators are not defined by subprogram annotations using only the previous set operations.

A theory of iterators can be specified as a generic virtual theory package (Section 5.2). Iterator theory can then be used to specify actual iterators.

Further Reading

The English requirements and Ada declaration of DIRECT_IO are in [Ada83] Chapter 14. Grady Booch's book on reusable software components in Ada contains dozens of commonly occurring Ada package declarations, which provide excellent targets for formal specification in Anna. The paper on Larch introduces a two-tiered methodology of specification whereby basic concepts are always specified separately from actual program units. This methodology was illustrated in Section 5.2 using virtual theory packages.

The collection of papers, edited by Gehani and McGettrick contains a wide selection of approaches to formally specifying systems and also introductions to some specification languages.

The SmallTalk language and system, described in the book by Goldberg and Robson, provides an environment for building new modules (called classes) from previous ones; it uses the inheritance tree (e.g., see Figure 5.2) to share code between classes and to keep track of changes in classes resulting from a change to an ancestor. Such techniques are often called "object–oriented." Section 5.6 introduced the idea that Anna package specifications can be manipulated and combined using SmallTalk–like operations (such as extension) as well as more powerful ones — a subject for further study. We will need environments that use the inheritance tree, analogous to the SmallTalk environment, to help us compose specifications from libraries of theories and implement them.

1. J.D. Ichbiah, et al. *The Programming Language Ada Reference Manual*. Springer-Verlag Lecture Notes in Computer Science, No. 155, 1983.
2. G. Booch. *Software Components with Ada*. Benjamin Cummings, Inc., 1987.
3. J.V. Guttag, J.J. Horning, and J.M. Wing. The Larch Family of Specification Languages. *IEEE Software*, September 1985.
4. N. Gehani and A.D. McGettrick. *Software Specification Techniques*, Addison-Wesley, 1986.
5. A.J. Goldberg and D. Robson. *SmallTalk-80: The Language and Its Implementation*. Addison-Wesley, 1983.

6

Annotation of Generic Units

Topics:

- *generic annotations and their meaning;*
- *generic formal parameter constraints;*
- *annotated generic units as reusable software components.*

A generic Ada unit is either a generic subprogram or a generic package. There are two kinds of annotations of a generic unit.

1. **Generic annotations.**
   These annotations are parameterized by the formal generic parameters of the unit. They can be placed in the specification or the body of a generic unit and are templates for annotations of instances of the unit.

2. **Generic parameter constraints.**
   These annotations are placed in the generic formal part of a generic unit. They constrain the actual parameters that may be substituted for the formal generic parameters in an instantiation. Only object annotations may be used to constrain generic instances, even though the generic parameters can be types and subprograms. As we shall see, this is not such a serious restriction as it may first seem.

6.1 Generic Annotations

An annotation of an Ada generic unit can be parameterized in exactly the same way as Ada permits the unit to be parameterized by formal generic parameters. An annotation containing formal generic parameters is called a *generic annotation*. Any annotation of an object, type, subprogram, or package can be a generic annotation. It must be placed either in the specification or in the body of an Ada generic unit. The formal generic parameters in a generic annotation are replaced by actual parameters when the unit is instantiated. A generic annotation is thereby converted to an annotation of the (nongeneric) instance.

Example: *A generic annotation of a generic subprogram declaration.*

```
    generic
       type ITEM is private;
       with function "*" (U, V : ITEM) return ITEM is <>;
    function SQUARING (X : ITEM) return ITEM;
--|    where return X*X;
```

Commentary

SQUARING is a template for each instance that can be constructed by the Ada operation of generic instantiation. This involves substituting an actual type for ITEM and an actual binary function (on the actual type) for "*".

When the Ada instantiation of SQUARING is done, it is applied also to the annotation. So the actual binary function will replace "*" in the annotation, yielding an instance of the annotation. For example,

```
function DOUBLE is new
      SQUARING (ITEM => INTEGER, "*" => "+");
```

will have the annotation

```
--| where return X+X;
```

where X must be an integer. From this, and the usual integer arithmetic, we can prove that DOUBLE computes 2*X where "*" is integer multiplication.

The Anna attributes of a generic package, such as the state type and the current state, are treated as being parameterized by the generic parameters. They denote the state type and current state of any instance of the package. Consequently, an annotation of a generic package is generic if it contains generic parameters or Anna package attributes of the generic package.

Example: *A generic stack specification.*

```
    generic
       type ITEM is private;
       MAXSTACK : POSITIVE;
    package STACK is

--:    function LENGTH return NATURAL;
--:    function "=" (S, T : STACK'TYPE) return BOOLEAN;

       procedure PUSH (X : in ITEM);
--|       where in STACK.LENGTH < MAXSTACK;
```

```
      procedure POP(E : out ITEM);
--|      where in STACK.LENGTH > 0;

--|   axiom
--|      for all ST : STACK'TYPE; X, Y : ITEM =>
--|         ST[PUSH(X); POP(Y)] = ST,
--|         ST[PUSH(X)].POP'OUT(E => Y).E = X,
--|         STACK'INITIAL.LENGTH = 0,
--|         ST.LENGTH ≤ MAXSTACK,
--|         ...;
   end STACK;
```

Commentary

The Ada generic stack package is a template — i. e. a parameterized unit. It cannot be called; it can only be instantiated. It denotes all instances that can be constructed by substituting actual parameters for the generic formal parameters ITEM and MAXSTACK.

The package attributes are treated as being parameterized by ITEM and MAXSTACK. For example, STACK'TYPE denotes the state type of any instance STACK. The instance

```
package SHORT_STACK   is new STACK(INTEGER, 10);
```

has a state type SHORT_STACK'TYPE, which is an instance of STACK'TYPE that denotes states of stacks of integers with maximum length 10. The corresponding instance of the generic current state STACK is SHORT_STACK.

If an annotation contains STACK'TYPE, it is a generic annotation that denotes all annotations that arise when the state type of the generic package is replaced by the state type of an instance.

The annotations of PUSH, POP, and the axioms are generic. They are templates for annotations of instances of STACK. For example, the annotation of PUSH is parameterized by MAXSTACK and by STACK'STATE.

Thus, SHORT_STACK.PUSH has the annotation

```
in SHORT_STACK.LENGTH < 10;
```

Similarly, the annotation of POP has STACK'STATE as a parameter. SHORT_STACK.POP therefore has the annotation

```
in SHORT_STACK .LENGTH > 0;
```

The axioms are also parameterized by ITEM and

MAXSTACK. The axioms for SHORT_STACK are instances of the generic axioms

```
--| axiom
--|     for all ST : SHORT_STACK'TYPE;
--|         X, Y : INTEGER =>
--|             ST[PUSH(X); POP(Y)] = ST,
--|             ST[PUSH(X)].POP'OUT(E=>Y).E=X,
--|             SHORT_STACK'INITIAL.LENGTH = 0,
--|             ST.LENGTH ≤ 10,
--|             ...;
```

Now, the question is how to interpret generic annotations. The underlying Ada generic unit is simply a *template* that may be instantiated but cannot be invoked — i. e., used in a computation. So, strictly speaking, a generic annotation does not constrain anything; it is also a template annotating an Ada template.

Indeed, one could claim not to understand generic annotations at all — nor Ada generic units — on the grounds that they do not have any meaning until instantiated. However, this view of generic annotations would not allow us to do any analysis of a generic specification prior to instantiation. A more practical interpretation is needed.

When constructing or analyzing a generic unit, we can think of it as if it is a nongeneric unit — and therefore executable. We can imagine, for example, that the generic parameters are actual entities declared outside the unit and visible to it. Ada83 hints at this interpretation in specifying the meaning of the name of a generic unit within the unit itself:

> ...Within the declarative region associated with a generic subprogram, the name of this program unit denotes the subprogram obtained by the *current instantiation* of the generic unit...

The italics are ours. Inside the Ada generic unit its name must be thought of as the name of an instance in order to allow recursive calls, etc. The idea is to interpret the context inside the boundary of a generic unit as an instance so that the normal language rules can be applied. Indeed, we may often construct a generic unit by first constructing an actual unit and then convert some of the (global or local) declarations to generic parameters.

We use a hypothetical nongeneric unit that "looks like" the generic one to define the meaning of generic annotations. The hypothetical unit can be viewed as a "most general" Ada instance of the generic unit. Here, "most general" means that the actual parameters used in the instantiation must not provide structure and operations that are not available in the generic formal parameter declarations.

To construct a hypothetical look-alike unit, the generic formal part of the Ada unit is replaced by new declarations of objects, types, and subprograms that match the generic formal parameters and have the same names.

The new declarations must not contain new constraints. The generic Ada unit and annotations are thus converted to a nongeneric unit and annotations, but look exactly as before. A generic annotation of an Ada generic unit is interpreted as having the same meaning as an identical nongeneric annotation of a hypothetical look-alike nongeneric Ada unit.

Example: *Interpretation of a generic annotation of a generic procedure body.*

1. *Generic unit.*

```
     generic
        type ITEM is private;
        with function "<=" (X, Y : ITEM)
               return BOOLEAN is <>;
        type INDEX is (<>);
        type ROW is array (INDEX range <>) of ITEM;

     procedure ORDER(A : in out ROW)
--|     where
--         Generic annotation containing formal generic parameters.
--         INDEX and <=.
--|          out (for all I, J : INDEX range A'RANGE =>
--|                                        I < J → A(I) <= A(J));
     is
           ...
--     The body is treated as if it were executable, and the annotation
--       places an out constraint on the body.

     end ORDER;
```

2. *Nongeneric version.*

```
--     New declarations using the same names and matching the generic
--     formal parameters.
     type ITEM is new T;                    --  T is any private type.
     function "<=" (X, Y : ITEM) return BOOLEAN;
     type INDEX is new INTEGER;
     type ROW is array (INDEX range <>) of ITEM;

     procedure ORDER(A : in out ROW)
--|     where
--         A nongeneric annotation that is syntactically identical to
--         the generic one above.
--|          out (for all I, J : INDEX range A'RANGE =>
--|                                        I < J → A(I) <= A(J));
     is
           ...
--           The annotation places an out constraint on the body.
     end ORDER;
```

Commentary

The generic formal parameters in (1) are converted to new declarations in (2), which are as general as possible. For example, T is any private type in the visible environment, and ITEM is a new private type derived from T. The generic function parameter is replaced by a similar function declaration with the same name — assuming we can avoid name clashes.

The generic formal parameter INDEX matches any enumeration or integer type. Inside the generic body of ORDER, operations common to integer and enumeration types may be assumed to apply to any match for INDEX. Here, for brevity, we have replaced parameter INDEX by a new type derived from INTEGER. The new type INDEX is a model for any integer type and does not satisfy any special properties such as having a finite number of elements. But it does make available special INTEGER operations. Strictly speaking, instead of INTEGER we should use an abstract type defined in a package that declares just those operations that are common to all enumeration and integer types.

Now we can use (2) to determine the meaning of annotations in (1). The generic body in (1) is interpreted as executable exactly as the nongeneric body in (2). The generic annotation in (1) is interpreted as placing the same constraint on (1) that the annotation in (2) places on the body in (2).

Under this view, we can analyze generic annotations in exactly the same way as nongeneric ones.

6.2 Generic Parameter Constraints

Object constraints may be placed in a generic formal part. These constraints must be satisfied by actual parameters that are matched to the formals when a generic unit is instantiated. Essentially, the instantiations are constrained. The constraints apply once — at instantiation.

There are three main points to explain about generic parameter constraints.

1. This feature of Anna is a simple generalization of Ada generic parameter declarations and has the same kinds of roles.

2. This kind of constraint is needed — it might be thought that it would not be useful since it restricts the applicability of a generic unit, but there are situations where such constraints are necessary.

3. Object constraints provide sufficient power of expression to make this feature useful.

Regarding the first point, let us begin by recalling a few details about the forms of Ada formal generic parameters. These parameters may be types, objects, or subprograms. Most of the forms of parameter declaration contain information about the formal object, type, or subprogram. For example, there are seven forms of type parameters for specifying a private type, array type, discrete type, and so on (Ada83, 12.1.2).

This information in generic parameter declarations plays two roles.

1. It imposes constraints that must be satisfied by the actual parameters at instantiation. An actual parameter that matches a formal private type must be a type for which assignment and equality are available, an actual parameter matching a formal array type must be an array type, etc.

2. The information may be assumed within the declaration and body of the generic unit. Inside the unit, assignment operations and equality tests may be applied to generic object parameters of a formal private type, and the attributes of array types may be assumed for generic object parameters of a formal array type.

Anna generic parameter constraints provide more general kinds of information and they play the same two roles.

Example: *An Ada package for small sets.*

```
    generic
       type BASE is (<>);
--           BASE is constrained to match a discrete type.

    package SMALL_SETS is

--     Declarations of SET, FULL, and EMPTY assume BASE
--     is discrete.
       type SET is array (BASE) of BOOLEAN;
       EMPTY : constant SET := (BASE => FALSE);
       FULL  : constant SET := (BASE => TRUE);

--     Set union.
       function "+" (LEFT : SET; RIGHT : SET)  return SET;

--     Element insertion.
       function "+" (LEFT : SET; RIGHT : BASE) return SET;

          ...   -- Other set operations.

    end SMALL_SETS;
```

Commentary

The Ada declaration of BASE constrains any actual parameter that matches it to be a discrete type. Conversely, this fact is assumed in the generic unit when using BASE as an index type for SET and as a choice in the aggregates for FULL and EMPTY. This representation of SETS will be inefficient if BASE has a large number of values, since the maximum number of elements that a given set can contain is fixed by its index constraint when it is declared. SMALL_SETS should be specified for use with small domains of values. An Anna generic parameter constraint can be used to restrict the instantiations to small discrete types.

Example: *Anna constraint on a generic formal type parameter.*

```
      generic
         MAX : POSITIVE := 100;
         type BASE is (<>);
--|      BASE'POS (BASE'LAST) – BASE'POS (BASE'FIRST) < MAX;
      package SMALL_SETS is

         type SET is array (BASE) of BOOLEAN;
--|         where A : SET => A'LENGTH < MAX;
         EMPTY : constant SET := (BASE => FALSE);
         FULL : constant SET := (BASE => TRUE);
--       Set union.
         function "+" (LEFT : SET; RIGHT : SET) return SET;
--       Element insertion.
         function "+" (LEFT : SET; RIGHT : BASE) return SET;
            ...  --  Other set operations.

      end SMALL_SETS;
```

Commentary

The constraint on BASE limits the number of elements in any actual type matched to it in an instantiation (role 1). There must be fewer than MAX elements. Note that this constraint on BASE is expressed by an Anna object constraint that relates the attributes to MAX, and not by a type annotation.

The constraint on BASE can be assumed in annotations of the specification and body of SMALL_SETS (role 2). Now, the type annotation on SET is a logical consequence of the constraint. Consequently, in analyzing this generic specification, we could choose to delete the type annotation. It will always be satisfied if the Ada instantiation of SMALL_SETS satisfies the Anna constraint on BASE.

What happens if an Ada instantiation does not satisfy an Anna constraint on a generic formal parameter? If the actual parameter does not satisfy the constraint, an Anna error exception is propagated during the instantiation. This has exactly the same effect as if the Ada package body tested the size of BASE in its sequence of statements and propagated an exception if it was too big.

The SMALL_SETS example illustrates the simple way that Anna generic parameter constraints extend the Ada idea of including constraining information in generic parameter declarations. This was the first point mentioned above. The example also shows the need for additional constraints in specifying generics. SMALL_SETS is intended for use only if its instances are restricted in ways that cannot be expressed in Ada. This was the second point.

And now the third point, the use of object constraints on generic formal parameters. First we give an example showing how this kind of a constraint can be used to require algebraic relationships between the generic parameters. This will illustrate the power of such annotations of generic units. Then we discuss the rationale for limiting constraints on generic formal parameters to object constraints only.

Example: *An object constraint expressing algebraic properties of formal generic subprogram parameters.*

```
    generic
        type ITEM is private;
        ZERO : in ITEM;
        with function "+" (X, Y : ITEM) return ITEM is <> ;
--|         for all U, V, W : ITEM =>
--|             ZERO+V = V,
--|             U+ZERO = U,
--|             (U+V)+W = U+(V+W);
--        Domain ITEM of values and the operation "+" are
--        constrained to be a semigroup with an identity (ZERO).
        type VECTOR is array (POSITIVE range <> ) of ITEM;

    package VECTOR_OPERATIONS is

        LENGTH_ERROR : exception;
--      Semigroup properties may be assumed in specifying and
--      implementing the operations.

        function SUM (A, B : VECTOR) return VECTOR;
--|         where
--|             return C : VECTOR =>
--|                 for all I : INTEGER range A'RANGE =>
--|                                                   C (I) = A (I)+B (I),
--|             A'LENGTH =
--|                 0 or A'LENGTH ≠ B'LENGTH =>
--|                                          raise LENGTH_ERROR;
```

```
      function SIGMA (A : VECTOR) return ITEM;
--|      where
--|         return if A'LENGTH = 0
--|                     then ZERO
--|                  else A (A'FIRST)+
--|                           SIGMA (A (A'FIRST+1 .. A'LAST))
--|                  end if;
                  ...

   end VECTOR_OPERATIONS;
```

Commentary

Instantiations of generic parameters ITEM, "+", and ZERO are constrained by the Anna object constraint in the generic formal part of the package. Suppose that when the package is instantiated, actual type T is substituted for ITEM, value FOO replaces ZERO, and operation "**" is substituted for "+". Then T, FOO and "**" must satisfy the constraint. Algebraically, "**" must be a semigroup over T with FOO as the identity.

In the specification of VECTOR_OPERATIONS it can be assumed that the vectors are over domains of items forming a semi-group. Such assumptions are routinely made (without specification) in Ada generics. Associativity, for example, would be a crucial assumption in any implementation of SIGMA — so an instantiation to a domain where "+" was not associative just would not work.

6.2.1 Rationale for restricting generic parameter annotations *

Why does Anna allow only object constraints on generic formal parameters? Why not permit type annotations and subprogram annotations? The main argument is that there is little loss of expressive power, while the annotation language is thereby simplified.

Remember one thing first : generic parameter constraints are checked at *instantiation.*

Let us go over the possibilities one by one. Obviously in the case of formal generic object parameters we have no more powerful alternative.

For formal types, type annotations are disallowed. This decision is based on the fact that there is actually no loss of generality, nor any increase in difficulty of checking consistency. For a generic formal type parameter the type constraint

```
      type T is ... ;
--|       where X : T => C(X);
```

is equivalent to the fully quantified object constraint (i. e., assertion)

```
--|     for all X : T => C(X);
```

Let us see why.

In the case of an ordinary[1] type declaration, weaker runtime checking methods can be applied for the type constraint. That is, the type constraint can be checked at runtime each time the value of an object is changed, and it is checked just for that value. But the fully quantified object constraint (assertion) must be checked or proved immediately when it is encountered. In the case of a generic formal type parameter, however, there is no difference. Both the type constraint on a generic formal type parameter and the fully quantified assertion must be checked at instantiation for all values of the actual type parameter. This will usually require mathematical proof that annotations of the actual type parameter imply the instance of the formal type constraint or the object constraint.

In addition to noticing the equivalence between type constraints and assertions in constraining instantiations, we can ask what kinds of constraints will be commonly used on generic formal type parameters. The seven allowed forms of Ada generic type definitions are such that the visible properties of the formal type most likely to be constrained are the attributes. If the constraint expressed by a type annotation depends only on the attributes, it is natural to choose an object constraint on those attributes — as in the SMALL_SETS example. It can be argued, therefore, that in practice object constraints would be used often even if type constraints were available.

Similar considerations apply to generic formal subprogram parameters. The argument here is that disallowing subprogram annotations is not as much of a restriction in practice as it may seem, while checking during instantiation that an actual subprogram satisfies a subprogram annotation for all inputs would generally require mathematical proof. In most cases, the kinds of properties of the formal subprograms that are assumed when a generic unit is constructed are algebraic properties, and subprogram annotations are usually inappropriate for expressing them. Algebraic properties can be expressed as object constraints.

So, for most practical purposes, object constraints are sufficient. Note, however, that checking whether an Anna instantiation is consistent with algebraic properties will be difficult unless the actuals are already specified to satisfy similar algebraic properties.

---

[1]That is, a type declaration as distinct from a generic type parameter.

The analogy between object constraints on generic formal subprogram parameters and package axioms should be noticed. They express the same kinds of relationships as axioms express for package subprograms. Package axioms express two meanings: They constrain the package body and promise properties to users of the package. Normally, an object constraint expresses only one meaning, a constraint. But an object constraint on generic formals constrains the actual parameters of any instantiation. As a logical consequence, the object constraint may be assumed within the generic unit.

Thus, for example, if generic formal subprogram parameters are constrained to satisfy algebraic properties, those properties can be assumed within the generic unit.

6.3 Annotated Generic Units as Reusable Software

Software is said to be "reusable" if it can be applied in different contexts. Ada generics provide a limited form of parameterization of program units, permitting them to be instantiated for use in different contexts. It is therefore natural to explore the role of Ada generics in constructing reusable software. As we have already seen, Ada generic parameters by themselves are inadequate because they do not express sufficiently powerful constraints on the contexts in which a generic unit is intended to be used. In this section, we illustrate the roles played by annotations of generic parameters in building reusable program units.

6.3.1 Generalization

To build a useful generic subprogram or package, we start with a nongeneric one having some proven application. We generalize it by replacing the types and operations it depends on by generic formal parameters.

Example: Generalizing a sorting procedure.

```
-- (1) Procedure to sort a vector of integers.
   type VECTOR is array (INTEGER range <>) of INTEGER;
   procedure SORT (A : in out VECTOR);

-- (2) Generic procedure to sort a vector of almost anything.
   generic
      type COMPONENT_TYPE is private;
      type INDEX_TYPE is (<>);
      type VECTOR_TYPE is array (INDEX_TYPE range <>)
                                          of COMPONENT_TYPE;
   procedure SORT (A : in out VECTOR_TYPE);
```

Commentary

The integer vector type in (1) has been generalized in (2) by three separate generic type parameters. Thus, (2) shows the first step in generalizing an Ada subprogram.

Having made this step, it will be found that the implementation of the body of SORT — and also an Anna specification of SORT — will require another generic parameter that generalizes the standard operation "<" on the integers. The generic "<" parameter must be a linear order over the component type if the generalized body is to work correctly. We will discuss this new generic parameter later.

6.3.2 Specifying generic contexts

During the process of converting a program to a generic unit, the underlying assumptions about the generic parameters can become quite complex. Whenever a type or operation is replaced by a generic parameter, the properties of it that are needed to ensure that the implementation of the unit behaves correctly must be expressed as constraints on that generic parameter. It is impossible to evolve very general generic versions of packages without incurring assumptions about properties of the generic parameters.

Expressing these assumptions as constraints on the generic formal parameters plays three crucial roles:

1. *The constraints specify the contexts in which the generic unit can be used.* If the unit is instantiated in other contexts that do not satisfy the constraints, the instantiation will not behave as intended.
2. *The constraints provide a means of judging how reusable the generic actually is.* If they constrain the instantiation very narrowly, then the unit is not very reusable.
3. *The constraints express explicitly the assumptions that the body of the generic unit may use.* It is possible to check or prove that the generic body does not overstep these assumptions (e. g., by requiring the parameters to satisfy properties not implied by the constraints).

Example: *The role of constraints on generic parameters.*

```
     generic
        type T is ...
        with function F ...
--|     C(T, F);         --  All instances of T and F must satisfy C.
```

```
package P is
   ...                  --  T and F can be assumed to satisfy C.
end P;

package body P is
   ...                  --  T and F can be assumed to satisfy C.
end P;
```

In the following example of a reusable sorting package[2] we give the Anna constraints on the generic parameters that are assumed by the actual Ada package. The intention of this example is to provide a generic sorting package that can be instantiated to sort an array of almost anything. The user has the flexibility to supply his own ordering function and equality test on the components, which must satisfy the Anna constraints given.

Example: *A reusable sorting package.*

```
generic
   type COMPONENT_TYPE is private;
   type INDEX_TYPE is (<>);
   type ARRAY_TYPE
      is array (INDEX_TYPE range <>)
                                    of COMPONENT_TYPE;
   with function "<"
            (LEFT, RIGHT : in COMPONENT_TYPE)
         return BOOLEAN is <>;
   with function EQUAL
            (LEFT, RIGHT : in COMPONENT_TYPE)
         return BOOLEAN is "=";

--  (1) EQUAL is required to be an equality relation.
--|     for all X, Y, Z : COMPONENT_TYPE =>
--|        EQUAL (X, X),                         -- Reflexive.
--|        EQUAL (X, Y) → EQUAL (Y, X),          -- Symmetric.
--|        EQUAL (X, Y) and EQUAL (Y, Z) → EQUAL (X, Z),
--|                                             -- Transitive.
--|        EQUAL (X, Y) and X < Z → Y < Z,
--                                   -- Indistinguishable by "<".
--|        EQUAL (X, Y) and Z < X → Z < Y;

--  (2) "<" is required to be a total order.
--|     for all X, Y, Z : COMPONENT_TYPE =>
--|        not X < X,                             -- Irreflexive.
--|        EQUAL (X, Y) or X < Y or Y < X,        -- Total.
--|        X < Y and Y < Z → X < Z;               -- Transitive.

   package SORT_UTILITIES is

      SORT_UTILITIES_VERSION : constant STRING := "1.0";
```

[2]Due to Geoff Mendal [5].

```
type SORT_ALGORITHM_TYPE is
   (QUICKSORT, RECURSIVE_QUICKSORT, BSORT,
    BUBBLE_SORT, BUBBLE_SORT_WITH_QUICK_EXIT,
    SELECTION_SORT, HEAPSORT, INSERTION_SORT,
    MERGE_SORT);
type PERFORMANCE_INSTRUMENTATION_TYPE
                         is range -1 .. SYSTEM.MAX_INT;

SORT_ARRAYS_LENGTH_MISMATCH : exception;

procedure SORT(
             SORT_ARRAY : in out ARRAY_TYPE;
             NUMBER_OF_COMPARISONS,
             NUMBER_OF_EXCHANGES : out
             PERFORMANCE_INSTRUMENTATION_TYPE;
             SORT_ALGORITHM : in
            SORT_ALGORITHM_TYPE := QUICKSORT);

...                          -- Other sorting subprograms.

end SORT_UTILITIES;
```

Commentary

This package contains a number of sorting algorithms, which may be selected by means of parameter SORT_ALGORITHM of SORT. Therefore the constraints on the generic parameters must imply all the properties that are used in proving the algorithms.

Constraint (1) on the generic parameters requires EQUAL to be an equivalence relation over the components and to have the substitution property in relation to "<". Constraint (2) requires "<" to be a total ordering of the components. Note that irreflexivity (**not** X < X) together with the other constraints in (1) and (2) implies that the **or** in the total ordering constraint must be exclusive (**xor**).

These constraints are the logically weakest ones that imply the assumptions that the package body makes about the generic parameters. Therefore they are necessary constraints on any set of actual parameters for the instantiation of the package to behave correctly.

In the process of generalizing an Ada unit, annotations of other units that it depends on may indicate constraints that must be placed on the generic parameters. These annotations express properties of the operations that are being replaced by generic parameters. If the properties are used in the implementation of the unit, then they are assumptions which the unit depends on. The generic parameters must be constrained to satisfy these assumptions. This application of annotations is most obvious when the operations used by the Ada unit are defined axiomatically. A simple example will suffice to illustrate this point.

In a sorting package that is specialized to sorting integer vectors, we may imagine that type INTEGER is defined in a version of package STANDARD that includes axioms as part of its specification. For example, one axiom of STANDARD might express the discreteness property of the integers:

```
--| axiom
--|     for all X : INTEGER => X < INTEGER'LAST →
--|         for all Z : INTEGER => X < Z →
--|                                          X+1 = Z or X+1 < Z;
```

This axiom of STANDARD may be assumed by the implementation of the package for sorting integer vectors. When the package is generalized, we must check if the axiom has been assumed. Suppose we find that operations "+1" and "<" have been used, and the axiom is needed to prove that the package body works correctly. Then, the generic parameters must be constrained to satisfy the axiom so that the same proof can be applied to the generalized body. Let us suppose the generalization is as follows:

Actual Concept		*Generic Formal Parameter*
INTEGER	*is generalized to*	COMPONENT_TYPE
INTEGER'LAST	*is generalized to*	MAX_COMPONENT_TYPE
"="	*is generalized to*	**function** EQUAL
"+1"	*is generalized to*	**function** NEXT
<	*is generalized to*	**function** <

Then one possible form of the constraint corresponding to the axiom is

```
--| for all X : COMPONENT_TYPE =>
--|     X < MAX_COMPONENT_TYPE →
--|         (for all Z : COMPONENT_TYPE =>
--|             X < Z → EQUAL(NEXT(X), Z) or NEXT(X) < Z);
```

This constraint is constructed from the axiom by replacing the actual concepts by the corresponding generic formal parameters in the table.

6.3.3 Generic theories

Finally, how can we encapsulate in theory packages the concepts used to annotate generic units?

- **Guideline: Generality of theories.**

  If a theory package is used to specify a generic unit, it must be "at least as generic" as the unit being specified.

Somewhat loosely, the guideline means that any list of actual parameters that provides a legal Ada instantiation of the generic unit is a sublist of a set of actual parameters that provides a legal instantiation of the generic theory. In addition, the Anna constraints on the formal generic parameters of the theory should not be more restrictive than those on the formals of the generic unit. Then, the theory can be instantiated to any context that the unit can be.

Here is one way to check the guideline informally. Treat the formal generic parameters of the unit as actual objects, types, and subprograms, and try to use them to instantiate the theory package. We should be able to do this without violating the Ada instantiation rules, although we may need additional actual parameters to complete the instantiation. We should then be able to prove the instantiated generic parameter constraints of the theory (the ones that are fully instantiated using only parameters of the unit) from the generic parameter constraints of the unit.

The guideline means that we must take care to generalize theory packages so that they are at least as generic as any of the application packages they will be used to specify.

A generalization similar to the SORT_UTILITIES example above can be applied to the sorting concepts theory package in Section 2.8. The generic version of sorting concepts would be used to annotate SORT_UTILITIES.

Example: *Generic theory package for searching and sorting.*

```
--: generic
--:     type COMPONENT_TYPE is private;
--:     type INDEX_TYPE is (<>);
--:     type ARRAY_TYPE is array (INDEX_TYPE range <>)
--:                                 of COMPONENT_TYPE;
--:     with function "<"
--:             (LEFT, RIGHT : in COMPONENT_TYPE)
--:         return BOOLEAN is <>;
--:     with function EQUAL
--:             (LEFT, RIGHT : in COMPONENT_TYPE)
--:         return BOOLEAN is "=";
        ...
--  Constraints on EQUAL and "<" as in previous example.

--: package SORTING_CONCEPTS is

--:     function "<=" (I, J : COMPONENT_TYPE)
--:     return BOOLEAN;
--|         where
--|         return EQUAL(I, J) or I < J;

--:     function ORDERED(A : ARRAY_TYPE) return BOOLEAN;
--|         where
--|         return for all I, J : A'RANGE => I ≤ J →
--|                                         A(I) <= A(J);
```

```
--: function PERMUTATION (A, B : ARRAY_TYPE)
--: return BOOLEAN;
--|     where
--|         in (A'LENGTH = B'LENGTH),
--|         return
--|             A'LENGTH = 0
--|                 or else
--|             (exist I : B'RANGE => A (A'FIRST) = B (I)
--|                     and
--|              if I = B'FIRST then
--|                  PERMUTATION
--|                      (A (INDEX_TYPE'SUCC (A'FIRST) ..
--|                                               A'LAST),
--|                       B (INDEX_TYPE'SUCC (I) .. B'LAST))
--|              elsif I = B'LAST then
--|                  PERMUTATION
--|                      (A (INDEX_TYPE'SUCC (A'FIRST) ..
--|                                               A'LAST),
--|                       B (B'FIRST .. INDEX_TYPE'PRED (I)))
--|              else
--|                  PERMUTATION
--|                      (A (INDEX_TYPE'SUCC (A'FIRST) ..
--|                                               A'LAST),
--|                       B (B'FIRST..INDEX_TYPE'PRED (I)) &
--|                       B (INDEX_TYPE'SUCC (I) .. B'LAST))
--|              end if);

--:     function SORTED (A : ARRAY_TYPE)
--:     return ARRAY_TYPE;
--|         where
--|         return B : ARRAY_TYPE =>
--|                         PERMUTATION (A, B) and ORDERED (B);

        ...             -- Other searching and sorting concepts.

--: end SORTING_CONCEPTS;
```

Commentary

This example results from generalizing type VECTOR in Section 2.8. The constraints on the formal generic parameters are the same as for SORT_UTILITIES. This version of sorting concepts can be instantiated in SORT_UTILITIES and used to specify SORT.

Note how the annotations of ORDERED and PERMUTATION are generalized. For example, the successor operator I+1 on INTEGERS (in the nongeneric version) is replaced by INDEX_TYPE'SUCC (I) in the general version. Virtual function "<=" is introduced to shorten some of the annotations.

Further Reading

Interest in reusable software is growing rapidly. We have included a few recent publications below. The first reference is a collection of papers from the ITT Workshop on Reusability in Programming: September 1983, chaired by Alan Perlis. The paper by Horowitz and Munson provides a good overview of the different methodologies involved in reusing software. The last four references discuss building reusable software in Ada and specifically discuss the applications of generics, which was our starting point in Section 6.3.

1. T. J. Biggerstaff and A. J. Perlis, editors. Special Issue on Software Reusability. *IEEE Transactions on Software Engineering*, SE–10 (5), September 1984.
2. E. Horowitz and J. B. Munson. An expansive view of reusable software. *IEEE Transactions on Software Engineering*, SE–10 (5), pp. 477–487, September 1984.
3. G. Booch. *Software Components with Ada.* Benjamin/Cummings,Inc., 1987.
4. A. Gargaro and T. L. Pappas. Reusability issues and Ada. *IEEE Software* 4 (4), pp. 43–51, July 1987.
5. G. O. Mendal. Designing for Ada reuse: a case study. *Proceedings of Second International Conference on Ada Applications and Environments*, pp. 33–42, April 8-10, 1986.
6. C. L. Braun, J. B. Goodenough, and R. S. Eanes. *Ada Reusability Guidelines*. Technical Report 3285–2–208/2, SofTech, Inc., April 1985.

7

Annotation of Operations on Composite Types

Topics:

- *array states;*
- *using array states in annotations;*
- *record states;*
- *access types and collections;*
- *using collection states in annotations.*

In this chapter we describe the additional features in Anna for specifying and annotating operations on arrays, records, and access objects (also sometimes called *pointers* for brevity). Such annotations require language features that are not available in Ada. Typically, to specify operations on composite objects, it is convenient to have expressions denoting the composite values in which only the important component values appear. The values of other components may be unknown or irrelevant. (Ada aggregates, for example, are complete composite values, and require all component values to be given.) *Array states* and *record states* are introduced in Anna for this purpose.

We also need expressions that denote parts of the Ada computation state that are not accessible to the Ada programmer. For example, in the case of an access type, we will define the concept of a *collection* of the objects designated by all the values of that access type. Collections enable us to write annotations that constrain side effects of pointer manipulations and aliasing between pointer structures. It is difficult to express such constraints without collections.

These new features are similar to the package state concept discussed in Chapter 4, so we have delayed describing these features until after the discussion of packages.

7.1 Array States

Specifications of operations on arrays and records often refer to values resulting from sequences of operations. To aid writing such specifications, expressions denoting the value of an array or record should contain the sequence of operations leading to that value. Since array and record types can be viewed as simple examples of Anna package state types, a notation similar to the successor state notation for package states suits this purpose very well. Anna provides such a notation in the form of two new kinds of expressions called *array states* and *record states*.

To explain array states, consider one-dimensional arrays of type VECTOR:

```
type VECTOR is array (INTEGER range <>) of INTEGER;
```

The value of a vector A after U has been placed in component I is denoted by an array state

```
A[I => U].
```

This is an expression of type VECTOR written in an Ada-like notation. Its value is defined more formally by the following indexing rule.

- **Indexing Rule**

```
A[J => V](K) = if K = J then V else A(K) end if.
```

Consequently, the following Ada assignment and Anna assertion are always consistent:

```
    A(I) := U;
--| A = in A[I => U];
```

Array state expressions may be used only in annotations. Here are some examples of their use.

Example: Values of array states.

```
    declare
        A : VECTOR(1 .. 3) : = (1, 2, 3);
    begin
        A(3) := A(3)-A(2);
--|     A = (1, 2, 1);                                    (1)
--|     A = in A[3 => in A(1)];                           (2)
--|     A[3 => A(3)+A(2)] = in A;                         (3)
    end;
```

Commentary

Assertion (1) gives the value of A as an Ada aggregate. Assertion (2) expresses that this value is equal to an array state that encodes a different computation on A to get the value. Assertion

(3) expresses another way to view the relationship between the initial and final values of A, again using our new notation.

Note that the modifiers **in** and **out** in an array state, as usual, refer to values at the beginning and end of the scope of the annotation.

The value of A after two operations, say assigning U to component I and V to component J, is denoted by the state

```
A[I => U][J => V].
```

This may be written equivalently as

```
A[I => U; J => V]
```

by applying the following composition rule.

- **Composition Rule**

```
A[I => U][J => V] = A[I => U; J => V].
```

The operations inside the square brackets are called *array store operations*. The left-hand expressions I and J must have values that are legal index values for A, and the right-hand expressions U and V must have values of its component type.

By applying the indexing rule

```
A[I => U; J => V](K) = if K = J then V
                       elsif K = I then U
                       else A(K) end if;
```

we see that the order of store operations is significant *if and only if* the same index value is used in more than one store operation. In this case, the rightmost store into a component hides other stores to that component. For example,

```
A[I => U; I => V](I) = V.
```

If I is not equal to J,

```
A[J => V; I => U] = A[I => U; J => V].
```

Here is another simple example of an assertion using an array state

Example: Swapping array components.

```
      begin
          Y := A(X);
          A(X) := A(X+1);
          A(X+1) := Y;
      end;
--|A = in A[X => in A(X+1); X+1 => in A(X)];
```

Commentary

The final value of A is asserted to be equal to an array state resulting from the initial state of A at the beginning of the block. Note that the array state on the right side of the equality does not express *how* the two array store operations are accomplished in the Ada text — there is no mention of temporary variable Y. In fact, the order of these store operations in the array state is not significant, and they can be reversed without changing the state. Also note that we can write this state as

```
in (A[X => A(X+1); X+1 => A(X)]);
```

the **in** modifier applies to all program variables in the state, namely A and X, but X does not change value in the block.

Next, we compare specifications of array operations using array states with specifications that do not use them.

Examples: Specifications of operation SWAP *on arrays.*

1. *Specification without use of array states.*

```
      function SWAP(A : VECTOR; I, J : INTEGER)
      return VECTOR;
--|       where return X : VECTOR =>
--|           X(I) = A(J) and X(J) = A(I) and
--|               (for all K : X'RANGE =>
--|                           K /= I and K /= J → X(K) = A(K));
```

2. *Specification using array states.*

```
      function SWAP(A : VECTOR; I, J : INTEGER)
      return VECTOR;
--|       where return A[I => A(J); J => A(I)];
```

Commentary

In the second specification, the new notation allows us to describe concisely and precisely what components are changed and what their new values are. The notation tells us exactly which components are changed and what their new values are. In the absence of array states, the returned value must be described by a compound boolean condition (first specification). The first specification can be deduced from the second by using the indexing rule for array states.

To summarize, the notation for array states consists of composing an array name, A, with a sequence of array store operations placed in square brackets, A[...]. This notation is similar to the Ada named format for array aggregates, but it deviates from array aggregates as follows: there does not have to be a store operation for every component, there can be more than one store operation for the same component, and **others** is not permitted in a store operation.

We emphasize that array states are not Ada expressions and therefore cannot appear in virtual Ada text — they can only appear in annotations. They can be used in slices to denote a contiguous segment of components of a one-dimensional array.

The array state notation applies generally to multidimensional arrays. The notation for store and index operations indicates the dimension. For example, if A is a two-dimensional array, the state that results when U is stored in position (I, J) is,

```
A[I, J => U].
```

The indexing rule is,

```
A[I, J => U](K, L) = if K = I and L = J
                          then U
                     else
                          A(K, L)
                     end if.
```

Runtime checking of an annotation containing an array state proceeds exactly as before for that kind of annotation. In general the value of the array state must be known when a check is made. There are different methods of computing array states for checking. The main problems involved in actually computing values of array states are (1) to avoid any effect on an actual array, and (2) efficiency concerns arising from repeatedly computing the same array value both in the actual computation and in the runtime checks. Some annotations can be checked by simplifying array state expressions without computing their values.

Similarly, if consistency proof methods are used, the composition and indexing rules for array states must be added to the set of proof rules.

The notation for array states is a special case of package successor state notation. Arrays are treated as state types of a simple kind of package that has the basic array operations as two of its operations, STORE_OP and INDEX_OP say, and in which the indexing rule is an axiom. For example, the states of instances of this package,

```
generic
   type INDEX is range <>;
   type COMPONENT is private;
package A is
   procedure STORE_OP(I : INDEX; U : COMPONENT);
   function  INDEX_OP(I : INDEX) return COMPONENT;
   axiom
      for all X : A'TYPE; I, J : INDEX;
              U : COMPONENT =>
             X[STORE_OP(I, U)].INDEX_OP(J) =
                    if I = J then
                       U
                    else
                       X.INDEX_OP(J)
                    end if;
end A;
```

behave exactly as we have described one-dimensional array states. (Array state V [I => X] corresponds to package state V [STORE_OP(I, X)], etc.) Of course, in order to model Ada array types accurately by state types of packages like A, we have to model all the Ada array type operations, dimensionality of arrays, and constrained arrays. In future languages where packages are types, arrays will be introduced as predefined packages.

7.2 Using Array States: QuickSort

In practice, the most common uses of array states are in defining properties of array manipulation concepts, and in detailed annotations of subprograms such as QuickSort. For example, array states may be used to construct annotations that compare an actual value of an array computed by the underlying program, with a value that would be computed if some other operations were performed. The following example of a version of QuickSort illustrates both uses of array states.

The example is presented in two stages. First, we give a plan for implementing the body using concepts from the sorting concepts package outlined in Section 2.5.3. A correctness proof for the plan is outlined using properties of the sorting concepts. These properties are promised by axioms involving array states in the sorting concepts package (they were not shown in Section 2.5.3). Finally, an implementation of the plan is given with detailed annotations supporting the correctness proof.

Since the sorting concepts package is quite large, we describe separately various parts of it — called *windows*. Here we introduce two new concepts related to *partitioning* a vector (i. e., a one-dimensional integer array): the *upper bound* and the *lower bound* of a vector. We show the definitions of these concepts, and some typical axioms, in another window of the sorting concepts package. Imagine that this window continues from the previous window in Section 2.5.3.

Example: *Another window in sorting concepts.*

```
--: package SORTING_CONCEPTS is
--:     ...                         -- Concepts shown previously in Section 2.6.

--:     function UPPER_BOUND (N : INTEGER; A : VECTOR)
--:     return BOOLEAN;
--|         where return for all I : A'RANGE => A (I) ≤ N;

--:     function LOWER_BOUND (N : INTEGER; A : VECTOR)
--:     return BOOLEAN;
--|         where return for all I : A'RANGE => A (I) ≥ N;

--:     function PARTITIONED (A : VECTOR; I : INDEX_TYPE)
--:     return BOOLEAN;
--|         where return
--|             if I isin A'RANGE then
--|                 UPPER_BOUND (A (I), A (A'FIRST .. I-1))
--|                     and
--|                 LOWER_BOUND (A (I), A (I+1 .. A'LAST))
--|             else
--|                 FALSE
--|             end if;

--:     ...                                               -- More concepts.

--:     axiom
--|         for all A : VECTOR;
--|                 I, J, L, U, P : INDEX_TYPE;
--|                 X : INTEGER =>
--                                                                    (1)
--|                     PERMUTATION (A, A [I => A (J);
--|                                        J => A (I)]);
--                                                                    (2)
--|                     ORDERED (A (L .. U)) and
--|                         L < P < U and
--|                     A (P-1) ≤ X ≤ A (P+1) →
--|                                 ORDERED (A [P => X] (L .. U));
--|         ...                                            -- More axioms.
--: end SORTING_CONCEPTS;
```

Commentary

In this window PARTITIONED is defined in terms of UPPER_ BOUND and LOWER_BOUND.

Axiom (1) expresses that the array resulting from swapping two components is a permutation of the original array. Axiom (2) expresses conditions under which a new component, X, can be inserted into an ordered array so as to maintain the ordering

property. In each case, array states provide a convenient and succinct notation.
Such axioms express properties of the sorting concepts that may be assumed in correctness proofs like the one below.

The body of QuickSort can be planned informally as follows:

Example: *An implementation plan for QuickSort.*

```
     procedure QUICKSORT (A : in out VECTOR)
--|      where out (A = SORTED (in A));
     is
-- Step 1: If A has less than two components, do nothing;

-- Step 2: Partition A using a component of A which eventually becomes A (J);
--
--|      out (PARTITIONED (A, J) and
--|      PERMUTATION (A, in A));

-- Step 3: QUICKSORT (A (A'FIRST .. J-1));
--|      out (A (A'FIRST .. J-1) =
--|                                SORTED (in A (A'FIRST .. J-1)));

-- Step 4: QUICKSORT (A (J+1 .. A'LAST));
--|      out (A (J+1 .. A'LAST) =
--|                                SORTED (in A (J+1 .. A'LAST)));

     end QUICKSORT;
```

It is easily proved that this implementation plan is correct. The intermediate assertions specify the outcomes of the planned steps in the computation. The assertions following the recursive calls at Steps 3 and 4 are the **out** annotation of QuickSort for the cases when the parameters are the slices, A (A′FIRST .. J−1) and A (J+1 .. A′LAST). They may be used as inductive assumptions to prove by induction on the length of A that this plan for QuickSort always satisfies the **out** annotation. We assume QuickSort sorts vectors of length 1, ..., A′LENGTH−1.

So, assuming the intermediate assertions are true, we must show that the **out** annotation is true after Step 4. To prove this in detail, we need other axioms of sorting concepts that relate PARTITIONED with PERMUTATION (we have not shown them in the window above):

```
--| for all A, B : VECTOR; J : INDEX_TYPE =>
--|     B (J .. B'LAST) = A (J .. A'LAST) and
--|     PARTITIONED (A, J) and
--|     PERMUTATION (B (B'FIRST .. J-1), A (A'FIRST .. J-1)) →
--|                PARTITIONED (B, J) and PERMUTATION (B, A);
```

(There is a similar axiom for permuting the upper segment of a partition.)

From these axioms, and the transitivity of PERMUTATION, we conclude at Step 4 that the initial and final values of A satisfy

> **out** (PERMUTATION (A, **in** A) **and** PARTITIONED (A, J) **and** ORDERED (A (A'FIRST .. J−1)) **and** ORDERED (A (J+1 .. A'LAST))),

which implies **out** (A = SORTED (**in** A)) for vectors of length, A'LENGTH. In this proof, the assertion at Step 2 is the crucial assumption; the rest follows by induction and the properties of the sorting concepts.

To implement this plan, we must decide how to do the partitioning at Step 2. The main idea in QuickSort is to choose a component of A and to construct two segments of a partition, a left-side consisting of components less than or equal to the chosen one, and a right-side of components greater than or equal to it. The segments start with the two end components, and are expanded by exchanging components that are out of place until the segments meet. Here is one version of the algorithm with array states used to annotate the fine details of the partitioning.

Example: *Using array states to annotate QuickSort.*

```
--: with SORTING_CONCEPTS; use SORTING_CONCEPTS;

-- This version of QuickSort uses half-exchanges.
    procedure QUICKSORT (A : in out VECTOR)
--|      where out (PERMUTATION (A, in A) and ORDERED (A));
    is
        FIRST : constant INTEGER range A'RANGE := A'FIRST;
        LAST : constant INTEGER range A'RANGE := A'LAST;
        I, J : INTEGER range A'RANGE;
        TEMP : INTEGER;

--  A0 is the input value of A.
--:      A0 : constant VECTOR := A;

    begin
        if FIRST < LAST then
            I := FIRST;
            J := LAST;
            TEMP := A (LAST);

-- Partition array with TEMP as the dividing element.
            while I < J loop
--                                                              (1)
--|               UPPER_BOUND (TEMP, A (FIRST .. I-1)) and
--|               LOWER_BOUND (TEMP, A (J+1 .. LAST)) and
--|               I ≤ J and PERMUTATION (A [J => TEMP], A0);
                 while A (I) <= TEMP and then I < J  loop
                 I := I+1;
                 end loop;
```

```
                A(J) := A(I);
--                                                          (2)
--|           PERMUTATION(A[I => TEMP], A0) and I≤J;
              while A(J) >= TEMP and then I < J loop
                  J := J-1;
              end loop;
              A(I) := A(J);
          end loop;
              A(J) := TEMP;
--                                                          (3)
--|           UPPER_BOUND(A(J), A(FIRST .. I-1)) and
--|           LOWER_BOUND(A(J), A(J+1 .. LAST)) and
--|           I = J and PERMUTATION(A, A0);

          QUICKSORT(A(FIRST .. J-1));
          QUICKSORT(A(J+1 .. LAST));
      end if;

  end QUICKSORT;
```

Commentary

Inductive assertion (1) and assertions (2) and (3) annotate the partitioning. At the beginning of each iteration of the outer loop, assertion (1) must be satisfied. The array state is used in

```
PERMUTATION(A[J => TEMP], A0)
```

to express that the current value of A on each iteration must have the property that it will be a permutation of the initial value A0 if TEMP is placed in Jth component. That is, if we perform the assignment,

```
A(J) := TEMP;
```

at that point, then A will be a permutation of A0. This use of array states in assertions (1) and (2) effectively documents the result of the half-exchanges (i. e., the inner loops and their following assignment) whereby there is always a duplicated component and the comparison component (in TEMP) is missing. The inner assertion (2) after the first half-exchange tells us that I is the position of the current duplicate. Assertion (1), which must be true initially and after each execution of the second half-exchange, tells us that J is the current position of the duplicate element. After the outer loop terminates, TEMP is restored. The assertion (3) at this point is a consequence of assertion, the loop test, and the semantics of array states:

```
-- If this assertions is true here:
--| PERMUTATION (A[J => TEMP], A0);
        A(J) := TEMP;
-- then this assertion is true here:
--| PERMUTATION (A, A0);
```

Assertion (3) implies the assertion after Step 2 in the previous plan for the body. The proof of correctness of the complete procedure now follows exactly the previous proof of the plan.

7.3 Record States

Record states provide the same facilities for annotating record operations that array states do for array operations. In describing record states we will assume the reader is already familiar with the previous two sections on array states.

Record states are names denoting record values. They also encode a sequence of operations leading to the value. Record states are formed by composing a record name, R, with a sequence of *record store operations* placed in square brackets; for example,

```
R[C => U; D => V]
```

where C, D are names of components of the record type, and U, V are expressions of the component types. Note that R can be an identifier or a record state. The sequence of store operations has a form similar to the named format for record aggregates with the following exceptions: an **others** clause is not permitted, two store operations may refer to the same component, and there does not need to be a store operation for every component. The order of operations in the sequence is significant only if the operations refer to the same component — just as for array states.

For examples of record states, consider the record type,

```
type BUFFER is
    record
        LENGTH : INTEGER range 0 .. MAX := 0;
        STORE : STRING(1 .. MAX);
    end record;
```

The following example specifies the state of a buffer, B, after an assignment to each of its components.

Example: A record state with an array state component.

```
        begin
           B.LENGTH := B.LENGTH+1;
           B.STORE(LENGTH) := 'A';
           ...
        end;
--| out (B = in B[LENGTH => in B.LENGTH+1;
--|               STORE => in B.STORE[in B.LENGTH+1 => 'A']]);
```

Commentary

In the annotation, the record state on the right side of the equality denotes the **out** value of B. The LENGTH component has the value,

```
in B.LENGTH+1,
```

and the STORE component has the value denoted by the array state,

```
in B.STORE[in B.LENGTH+1 => 'A'].
```

These are the significant changes to the value of B, and reference to other subcomponents can be omitted by using the state notation.

Record states obey rules similar to those for array states.

- **Composition Rule**

```
R[C => U][D => V] = R[C => U; D => V]
```

- **Selection Rule**

```
R[C => U].C = U, R[C => U].D = R.D
```

The selection rule implies that the order of two record store operations is significant if and only if they apply to the same component. In this case the rightmost operation hides the other one.

These rules imply that the store operations to different components can be reversed without affecting the record state. For example,

```
B[LENGTH => B.LENGTH+1; STORE =>
                            B.STORE[B.LENGTH+1 => 'A']] =
B[STORE => B.STORE[B.LENGTH+1 => 'A'];
                                    LENGTH => B.LENGTH+1]
```

Note that record store operations are treated as subexpressions within a record state — just like expressions in a record aggregate. They are all evaluated in the context in which the record state expression appears. In these record states, B.LENGTH always denotes the value of the LENGTH component of B — not the LENGTH component of B[LENGTH=> B.LENGTH+1] for example.

Two record states are equal if they represent the same record value.

Example: *Using record states in annotations.*

```
--: function MAKE_ROOM(B : BUFFER; P : POSITIVE)
--: return STRING;
--|     where
--|         B.LENGTH < B.STORE'LAST,
--|         P isin B.STORE'FIRST .. B.LENGTH,
--|         return X : STRING =>
--|             X'LENGTH = B.STORE'LENGTH+1    and
--|             X(B.STORE'FIRST .. P-1) =
--|                        B.STORE(B.STORE'FIRST .. P-1) and
--|             X(P+1 .. B.LENGTH+1) =
--|                                  B.STORE(P .. B.LENGTH);

    procedure INSERT(C : CHARACTER;
                     P : POSITIVE;
                     B : in out BUFFER)
--|     where
--|         in B.LENGTH = B.STORE'LAST => raise NO_ROOM,
--|         P isin B'FIRST .. B.LENGTH,
--|         out (B = in B[STORE =>
--|                            MAKE_ROOM(in B, P) [P => C];
--|                             LENGTH => in B.LENGTH+1)]);
    is
    begin
        if B.LENGTH = B.STORE'LAST then
            raise NO_ROOM;
        end if;
        if P in B.STORE'FIRST .. B.LENGTH then
            B := (LENGTH => B.LENGTH+1,
                  STORE => B.STORE(B.STORE'FIRST .. P-1)
                       & C & B.STORE(P .. B.STORE'LAST-1));
        end if;
        return;
    end INSERT;
```

Commentary

The **out** annotation of INSERT uses a record state to specify the final value of the buffer. The length component is incremented, and a character is inserted in the store component. The operation on the store is specified by an array state,

```
MAKE_ROOM (in B, P) [P => C],
```

in which a store operation, [P => C], is applied to an array state resulting from a MAKE_ROOM operation. MAKE_ROOM is a virtual function defining the process of shifting components to the right to make room at P. In the body of INSERT, the change to B is computed as a single record aggregate. It must contain a STORE component covering the range of the STORE in the buffer type. This is computed as the string catenation,

```
B.STORE(B.STORE'FIRST .. P-1)
    & C & B.STORE(P .. B.STORE'LAST-1).
```

The specification, however, certainly does not require copying of all components in the STORE. The problem of finding a more efficient implementation is left to the reader.

7.3.1 Variant record states *

The sequence of store operations in the state of a variant record must obey restrictions corresponding to the Ada rules for variant records. First, since the discriminant is a component, a record state may contain a store operation for the discriminant. A record state may thereby express a change of discriminant value. A state, R[C => U], is legal only if C is the name of a component in the variant corresponding to the values of the discriminants in R. Consequently, a store operation in a record state is legal only if the component it refers to is a component of the values associated with the current discriminants.

Example: *Legal and illegal variant record states.*

```
type NUMBER(D : BOOLEAN := TRUE) is
    record
        case D is
            when TRUE => B : INTEGER;
            when FALSE => C : FLOAT;
        end case;
    end record;
```

```
      NUM : NUMBER;          -- Default discriminant value is TRUE.
begin
      NUM := (D => FALSE, C => 1.0);
--| NUM = in NUM[C => 1.0]                -- (1) Illegal record state.
--| NUM = in NUM[D => FALSE;
--|                C => 1.0];              -- (2) Legal record state.
--| NUM = in NUM[C => 1.0;
--|                D => FALSE];            -- (3) Illegal record state.
end;
```

Commentary

In assertion (1) the record state is illegal because the discriminant value of **in** NUM is TRUE; the component C does not exist for the variant corresponding to that value. The state in (3) is illegal for the same reason even though the discriminant is changed by a later store — the order is significant. In (2) the state is legal since the first store operation changes the discriminant value to the variant case for which C is a component.

In Ada, a change to the value of a discriminant component can be made only by an assignment of a complete record value to the variable. This is not reflected in the Anna restrictions on record states. Thus, in the previous example the record states shown below are all legal expressions even though some of them denote illegal Ada record values:

```
in NUM[D => FALSE],
in NUM[D => FALSE; C => 1.0],
in NUM[D => FALSE; C => 1.0; D => TRUE].
```

Selection on the state of a variant record is defined only if the component exists for that variant represented by the state. For example,

```
in NUM[D => FALSE; C => 1.0; D => TRUE].C
```

is not defined.

7.4 Access Types and Collections

The objects designated by the values of an access type form a *collection* associated with that access type. Each access type has a collection associated with it. The collections associated with different access types never have an object in common.

In Ada, collections cannot be directly referenced by a program (unlike some other languages such as an early version of Pascal and Euclid). However, if an Ada program allocates and manipulates objects of an access type, it will cause changes in the state of the associated collection. In many cases the results and effects — including side effects — of such programs can only be specified by annotations on the state of the collection. Therefore, in Anna the collection associated with an access type is made available for use in annotations as an attribute of the access type.

An access type T has an attribute T′COLLECTION whose state (or value) at any point in a computation contains all objects that it is possible to designate by values of T together with the values (if any) of designated objects. The collection state also contains an allocation status (true or false) for each object indicating if the object is currently allocated or not. The value of T′COLLECTION is called the *current state* of the collection. If the value of a designated object changes, or if a new object is allocated, the state of the collection is changed. The type of the collection states is another attribute of T, T′COLLECTION′TYPE. It is treated as a private type. Anna provides an equality operator on collection states, as with any type. Anna also provides a successor state notation for collection states resulting from sequences of operations on the access objects. This allows us to write annotations that compare collection states before and after access type operations.

7.4.1 Collections

In this section we describe an intuitive model of collections and how collections are changed by operations on access type objects (pointers). We model an access type as an unbounded set of values — although an implementation may impose a bound. These values are not available in Ada or Anna, but we may suppose, for discussion, that the values of the access type can be enumerated as $\mathbf{v}_1, \mathbf{v}_2, \mathbf{v}_3, \ldots$.

A quantified expression with a quantifier over an access type, T, is a statement about this set of values, $\mathbf{v}_i$. For example

```
for all X : T => A(X);
```

means "for all access values $\mathbf{v}_i$, $A(\mathbf{v}_i)$ is either defined and true or else undefined."

A collection can be modeled as an unbounded array of objects. Each of the $\mathbf{v}_i$'s designates a unique object in the collection. Thus, the "components" of the collection are the designated objects, and the "index values" are the $\mathbf{v}_i$'s. A component in the collection may have a value, which is always of the *designated* type. It also has a *status* which is true if it has been allocated, and false otherwise. A state of the collection contains whatever values have been assigned to its components and also the status value of each component. Some components in a state will be uninitialized and others will not be allocated.

Suppose that an access type variable X has a value $\mathbf{v}_i$. We say that X designates an object in a collection state if the status of the object designated by $\mathbf{v}_i$ is true in that state. Ada is designed so that if X has a value that is not **null**, then it always designates an object in the *current* state of the collection. Remember, however, that Anna allows us to express whether or not X designates an object in some other collection state.

Consider a simple example of mutually dependent type definitions.

```
type WORD;
type SET is access WORD;
type WORD is   record
                  ITEM : INTEGER;
                  NEXT : SET;
               end record;
```

Values of type SET designate objects of type WORD. The collection associated with SET is SET′COLLECTION, an attribute of SET. Its value is called the *current state* of the collection associated with SET. It contains all the WORDs that can be designated by values of type SET together with their current values and allocation status. The number of WORDs in SET′COLLECTION is not bounded in Anna — an implementation may impose a bound.

Let us see how we can model the changes in SET′COLLECTION as a result of operations on SETS. We will trace the changes that happen as elements are added to a set.

Example: Adding an element to a set.

```
procedure ADD (ELEMENT : in INTEGER;
               THE_SET : in out SET)
is
   INDEX : SET := THE_SET;
begin
--    Check if the element is already in the set.
   while INDEX /= null loop
      if INDEX.ITEM = ELEMENT then
         return;
      end if;
      INDEX := INDEX.NEXT;
   end loop;

--    If not, add the element to the set.
   THE_SET := new WORD'(ITEM => ELEMENT,
                        NEXT => THE_SET);
exception
   when STORAGE_ERROR => raise OVERFLOW;
end ADD;
```

For discussion, suppose the SET access type values can be enumerated as $\mathbf{v}_1$, $\mathbf{v}_2$, $\mathbf{v}_3$, ... Informally, we will use an aggregate-like notation to represent states of the collection; we will represent only those objects that have been allocated and have values. This notation is *not* Anna.

Suppose that prior to a call to ADD we have a collection in which two WORDs have been allocated and have values. The current state (or value) of the collection can be written:

SET'COLLECTION = ($\mathbf{v}_1$ => (1, $\mathbf{v}_2$), $\mathbf{v}_2$ => (2, **null**),
others => **not** ALLOCATED)

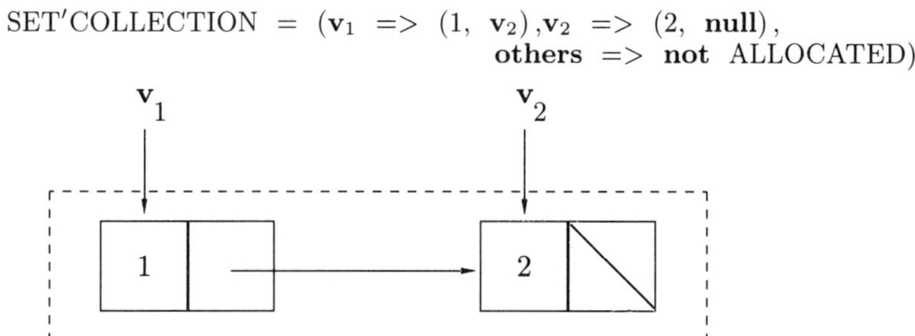

Consider the execution of a call, ADD(3, U), where the value of U is $\mathbf{v}_1$, that is U.**all** = (1, $\mathbf{v}_2$). During the loop to check if the element is already in the set, the collection state does not change because the values of all words remain unchanged, and no new words are allocated. Certainly the value of INDEX is changed as it iterates over the set, but the collection state remains constant. But if the assignment to U is completed, a new word is allocated. Suppose it is designated by $\mathbf{v}_3$. Then the new value of U is $\mathbf{v}_3$ so that U.**all** = (3, $\mathbf{v}_1$), and the collection state changes to:

SET'COLLECTION = ($\mathbf{v}_1$ => (1, $\mathbf{v}_2$), $\mathbf{v}_2$ => (2, **null**),
$\mathbf{v}_3$ => (3, $\mathbf{v}_1$), **others** => **not** ALLOCATED),

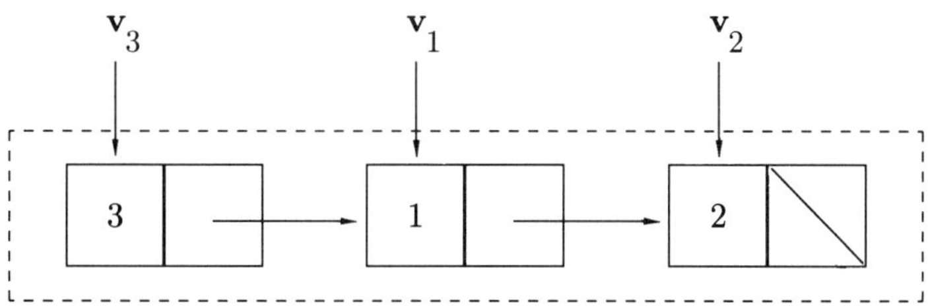

Suppose now that a set variable V has the value $\mathbf{v}_2$, and consider a second call, ADD(3, V), with the previous state of the collection as the input state. In this case the collection state will change to:

SET'COLLECTION = ($\mathbf{v}_1$ => (1, $\mathbf{v}_2$), $\mathbf{v}_2$ => (2, **null**),
$\mathbf{v}_3$ => (3, $\mathbf{v}_1$), $\mathbf{v}_4$ => (3, $\mathbf{v}_2$),
others => **not** ALLOCATED).

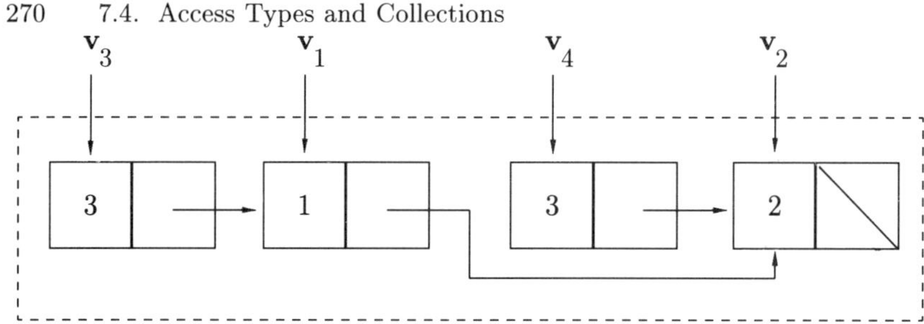

The new value of V is $\mathbf{v}_4$. It so happens in this example that the two sets, represented by variables U and V, share the word designated by $\mathbf{v}_2$.

Anna provides an equality relation between collection states. Two collection states are equal if the same objects have been allocated in both states, and any object has the same value in both states or its value is undefined in both states.

We will give a formal specification of equality later, but first let us see how to use it. The ability to test collection states for equality allows us to express some powerful constraints on what a subprogram must and must not do. As an example, consider the set membership test:

Example: *Set membership specification using collections.*

```
   function IS_MEMBER (ELEMENT  : in ITEM;
                       THE_SET  : in SET) return BOOLEAN;
--|   where return if THE_SET = null then FALSE
--|                else (THE_SET.ITEM = ELEMENT or else
--|                   IS_MEMBER (ELEMENT, THE_SET.NEXT)
--|                end if,
--|                SET'COLLECTION = in SET'COLLECTION;
   is
      I : SET := THE_SET;
   begin
      while I /= null loop
         if ELEMENT = I.ITEM then
            return TRUE;
         end if;
         I := I.NEXT;
      end loop;
      return FALSE;
   end IS_MEMBER;
```

Commentary

The return annotation specifies the boolean value of the function. The second annotation uses "=" on collection states to specify that the current state of the collection must remain invariant throughout the computation of the body.[1] The function

[1]Not to be confused with an **out** annotation which constrains only the final

cannot have a side effect on the collection. This means that the value of every WORD so far allocated at the moment of call must not change and no new words can be allocated. So the function cannot do any local bookkeeping such as reordering the set while testing for membership, or making a new copy. Note, by the way, that an alternative **return** annotation using an existential quantifier over WORDs would require a concept of *reachability* between WORDS. For example,

```
return exist X : WORD =>
    REACHABLE(THE_SET, X) and X.ITEM =
                                        ELEMENT
```

uses REACHABLE to encapsulate the explicit recursion along the WORDs in the set.

It is not easy to express invariant constraints of the kind illustrated above without using collections. Consider using the following annotation to express that all objects accessed by SET pointers must be invariant:

```
for all X : SET => X.all = in (X.all).                    -- (1)
```

This actually expresses that the values of those objects having a defined value before a call to IS_MEMBER (i. e., **in** (X .**all**) is defined) must remain invariant during the call. But it says nothing about objects allocated during the call. For example, suppose we execute the allocation

```
Y := new WORD'(E)
```

during a call, and suppose the final value of Y is **v**. Before the call, the WORD designated by **v** was not allocated so **v . all** was undefined. Now, to compute the value of the annotation (1) at any state during the call, consider the case when the logical variable, X, has the value **v**. This case of the annotation is

```
v.all = in (v.all).
```

Since the right side value is undefined, the equality is undefined and does not affect the value of the quantified expression (1) (see Section 1.2) . So our constraint, (1) , is not affected by the allocation. It would permit allocations during a call to the set membership test.

---

computation state.

7.4.2 Collection states and operations

Now we come to the Anna notation for collection state expressions, and for operations on collections.

The states of a collection resulting from operations on the access objects are represented in Anna by names (i.e., primary expressions) called *collection states*. This provides a notation similar to array states for expressing the value of a collection. A collection state has the form

```
C[X => E; ... ],
```

where C is a collection state, and a sequence of *store* operations appears in the square brackets. X is called the *index* expression of the store operation, and E is the component expression. The store operations are restricted to operations that have an effect on the collection state. The type of the index expression, X, must be either the *access* type or the *designated* type or one of its component types. If the type of X is the designated type (or a component type), then X must consist of operations on the access type. The role of the index expression in the notation is to indicate which designated object (component) in the collection is changed. The index expression is optional and can be omitted, in which case the component expression, E, must be an allocator for the access type. If the index expression is a selected or indexed component, then the component expression must be of a compatible type.

Below we give some examples of collection states. Suppose that C is the initial state of SET'COLLECTION before an assignment or allocation to a SET variable, X. In each case the final state is written as follows:

operation	**resulting collection state**
X.**all** := E;	C[X => E]
X.ITEM := 5;	C[X => X.**all**[ITEM => E]] *or* C[X.ITEM => 5]
X := **new** WORD;	C[**new** WORD]
X := **new** WORD'(5, **null**);	C[**new** WORD'(5, **null**)]
IS_MEMBER(5, **new** WORD'(5, **null**))	C[**new** WORD'(5, **null**)]

The basic notation always has an access type expression in the index position. However, Ada expressions denoting components of the designated type are also allowed in index positions as shorthand to reduce complexity of the component expressions. Consequently the same collection state can be represented in different ways. For example, we can write

```
C[X.ITEM => 5]
```

as a shorthand for the basic notation

```
C[X => X.all [ITEM => 5]].
```

Substitution of equal terms in an index expression of a store operation is allowed only when the index is of the access type — i. e., equality substitution is allowed in the basic notation but not in shorthands. For example, if access variables X and Y are such that X ≠ Y and X.ITEM = Y.ITEM then substitution in the shorthand form of the collection state would equate C[X.ITEM => E] and C[Y.ITEM => E].

• The NEXT attribute

The Anna 'NEXT attribute of an access type T returns the value of an allocator as a function of the collection state. If C is the state of the collection of T, then:

```
new T = C'NEXT.
```

Consequently, after an assignment, X := **new** WORD' (5, **null**), we have,

```
SET'COLLECTION = C[new WORD'(5, null)] and
                  X = C'NEXT.
```

This attribute allows annotations relating access values to collection states. It is useful in proofs of correctness.

• Membership test

The Anna membership test, **isin**, can be applied to collections. The membership test, X **isin** C, takes as arguments an access type object X and a collection state C of the collection type associated with the access type — e. g., X is of type SET and C is of type SET'COLLECTION'TYPE. The test is true if X designates an object in C that has been allocated. Consequently, for any access value Y and collection state C:

```
Y isin C → Y ≠ C'NEXT.
```

Also, if Y is a program variable and C is the current state of the collection, then:

```
Y isin C ↔ Y /= null.
```

As an example of using the membership test for collection states, consider specifying the previous example of adding an element to a set.

Example: *Specification for adding an element to a set.*

```
--: function NEW_WORD (X : SET;
--:                    C1, C2 : SET'COLLECTION'TYPE)
--: return BOOLEAN;
--|    where return X isin C1 and X not isin C2;

    procedure ADD (ELEMENT : in INTEGER;
                   THE_SET : in out SET);

--|    where not IS_MEMBER (ELEMENT, in THE_SET) or else
--|                SET'COLLECTION = in SET'COLLECTION,
--|       out (IS_MEMBER (ELEMENT, THE_SET)),
--|       out (for all I : INTEGER  =>
--|              IS_MEMBER (I, in THE_SET) →
--|                         IS_MEMBER (I, THE_SET),
--|       out (for all X : SET =>
--|              NEW_WORD (X, SET'COLLECTION,
--|                           in SET'COLLECTION) →
--|                              X.ITEM = ELEMENT),
--|       out (for all X, Y : SET =>
--|              (NEW_WORD (X, SET'COLLECTION,
--|                              in SET'COLLECTION)
--|                      and
--|               NEW_WORD (Y, SET'COLLECTION,
--|                      in SET'COLLECTION)) → X = Y);
```

Commentary

The Anna membership test, **isin**, is used to define the virtual concept of a "new word": X designates a word that is allocated in collection state C1 but is not allocated in collection state C2. The specification of ADD has two cases. In the first case, the collection must remain invariant throughout the call if the element is already in the set.[2] In the second case, the **out** annotation specifies that the element is placed in the set, and also that all previous members remain. In addition, it is specified that any new word that is allocated must have the element as its ITEM component. And lastly, it is specified that only one new word is allocated.

The only implementation details that are left open are the actual test for membership (e. g., by an iterative loop), and where in the list representation of THE_SET the element is added (e. g., it could be inserted into the middle of the list or added at the front of the list) . We would expect to see the kind of detailed

[2]This is an invariant constraint on the body of ADD, not just an **out** annotation.

specification shown in this example only at the implementation level within the body of a sets package that encapsulates set operations.

• Indexing operations

Variables of the access type may be used as indices into a collection state. If C is a collection, then C (X) denotes the value of the object that X designates in the state C. In particular, C (X) and X .**all** represent the same value if C is the current state of the collection. For example, if X is a SET variable and C is a collection of type SET'COLLECTION'TYPE, the following equalities are true:

```
C[X => E](X) = E,
C[X.ITEM => I](X).ITEM = I,
X = C'NEXT → C[new WORD'(5, null)](X) = (5, null).
```

There are rules for collection operations that play a role in defining the semantics of collection states similar to the rules for array store and indexing operations. The rules for indexing on collection states are similar to arrays — e. g., the rightmost collection operation hides any other operations on the same access variable or designated component. For example,

```
X = SET'COLLECTION'NEXT →
      SET'COLLECTION[new WORD'(5, null);
                              X.ITEM => 3](X) = (3, null).
```

Collection states also obey other rules. For example, there are rules specifying conditions under which collection operations commute, e. g.,

```
Y isin C → C[Y => E; new T] = C[new T; Y => E].
```

The indexing rules are messy to state in a general form because they must allow for arbitrary indexing or selection operations on the designated objects, depending on the type declarations.

• Equality operator

The equality operator is defined on collection states. Recall that in the case of array states this is the Ada equality on array values. But for collections, there is no predefined Ada operation, so the Anna equality operation must be defined. We have already described it informally. A formal definition can be given as follows.

Example: *Formal specification of equality on collections.*

```
--: function "=" (C1, C2 : T'COLLECTION'TYPE)
--: return BOOLEAN;
--|     where
--|         return (for all X : T => (X isin C1 ↔ X isin C2)
--|                                   and then C1(X) = C2(X));
```

Collections can be specified as (instances of) a generic package similarly to the package specification for arrays outlined in Section 7.1. The designated type is a generic parameter, and the package declares the access type as a private type. States of a collection are states of the package, and the rules for collection states are expressed as axioms of the package.

Runtime checking of annotations that use collection states requires an implementation of collections. A collection is implemented as a virtual data structure. It has the same visibility (in annotations) as the associated access type. Its states are updated each time an access type operation is performed. This virtual implementation allows expressions with collection states to be evaluated by the checking functions for the annotations.

7.5 Using Collections

Programming with access types has incurred much fear and criticism over the years. Many writers have been concerned about the problems of "dangling pointers," aliasing of pointer parameters, and unexpected side effects. This accumulation of bad press is accentuated by a style of "programming by side effect" which seems to accompany pointer manipulation in general, no matter which programming language is used — it is a way of life in such languages as Lisp. It is therefore quite understandable that access types are regarded as "dangerous" in current literature on security aspects of systems implemented in Ada. Indeed, some proposed "secure subsets" of Ada have considered deleting access types from the language altogether.

So, some of the most important applications of collections are their use in annotations to constrain against side effects and aliasing — i. e., sharing of substructures between pointer structures. As an example, let us continue to study the annotation of set operations using the linked list structure representation. Bear in mind that SET would usually be declared as a private type in the visible part of a sets package. Our examples involve specifying these operations at a level where the full declaration of SET as an access type, and the associated collection, are visible. This would be in the hidden part of a sets package, encapsulating the set operations.

Suppose we start with an informal specification such as,

```
      procedure COPY (S : in  SET; T : out SET);
--|      where ... to be completed ... ;
--    The set T is equal to the set S,
--    T has no structure in common with any existing set.
```

The first specification cannot be expressed by the Ada "=" operation between parameters S and T because they access type objects. Equality of the access type values is not necessary for equality of the sets represented by those values. First we must specify set equality. This can be done using the set membership function defined previously.

Example: Specification of a set equality test without side effects.

```
      function IS_EQUAL(S, T : in SET) return BOOLEAN;
--|      where
--|         return for all X : ITEM =>
--|            IS_MEMBER(X, S) ↔ IS_MEMBER(X, T),
--|            SET'COLLECTION = in SET'COLLECTION;
```

Commentary

We have specified set equality using the set membership function. In relative specifications such as this, it is important to include a constraint against side effects — as the second annotation on the collection does here. Note that a similar "no side effects" constraint is placed on the set membership function (see the specification in Section 7.4.1).

The **return** annotation in this example is true if the boolean expression is either true or undefined for each value of ITEM. It constrains the body of IS_EQUAL to return a *value* satisfying the quantified expression. It does not, however, imply that the side effect constraint on the IS_MEMBER function applies here. Therefore, the second specification is *not* redundant.

Next, we discuss the second specification of COPY. The COPY procedure is intended to make a new copy of its **in** parameter S. To ensure that this copy will not have structure in common with another set, it is sufficient to specify that the copy, T, must be *new* — not in the collection when a call begins — and that the structure of an existing set is not changed.

Example: Specifying that a set is not represented in a collection state.

```
--: function NEW_SET(T : SET; C : SET'COLLECTION'TYPE)
--: return BOOLEAN;
--|     where
--|         return T = null or else
--|                    (T not isin C and NEW_SET(T.NEXT, C));
```

Commentary

T is a new set relative to the collection state C if each WORD in the structure representing T is not allocated in C.
Note that NEW_SET must be virtual since it has a collection type parameter.

If COPY does not change the value of any WORD that is already allocated in the input collection, then an existing set structure cannot be changed to share common structure with the new set, T (or with any other set). One way to express this specification is to define a more general concept of one collection state being a subcollection of another.

Example: Defining a concept of subcollection.

```
--: function SUB_COLLECTION(C, D : SET'COLLECTION'TYPE)
--: return BOOLEAN;
--|     where
--|         return (for all X : SET =>
--|                   X isin C → X isin D and then C(X) = D(X));
```

Commentary

If a WORD is allocated in C then it must be allocated in D, and it must have the same value in both collection states.

The specification of the set copying operation can be expressed formally using set equality and the NEW_SET and SUB_COLLECTION tests.

Example: Specification and annotation of copying a set.

```
    procedure COPY(S : in SET; T : out SET)
--|     where
--|         out (IS_EQUAL(S, T)),
--|         out (NEW_SET(T, in SET'COLLECTION)),
--|         out (SUB_COLLECTION
--|                  (in SET'COLLECTION, SET'COLLECTION));
    is
        I : SET := S;
        J : SET;
--       Save the in state of the collection.
--:     IN_COLLECTION : SET'COLLECTION'TYPE :=
--:                                         SET'COLLECTION;
```

```
begin
   if S = null then
      T := null;
   else
      T := new WORD'(ITEM => I.ITEM, NEXT =>
                                                      null);
      J := T;
      I := I.NEXT;
--    Invariant over the loop.
--|      with
--|      for all X : SET =>
--|         X isin SET'COLLECTION →
--|            (X isin IN_COLLECTION and
--|                              IN_COLLECTION(X) = X.all)
--|         or
--|         (NEW_SET(X, IN_COLLECTION) and
--|                               IS_MEMBER(X.ITEM, S-I));
      while I /= null loop
         J.NEXT := new WORD'
                        (ITEM => I.ITEM, NEXT => null);
         J := J.NEXT;
         I := I.NEXT;
      end loop;
   end if;
exception
   when STORAGE_ERROR => raise OVERFLOW;
end COPY;
```

Commentary

The first specification requires set equality between S and T. The second requires the copy, T, to be a new set. It requires a "new" copy by disallowing any prior allocated value existing at the time of a call. It excludes cheating by assigning the access value of S to T. The third specification requires the input collection state to be a subcollection of the final state.

If all set structures are disjoint when COPY is called, then the second and third specifications together ensure disjointness of all set structures upon termination. The role of these two specifications is simply to constrain the implementation to maintain disjointness. This property is important in implementing other set operations such as deletion of an item from a set. (Sharing of list structure between sets will make it difficult to delete an item from one particular set.)

The invariant annotation of the loop constrains the effect of the loop body on the collection state. When the loop terminates normally the invariant implies the procedure specifications. This can be proved by induction on the number of members of SET.

Note that only the first **out** subprogram annotation is needed to specify *what* COPY does. All the other annotations express powerful constraints on its computation that are not expressed in the Ada code itself, although they are critical to correctness of a sets package.

Sharing of structure designated by access values is a particularly common case of *aliasing* between parameters. It is important to be able to specify that actual parameters of a call not be aliases, since most subprograms will not produce specified results in the presence of aliasing — i. e., "no aliasing" is often an unstated requirement. In the copying example, the NEW_SET specification is a sufficient condition for "no aliasing" between T and any existing set. A necessary and sufficient condition is not so easy to express.

Let us consider the problem of specifying in general that the representations of two sets, X and Y, be structurally disjoint. Such a specification cannot be a function of the values of X and Y only. This is so because if we change the NEXT component of a WORD in the list structure representing X or Y, we can introduce a common substructure without changing the values of either X or Y — neither their "set" values nor their "access" values need be changed by the surreptitious introduction of a common substructure. It only makes sense to talk about two sets having "structurally disjoint representations" in a given state of the collection where the values of all relevant access objects are represented. So the concept of disjointness for SETs cannot be specified without collections.

Example: *Specifying that sets* X *and* Y *are represented by disjoint structures.*

```
--: function DISJOINT_STRUCTURE(X, Y : SET;
--:                               C : SET'COLLECTION'TYPE)
--: return BOOLEAN;
--| where
--|    return
--|       X = null or Y = null or
--|       (X /= Y and
--|       DISJOINT_STRUCTURE(X, C(Y).NEXT, C) and
--|       DISJOINT_STRUCTURE(C(X).NEXT, Y, C)         );
```

Commentary

The DISJOINT_STRUCTURE concept specifies that two sets are represented by disjoint structures in a given collection state — not necessarily the current collection. It is easily proved that this concept is a function — it satisfies equality substitution for all parameter values:

```
U = X and V = Y and C = D →
    DISJOINT_STRUCTURE(U, V, C) =
                      DISJOINT_STRUCTURE(X, Y, D)
```

However, suppose we try to specify the same function without using collections as follows:

```
    function DISJOINT_LISTS(X, Y : SET)
    return BOOLEAN;
--| where
--|     return
--|         X = null or Y = null or
--|         (X /= Y and
--|         DISJOINT_LISTS(X, Y.NEXT) and
--|         DISJOINT_LISTS(X.NEXT, Y)          );
```

This specification uses not only the formal parameters, X and Y, but also other values X.NEXT and Y.NEXT. We can implement DISJOINT_LISTS recursively following the specification. But, the result of a call, DISJOINT_LISTS(X, Y), will return different values at different times for the same parameter values of X and Y — it does not satisfy equality substitution. Essentially, it is not a function of its parameters, but relies also on the collection state, which is referenced implicitly in the expressions X.NEXT and Y.NEXT.

Many other concepts used in describing pointer manipulation algorithms — such as the reachability between cells in a list structure — depend similarly on the collection state. So it turns out that collections play a basic role in specifying pointer manipulation algorithms and annotating the details of their implementations.

Further Reading

The collection concept started with an early Pascal concept by Wirth called a *reference class*, which was present in the 1971 paper on Pascal. Reference classes were not included in later versions of Pascal. Reference Classes were defined axiomatically and implemented in the Stanford Pascal Verifier system as an annotation feature in the mid–1970's (see Appendix C(4)). Later on, a similar concept called a *collection* was included in Euclid and other languages, and is mentioned in the Ada reference manual. Up to now, the literature on collections has appeared only in research journals. A few of these papers are listed below.

1. B. W. Lampson, J. J. Horning, R. L. London, J. G. Mitchell, G. L. Popek. Report on the programming language Euclid. *ACM SIGPLAN Notices*, 12(2), February 1977.

2. C. A. R. Hoare, N. Wirth. An axiomatic definition of the programming language Pascal. *Acta Informatica*, Vol 2, pp. 335–355, 1973.
3. D. C. Luckham, N. Suzuki. Verification of array, record, and pointer operations in Pascal. *ACM Transactions on Programming Languages and Systems*, 1(2), pp. 226–244, October 1979.
4. N. Wirth. The programming language Pascal. *Acta Informatica*, Vol 1(1), pp. 35–63, 1971.

8

Annotation of the Hidden Parts of Packages

Topics:

- *modified type annotations;*
- *annotation of hidden type definitions;*
- *stability constraints, application to abstract types;*
- *Anna model of package states, annotation of package states, package state stability;*
- *annotation of hidden subprogram bodies;*
- *consistency of package implementations;*
- *packages as types.*

Let us assume that at a particular stage in the design of the program, an Anna specification of an Ada package has been constructed. At some later stage it will be necessary to construct a hidden part (i. e., an Ada package private part and body) that satisfies this visible specification. When faced with this situation, a number of questions immediately come to mind.

- What kinds of annotations are useful in documenting a package hidden part?
- How are the hidden annotations related to the visible ones?
- Can the visible specification be used as an implementation plan to guide the construction of a hidden part that satisfies it?

These three questions are each the subject of a separate chapter. This chapter describes the special annotations for package hidden parts and the predefined structure of the Anna package state type. Chapters 9 and 10 describe a methodology for implementing package hidden parts so that they are consistent with their visible specifications. Chapter 9 describes how to define the relationship between visible specifications and the package hidden part. This is called *interpreting* the visible specifications. Interpretation is possible only if the package hidden part has adequate annotations, which are also described in Chapter 9. Chapter 10 outlines processes for implementing a package hidden part using a package specification as a guide.

Let us start by listing the special features in Anna for annotating package hidden parts. First of all, there is a new kind of type annotation, called a *modified type annotation*. Its main purpose is to express an important property of the hidden part of many packages called *stability*. Secondly, the Anna package state type has a predefined hidden structure. It is defined by an implicit virtual full declaration of the package state type as a record within the hidden part of the package. This defines the semantics of Anna package states in a natural way that is compatible with Ada language rules. Type annotations, including modified ones, may be applied to this implicit state type declaration — even though the declaration is implicit and does not appear syntactically in the package. Thirdly, the hidden subprogram annotations of a subprogram body are required to be logically consistent with the visible annotations of the corresponding subprogram specification. Essentially, requiring *logical consistency* between visible and hidden subprogram annotations is an Anna rule that generalizes the Ada rule requiring *syntactic conformance* between visible and hidden subprogram specifications. We will see that requiring logical consistency has practical repercussions on how we annotate package bodies.

The reader should review Section 4.1 on annotations and package structure. Recall that annotations in the visible part of a package are visible both outside the package and in the hidden part. To the user, visible annotations specify how to call the package operations and what results to expect (Chapter 4). To the implementor of the hidden part, the visible annotations are constraints. For example, an annotation of a visible subprogram declaration constrains the hidden subprogram body. Figure 8.1 shows the various levels of annotations in a simple package — one without nested packages. Note that the Ada private part is pictured as part of the package body.

Annotation of a package hidden part may be undertaken with various goals in mind. The simplest goal is to document properties of the implementation that are not specified in the visible part — the so-called "implementation details." Generally, a package specification will leave the implementor a great deal of freedom to choose data structures and algorithms. These choices are made not only to satisfy the visible specifications, but also to satisfy various aspects of efficient execution, such as timing and storage allocation, which are often not mentioned in the visible specification. The first goal, therefore, is to specify the additional properties with annotations in the hidden part of the package. Examples of such annotations are given in this chapter. Consistency between the hidden part and all of the annotations that apply to it — both visible and hidden — can be checked by runtime checking methods. This is discussed in Section 8.4.

A more ambitious goal is to give hidden annotations that are sufficient to enable consistency between specification and hidden part to be established by proof methods. Towards this goal, an important concept is *interpretation* of visible specifications. An *interpretation* of a visible specification is a set of constraints on the hidden types, objects, and subprogram bodies of a package that imply consistency. Since a visible specification cannot refer to hidden details, an interpretation of it is not usually immediately obvious but must be constructed.

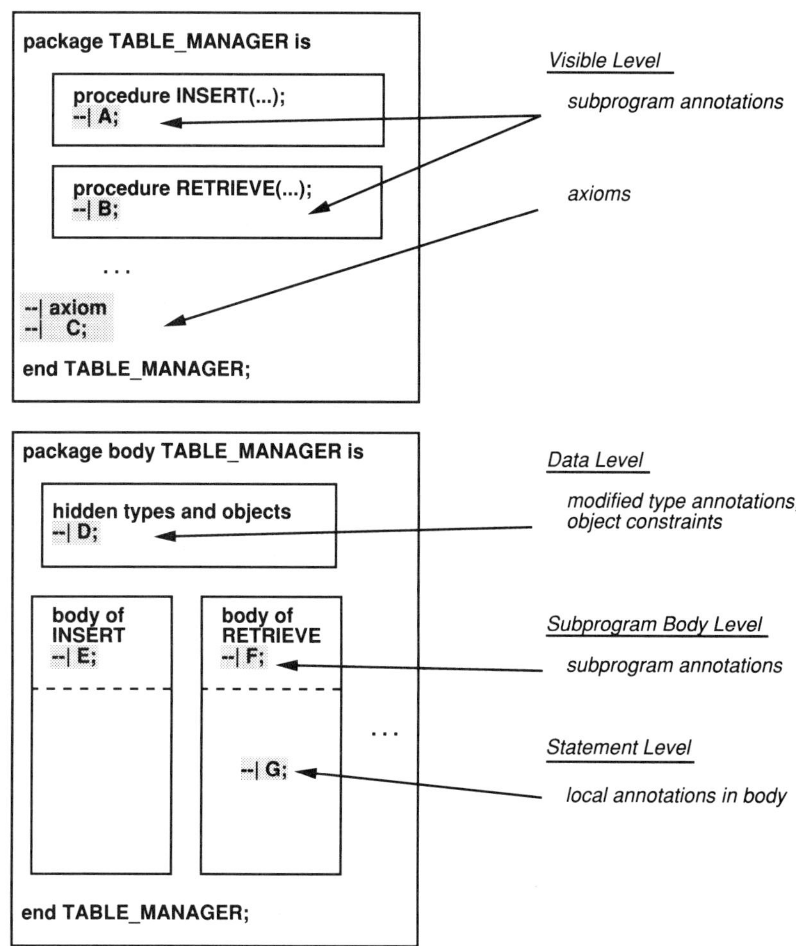

FIGURE 8.1. Levels of annotations.

Generally speaking, an interpretation of an Anna package specification can be constructed from a combination of two things: (1) the Ada full type definitions of private types together with their Anna constraints (this includes the predefined Anna package state type) and (2) hidden annotations of the basic functions of the specification. Chapter 9 is devoted to illustrating the use of hidden annotations to compute an interpretation of a visible specification. Chapter 10 shows how an interpretation can be used to guide the implementation of a package body.

8.1 Modified Type Annotations

Modified type annotations apply to types and subtypes that are declared in the visible part of a package. They constrain the values of a type, but permit variables of the type to have values that violate the constraint temporarily. Violations may occur only during computations of subprograms of the package. This kind of relaxed constraint is useful for annotating private types of a package, and in particular the state type of a package.

A *modified type annotation* is written exactly as a normal type annotation except that it is prefaced by the reserved words **in out**:

```
     type T is ... ;
--|     where in out X : T => C(X);
```

A modified type annotation may be applied to a type only if that type has a visible declaration in a package specification. Remember that private types have separate visible and hidden declarations, so a modified type annotation can be used to constrain a visible type declaration of a package, a hidden full declaration of a private type, or a package state type. The modifier notation **in out** is used to indicate that constraint C (X) must hold whenever entering and leaving the package body.

The domain of values of the type is constrained by a modified type annotation exactly as if the annotation was a normal type constraint. However, while the normal type annotation

```
     type T is ... ;
--|     where X : T => C(X);
```

requires objects of type T to have values satisfying C at every observable state, a modified type annotation,

```
     package P is
       ...
       type T is ... ;
--|       where in out X : T => C(X);
       ...
     end P;
```

requires the constraint to be satisfied only at the states when the thread of control is outside of the package. This includes the states when a subprogram of P is called, when its computation terminates normally, and also when the sequence of statements in the body of P terminates normally (at the elaboration of P). The constraint is not required to hold when an exception is propagated by a package subprogram.[1]

---

[1]Propagation annotations can be used to constrain values of the type when exceptions are propagated out of the package.

Example: A modified type constraint applied to buffers.

```
generic
   type ITEM is private;
   MAX : POSITIVE;
package BUFFER_MANAGER is

   type BUFFER is private;
   procedure READ(B : in out BUFFER; X : out ITEM);
   procedure WRITE(B : in out BUFFER; X : ITEM);
   ... ;                          -- Other operations are omitted.

private

   type STORE is array (1 .. MAX) of ITEM;
   type BUFFER is
      record
         S : STORE;
         IN_PTR, OUT_PTR, LENGTH : NATURAL := 0;
      end record;
--|   where in out B : BUFFER =>
--|      B.IN_PTR = (B.OUT_PTR+B.LENGTH) mod MAX;

end BUFFER_MANAGER;
```

Commentary

The record type that implements buffers contains an array, the length of the buffer, and components IN_PTR and OUT_PTR, which are the indices of the last and first items of the buffer. The modified annotation places a constraint on buffer records. It defines those records that are "stable buffers." A buffer record must be stable in every observable state when control is outside the package. The constraint is not required to hold during a package operation on a buffer. Suppose a buffer B is passed as a parameter to operation READ, for example. READ will increment B.OUT_PTR, decrement B.LENGTH, and finally return B.S(OUT_PTR). Each change to the record can be made without having to satisfy the constraint. When all the changes have been made and operation READ terminates, the record must be a stable buffer. Once control is outside the package, B remains stable. So the next time a package operation receives it as an **in** value, it can assume that the buffer record is stable.

In the BUFFER_MANAGER example, the modified type annotation constrains the hidden record structure of BUFFERs. We can reason by induction on the number of operations on a BUFFER that its implementation as a record is always stable between operations, provided an operation on it did not terminate by propagating an exception. In exceptional situations we have a choice. Either we allow the BUFFER_MANAGER to destroy a buffer, in which case buffers are stable only in the absence of exceptions, or we can program the operations to maintain stability when they propagate exceptions. If we choose the latter, we can specify that the operations maintain stability when they propagate exceptions by weak propagation annotations on their bodies with the stability constraint as the propagation condition. An inductive proof of stability can then be extended to apply in case of exception propagation.

The modified type annotation does not constrain exceptional behavior, so it can be used to specify packages in either case — those that work only for normal termination and those that also work for abnormal termination.

8.1.1 Stability constraints

A property of a package is *stable* if it holds whenever any operation of the package terminates normally but it need not hold during the computation of an operation. A stability constraint, namely a constraint that specifies a stable property, is precisely expressed by a modified type annotation, as we saw in the previous BUFFER_MANAGER example.

An important class of packages whose implementation usually involves stability of data is the class of *abstract type packages*. Typical examples are packages defining complex numbers, sets, lists, queues, and trees. An abstract type package binds together a type name and the operations on that type and hides its implementation. The data type is declared as a private or limited private type, together with the appropriate operations. Generally, the state of this kind of package is trivial. A user may declare objects of the type and apply the package operations to them. Calls to the operations appear to the user as "atomic," just like the standard assignment operation.

The hidden part of an abstract type package contains a full declaration for the type and the bodies of the operations. The hidden type declarations define the data structure representation for the type. This data structure usually must satisfy a stability constraint in order for the hidden bodies of the operations to work correctly.

Modified type annotations not only express stability, they are useful in the top-down planning of implementations of packages such as abstract types.

Consider package SETS that is specified in Section 5.4. Recall that the private part was omitted from the Anna specification. Abstract type SET may be represented by many different structures, for example by an *ordered* linked list or a *balanced* binary tree. Properties like *orderedness* and *balanced* must be stable. An operation on a set, such as adding or deleting an element, may temporarily disturb the *orderedness* or *balance* of the representation. But the property must be restored upon termination of the operation.

The first step towards implementing the SETSi package specification is to define a data representation for type SET. At this point, it is important to specify all the assumptions about the data that will be required for the correct functioning of each of the subprogram bodies. This will be expressed by a modified type annotation.

- **Guideline: Planning with stability constraints.**

  The full definition of a private type should have a modified type annotation that expresses all assumptions made by package operations about the representation of values of the type.

The modified type annotation behaves like a global **in** and **out** annotation on all operations. So it can be used as a "global reminder" when each individual subprogram body is being implemented. (It is all too easy, when implementing one body, to forget to leave data in a condition that is assumed by another body.)

Example: *Sets package (from Section 5.4) – private part with annotations.*

```
        generic
            type ELEM is private;
        package SETS is

            type SET is limited private;

--          Basic concepts.
            function IS_MEMBER(E : ELEM; S : SET)
            return BOOLEAN;
            function IS_FULL(S : SET) return BOOLEAN;
            function CARDINALITY(S : SET) return NATURAL;

--          Exceptions and constants.
            SET_FULL : exception;
            NULL_SET : constant SET;

--          Relations on sets.
            package SET_EQUAL is
                function "=" (S, T : SET) return BOOLEAN;
--|                 where return (for all E : ELEM =>
--|                     IS_MEMBER(E, S) ↔ IS_MEMBER(E, T));
            end SET_EQUAL;

            function IS_EMPTY(X : SET) return BOOLEAN;
--|           where return (for all E : ELEM =>
--|                                           not IS_MEMBER(E, X));
```

```
--        Set operations.
          procedure ADD(E : in ELEM; S : in out SET);
--|         where
--|             IS_FULL(S) => raise SET_FULL,
--|             out (for all U : ELEM => IS_MEMBER(U, S) ↔
--|                                   U = E or IS_MEMBER(U, in S));

          procedure REMOVE(E : in ELEM; S : in out SET);
--|         where
--|             out (for all U : ELEM => IS_MEMBER(U, S) ↔
--|                               IS_MEMBER(U, in S) and U /= E);

          function "+" (X, Y : SET) return SET;
--|         where
--|             raise SET_FULL,
--|             return Z : SET =>
--|                 (for all U : ELEM => IS_MEMBER(U, Z) ↔
--|                        IS_MEMBER(U, X) or IS_MEMBER(U, Y));

          function "–" (X, Y : SET) return SET;
--|         where
--|             return Z : SET =>
--|                 (for all U : ELEM => IS_MEMBER(U, Z) ↔
--|                 IS_MEMBER(U, X) and not IS_MEMBER(U, Y));

                  ...
--        Other set operations and axioms are omitted, see Section 5.4.

      private                                    -- Beginning of hidden part.

          MAX_SET_SIZE : POSITIVE := 500;
          subtype ELEM_RANGE is POSITIVE
              range 1 .. MAX_SET_SIZE;
          type ELEM_ARRAY is array (ELEM_RANGE) of ELEM;

          type SET_REC is
              record
                  LAST_ELEM : ELEM_RANGE;
                  ELEMENTS  : ELEM_ARRAY;
              end record;
--|               where in out (S : SET_REC =>
--|                   (for all I, J : 1 .. S.LAST_ELEM =>
--|                I /= J → S.ELEMENTS(I) /= S.ELEMENTS(J)));

          type SET is access SET_REC;
--|           where in out (S : SET =>
--|               (S /= null → S.LAST_ELEM'DEFINED and
--|                   (for all I : 1 .. S.LAST_ELEM =>
--|                                    S.ELEMENTS(I)'DEFINED));

          NULL_SET : constant SET := null;

      end SETS;
```

Commentary

There is one "Adaism" in this example, which we discuss before getting down to the real issues, namely the purpose of the nested package SET_EQUAL. We want to declare an abstract "=" on SETs. Our intention is to provide a hidden definition of the abstract "=" in terms of the Ada predefined "=" operation on the type that implements SET in the hidden part of the package. If we just declared the abstract "=" as an operation of package SETS it would hide the predefined "=" on the implementation type. Nesting it as an operation of a "dummy" package SET_EQUAL makes both "=" operations visible in the hidden part.

Skim over the type declarations in the private part. A value of abstract type SET is *represented* by a record consisting of an array and an integer that gives the number of elements in the set. Let us call this a *set record.*

Abstract type SET is *implemented* by an access type that designates set records. (Such implementation decisions are routinely made to ensure that abstract SET parameters are passed by reference, but that does not concern us here.)

Now let us discuss the constraints. Our first constraint is that the representation of a set must contain only one copy of an element. This is expressed by the type constraint on the array component of SET_REC. It is unnecessary to require this constraint during the processing of set values by the set operations, and to do so may be overly restrictive. Therefore the type constraint is modified by **in out**. When an operation is called, an input set record may be assumed to satisfy the constraint, and it must again satisfy it whenever that operation terminates normally.

The global role of this annotation can be clearly seen. It will be an important **out** constraint for operations that extend a set, such as ADD and "+", since it requires that they check to see if a supposed "new" element is already in the set representation before adding it. It will be a simplifying **in** assumption for operations that reduce a set, such as REMOVE and "−", since it implies that only one copy of an element need be removed from a set representation.

Note that a linear ordering operator on the generic type of the elements could have been a second generic (function) parameter of the sets package. Sets could then have been represented by *ordered* arrays, which would greatly improve the efficiency of the membership and equality operators. The *ordered* requirement would be a second constraint expressed by the modified annotation of SET_REC.

The second modified type annotation constrains access type SET. It requires all non-null access values of that type to designate set records whose components have defined values. Taken in conjunction with the Ada type definitions, this implies that an empty set can only be represented by **null**. This is an important **out** constraint to be satisfied by all operations that reduce sets. If a set is reduced to the empty set, say by deleting an element, its access pointer must be assigned **null**.

The two modified type constraints in this example could be combined and placed on the access type to express an equivalent constraint.

Although SET is *implemented* by an access type, equality must be defined as a function of the structure that *represents* the set. In this example, operator "=" is declared, nested in SET_EQUAL for visibility reasons given above. Its body will appear in the package body of SETS. The flexibility to do this can only be achieved (in the present version of Ada [Ada83]) if SET is specified as a **limited private** type. For only then do we have the ability to define an Ada equality operator for values of type SET. Equality of the access type values (which is what would be imposed if the type was only **private**) would be incorrect, as would equality on record type SET_REC. Anna requires all equality operators to satisfy the equality axioms (Section 4.5).

Last remark: this example elicits debate at the level of Ada style. Some people feel that MAX_SET_SIZE and its initial value should be generic parameters (Chapter 6). If we did this, we would need to specify the meaning of the new generic parameters (small exercise for reader). In our opinion, the use of 500 is a detail of a particular implementation of IS_FULL.

In this example we have illustrated the use of modified type annotations in the Ada private part. Other kinds of annotations may also be useful in a private part. These might include annotations of subprogram declarations, unmodified type annotations, and object constraints. Their scope is the hidden part of the package. Also, modified type annotations can be used in the Ada package body, usually to constrain the package state type.[2]

8.1.2 Changing values of composite types

Modified type annotations provide an elegant solution to the updating problem for composite types that is discussed in Section 1.10. The problem is to change values of a composite type efficiently when the type is subject

---

[2]An example is given later.

to an unmodified constraint relating two or more of its components. Ideally, one would like to "turn off" the constraint check while an updating operation is in progress by using a modified constraint instead.

To do this, the type and all the operations that change its values must be encapsulated in a package. The unmodified type annotation is replaced by a modified one with an identical constraint. The goal is to make the type and the operations visible, but, at the same time, to ensure that updating of values is always done in the package body.

Usually, the type will be declared as a private type, and the unmodified type annotation will be replaced by a hidden modified one on the full type declaration, as in our previous examples. On the other hand, if the type is not private, and its structure is visible, the modified annotation will also be visible. So the constraint will apply "unmodified" to all operations on values of the type performed outside the package. Operations that make component-at-a-time changes must be in the Ada package body.

The constrained interval type in Section 1.10 can be encapsulated as follows.

Example: *Manipulating the interval type.*

```
    package REAL_INTERVAL_OPS is

        type INTERVAL is private;
        function LEFT_END (X : INTERVAL) return REAL;
        function RIGHT_END (X : INTERVAL) return REAL;
        procedure UPDATE (X : in out INTERVAL;
                          LEFT, RIGHT : REAL);

--| axiom
--|     for all I : INTERVAL => LEFT_END (I) ≤ RIGHT_END (I),
        ... ;        -- Other axioms relating the operations are omitted.

    private

        type INTERVAL is
            record
                LEFT_POINT, RIGHT_POINT : REAL;
            end record;
--|         where in out X : INTERVAL =>
--|                          X.LEFT_POINT ≤ X.RIGHT_POINT;

    end REAL_INTERVAL_OPS;
```

Commentary

The interval type declaration of Section 1.10 has been encapsulated in a package. The package axiom promises to the outside world that the left end of an interval is at most its right end. The modified type annotation permits operation UPDATE to vi-

olate this ordering temporarily. It can do component-at-a-time updates.
In the next section we see that, in this example, the modified type annotation is one formulation (within the package hidden part) of the constraint imposed on the package hidden part by the axiom.

8.1.3 Semantics of modified type annotations *

In this section, we repeat the definition of modified type annotations in more detail so that we can see what constraints apply to recursive package operations and how runtime checking works.[3]

Suppose the modified type annotation is in the visible part of a package P:

```
         package P is
            type T is ...;
--|            where in out X : T => C(X);
            procedure Q(A : in out T);
               ...
         end P;
```

For discussion, we divide the scope of T into two parts: (1) the outside part — i. e., any point in its scope outside of P or in the visible part of P, and (2) the hidden part of P.

In the outside part of its scope, the modified constraint has the same meaning as if it were an ordinary type annotation — i. e., the value of any object (or parameter) of type T in the outside part must satisfy the constraint C in any observable state.

In the hidden part of its scope, we can give a precise definition of the meaning of a modified type annotation by defining a set of subprogram and object annotations that impose an equivalent constraint on the hidden part.

Consider a typical example where the modified type annotation is in the hidden part of the scope: type T is private, and the modified annotation constrains a hidden full declaration of T in the private part.

```
package P is
   type T is private;
   procedure Q(A : in out T);
      ...
```

[3]The subsection can be skipped.

```
     private
         type T is ... ;
--|          where in out X : T => C(X);
         ...
     end P;
```

Let Q be a visible subprogram of package P. The effect of the modified annotation on computations of Q is equivalent to additional hidden **in** and **out** annotations on the body of Q that require each parameter and global variable of Q of type T to satisfy C. For example,

```
     package body P is
         X : T;

         procedure Q(A : in out T)
--|          where
--|              in (C(A)),
--|              in (C(X)),
--|              out C(A),
--|              out C(X),
--|                  ...            -- Other annotations of the body of Q.
         is ... end Q;               -- Body of Q changes both A and X.
         ...
     end P;
```

Also, it has the effect of placing a result annotation on the bodies of visible functions that return values of type T and an **out** annotation on the sequence of statements of the package body, for each variable of type T that may be affected when the body is elaborated.[4]

There can be references in the hidden part of the scope to global variables of type T situated in the outside part, or calls to outside subprograms with parameters of type T (e. g., procedure Q above could be recursive). These cases are dealt with as follows. A subprogram body that refers to an outside global variable must satisfy **in** and **out** subprogram annotations on that global variable as described above for global variables in general. However, if the modified annotation is in the outside part of the scope then the normal type constraint on the outside scope will make these annotations unnecessary. A call in the hidden part to a visible subprogram of P must satisfy the **in** annotations of the body of that visible subprogram, so values of type T passed at a hidden call to an outside subprogram must be stable.

Runtime checking of a modified type annotation involves checking the outside part of its scope in exactly the same way as an ordinary type annotation is checked; but only the equivalent set of object and subprogram annotations are checked in the hidden part.

---

[4]These additional annotations must also be added to the bodies of visible subprograms that belong to other packages nested in P.

8.2 Representation of Package States

The Anna package attributes *state type* and *current state* provide a means of using the concept of "package state" in the visible specification. The state type is treated as an Ada private type, except that "=" can be redefined. The current state is treated as a virtual function that returns a value of the state type.[5]

Anna specifies an implicit virtual full type declaration for the state type as a record inside the package hidden part and a position of that declaration. Also, an implicit virtual function body for the current state attribute is specified that returns the aggregate of hidden values that comprise the current state. These implicit declarations allow us to describe: (1) rules for using state types that are analogous to the Ada rules for using private types, and (2) ways of specifying the hidden properties of states by using type and modified type annotations.

- **Representation of Anna package state types**

  A package state type is represented in the Ada package body as a record type with components whose values are the values of all the hidden objects [6] *in the package.*

A simple example of a package with a nontrivial state is the table manager package studied in Chapter 4 (see Section 4.4). This package is, in essence, a composite object for storing data. When a package body is constructed, the structure of the state type and the components of the current state are determined automatically. Here is a possible body for table manager showing the Anna representations.

Example: *Structure of the state of a table manager package body.*

```
-- Suppose the table manager package body is implemented as follows:

      package body TABLE_MANAGER is

          type TABLE_TYPE is array (0 .. 1000) of ITEM;
          TABLE : TABLE_TYPE;
          LAST_ITEM : INTEGER := -1;

--:       function FULL return BOOLEAN;
          ...                                                -- Annotations.
--:       function MEMBER(X : ITEM) return BOOLEAN;
          ...                                                -- Annotations.
```

[5]See Section 4.6.

[6]Remember this includes variables, states of packages, and access type collections.

```
        procedure INSERT (NEW_ITEM : in ITEM)
           is ... end INSERT;

        procedure RETRIEVE (FIRST_ITEM : out ITEM)
           is ... end RETRIEVE;

     end TABLE_MANAGER;

-- Then the state type of table manager is represented as if it had a full decla-
-- ration:

--:      type TABLE_MANAGER'TYPE is
--:         record
--:            TABLE : TABLE_TYPE;
--:            LAST_ITEM : INTEGER := -1;
--:         end record;


-- The current state attribute is represented as if it had a virtual function body
-- that returns a record aggregate value:

--:      function TABLE_MANAGER'STATE
--:      return TABLE_MANAGER'TYPE
--|         where return TABLE_MANAGER'TYPE'
--|                                          (TABLE, LAST_ITEM);
--:      is
--:      begin
--:         return TABLE_MANAGER'TYPE' (TABLE, LAST_ITEM);
--:      end;

-- The initial state attribute is represented as having the record aggregate value:

         TABLE_MANAGER'TYPE' (INITIAL_TABLE, -1)

-- Where INITIAL_TABLE is an arbitrary array value.
```

Commentary

The state type is represented as a record type whose components correspond in name and type to the hidden Anna objects. The current state is represented as a function that returns the current record aggregate value of the state. The initial state is the record aggregate of initial component values, if they exist. In this example, TABLE has no initial value, so the name INITIAL_TABLE is introduced to denote an arbitrary value for it.

It should be emphasized that the implicit virtual declarations defining the state type and current state representations are completely determined once the package body is given. Different bodies for the same package will usually have different representations of "state."

8.2.1 RESTRICTIONS ON USING PACKAGE STATES *

The use of package state attributes within the package is subject to restrictions, some of which were described in Section 4.6.1. There are two reasons for these restrictions:

1. The state concept must fit into the Ada language rules for packages. This means, for example, that the rules for *using* the state attributes must not allow the state to be used in a computation — i. e., used in a way that requires it to have a value — before the package body is elaborated.
2. The definition of a package state type must not be circular.

The Ada rules for using private types ([Ada83], 7.4.1(4)) are easily extended to define the use of 'TYPE, 'STATE, and 'INITIAL in virtual text and annotations. Here we describe how the Anna restrictions are related to the Ada restrictions.

Anna postulates the existence of two implicit type declarations for the package state type. The first is a private type, and the second is a corresponding full type declaration.

For a package P, the first implicit declaration is a private type declaration of P'TYPE at the beginning of the package visible part. The visibility of P'TYPE and the restrictions governing its use in virtual text follow those for an Ada private type declared at that position ([Ada83], 7.4.1). In the *visible part* of P, the name P'TYPE can only occur in virtual text in a deferred constant declaration, a type or subtype declaration, a subprogram specification, and an entry declaration. In annotations its use as a type name is not restricted, e. g., it may be used in a quantifier declaration in an axiom.

The second implicit declaration is a full type declaration for P'TYPE in the *hidden part* of P. This is a record type having a component corresponding to each actual and virtual object declared in the hidden part of P. Each component has the same type and name as the corresponding object. The position of this full type declaration is immediately following all the hidden object declarations in P, and is therefore usually in the Ada body of P rather than in the private part. After that position, the full type declaration is considered to be visible.

In the *hidden part* of P, the use of P'TYPE in virtual text is even more restricted than an Ada private type. In virtual text, it may be used only in a subprogram specification or an entry declaration. It may not be used in type or object declarations — if this were allowed, objects of the state type could become part of the state, an obvious circularity. These restrictions prevent circular record type definitions in the implicit full declaration of the state type. The use of P'TYPE as a type name in annotations is not restricted.

Similarly, Anna assumes the existence of implicit function and function body declarations for the current state attribute. The function declaration is assumed to follow immediately the implicit private declaration of the state type. Then, restrictions on using the current state of a package follow from Ada rules by treating P'STATE as a visible virtual function returning values of the state type. The most important restriction is that P'STATE may not be called before the package body of P is elaborated. A corresponding implicit virtual function body simply returns the current record aggregate representing the state.

P'INITIAL is treated as having an implicit deferred constant declaration and a corresponding full declaration in the hidden part. P'INITIAL may not be used in computing a virtual expression until the body of P is elaborated.

Three points about the Anna representation of states should be emphasized. First, the components of the package state include not only "objects" in the Ada sense, but also collections associated with hidden access types and states of packages nested in P. Second, the representation assumes that the implicit full declaration is placed in the basic declarations of the hidden part, *after* all declarations of hidden "objects." This requires a minor relaxation of the Ada rules for positioning full type declarations of private types, since in general it will be in the body rather than in the private part. Also, we note that Anna'87 assumes the local packages are always declared as basic declarations, so that the full state type declaration can be a basic item (Anna'87, 7.7.1). It is reasonable to delete this assumption and allow the state type to be a later declarative item, since Ada allows some basic declarations to occur after later declarative items — task objects and anonymous task types can be later declarative items in Ada. Third, remember that the virtual type and function declarations for P'TYPE, P'STATE, and P'INITIAL are *implicit*. Their purpose is to define the rules of use of these attributes; they do not actually exist in the text of P.

Example: *Implicit type declarations defining the use of a package state type.*

```
    package P is
--:     type P'TYPE is private;   -- Implicit virtual type declaration.
--:     function P'STATE return P'TYPE;          -- Implicit virtual
        ...                                              -- function.

    private
        X : T1;            -- An object declaration in the private part.
    end P;

    package body P is
```

```
      type T2 is access T1;              -- A hidden access type.
      Y : T3;                            -- Another hidden object.
      package Q is      -- A package Q nested in the body of P.
        ...
      end Q;                    -- Q is the last object declaration.

--:   type P'TYPE is         -- Implicit virtual full type declaration.
--:      record
--:         X  : T1;
--:         T2 : T2'COLLECTION'TYPE;
--:         Y  : T3;
--:         Q  : Q'TYPE;
--:      end record;

--     Implicit current state function.
--:   function P'STATE return P'TYPE is
--:   begin
--:      return P'TYPE' (X, T2'COLLECTION'STATE,
--:                      Y, Q'STATE);
--:   end;
      ...     -- Other declarations and sequence of statements of P.

      end P;
```

Commentary

The implicit full type declaration is placed immediately after all the local objects that comprise the state of P. That is, it is placed immediately after the declarations of X and Y, the local collection, T2'COLLECTION, and the local package Q.

From this position until the end of the package body, the implicit full declaration is considered visible. Also, the standard Ada rules for private types apply to the state type. If virtual variables of the state type (e. g., parameters of a virtual subprogram) appear where this declaration is visible, their components are visible and the standard record operations can be performed on them. This facility is important, for example, in redefining equality between states by a virtual body for "=" (see example in Section 9.1).

We have also shown an implicit body for the current state function that returns the record aggregate value of the current state of the package. After the body of P is elaborated, expressions containing P'STATE can be evaluated.

8.2.2 Hidden State Property

The Anna representation of package state satisfies the *hidden state* property described in Section 4.6. That is, an Anna package state has components corresponding only to the hidden objects of the package.

If an Ada package is to be consistent with the Anna state representation, it must be restricted in some way, since Ada visibility rules allow package bodies to reference global variables. The set of those objects (Anna sense) whose values or states can influence the behavior of the Ada package operations (including elaboration of its body) must be hidden.

There are many ways to formulate sufficient restrictions that imply consistency with the hidden state property. Perhaps the simplest restriction (repeating Section 4.4) is that a package body must not refer to any objects declared outside of the body whose values can change. This disallows use of outside variables, access types, or nongeneric packages whose states are not constant. It does allow use of outside constants and types (except access types), generic units, and outside packages with trivial states such as package STANDARD or a rational numbers package. It would prohibit use of an outside Symbol_Table — a generic symbol table must be instantiated within the body.

If an Ada package does not satisfy the hidden state property, it can still be specified using visible annotations (constraints on types, objects, and subprograms, and also axioms), but the Anna package state attributes should not be used.

Summary

The concept of an abstract package state is simple and intuitive. The Anna representation of it as a record type allows us (1) to define rules for using the package attributes that follow from the Ada rules for private types and (2) to enable construction of the hidden constraints corresponding to visible specifications that use these attributes.

8.3 Annotation of Hidden Package States

There are two ways in Anna to specify local properties of a package state in the body of the package. The first is by declarative object constraints on the variables that make up the state. The second is by a type constraint on the package state type.

Example: Table manager body with constraints on its variables.

```
    package body TABLE_MANAGER is

        type TABLE_TYPE is array (0 .. 1000) of ITEM;
        TABLE : TABLE_TYPE;
        LAST_ITEM : INTEGER := -1;

--|      for all I, J : 0 .. LAST_ITEM =>
--|          I < J → TABLE(I) /= TABLE(J) and
--|                  TABLE(I).PRIORITY <= TABLE(J).PRIORITY;
```

```
      ...                                          -- Virtual functions.

      procedure INSERT (NEW_ITEM : in ITEM)
      is
         ...
      end INSERT;

      procedure RETRIEVE (FIRST_ITEM : out ITEM)
      is
         ...
      end RETRIEVE;

   end TABLE_MANAGER;
```

Commentary

The variables TABLE and LAST_ITEM that make up the state are specified to satisfy an object constraint. The values of the two variables are related by the constraint. The constraint itself requires (1) no duplication of items and (2) items to be ordered by their priority.

This constraint is not implied by the package specification. It expresses properties of the local data that concern the implementation. These properties can be assumed by procedures INSERT and REMOVE. The constraint applies to every observable computation state in its scope. So each operation performed by the procedures on the local data must satisfy it. There is little room for efficient updating.

Note that this object annotation constrains only the actual variables in the package body. It constrains the current state value, but not the state type. Consequently, it would be possible to declare a virtual variable of the state type, TABLE_MANAGER'TYPE, and assign to it an aggregate value that contains duplicate items in the TABLE component.

The second method of annotating hidden states is supported by a special feature. Anna allows the use of a type or modified type annotation to constrain the implicit full declaration of the state type. A type annotation constraining P'TYPE may appear in the hidden declarative part of P, without the type declaration being present. It contains the implicit full declaration of P'TYPE, and must be placed at a position where that declaration could occur. This is the only situation in which a type annotation may be used without a type declaration.

This is how such an annotation would look in the schematic example of the previous section.

Example: *Annotation of the implicit full declaration of a package state type.*

```
--   Refer to the example in Section 8.2.1.
     package body P is       -- Basic declarations in the body of P.
        type T2 is access T1;                       -- An access type.
        Y : T3;                                  -- Another hidden object.
        package Q is       -- A package Q nested in the body of P.
           ...
        end Q;

--|     where Z : P'TYPE => C(Z.X, Z.T2, Z.Y, Z.Q);

        ...      -- Other declarations and sequence of statements of P.

     end P;
```

Commentary

The state type annotation is placed in the position where the implicit full declaration occurs — immediately after all the local objects that comprise the state of P. It constrains all values of the state type. In particular, record aggregates of the form,

P'TYPE'(X, T2'COLLECTION'STATE, Y, Q'STATE)

must obey the constraint C since they are values of the state type. These aggregates are the values returned by the current state attribute, P'STATE. Therefore, the values of the variables X and Y, and the states Q'STATE and T2'COLLECTION'STATE must always *simultaneously* satisfy C whenever the package state of P can be observed — i. e., whenever P'STATE can be called.

Anna state type annotations allow us to express *stability* constraints on the state — a *modified* annotation of the state type is used.

Example: *Table manager body with a modified annotation of its state type.*

```
package body TABLE_MANAGER is

   type TABLE_TYPE is array (0 .. 1000) of ITEM;
   TABLE : TABLE_TYPE;
   LAST_ITEM : INTEGER := -1;
```

```
--| where
--|    in out  X : TABLE_MANAGER'TYPE =>
--|       for all; I, J : 0 .. X.LAST_ITEM =>
--|          I < J → X.TABLE(I) /= X.TABLE(J) and
--|          X.TABLE(I).PRIORITY <= X.TABLE(J).PRIORITY;

         ... -- Virtual functions INSERT and RETRIEVE.

   end TABLE_MANAGER;
```

Commentary

The modified type annotation applies to the implicit state type declaration for table manager shown in Section 8.2. Values of variables, subprogram parameters, and functions must satisfy the constraint, except where it is relaxed because it is modified. Such values are record aggregates. In particular, values of the current state function attribute TABLE_MANAGER'STATE are constrained. Since these values are aggregates of the form TABLE_MANAGER'(TABLE, LAST_ITEM), variables TABLE and LAST_ITEM are also constrained.

The stability type constraint allows INSERT and RETRIEVE to change variables TABLE and LAST_ITEM temporarily. During their computations, the components of TABLE within the quantified range 0 .. LAST_ITEM might not be in order of priority, or might be duplicated. When the computations terminate, TABLE and LAST_ITEM must again be the components of a stable state. INSERT and RETRIEVE can also assume, when they are called, that the state will be stable because the data are hidden and they are the only ones that can alter it.

8.4 Annotation of Package Subprogram Bodies

The main question to be decided when annotating a package body is what properties of the entities in the body should be expressed by annotations. When annotating hidden subprogram bodies we should remember two guidelines.

- **Guideline: Annotations of package subprogram bodies.**

  Annotations of subprogram bodies in the body of a package should document properties that depend on the hidden data representation and are not obvious consequences of the visible specifications.

We need not repeat the visible specifications, but we do need to say "what's new" about the algorithms implemented in the package body. To support this idea, Anna does not require that the visible annotations of a package subprogram be repeated for the body of that subprogram. The conformance rule that applies generally to annotations of subprogram specifications and their bodies is not required for package operations. The only requirement imposed is that the visible and hidden annotations be logically consistent.

- **Guideline: Consistency of visible and hidden subprogram annotations.**

  Annotations of a subprogram body in the body of a package should be consistent with the visible annotations of the subprogram declaration.

Consistency of visible and hidden annotations of a subprogram means that there must exist values of the subprogram parameters that satisfy the conjunction of the visible and hidden **in** conditions, and similarly there must exist values that satisfy the conjunction of the visible and hidden **out** conditions. The following example illustrates this point.

Example: Consistency of visible and hidden subprogram annotations.

```
    package P is
        procedure Q (X : in out T);
--|         where in (C (X)),
--|                 out D (X);
            ...
    end P;

    package body P is
        procedure Q (X : in out T)
--|         where
--                  The annotations C and D apply to the body of Q;
--                  they do not need to be repeated here.
--|                in (E (X)),
--|                out (F (X));
        is
            ...
    end P;
```

Commentary

The hidden annotations E and F should document hidden properties of the implementation. There is no need to repeat C or D for the body. However, E should be consistent with C; there should exist values V such that C (V) **and** E (V) is true. Similarly, D **and** F should be consistent. The subprogram body of Q may assume C **and** E as **in** conditions and must satisfy D **and** F as **out** conditions when it terminates normally.

The first step in the process of constructing a package hidden part is to choose the data representations for the private types and for the local data of the package body. At this stage, the hidden type and object constraints are defined. This will usually involve specifying stable properties.[7]

The second step is the implementation of the bodies of the package operations. Annotations of these bodies should specify hidden properties of their implementation and should provide formal explanation of their algorithms. Typically, these hidden annotations will employ techniques illustrated in Chapter 2, such as inductive assertions.

Below is an annotated body for package SETS. It assumes the hidden type definitions given in Section 8.1.1 that *represent* SETS by *set records*, together with the stability constraints. These constraints play the planning role suggested in the guideline of Section 8.1.1. They express globally in the hidden part the assumptions that each subprogram body can make about the data and must honor.

Example: *Sets package body with annotations.*

```
-- The sets package body.
   package body SETS is

--      Basic functions.
        function IS_MEMBER(E : ELEM; S : SET)
        return BOOLEAN
--|         where
--|             return S /= null and then
--|                 (exist I : 1 .. S.LAST_ELEM =>
--|                                         S.ELEMENTS(I) = E);
        is
        begin
            if S = null then
                return FALSE;
            end if;
            for I1 in 1 .. S.LAST_ELEM loop
                if S.ELEMENTS(I1) = E then
                    return TRUE;
                end if;
            end loop;
            return FALSE;
        end IS_MEMBER;

        function IS_FULL(S : SET) return BOOLEAN is
--|         where
--|             return S /= null
--|                 and then S.LAST_ELEM = MAX_SET_SIZE;
        begin
            return S /= null
                and then S.LAST_ELEM = MAX_SET_SIZE;
        end IS_FULL;
```

[7]See the guideline in Section 8.1.1.

```
        function CARDINALITY(S : SET) return NATURAL
--|        where
--|            return (if S /= null then 0
--|                                          else S.LAST_ELEM end if);
        is
        begin
           if S = null then
               return 0;
           else
               return S.LAST_ELEM;
           end if;
        end CARDINALITY;
--      End of basic functions.

        package SET_EQUAL is

           function "=" (S, T : SET) return BOOLEAN
           is
               ACCUMULATED_EQUAL, TEMP_EQUAL : BOOLEAN;
               S_INDEX, T_INDEX : NATURAL;
           begin
               if SETS."=" (S, null) or SETS."=" (T, null) then
                   return SETS."=" (S, null) and
                                                   SETS."=" (T, null);
               end if;
               ACCUMULATED_EQUAL :=
                   S.LAST_ELEM = T.LAST_ELEM;
               S_INDEX := 0;
               while ACCUMULATED_EQUAL and
                       S_INDEX < S.LAST_ELEM loop
                   TEMP_EQUAL := FALSE;
                   S_INDEX := S_INDEX+1;
                   T_INDEX := 0;
                   while not TEMP_EQUAL and
                           T_INDEX < T.LAST_ELEM loop
                       T_INDEX := T_INDEX+1;
                       TEMP_EQUAL := TEMP_EQUAL or
                           S.ELEMENTS(S_INDEX) =
                                       T.ELEMENTS(T_INDEX);
                   end loop;
                   ACCUMULATED_EQUAL :=
                      ACCUMULATED_EQUAL and TEMP_EQUAL;
--|              ACCUMULATED_EQUAL →
--|                 for all I : 1 .. S_INDEX =>
--|                           IS_MEMBER(S.ELEMENTS(I), T);
               end loop;
               return ACCUMULATED_EQUAL;
           end "=";

        end SET_EQUAL;
```

```
        function IS_EMPTY (X : SET) return BOOLEAN is
        begin
           return X = null;
        end IS_EMPTY;

--      Set constructors.
        procedure ADD (E : ELEM; S : in out SET)
--|        where
--|           out (in S = null → S =
--|                                     in SET'COLLECTION'NEXT),
--|           out (in S /= null → S = in S),
--|           out (for all T : SET =>
--|                                 T /= S → T.all = in T.all);
        is
           FOUND : BOOLEAN := FALSE;
        begin
           if S = null then
              S := new SET_REC;
              S.LAST_ELEM   := 1;
              S.ELEMENTS (1) := E;
           else
              for I1 in 1 .. S.LAST_ELEM loop
                 FOUND := S.ELEMENTS (I1) = E;
                 if FOUND then return; end if;
              end loop;
              if S.LAST_ELEM = ELEM_RANGE'LAST then
                 raise SET_FULL;
              else
                 S.LAST_ELEM := S.LAST_ELEM+1;
                 S.ELEMENTS (S.LAST_ELEM) := E;
              end if;
           end if;
        exception
           when STORAGE_ERROR => raise SET_FULL;
        end ADD;

        procedure REMOVE (E : ELEM; S : in out SET)
--|        where
--|           out (S /= in S or S /= null),
--|           out (for all T : SET =>
--|                                T /= S  → T.all = in T.all);
        is
           LOCATION : NATURAL := 0;
        begin
           if S /= null then
              for I1 in 1 .. S.LAST_ELEM loop
                 if S.ELEMENTS (I1) = E then
                    LOCATION := I1;
                 end if;
                 exit when LOCATION > 0;
              end loop;
```

```
            if LOCATION > 0 then
               if S.LAST_ELEM = 1 then
                  S := null;
               elsif LOCATION = S.LAST_ELEM then
                  S.LAST_ELEM := S.LAST_ELEM-1;
               else
                  S.ELEMENTS
                     (LOCATION .. S.LAST_ELEM-1) :=
                  S.ELEMENTS
                     (LOCATION+1 .. S.LAST_ELEM);
                  S.LAST_ELEM := S.LAST_ELEM-1;
               end if;
            end if;
         end if;
      end REMOVE;

      function "+" (X, Y : SET) return SET
--|      where
--|         return
--|            if X = null then Y
--|            elsif Y = null then X
--|            else in SET'COLLECTION'NEXT end if;
      is
         TEMP_SET : SET;
      begin
         if X = null then
            return Y;
         elsif Y = null then
            return X;
         else
            TEMP_SET : = new SET_REC'(X.all);
            for I1 in 1 .. Y.LAST_ELEM loop
               ADD(Y.ELEMENTS(I1), TEMP_SET);
            end loop;
            return TEMP_SET;
         end if;
      exception
         when STORAGE_ERROR => raise SET_FULL;
      end "+";

--:   function SUBSET(X, Y : SET) return BOOLEAN;
--|      where
--|         return for all E : ELEM =>
--|                     IS_MEMBER(E, X) → IS_MEMBER(E, Y);

      function "-" (X, Y : SET) return SET
--|      where
--|         return
--|            if SUBSET(X, Y) then null
--|            elsif Y = null then X
--|            else in SET'COLLECTION'NEXT end if;
```

```
    is
        TEMP_SET : SET;
    begin
        if X= null then
            return null;
        elsif Y = null then
            return X;
        else
            TEMP_SET := new SET_REC'(X.all);
            for I1 in 1 .. Y.LAST_ELEM loop
                REMOVE(Y.ELEMENTS(I1), TEMP_SET);
                exit when TEMP_SET = null;
            end loop;
            return TEMP_SET;
        end if;
    end "–";

        ...                              -- Bodies of other set operations.

end SETS;
```

Commentary

The *basic* functions of the specification are IS_MEMBER, IS_FULL, and CARDINALITY. Their values are not defined by visible subprogram annotations. They are used in the visible specifications of the other operations. The specification of package SETS is *relative* to this nucleus of visible operations. We have provided hidden annotations that define their values uniquely in terms of the hidden data types, even though some of these annotations duplicate the Ada code in the bodies.

There are two reasons for detailed hidden annotations of basic functions. One has to do with studying consistency of the hidden part, which we deal with later. The other reason is to provide notation for expressing other hidden annotations concisely — e. g., see the inductive assertion in the body of the "=" relation.

The implementation also depends on predefined operations of the types used to represent SETs, particularly the predefined relation "=" on the access type, SET. As explained previously, we have nested the visible abstract "=" on the limited private type SET in package SET_EQUAL so as not to hide access type "=". In the body of SET_EQUAL, the access type equality must be referred to by its fully qualified Ada name, SETS . "=".

The first thing to note about this example is that the subprogram annotations of the bodies of ADD, REMOVE, etc. express only how the hidden data structures are manipulated. The annotations of ADD, for example, specify that if parameter S is empty, then a new set record is allocated; otherwise, the access value pointing to the old set record is returned. No hidden specification requires E to be added to S; this is implied by the visible specification.

An important concern of this implementation is that set operations do not have side effects. This is implied by two kinds of constraints in the package body.

First, annotations of procedures ADD and REMOVE require that all *set values* other than parameter S remain unchanged — e. g.,

```
out (for all T : SET =>
                   T /= S → T.all = in T.all).
```

This is a quantification over all access values of type SET. It will be true if for each access value other than S, the values it designates in the **in** and **out** states of SET′COLLECTION are both undefined or are the same. This is a powerful constraint. It will be satisfied if the procedures do not change any set record other than the one for S.

Secondly, some annotations imply that *no sharing of representation* between abstract sets can result from parameter values. Their purpose is to ensure that nonempty abstract sets are represented by distinct set records. Consider the annotations of ADD and REMOVE, each of which have set parameters of mode **in out**. The annotation of ADD says that the **out** value of S must be its **in** value unless the **in** value is **null**; in this latter case the **out** value of S must designate a new set record. A similar annotation applies to the body of COPY (not shown here). The annotation of REMOVE allows its parameter value to be changed only to **null**. Consequently, these procedures cannot change their parameters to point to a set record that represents some other set. Similar annotations apply to "+" and "−". It follows by induction that distinct sets will always be represented by different records even if they are equal.

Finally, note the role of the stability constraints on sets and set records given in Section 8.1.1. Each subprogram body assumes the constraints are true of its parameters on input, and returns values that satisfy the constraints on output. REMOVE, for example, makes full use of the assumption that an element can occur at most once in a set record — it removes only one component. On the other hand, ADD makes sure that an element is not already in a set record before inserting it. And "=" only tests for set inclusion given that the LAST_ELEM indices are equal.

8.5 Establishing Consistency

A package implementation is *consistent* if it satisfies both the visible specification of the package and the hidden annotations.

When we annotate and construct package hidden parts, we must have in mind a strategy by which we propose to approach the problem of consistent implementation, and a method by which we propose to check consistency. The *basic functions* of the specification — see Chapter 5 — are a key element in building consistent package hidden parts and in establishing consistency.

In specifying a package, we follow a process of assuming a set of basic functions as given or understood and using them to define the other package operations. We can use the same strategy to break up the consistency problem into separate pieces. Since visible specifications contain calls to basic functions, we want to establish confidence in the basic functions first. Then, when an inconsistency between a visible specification and the package hidden part arises, calls to basic functions can be excluded from the search for a cause of the inconsistency. We can concentrate on the bodies of nonbasic subprograms.

- **Guideline: Divide and conquer the consistency of package implementations.**

  First ensure that the basic functions are correct. Then establish the consistency of the package hidden part.

When there are no basic functions in a package, this guideline reduces simply to first establishing the consistency of those packages upon which the current package depends for its basic concepts. When basic functions are declared in a package, they are not given explicit **return** annotations; following guidelines deal with correctness in this case.

Let us consider the method of runtime checking. The visible subprograms of the package are executed on test data. The visible specifications and hidden annotations are executed at appropriate points in the computation to see if the observable computation states satisfy them. To do this, all basic functions must be implemented.

- **Guideline: Runtime checking of consistency of package bodies.**

  To use runtime checking, all basic functions of the visible specification must be executable. Therefore, bodies must be provided for the virtual basic functions, as well as for the actual ones.

For example, the Ada rules require a body for IS_MEMBER in the SETS package body since it is an actual subprogram. On the other hand, the TABLE_MANAGER (Section 4.5) has a virtual basic function MEMBER.

Anna rules do not require a virtual body, but the guideline tells us to supply a virtual body for it, if we want to use runtime checking.

Checking a call to a package subprogram will proceed, roughly, as follows. First the visible **in** annotations of the subprogram are checked. This may involve computing an expression with a call to a basic function, e. g., **not** IS_MEMBER (1, MY_SET). Then the hidden **in** annotations of the subprogram body are checked (these may include modified type annotations that apply to **in** parameter values). Next, local annotations of the subprogram body are checked as the computation progresses. Finally, hidden and then visible **out** annotations are checked.

There are three guidelines we can follow to increase our confidence in the implementation of the basic functions.

- **Guideline: Specify the hidden values of basic functions.**

  All basic functions in the package specification should have hidden **return** *annotations in the package body that define the values they return.*

Since there are no visible **return** annotations, our intuitive understanding of basic functions should be expressed at the hidden level of a package. This allows us to apply both runtime checking and consistency proof methods to bodies of basic functions. Without hidden **return** annotations, we have no way to compare a basic function body with our intentions.

We will see in Chapter 9 that this guideline is crucial in applying proof methods to consistency of package implementations.

- **Guideline: Implement basic functions as simply as possible.**

  All basic functions in the package specification should have as simple an implementation as possible, at the expense of efficiency.

Simplicity reduces the likelihood of errors. Efficiency of virtual basic functions is not important. More efficient implementations of actual basic functions can be introduced at a later step, after consistency testing.

- **Guideline: The hidden annotations and bodies of subprograms should have the same dependencies as the visible specifications.**

  In particular, the hidden annotations and Ada bodies of basic functions must not call a nonbasic subprogram.

Basic functions may be mutally recursive. But if their hidden annotations or bodies call nonbasic subprograms, we can no longer establish correctness of basic functions by runtime checking *before* analyzing the nonbasic ones.

Having implemented and tested the basic functions, we can proceed to implement the nonbasic subprograms and test them by runtime checking. A recipe for developing consistent package implementations that follows the divide-and-conquer strategy with basic functions is given in Section 10.2.

The use of proof methods in implementing packages is studied in Chapter 9 and is illustrated by example in Section 10.3. The methods described in Chapter 9 assume an even stronger guideline than the previous one for hidden annotations of basic functions.

Digression

We digress briefly to discuss the consistency of packages in a little more detail. Consistency of a package implementation can be separated into two problems.

1. **External consistency**
   The computation states of the hidden implementation that are observable[8] from outside the package must satisfy the visible annotations of the package. This means that states in which subprograms are called and terminate, either normally or by propagating exceptions, as well as the initial computation state when the package is elaborated, must satisfy the visible annotations that apply to them.

2. **internal consistency**
   The computation states of the hidden implementation that are observable from within the hidden part must satisfy the hidden annotations. That is, states that result from elaboration of declarations or execution of simple statements in the hidden part must satisfy the hidden annotations.

In general these two problems can be independent. An implementation of a package may be externally consistent with the visible specification but internally inconsistent (or conversely). For example, an n ** 2 implementation could have hidden annotations requiring it to take n log n steps.

In practice it is useful (e. g., in testing and debugging packages) to provide hidden annotations so that internal consistency implies external consistency. One way to achieve this is to provide hidden annotations that express subgoals towards satisfying the visible annotations. We will discuss how to do this in the next chapter.

8.6 Redefinition of Equality

Equality on a limited private type or an Anna package state type may be redefined. This deviates from Ada rules for "=" since the package state type is not a limited type. So we give a short example.

---

[8] See Section 1.2.

To redefine "=", a declaration of function "=" is included in the package specification that contains the limited private type.[9] Then, a body defining the new "=" may be declared in the package body. As we saw in Section 4.5.1, this user-defined equality must satisfy the Anna axioms for equality.

Here is an example of a function body that redefines the equality operation on the state type of package TABLE_MANAGER.

Example: *Redefinition of equality on the table manager state type.*

```
    package body TABLE_MANAGER is

        type TABLE_TYPE is array (0 .. 1000) of ITEM;
        TABLE : TABLE_TYPE;
        LAST_ITEM : INTEGER := -1;

--| where
--|     in out X : TABLE_MANAGER'TYPE;
--|         for all I, J : 0 .. X.LAST_ITEM =>
--|             I < J → X.TABLE(I) /= X.TABLE(J) and
--|             X.TABLE(I).PRIORITY <= X.TABLE(J).PRIORITY;

--:     function "=" (S, T : TABLE_MANAGER'TYPE)
--:     return BOOLEAN
--|         where
--|             S.LAST_ITEM = T.LAST_ITEM and then
--|             for all I : 0 .. S.LAST_ITEM =>
--|                                     S.TABLE(I) = T.TABLE(I);
        is ... end "=";
        ...

    end TABLE_MANAGER;
```

Commentary

The Anna predefined "=" is the identity relation on states. This requires the LAST_ITEMs of two states to be equal and requires equality of *all* components of the TABLEs in two states.

Our new definition of "=" differs from the identity by requiring equality of only the components of the TABLEs corresponding to indices up to the LAST_ITEM.

To show that our new equality satisfies the TABLE_MANAGER specification, we must show that all the Anna axioms of equality (Section 4.5.1) are satisfied by the body of TABLE_MANAGER (next chapter).

[9]See the TABLE_MANAGER specification in Section 4.5.

8.7 Packages as Types

The introduction in Anna of package state types allows us to declare variables of state types and to apply the package operations to them as described in Section 4.4.1.

We can compute calls such as S . F, where F is a function of package P and S is some state of P that is not necessarily its current state. Such calls, of course, can only occur in annotations and virtual text. In effect, a package P is treated as a type declaration of a new composite type P'TYPE whose operations are the operations of P.

Here we describe how the Anna representation of state types given in Section 8.2 allows us to define the hidden values returned by calls such as S . F.

In Section 8.2, we saw that a variable of a package state type has as a hidden structure a state record aggregate. Thus, if we declare,

```
MY_TABLE : TABLE_MANAGER'TYPE :=
                                   TABLE_MANAGER'INITIAL;
```

somewhere outside the package body,[10] MY_TABLE has a hidden record structure with components TABLE and LAST_ITEM. If MY_TABLE is a parameter of a subprogram call (as we shall discuss in a moment), then its hidden structure is visible in the subprogram body and can be subjected to standard record operations such as MY_TABLE . TABLE. This is analogous to the Ada rules for private types.

In Section 4.3 we saw that package subprograms are treated in Anna as having an implicit state type parameter.

- **Implicit state parameter of package subprograms**

  Subprograms of a package have the package state as an implicit parameter. This means that whenever a name of a hidden object of the package appears in a subprogram body or an annotation of a subprogram body, it is treated as the name of a component of the implicit state parameter.

This treatment enables us to compute the hidden values of calls such as S . F, where F is a function of package P and S is some arbitrary state of P.

Consider the body of TABLE_MANAGER (Section 8.2) with some annotations of its subprogram bodies:

[10]It must be declared *outside* the package for reasons given in Section 8.2.1.

```
    package body TABLE_MANAGER is

        type TABLE_TYPE is array (0 .. 1000) of ITEM;
        TABLE : TABLE_TYPE;
        LAST_ITEM : INTEGER := -1;
        ...
--:     function MEMBER(X : ITEM) return BOOLEAN;
--|         where
--|             return (exist I : 0 .. LAST_ITEM =>
--|                                             TABLE(I) = X);
        ...

    end TABLE_MANAGER;
```

The names of local variables TABLE and LAST_ITEM in the annotations of MEMBER are interpreted as referring to the components of an implicit state parameter. So MEMBER is treated as though it had the implicit declaration

```
--: function MEMBER(X : ITEM;
--:                      STATE : TABLE_MANAGER'TYPE)
--: return BOOLEAN;
--|     where
--|         return (exist I : 0 .. STATE.LAST_ITEM =>
--|                                       STATE.TABLE(I) = X);
```

A call STATE.MEMBER(X) is interpreted as a call to the implicit subprogram MEMBER(X, STATE). Therefore, the result of a call

```
    MY_TABLE.MEMBER(X)
```

is

```
    exist I : 0 .. MY_TABLE.LAST_ITEM =>
                                  MY_TABLE.TABLE(I) = X).
```

This interpretation of package subprograms has the property that whenever a call is executed in the current state, the values resulting from the actual Ada computation are the same as those that would result from calling the interpretation of the subprogram with the implicit state type parameter.

Let us consider another example of an interpretation of a subprogram. Some of the annotations of the procedure body of INSERT in TABLE_MANAGER are:

```
    procedure INSERT (NEW_ITEM : in ITEM)
--|    where ...
--|       out (not (in MEMBER (NEW_ITEM)) →
--|          TABLE = in TABLE [in LAST_ITEM+1 =>
--|                                            NEW_ITEM]
--|          and
--|          LAST_ITEM = in LAST_ITEM+1);
    is
    ...                                   -- Body of INSERT.
```

The annotations refer to the **in** and **out** values of local variables of the package body. The local variables are components of the current state. In fact, INSERT is specified to have a side effect on the current state. Note also that the call to MEMBER is in the **in** state.

The Anna interpretation of INSERT is an implicit declaration with a state type parameter of mode **in out**. Side effects on the current state are interpreted as operations that change the value of this parameter.

```
    procedure INSERT (NEW_ITEM : in ITEM;
                      S : in out TABLE_MANAGER'TYPE)
--|    where ...
--|       out (not (in S.MEMBER (NEW_ITEM)) →
--|         S.TABLE = in S.TABLE [in S.LAST_ITEM+1 =>
--|                                            NEW_ITEM]
--|         and
--|         S.LAST_ITEM = in S.LAST_ITEM+1);
    is
    ...                                   -- Body of INSERT.
```

According to this interpretation, if X is not a member of MY_TABLE, the effect of call MY_TABLE . INSERT (X) is to change the value of MY_TABLE. The result of the call will be to make X a component of MY_TABLE . TABLE and to increment MY_TABLE . LAST_ITEM.

Further Reading

Plenty of examples of Ada package specifications and corresponding bodies can be found in Booch's book. These provide excellent exercises for annotation. In annotating the bodies, the reader will become aware that many of the bodies satisfy "unconscious constraints" that are never mentioned in the accompanying explanation, such as operations on one set not having a side effect on any other set.

A concept similar to our *stability* constraint applied to package states is Hoare's concept of *data invariant*. This was introduced as an aid to proving the correctness of data abstractions represented by Simula Classes. As we have seen in Section 8.1.1, the data invariant idea applies more generally in Ada packages, not just to package states, but to any type exported by a package.

1. G. Booch. *Software Components with Ada.* Benjamin/Cummings, Inc., 1987.
2. C. A. R. Hoare. Proof of correctness of data representations. *Acta Informatica*, Vol. 1, pp. 271–281, 1972. Also published in the collection of papers, *Programming Methodology* edited by D. Gries, Springer-Verlag, 1978.

9

Interpretation of Package Specifications *

Topics:

- *what interpretations are;*
- *why interpretations are useful;*
- *adequate hidden annotations of a package;*
- *constructing interpretations of visible specifications;*
- *interpretation of subprogram annotations;*
- *full specification of subprogram bodies in a package;*
- *interpretation of axioms;*
- *interpreting dependent specifications.*

Each visible annotation in a package specification imposes a constraint on the package hidden part. This constraint is expressed by a hidden annotation, which is called *an interpretation* of the visible annotation. The interpretation of an annotation of a private type is an annotation of the corresponding full type definition. The interpretation of an annotation of a subprogram is an annotation of the subprogram body. The interpretation of an axiom is, in the most general case, a modified type constraint on the state type. However, interpretations of axioms are often equivalent to fully quantified boolean assertions.

Interpretations have two important applications. First, they can be used to guide the construction of a package body. Secondly, they can be used to divide the complicated problem of proving (as opposed to checking at runtime) consistency between the visible and hidden parts of a package into simpler problems.

Interpreting visible annotations is a nontrivial process for humans. In all but the simplest examples, the number of details involved makes the chance of errors likely. Luckily, constructing interpretations is automatable. In this chapter, we outline how to do it in simple cases. Examples of interpreting subprogram annotations and axioms are described. The goal of this chapter is to give the reader an idea of what interpretations look like and how they can be applied in the process of constructing a package hidden part. This chapter provides an introduction to the topic and motivation for the next chapter, which integrates interpretation into the process of constructing the hidden part of a package. It will be quite clear that the use of interpretations in general can be — and must be — supported by automated tools. A definitive treatment of general methods of constructing interpretations is beyond the scope of our discussion.

9.1 Why Interpretations Are Useful

Let us digress for a moment to discuss why it is useful to have interpretations available when constructing a package body. Suppose we are given the package specification SETS with the private part in Section 8.1.1, and that we are about to implement subprogram bodies for ADD and REMOVE. These procedures will be implemented as operations on set records. But their visible specifications do not mention set records; they are specified entirely in terms of IS_MEMBER. How do we decide, for example, which procedure should increase the value of a LAST_ELEM component of a set record, and which should reduce it? Obviously we would like to guard against a misunderstanding whereby the meanings of the two operations are reversed!

Such decisions must be based on an earlier decision about how to represent an abstract set by a set record — i. e., how the basic IS_MEMBER function is interpreted on set records.

Now consider what happens if we disregard the interpretations of the visible specifications of ADD or REMOVE. This means that we disregard how the specification

```
--: procedure ADD(E : in ELEM; S : in out SET);
--|    where out (for all U : ELEM =>
--|       IS_MEMBER(U, S) ↔ (U = E or IS_MEMBER(U, in S));
```

can be expressed as an equivalent annotation involving internal set record structures. Similarly, we disregard the specification for REMOVE. If we do this, we must guess how to implement the bodies, because we have no other information about ADD and REMOVE. When we are finished, we will test them against the visible specifications. That is, we would implement bodies for ADD and REMOVE and then execute both their bodies and their visible specifications independently on test cases and compare the results. [1]

This approach is rather haphazard. It has the drawback that misunderstandings will not be detected until we have finished an implementation. [2]

Suppose, on the other hand, that we do consider the interpretations of the visible specifications. The one above, for example, is interpreted (in the SETS package body where the set record representation and the hidden specification of IS_MEMBER are visible — see Sections 8.1.1 and 8.4) as

---

[1] This assumes we write a body for IS_MEMBER.

[2] The most expensive software errors are those that go undetected for the longest time.

```
--: procedure ADD (E : in ELEM; S : in out SET)
--|     where
--|         out (S /= null and
--|             (for all U : ELEM =>
--|             (exist I : 1 .. S.LAST_ELEM =>
--|                                     S.ELEMENTS (I) = U) ↔
--|             (U = E or (in S /= null) and then
--|                 (exist J : 1 .. in S.LAST_ELEM =>
--|                                 in S.ELEMENTS (J) = U))));
    is ... end ADD;
```

This interpretation, together with the stability constraint on set records (i.e., they do not have duplicate elements, see Section 8.1.1), allows us to prove that

out (S.LAST_ELEM ≥ **in** S.LAST_ITEM),

so we won't have the misunderstanding alluded to above!

Interpretations involve the internal operations — such as selection, indexing, equality on set records, and on the access type SET. They give us the input assumptions and output goals for the subprogram bodies, but expressed in terms of the same operations that are used to implement the bodies. Many possible "wrong" implementations are thereby eliminated from consideration. Indeed, programmers probably do carry out a process of interpretation subconsciously, but not always correctly or completely.

Consequently, we argue that it is important to develop practical methods for constructing interpretations of visible specifications. There are several other benefits. First of all, such methods can be automated, leading to tools for constructing interpretations automatically. Errors due to incorrect interpretation can be eliminated. We will then be able to use correct and complete interpretations of visible specifications as plans to guide our implementation of a package body.

Automation may be taken a step further. In many cases, the interpretations of visible subprogram annotations can be easily transformed into executable subprogram bodies, as we shall see. This would give us a two-step method of automating the transformation of visible subprogram annotations into hidden subprogram bodies that satisfy them.

Visible subprogram annotations	*Step 1* ⟹ *interpretation*	Hidden subprogram annotations	*Step 2* ⟹ *transformation*	Subprogram body

Finally, interpretations provide a vital link in proving consistency between the visible and hidden parts of a package. The visible and hidden parts are consistent if the hidden implementation satisfies the interpretation of the visible annotations.

This ends our digression. The rest of this chapter deals with Step 1; Chapter 10 deals with Step 2.

9.2 Constructing Interpretations *

Consider any visible annotation A (X, F) in the specification of a package P:

```
    package P is

        type T is private;
        function F ... ;
        ...
--|     A (X, F);
        ...
    end P;
```

A (X, F) is a boolean expression that contains a variable X and calls to a function F. Let us assume, to make the discussion interesting, that X is a variable of a private type T in P, and F is a function in P.

The interpretation of A (X, F) is another annotation, say **I** (A (X, F)), in the hidden part of P. It annotates the corresponding entity as shown in the table below and Figure 9.1.

Example: Correspondence between visible annotations and their interpretations.

Visible annotation of P	Interpretation in hidden part of P
A annotates private type T.	**I** (A) annotates full type declaration of T.
A annotates subprogram Q.	**I** (A) annotates body of Q.
A is an axiom of P.	**I** (A) is a modified constraint on the hidden state type of P. When the state is trivial, it is equivalent to a hidden boolean assertion.

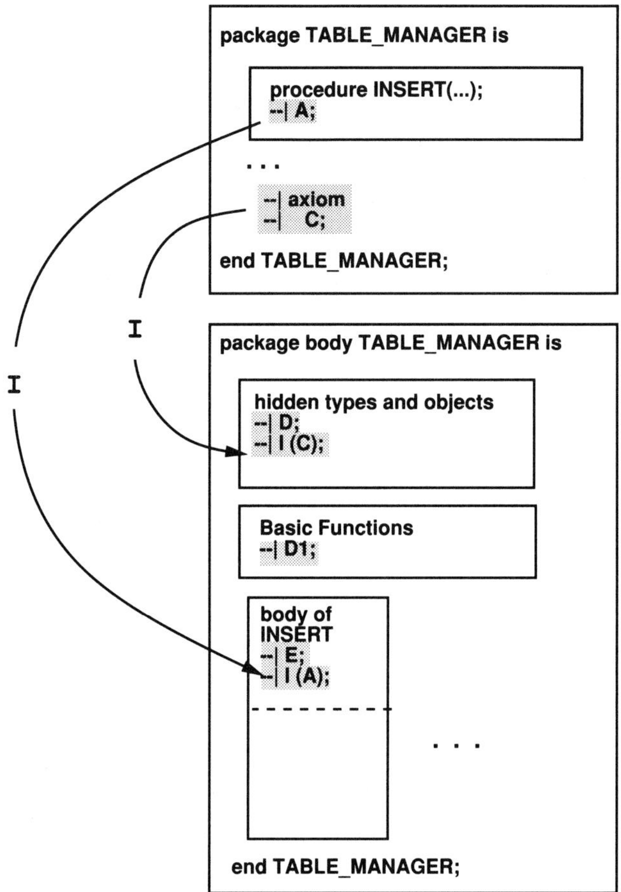

FIGURE 9.1. Interpretation of visible package annotations.

To construct an interpretation **I** (A (X, F)), the abstractions of P that appear in A are replaced by their implementations. To do this, the first step must be to specify implementations of the private types and basic functions (Section 5.1) of P in the hidden part according to the guideline below.

To simplify the interpretation process, we assume that all basic concepts are either standard Ada and Anna predefined concepts or functions declared in P itself.[3] So the specification of P does not depend on other packages (Section 5.6). Under this assumption, the process will work if there are *adequate hidden annotations* in P:

- **Guideline: Adequate hidden annotations for interpretation.** [4]

  1. *All full type declarations of private types should have type or modified type annotations that express any intended constraints on the representation of the types (including the package state type).*
  2. *All basic functions in the package specification should have hidden result annotations of their bodies that define the values they return. In the case of virtual basic functions, these annotations will apply to a virtual body, if there is one, or to a virtual stub.*

  These hidden annotations should use only predefined operations of Ada and Anna (such as the operations of hidden types), and hidden operations declared in the package body.

So first of all, we must provide hidden annotations that are adequate in this sense. The annotations of bodies of basic functions, which will be result annotations and possibly also **in** annotations, define an interpretation of the basic functions. If the basic functions are virtual, bodies need not be given, so their interpretation may provide the only definition of their values. For example, adequate annotation of package SETS requires that hidden annotations that define values of IS_MEMBER, IS_FULL, and CARDINALITY must be given in the SETS package body.

Our criteria for adequate annotation disallow annotating basic function bodies using visible functions. For example, specifying the body of IS_MEMBER using SET . "=" is not allowed. The idea is to disallow recursive and mutually recursive specification of basic function bodies — "=" is specified in terms of IS_MEMBER in the visible part of SETS. The simple recipe for interpretation below won't work without this restriction. Other recipes do allow mutually recursive definitions of basic functions.

The main steps in computing **I**(E) for an expression E are sketched in the following recipe. We use some shorthand notation in the recipe:

---

[3]Eliminating this assumption is discussed in Section 9.6.

[4]This guideline combines the guidelines in Sections 8.1.1 and 8.5.

1. The notation "...E ..." before "*is*" indicates an expression E that occurs within a larger expression in the visible part of P. The notation "...F ..." after "*is*" indicates that E has been replaced by F in the interpretation of the larger expression.

2. If the full definition of a private type T has a modified type annotation, we denote the boolean constraint of the annotation by IS_T. Thus, IS_T (X) means that the value of X satisfies the constraint.

- **Recipe for I** (E)

  The following general steps are applied recursively to subexpressions of E.

  1. **Eliminate abstract types.**

     (a) Each program variable or expression X whose type is a private type T (including the package state type) is interpreted as a variable or expression X of the corresponding full type declaration. As a consequence, the operations of the full type can be applied to X at other steps of the recipe. A deferred constant is replaced by its hidden value. If there is a type or modified type annotation of the full type declaration, then a premise IS_T (X) is added to the interpretation of the expression in which X occurs:

     I (... X ...) *is*
     IS_T (X) $\rightarrow$ ... X ...

     (b) A special case of this step applies to interpreting selection on state type expressions, such as S . E, since hidden variable names are interpreted as component selection on the state type records (Section 8.7). Suppose the hidden representation of the state type is a record with components U and V. If

     I (E) *is* ... U, ... V, ...

     then

     I (S . E) *is* IS_T (S) $\rightarrow$ ... S . U, ... S . V, ...

     (c) Each quantifier over a private type T is interpreted by an identical quantifier over the full type definition of T, together with a premise that the values of the logical variable satisfy IS_T:

```
I (for all X : T => C(X)) is
for all X : T => IS_T(X) → I (C(X)).

I (exist X : T => C(X)) is
exist X : T => IS_T(X) and I (C(X)).
```

2. **Eliminate functions.**
   Functional terms that contain visible functions are replaced by boolean expressions that define those terms. To do this, we use the *function call rule* described below, which allows us to replace a call to a function by an appropriate instance of annotations of that function.

   Let F be a visible function. To simplify notation, suppose F has one formal parameter Z (say). Let **In_F**(Z) denote the conjunction of the input annotations and negated propagation conditions of both the visible declaration of F and the body of F. Similarly, let **Out_F** (Z, Y) denote the conjunction of visible and hidden return annotations of F. Suppose F returns values of type T.

   – **Function call rule**

   (a) If the values of F are specified implicitly by (a conjunction of) result annotations, which we represent in the form

   ```
   return Y : T => Out_F (Z, Y),
   ```

   then:

   ```
   I (... F(X) ...) is
     IS_T(X) and In_F (X) →
        (for all Y : T =>
          Out_F (X, Y) and IS_T(Y) → ... Y ...),
   ```

   where the type of X and Y is the full type definition T and ...Y ... denotes the result of applying the recipe to the expression after F(X) is replaced by Y.

   (b) If the values of F are specified explicitly by a result expression

   ```
   return Result_F(Z),
   ```

   then:

   ```
   I (... F(X) ...) is
     IS_T(X) and In_F(X) →
       IS_T(Result_F(X)) and ... Result_F(X) ...
   ```

3. **Map visible annotations to hidden annotations.**
By applying the two elimination steps recursively, a visible annotation is converted to an annotation of the hidden part of a package. The final step in constructing an interpretation is to apply the interpreted annotation as a constraint on the appropriate hidden entity (see Figure 9.1). We call this step *mapping*.
The mapping between visible and hidden annotations follows the table above. For example, **in** and **out** annotations of a subprogram map to **in** and **out** annotations of the subprogram body. A visible result annotation whose type is T maps to a result annotation of the corresponding function body, having as type the full type definition of T, and specifying a value that satisfies IS_T:

```
I (return X : T => C(X)) is
return X : T => IS_T(X) and I (C(X)).
```

An axiom A maps to a hidden modified annotation

```
where in out S : P'TYPE => I(A(S))
```

of the package state type in the declarative part of the package body, placed after the implicit full state type declaration. If the state type is trivial, this interpretation is equivalent to a purely logical assertion (no program variables), **I**(A), in the declarative part of the package body.

- **end recipe.**

Commentary

The steps of the recipe are applied successively to a visible annotation. Abstract types are replaced by their hidden representations, which allows the hidden type operations to be applied to variables and expressions of those types. Calls to visible functions of the package are replaced by expressions that specify their hidden values. Each kind of annotation is mapped to the corresponding kind of hidden annotation. The linear visibility rules of Ada, which apply to annotations, ensure that circularities in the applications of the steps do not occur.
The order of applying the steps is left open. One strategy is to eliminate abstract types and then eliminate all visible functions. The ability to eliminate all visible functions by the function call rule depends on each visible function having a result annotation that defines the value it returns. Nonbasic functions are replaced by their visible result annotations, and those expres-

sions contain basic functions which are then replaced by their hidden result annotations.
The final result is a hidden annotation that contains no references to the abstractions (private types and visible subprograms) of the package. Concrete entities (e. g., integer variables, record types) that are declared in the Ada visible part of a package will, of course, remain in a hidden interpretation. Otherwise, an interpretation will refer only to the predefined Ada and Anna types and operations used to implement the hidden part and other hidden operations that may be nested in the package.

The steps of the recipe are loose, informal descriptions of formal proof rules, which we do not present here. However, a few words of explanation are in order.

The function call rule expresses that any value Y that satisfies the conjunction of **return** annotations of the specification and body of F when the actual parameter is X is an interpretation for F (X). When the result type returned by F is not subject to an Anna type constraint, the premise IS_T (Y) will not appear in the interpretation. Also, when the function is defined explicitly by a hidden result expression, the quantifier over the result value is unnecessary.

The step for eliminating abstract types contains a special clause for package states whenever they are part of a selection, as in S . F. In this case, F will be replaced by its hidden result annotation. Names of hidden variables of the package must then be interpreted as selections of corresponding components of the hidden value of the state S. This follows the semantics of hidden states described in Section 8.7. Whenever state S is the current state P'STATE, the values of the components are the values of the hidden variables — i. e., P'STATE . L = L.

We note also that **I**(C (X)) has the logical form

```
IS_T (X) → ... .
```

So whenever IS_T (X) is false the interpretation is true. Thus, the hidden value of X is constrained only when the type constraint is true — i. e., when X is stable.

The mapping of axioms to modified type constraints expresses the meaning of axioms: they express properties that must be satisfied by package states that are visible outside the package. They do not have to hold while a package state is being updated.

Also, when the state is trivial (i. e., constant) an axiom will map to a modified type constraint that is equivalent to a hidden boolean assertion that contains no program variables. In such cases, the axiom is satisfied by the hidden implementation if the boolean assertion is true.

Finally, we can choose when to apply the function call rule so a call to a basic function can be left uninterpreted and used as a notational shorthand for the hidden result expression. Delaying the elimination of some basic functions may help in processing and analyzing interpretations.

To make up for the sketchiness of our recipe, we give a number of examples of interpretations.

Examples of interpretations of visible annotations

1. Consider package SETS of Section 8.1.1. Type SET has a stability constraint. A visible variable S of type SET is interpreted as a hidden variable with a stable composite value of type SET. Thus, the interpretation of S is an access type variable that satisfies stability constraint IS_SET (S):

```
--: function IS_SET (S : SET) return BOOLEAN;
--|     where return S /= null → S.LAST_ELEM'DEFINED
--|           and
--|          (for all I : 1 .. S.LAST_ELEM =>
--|                               S.ELEMENTS (I)'DEFINED)
--|           and
--|          (for all I, J : 1 .. S.LAST_ELEM =>
--|          I /= J → S.ELEMENTS (I) /= S.ELEMENTS (J));
```

2. To interpret a functional term in a visible annotation of package SETS, say,

   ```
   ... IS_MEMBER (E, S) ...
   ```

   we apply both elimination steps of the recipe.

   At the first step, S is interpreted using elimination of abstract types:

   ```
   IS_SET (S) → ... IS_MEMBER (E, S) ...
   ```

   where S is an access type variable that designates a set record.

   At the second step, the function call rule is used to replace the term IS_MEMBER (E, S) by the hidden result annotation of IS_MEMBER (Section 8.4), instantiated to the actual parameters E and S:

   ```
   IS_SET (S) → ... (S /= null and then
                     exist I : 1 .. S.LAST_ELEM =>
                            S.ELEMENTS (I) = E) ... ;
   ```

3. As a slightly more complex example, consider constructing an interpretation

```
I(...  "+" (X, Y) ...).
```

At the first step, elimination of abstract types is applied to the parameters X and Y of type SET:

```
IS_SET (X) and IS_SET (Y) → ...  "+" (X, Y) ...
```

where the type of X, Y, and "+" (X, Y) is the access type SET.

At the next step, the function call rule is applied, using the conjunction of the visible and hidden annotations of "+" (Sections 8.1.1 and 8.4):

```
IS_SET (X) and IS_SET (Y). →
    (for all Z : SET =>
          if X = null then Z = Y
          elsif Y = null then Z = X
          else Z = in SET'COLLECTION'NEXT and
             (for all U : ELEM =>
                  IS_MEMBER (U, Z) ↔
                      IS_MEMBER (U, X) or
                      IS_MEMBER (U, Y))
          end if
          and IS_SET (Z)
             → ... Z ... ).
```

Finally, interpretations of the terms that contain IS_MEMBER are constructed by applying the function call rule again, as in the previous example. This can result in a lengthy and very detailed hidden annotation. We can choose to delay applying the function call rule until we want to see the details — i. e., the calls to IS_MEMBER can be treated as abbreviations for instances of the boolean result expression.

4. Consider package TABLE_MANAGER, whose specification is given in Section 4.5 and whose body is outlined in Section 8.2. A visible variable TM of the state type is interpreted as a variable of record type TABLE_MANAGER'TYPE, with a stable value. Therefore it must satisfy IS_TABLE (TM), where

```
--: function IS_TABLE (TM : TABLE_MANAGER'TYPE)
--: return BOOLEAN;
--|      where return
--|          (for all I, J : 0 .. TM.LAST_ITEM =>
--|           I < J → (TM.TABLE (I) /= TM.TABLE (J)
--|           and
--|           TM.TABLE (I).PRIORITY <=
--|                                 TM.TABLE (J).PRIORITY));
```

5. Let us apply the recipe to an expression, supposing it to be an axiom of the TABLE_MANAGER specification:

```
axiom
for all TM : TABLE_MANAGER'TYPE => not TM.FULL;
```

By elimination of abstract types,

```
for all TM : TABLE_MANAGER'TYPE =>
                          IS_TABLE(TM) → not TM.FULL;
```

where TM is a variable of the record type that represents the state type. (Note that TM.FULL is Anna notation for selection on a state and is not legal Ada.) Assume that the body of FULL in TABLE_MANAGER has a hidden result annotation:

```
--: function FULL return BOOLEAN;
--|     where return LAST_ITEM = 1000;
```

where LAST_ITEM is a local variable of the package body.

Then we eliminate FULL using the function call rule and apply the special step for selection on package states to interpret TM.FULL:

```
for all TM : TABLE_MANAGER'TYPE =>
          IS_TABLE(TM) → TM.LAST_ITEM /= 1000.
```

At the mapping step, this annotation is added to the type constraints on TABLE_MANAGER'TYPE as a modified constraint:

```
where in out TM : TABLE_MANAGER'TYPE =>
          IS_TABLE(TM) → TM.LAST_ITEM /= 1000.
```

Thus, the interpretation of the axiom constrains LAST_ITEM components of states of TABLE_MANAGER to be not equal to 1000 at computation states that are observable outside the package.

6. Let us interpret one of the visible annotations of INSERT of the TABLE_MANAGER specification. In order to shorten the notation, we have abbreviated TABLE_MANAGER to T_M:

```
   procedure INSERT(NEW_ITEM : ITEM);
--|  where
--|     out (not in T_M.MEMBER(NEW_ITEM) →
--|                        T_M.MEMBER(NEW_ITEM) );
```

The annotation refers to **in** and **out** values of the package state. The interpretation will be an annotation of the body of INSERT in the body of TABLE_MANAGER.

First we eliminate the abstract state type. This gives us the hidden annotation

```
out (IS_TABLE(in T_M) and IS_TABLE(T_M) →
    (not in T_M.MEMBER(NEW_ITEM) →
                          T_M.MEMBER(NEW_ITEM)));
```

in which the type of the state expressions is now the hidden record type representing package states, so the record operations can be applied to them.

Virtual basic function MEMBER must have a hidden result annotation that defines its value (guideline on adequate annotations). We may suppose this to be

```
--: function MEMBER(X : ITEM) return BOOLEAN;
--|     where return exist I : 0 .. LAST_ITEM =>
--|                                   TABLE(I) = X;
```

Next, the two calls to MEMBER are eliminated. Each call is replaced by the result annotation instantiated to the actual parameter of the call. Both calls occur in selections on states, so the local variables in the annotations that replace these calls are interpreted as component selections on the states (recipe, Step 1 (b)).

```
out (IS_TABLE(in T_M) and IS_TABLE(T_M) →     -- (1)
    (not (exist I : 0 .. in T_M.LAST_ITEM =>
                   in T_M.TABLE(I) = NEW_ITEM) →
         (exist I : 0 .. T_M.LAST_ITEM =>
                      T_M.TABLE(I) = NEW_ITEM)));
```

At the mapping step, this becomes a hidden **out** annotation of the body of INSERT. It specifies the effect of INSERT when called in any state T_M.

We may use the representation of TABLE_MANAGER'TYPE to replace the state variables by record aggregates. For example, the current state T_M has as value an aggregate of local variables (TABLE, LAST_ITEM). Selection on these state record aggregates satisfies the following equalities:
(A, B).TABLE = A and (A, B).LAST_ITEM = B.
These equalities may be used to simplify (1). Finally, we may write the interpretation as an annotation of the body of INSERT as follows:

```
        procedure INSERT (NEW_ITEM : ITEM)
--|        where
--|            out (IS_TABLE((in TABLE, in LAST_ITEM))
--|                 and
--|                 IS_TABLE((TABLE, LAST_ITEM)) →
--|                 (not (exist I : 0 .. in LAST_ITEM =>
--|                                in TABLE(I) = NEW_ITEM) →
--|                     (exist I : 0 .. LAST_ITEM =>
--|                                    TABLE(I) = NEW_ITEM)));
        is ...
```

9.3 Interpreting Subprogram Annotations *

Here, we give two examples of interpreting visible subprogram annotations from package SETS (see Section 8.1.1). The examples are constructed according to our recipe. But we also apply some logical and algebraic rules, which allow us to rewrite the raw interpretations in simpler forms.

These examples illustrate the plausibility of providing tools to aid in the two-step process, mentioned at the end of Section 9.1, for transforming visible specifications into executable bodies.

It is assumed that the hidden data types are already chosen and the basic functions have been defined in the hidden part. An interactive tool would then be used to construct interpretations and aid in transforming them into Ada code. The user would supply additional implementation details that are not contained in the interpreted visible specifications. In these examples, the correspondence between the interpretations of the visible subprogram annotations and the subprogram bodies[5] is so close that the two-step transformation could be completely automatic.

The examples assume that type SET has the full definition with the stability constraints specified in Section 8.1.1.

Example: Interpretation of the visible result annotation of "=" *for* SETS.

The visible result annotation of "=" is :

```
    function "=" (S, T : SET) return BOOLEAN;
--|     where return (for all E : ELEM =>
--|                        IS_MEMBER(E, S) ↔ IS_MEMBER(E, T));
```

Replacing S, T, and IS_MEMBER by their interpretations, as shown in the example in Section 9.2, and simplifying yields the following result an-

[5]See the sets package body in Section 8.4.

notation of the body of "=":

```
    function "=" (S, T : SET) return BOOLEAN
--|     where return IS_SET(S) and IS_SET(T) →
--|         if S = null or T = null then
--|             S = null and T = null
--|         else
--|             for all E : ELEM =>
--|                 (exist I : 1 .. S.LAST_ELEM =>
--|                                         S.ELEMENTS(I) = E)
--|                  ↔
--|                 (exist J : 1 .. T.LAST_ELEM =>
--|                                         T.ELEMENTS(J) = E)
--|         end if;
    is ... end;                                -- Body of "=".
```

Commentary

The interpretation in the conditional expression form shown here could have been used as a plan for the Ada body of "=" (Section 8.4). For example, the Ada body consists of a conditional statement that corresponds exactly to the Anna conditional expression in the interpretation. The nested loop in the **else** part of the body is a straightforward way of implementing the test for equivalence of the two existentially quantified expressions.

Note that correctness of the Ada body depends on the two premises that S and T satisfy IS_SET — the loops only search for components in the range 1 .. LAST_ELEM.

In general, interpretation of visible specifications involves algebraic manipulation of boolean expressions. These manipulations could be performed by automated tools, which at the moment are experimental but may be part and parcel of programming environments within a few years.

Here is another example: let us interpret the visible result annotation of the "+" operation in SETS.

Example: Interpretation of the result annotation of operation "+".

The visible result annotation of "+" is :

```
    function "+" (X, Y : SET) return SET;
--|     where
--|         return Z : SET =>
--|             for all U : ELEM =>
--|                 IS_MEMBER(U, Z) ↔ IS_MEMBER(U, X)
--|                                     or IS_MEMBER(U, Y);
```

The recursive recipe will replace abstract type SET and calls to

IS_MEMBER, as in the examples in Section 9.2. This gives us an interpretation in which SET variables X, Y, and Z are access type variables:

```
--| return Z : SET => IS_SET(X) and IS_SET(Y) →
--|     IS_SET(Z) and
--|     for all U : ELEM =>
--|     (Z /= null and then
--|         (exist I : 1 .. Z.LAST_ELEM =>
--|                                      Z.ELEMENTS(I) = U))
--|      ↔
--|     (X /= null and then
--|         (exist I : 1 .. X.LAST_ELEM =>
--|                                      X.ELEMENTS(I) = U))
--|      or
--|     (Y /= null and then
--|         (exist I : 1 .. Y.LAST_ELEM =>
--|                                     Y.ELEMENTS(I) = U));
```

The expression that defines the resulting values can be rewritten as a logically equivalent conditional boolean expression:

```
      function "+" (X, Y : SET) return SET
--|        return Z : SET => IS_SET(X) and IS_SET(Y) →
--|            IS_SET(Z) and
--|            if X = null then Z = Y
--|            elsif Y = null then Z = X
--|            else
--|                for all U : ELEM =>
--|                   (exist I : 1 .. Z.LAST_ELEM =>
--|                                           Z.ELEMENTS(I) = U) ↔
--|                         (exist I : 1 .. X.LAST_ELEM =>
--|                                           X.ELEMENTS(I) = U) or
--|                         (exist I : 1 .. Y.LAST_ELEM =>
--|                                              Y.ELEMENTS(I) = U)
--|            end if;
       is ... end "+";                   -- Body of "+"; see Section 8.4.
```

Commentary

The visible specification of "+" in terms of IS_MEMBER has been interpreted as a result annotation in terms of set records. It annotates the body of "+". The form of this annotation corresponds closely to the form of the final Ada implementation of the body of "+" in Section 8.4. Note that the **else** part of the body constructs a set Z that satisfies the existentially quantified constraints in the **else** part of the annotation. Correctness of the Ada body depends on the assumption IS_SET(X) (i.e., no duplicate elements in X) and on the visible specification for ADD (i.e., that it won't add a duplicate member to a set).

Looking back at the previous two examples, we can see some other applications of interpretations beyond their use as an implementation guide. First of all, they give us a way to apply consistency proofs. The problem, in one step, is to prove that a subprogram body is consistent with a visible specification. Interpretation allows us to break the problem into two steps. First interpret the visible specification and then prove consistency between the interpretation and the body.

Secondly, interpretations may be used in conjunction with runtime checking to "zero in" on bugs. Suppose it is discovered by runtime checking that the body of "+" is inconsistent with its visible specification. (To do runtime checking, execute the visible specifications to check the parameter values before and after calls.) This tells us that there is an inconsistency between three things: (1) the visible specification, (2) the body of IS_MEMBER, and (3) the body of "+". The interpretation of the visible specification was not actually needed to do the runtime checking. But now it allows us to divide the debugging problem into smaller pieces. An inconsistency must exist (i) between the hidden annotation of IS_MEMBER and its body or (ii) between the interpretation of the visible specification of "+" and the body of "+" (or both (i) and (ii)). So now we would start testing these two subproblems on the same data. Methodologically, one should put more confidence in (i) and look for an inconsistency in (ii) first.

9.4 Full Specifications of Subprogram Bodies *

Writing the body of a package subprogram may seem like herding a flock of sheep. It must satisfy annotations that are the logical conjunction of (1) the interpretation of its visible specification, (2) modified constraints on the types of its parameters and global variables, and (3) its hidden annotation. We will refer to this set of annotations as the *full specification* of the subprogram body. Now that we know how to construct interpretations, we can face the problem of becoming good shepherds!

One technique for constructing a package body is to construct the full specifications of its subprograms first. Each full specification is a complete list of the assumptions and goals for a subprogram body. It is often useful, as we illustrate below, to study the flock before trying to herd it, so to speak. This is probably what most programmers try to do, in a somewhat intuitive and subconscious manner. But the complexity of full specifications is such that studying them must be approached methodically.

As an example, we construct the full hidden specification for the body of "+" in SETS. Below, we have written the whole specification, combining the interpretation of the visible annotations (Section 9.3), the modified type annotation on type SET (Section 8.1.1), and the hidden subprogram annotation (Section 8.4).

Example: *Full hidden specification of the body of "+" in* SETS.

```
    function "+" (X, Y : SET) return SET
--|     where
--|         raise SET_FULL,
--  In conditions implied by the modified type annotations.
--|         X /= null → X.LAST_ELEM'DEFINED and
--|               (for all I : 1 .. X.LAST_ELEM =>
--|                              X.ELEMENTS(I)'DEFINED) and
--|         for all I, J : 1 .. X.LAST_ELEM =>
--|              I /= J → X.ELEMENTS(I) /= X.ELEMENTS(J),
--|         Y /= null → Y.LAST_ELEM'DEFINED and
--|               (for all I : 1 .. Y.LAST_ELEM =>
--|                               Y.ELEMENTS(I)'DEFINED) and
--|         for all I, J : 1 .. Y.LAST_ELEM =>
--|             I /= J → Y.ELEMENTS(I) /= Y.ELEMENTS(J),
-- Return annotation combining the interpretation of the visible annotation of
-- "+" with the hidden annotations of "+" and the modified type annotation.
--|         return Z : SET =>
--|         if X = null then Z = Y
--|         elsif Y = null then Z = X
--|         else
--|             Z = in SET'COLLECTION'NEXT
--|             and
--|             Z.LAST_ELEM'DEFINED
--|             and
--|               (for all I : 1 .. Z.LAST_ELEM =>
--|                                   Z.ELEMENTS(I)'DEFINED)
--|             and
--|               (for all I, J : 1 .. Z.LAST_ELEM =>
--|              (I /= J → Z.ELEMENTS(I) /= Z.ELEMENTS(J)))
--|             and
--|               (for all U : ELEM =>
--|                   (exist I : 1 .. Z.LAST_ELEM =>
--|                       Z.ELEMENTS(I) = U) ↔
--|                       (exist I : 1 .. X.LAST_ELEM =>
--|                                    X.ELEMENTS(I) = U)
--|                       or
--|                       (exist I : 1 .. Y.LAST_ELEM =>
--|                                   Y.ELEMENTS(I) = U))
--|          end if;
    is
       ...                -- Body of "+" as before; see Section 8.3.
    end "+";
```

Commentary

We have arrived at this full specification by: (i) applying our recipe to interpret the visible specification as in Section 9.3, (ii) adding the list of hidden annotations, (iii) adding hidden **in** and **result** annotations that express the stability constraints on the

SET parameters and the return value, and, finally, (iv) rewriting the full specification in an equivalent form by applying logical equivalences for boolean expressions with quantifiers.

This full specification provides us with a complete checklist of constraints the body must satisfy. It is worthwhile taking a moment to compare it with the body for "+" in Section 8.4. Are all the **in** annotations used in the body? Note that the body uses the assumption that X is stable in constructing X+Y by not checking for repetitions in X. Repetitions in Y would not affect the result.

Is it true that the constructed value always satisfies the **return** annotation on Z above?

Of course, we do not have to expand all the calls to type predicates and basic functions at one time in displaying a full hidden specification. The reader should imagine analyzing the full hidden specification of "+" with an interactive tool that will present the result expression corresponding to a call to a type predicate or basic function upon demand. This improves understandability and allows details to be considered separately.

The complexity of full hidden specifications of package subprograms makes it especially important to consider rewriting them in different, logically equivalent forms. Some of these might suggest quite different implementations of the body. Consider for example relation "=" in SETS.

Example: *Different forms of the full specification of "="*.

The visible **return** annotation is:

```
     function "=" (S, T : SET) return BOOLEAN;
--|      where return (for all E : ELEM =>
--|                          IS_MEMBER(E, S) ↔ IS_MEMBER(E, T));
```

One form of the full specification, consists of the interpretation of the return annotation and the stability constraint on set records:

```
--|    ...        -- Input conditions – stable properties of S and T.
--|  return for all E : ELEM =>
--|     (S /= null and then
--|          (exist I : 1 .. S.LAST_ELEM =>
--|                                       S.ELEMENTS(I) = E)) ↔
--|     (T /= null and then
--|          (exist J : 1 .. S.LAST_ELEM =>
--|                                          S.ELEMENTS(J) = E)),
--|  out (...);                   -- Stable properties of S and T.
```

The stability property of set records, which requires no repetitions of components, implies an alternative form:

```
--|     ...          -- Input conditions – stable properties of S and T.
--| return (S = null ↔ T = null) or
--|     (S.LAST_ELEM = T.LAST_ELEM and
--|      PERMUTATION(S.ELEMENTS(1 .. S.LAST_ELEM),
--|                  T.ELEMENTS(1 .. T.LAST_ELEM))),
--| out (...);                    -- Stable properties of S and T.
```

Commentary

The first form would probably lead to the implementation of the body of "=" given in Section 8.4, which contains nested loops corresponding to the two existentially quantified expressions.

The second form accentuates the fact that the set records need not be identical for "=" between sets to be true. It suggests a somewhat different implementation of the body, possibly reusing an existing subprogram body for testing to see if two arrays are permutations.

Proof that the two result annotations are equivalent for stable sets is probably easier if we use a definition of PERMUTATION such as the one based on COUNT in Section 2.5.3.

9.5 Interpreting Package Axioms *

Axioms provide a convenient way to express algebraic relationships between the visible subprograms in a package specification. Viewed from outside the package, they express invariant relationships between subprograms that may be assumed by the user. Internally, they are interpreted as modified type constraints in the package hidden part.

In this section we give some examples of interpretations of axioms. These examples use the TABLE_MANAGER specification in Section 4.5 and the body given below in the next example.

Construction of interpretations of axioms follows the recipe. So, to interpret an axiom A, we must first carry out the following steps in annotating the package body:

1. Give adequate hidden annotations for all basic concepts.
2. Construct full specifications for the bodies of subprograms that are called in axiom A.

As we shall see, the resulting modified type constraint is a universally quantified boolean expression that relates the components of the state and values of subprogram parameters. (An axiom does not constrain visible program variables because program variables in axioms are replaced by their values when the axioms are elaborated; see Section 4.5.) We must prove that the interpretation of an axiom is satisfied by all states that are observable outside of the package.

- **Consistency of axioms with package hidden parts**

  A package hidden part is consistent with an axiom if the modified type constraint that is the interpretation of the axiom is a logical consequence of the full hidden specifications of the operations occurring in it, and bodies of those operations are consistent with their specifications.

This is a sufficient criterion for consistency. If the modified type constraint turns out not to be true, the type and subprogram annotations in the package body should be changed accordingly, so that it is true. We shall discuss this and an alternative strategy for achieving consistency after the examples below, which include a simple example where the interpretation of an axiom indicates a change in a package body.

Interpretations are useful in structuring the proof of consistency of axioms with package hidden parts into separate problems. Construction of the interpretation of an axiom assumes that the subprograms satisfy their subprogram annotations. The consistency proof problem is thereby reduced to two subproblems:

1. Prove the interpretation of the axiom.
2. Prove that subprogram bodies satisfy their hidden specifications.

However, as we shall see in this section, interpretations of package axioms can be very complex boolean expressions. In general, formulas of this complexity require automated processing to ensure correct construction, algebraic simplification, and proof. We shall return to this point at the end of the section.

For the purposes of illustration, we consider two kinds of axioms. (1) Axioms that express properties of a deferred constant and thus constrain the value of the constant. (2) Axioms that express an algebraic relationship between subprograms that must hold for all values of their parameters and the package states.

Let us start by viewing the body of package TABLE_MANAGER at a preliminary stage in its implementation.

Example: *Outline of a table manager body with interpretations of visible annotations.*

```
package body TABLE_MANAGER is

   type TABLE_TYPE is array (0 .. 1000) of ITEM;
   TABLE : TABLE_TYPE;
   LAST_ITEM : INTEGER := -1;
```

```
--|     where in out( X : TABLE_MANAGER'TYPE =>
--|           for all I, J : 0 .. X.LAST_ITEM =>
--|              I < J → X.TABLE(I) /= X.TABLE(J) and
--|              X.TABLE(I).PRIORITY <=
--|                                   X.TABLE(J).PRIORITY);

--:     function FULL return BOOLEAN;
--|        where return LAST_ITEM = 1000;

--:     function EMPTY return BOOLEAN;
--|        where return LAST_ITEM = -1;

--:     function MEMBER(X : ITEM) return BOOLEAN;
--|        where return (exist I : 0 .. LAST_ITEM =>
--|                                          TABLE(I) = X);

--:     function "=" (X, Y : TABLE_MANAGER'TYPE)
--:     return BOOLEAN;
--|        where return X.LAST_ITEM = Y.LAST_ITEM and
--|                 for all I : 0 .. X.LAST_ITEM =>
--|                                X.TABLE(I) = Y.TABLE(I);

        procedure INSERT(NEW_ITEM : in ITEM)
--|        where
--|           FULL => raise TABLE_FULL,
--|           raise TABLE_FULL => TABLE = in TABLE,
--|           in NEW_ITEM.PRIORITY'DEFINED,
--|           out (in MEMBER(NEW_ITEM) →
--|                 TABLE = in TABLE and
--|                 LAST_ITEM = in LAST_ITEM),
--|           out (not (in MEMBER(NEW_ITEM)) →
--|                 TABLE = in TABLE[LAST_ITEM+1 =>
--|                                          NEW_ITEM]
--|                 and
--|                 LAST_ITEM = in LAST_ITEM+1);
        is
        ...                                -- Body of INSERT.

        end INSERT;

        procedure RETRIEVE(FIRST_ITEM : out ITEM)
--|        where
--|           in EMPTY => raise TABLE_EMPTY,
--|           raise TABLE_EMPTY => TABLE = in TABLE,
--|           out (not MEMBER(FIRST_ITEM)),
```

```
--|             out (for all X : ITEM =>
--|                  MEMBER(X) → X.PRIORITY >=
--|                                   FIRST_ITEM.PRIORITY);
        is
        ...                               -- Body of RETRIEVE.
        end RETRIEVE;

    end TABLE_MANAGER;
```

Commentary

This example shows the body of TABLE_MANAGER at the first step in its development. Result annotations for the basic functions FULL, MEMBER, and "=" have been given. The visible subprogram annotations for INSERT and RETRIEVE that are given in Section 4.5 have been interpreted. At this stage, *before* subprogram bodies are implemented, the axioms of the package should be interpreted.

We have tried to make the subprogram annotations more readable by abbreviations. First of all, calls to basic functions FULL and MEMBER (X) have not been replaced by their result annotations — they are left uninterpreted. A new function, EMPTY, is defined to make the annotations of RETRIEVE more readable. Secondly, the stability constraint on the state type implies **in** and **out** subprogram annotations that constrain the values of the current state components TABLE and LAST_ITEM. These **in** and **out** annotations imply the constraints IS_T(X), which are added as premises to interpretations by the recipe; so we have omitted the premises.

Note that one of the **out** annotations of INSERT uses an array state to indicate the change to TABLE. This is not the interpretation of a visible annotation, according to our recipe. It is a more precise hidden annotation that implies the interpretation of a visible **out** annotation, which is,

```
--| out (not (in MEMBER(NEW_ITEM)) →
--|         exist I : 0 .. LAST_ITEM =>
--|                              TABLE(I) = NEW_ITEM);
```

We can always add hidden **out** annotations that imply interpretations of visible **out** annotations. Stronger **in** annotations, on the other hand, have to be honored by all subprograms and so are best expressed by type stability constraints.

Example: *Interpreting an initial state axiom.*

The table manager specification in Section 4.5 contains the axiom

```
axiom                                                    -- (1)
for all X : ITEM =>
   not TABLE_MANAGER'INITIAL.MEMBER(X).
```

The interpretation of this axiom in the body of the table manager is

```
where in out TM : TABLE_MANAGER'TYPE =>                  -- (2)
      for all X : ITEM =>
            not (exist I : 0 .. -1 => INITIAL_TABLE(I) = X).
```

Commentary

The axiom (1) expresses a property of the initial state. The initial state is a deferred constant of the virtual private state type. Its hidden value (Section 8.2) is an aggregate,

```
TABLE_MANAGER'TYPE'(TABLE =>
                  INITIAL_TABLE, LAST_ITEM => -1),
```

where INITIAL_TABLE is an unspecified array that denotes the initial value of TABLE when the table manager body is elaborated.

Following the recipe, there are four steps in transforming the axiom to its hidden interpreation: (*i*) elimination of the deferred constant (replacement by its hidden aggregate value), (*ii*) elimination of the visible MEMBER function (replacement by its hidden result annotation given in the previous example), (*iii*) interpretion of selection on a state type expression (local variables are interpreted as components of the state), and (*iv*) mapping to a modified type constraint. The result is the interpretation (2).

Although (2) is a modified type constraint on the state type, it does not constrain the general state value TM in the quantifier, but instead constrains only INITIAL_TABLE. So, all values of the state type will satisfy it if the initial value, INITIAL_TABLE, satisfies it. In fact, (2) is equivalent to an object constraint on the initial value of hidden variable TABLE. Furthermore, (2) is true irrespective of the components of INITIAL_TABLE because the range of the existential quantifier is empty. Therefore, the hidden implementation satisfies it.

It is instructive from the viewpoint of using axioms to guide an implementation to consider what would happen if LAST_ITEM were initialized to 0 instead of – 1. This decision can be checked by interpreting axiom (1).

The interpretation of the axiom would be

```
for all X : ITEM =>
        not (exist I : 0 .. 0 => INITIAL_TABLE(I) = X),
```

which simplifies to

```
for all X : ITEM => INITIAL_TABLE(0) /= X.
```

This constraint requires the initial value of TABLE (0) not to be a member of type ITEM. Although the value of TABLE (0) is uninitialized, Ada semantics do not imply **not** TABLE (0)'DEFINED.

The inequality will be false for some value of X unless TABLE (0) does not have a value — in which case the inequality is always undefined and the quantified expression is then true. Ada does not require compilers to ensure that uninitialized variables do not have defined values.

Indeed, trying to check this constraint at runtime reveals a problem: a runtime check for this constraint will result in an erroneous Ada program, just as any Ada program whose result depends on an uninitialized variable is erroneous. Consequently, when faced with such an interpretation of a visible annotation, the implementor should be guided to change the implementation.

The table manager specification (Section 4.5) contains the following axiom:

Example: *Interpreting an algebraic relationship between subprograms.*

```
for all TM : TABLE_MANAGER'TYPE; I, J : ITEM =>
   TM [INSERT (I); RETRIEVE (J)] =
           if not TM.LEAST_PRIORITY (I) then
               TM [RETRIEVE (J); INSERT (I)]
           elsif not TM.MEMBER (I) then TM
           else   TM [RETRIEVE (J)]
           end if;
```

Commentary

The "=" operator is the equality between states.

Let us construct an interpretation of this axiom for the body of table manager given at the beginning of this section. The axiom contains successor states, which represent the results of two package operations performed in different orders. In general, the interpretation of each successor state will be a conditional expression, the cases of which express the alternative results of the package operations. Application of the recipe will lead to nested conditional expressions. To simplify our notation, we first introduce new names for the various states in the axiom.

```
TM1  =  TM [INSERT (I) ] ,                                    -- (1)
TM2  =  TM1 [RETRIEVE (J) ] ,
TM3  =  TM [RETRIEVE (J) ] ,
TM4  =  TM3 [INSERT (I) ] .
```

The axiom may be written equivalently as

```
for all TM, TM1, TM2, TM3, TM4 : TABLE_MANAGER'TYPE;
    I, J : ITEM =>
    {conjunction of equations (1)} →                          -- (2)
        TM2 = if not TM.LEAST_PRIORITY (I) then TM4
              elsif not TM.MEMBER (I) then TM
              else TM3
              end if;
```

The next step is to interpret the subexpressions in axiom (2), most of which appear in the equations of (1) that are added as premises in (2).

For example, suppose we apply the recipe to interpret the first equation, TM1 = TM [INSERT (I)]. The successor state notation is a shorthand for application of a 'NEW_STATE function to a state (Section 4.4.2). The right side is a functional expression of the form TM . INSERT'NEW_STATE (I). We must first construct a hidden specification for this function attribute before we can use it to interpret visible expressions. Its **in** and **return** annotations can be constructed easily from those for INSERT (it has the same **in** annotations and a result annotation that specifies the record aggregate of values specified in **out** annotations of the procedure). A hidden specification for INSERT'NEW_STATE (at a position where the full definition of the state type is visible) is as follows:

```
--:       function INSERT'NEW_STATE (NEW_ITEM : in ITEM)
--:       return TABLE_MANAGER'TYPE;
--|          where
--|             FULL => raise TABLE_FULL,
--|             raise TABLE_FULL => TABLE = in TABLE,
--|             in NEW_ITEM . PRIORITY'DEFINED,
--|             return
--|                 if in MEMBER (NEW_ITEM) then
--|                      (in TABLE, in LAST_ITEM),
--|                 else
--|                      (in TABLE [LAST_ITEM+1 => NEW_ITEM],
--|                         in LAST_ITEM+1 );
--|                 end if;
```

where the aggregates in the **return** annotation specify the state values returned by the function.

Now we apply the recipe to

```
TM1  =  TM . INSERT'NEW_STATE (I) .
```

At the first step, elimination of the abstract state type allows us to apply record selection operations of the hidden state record type to TM1 and TM (for brevity we omit the type constraint premises for TM1 and TM below).

Next, we apply the function call rule using the annotations

```
        In_INSERT'NEW_STATE
and
        Result_INSERT'NEW_STATE
```

shown above. **In**_INSERT requires that I.PRIORITY'DEFINED is true in TM and that FULL is not true in TM, so that no exception is propagated. **Result**_INSERT is a conditional expression in which the values returned on each branch of the conditional correspond to the cases when I is or is not a member of TM.

Omitting the type constraint premises, the result of the function call rule is

```
In_INSERT (I)  →  TM1  =  TM . Result_INSERT (I);
```

Interpreting local variables in **Result**_INSERT as selections on TM, distributing equality inside the conditional result expression, and applying the function call rule again to FULL and MEMBER, the interpretation is

```
                                                          -- (3-1)
I.PRIORITY'DEFINED and TM.LAST_ITEM /= 1000 →
 if exist X : 0 .. TM.LAST_ITEM =>
                                        TM.TABLE (X) = I then
     TM1 = TM
 else
     TM1.TABLE = TM.TABLE [TM.LAST_ITEM+1 => I]
     and
     TM1.LAST_ITEM = TM.LAST_ITEM+1
 end if;
```

Commentary

Similar interpretations can be given for the other equations in (1), (call these (3–2), ... (3–4)) as well as the other subexpressions in (2).

The final interpretation is mapped into a modified type constraint on the Anna implicit full declaration of the package state type. It is added to the other modified constraints in the TABLE_MANAGER body. In a somewhat abbreviated form this constraint is

```
  where in out (TM : TABLE_MANAGER'TYPE =>                    -- (4)
     for all TM1, TM2, TM3, TM4 : TABLE_MANAGER'TYPE;
            I, J : ITEM =>
Conjunction of conditional expressions (3–1), ... (3–4) →
            TM2 =
               if (exist X : ITEM; Y : 0 .. TM.LAST_ITEM =>
                     TM.TABLE(Y) = X
                     and
                     X.PRIORITY < I.PRIORITY)  then
                        TM4
               elsif not (exist X : 0 .. TM.LAST_ITEM =>
                                     TM.TABLE(X) = I) then
                        TM
               else
                        TM3
               end if);
```

Commentary

This is a constraint on the hidden states TM. We can try to prove it using the standard properties of equality, array access operations, etc., and also we may assume that the state variables TM, TM1, ... satisfy the other type constraints (we omitted the type constraint premises). If we can prove that it is true we can then conclude that all states satisfy it.

Let us review the construction of this interpretation. We started with an algebraic relationship between the abstractions (state type and subprograms) of package TABLE_MANAGER. This algebraic relation is an invariant of the abstract specification — it must be true in all computation states observable outside the package.

We used the full hidden subprogram annotations of MEMBER, FULL, INSERT, and RETRIEVE to eliminate these visible subprograms by applying the function call rule. The interpretation is thereby a boolean combination of the full hidden annotations of the subprogram bodies. Thus, an algebraic invariant between subprograms maps into a boolean type constraint that combines the annotations of the subprogram bodies.

Strategies for Consistency

If the interpretation of an axiom turns out not to be provable, then some states may violate it. This indicates that the visible axiom is not a consequence of the hidden annotations of the bodies of the visible subprograms. In this situation, there are two main courses of action.

1. Distribute the modified type constraint as additional **in** and **out** annotations on the subprogram bodies, as outlined in Section 8.1.3. However, since the interpretation of an axiom is usually a compli-

cated formula, this course of action is unlikely to help in planning the subprogram implementations.

2. Change one or more hidden annotations of subprogram bodies so that the type constraint is provable. Often, small changes to the existing hidden annotations will be sufficient.

There is good cause to interpret and prove an axiom as soon as hidden annotations for all the subprograms that it refers to have been constructed and before the subprogram bodies are written. This will avert errors in planning a package implementation as early as possible.

We return to the topic of strategies for consistent implementation of packages in Chapter 10.

Automated Assistance

Automation of interpretation of axioms like the ones above, and their proof, is within the current capabilities of automatic program verifiers. However, automatically constructing a counter example to a complex logical formula is another matter. "Trouble shooting," when proofs are not forthcoming, is beyond the capabilities of current automated techniques.

Hopefully, research in the area of proof and counter-example construction will progress. If so, we can expect that future implementors of packages will be able to request interactively the interpretation and proof of axioms they are trying to implement. They should get counter examples when interpretations of axioms are not true for all states.

At present, runtime checking tools[6] provide the most promising automated methods of finding inconsistencies involving algebraic axioms in packages.

9.6 Interpreting Dependent Specifications *

So far we have dealt only with packages that contain the declarations of all the basic concepts used in their specifications. What happens if the package specification depends on other packages? What constitutes adequate hidden annotation, and how can we construct the hidden constraints corresponding to visible annotations that call operations of other packages? The recipe of Section 9.2 can be used to construct an interpretation, but now it will contain calls to functions in other packages. Usually it does not result in a very useful guide to implementation. Other recipes may yield more useful guides.

In this section we consider an example of a dependent package that is specified by associating its private type with a private type of a theory

[6]See Appendix B.

package — i. e., specification by association (see Section 5.6.2). We refer to the theory package as the *theory* and the actual package whose specifications depend on it as the *actual package*. We show how to give hidden annotations specifying the basic MAP function that associates the actual private type with the private type in the theory. If MAP is implemented to satisfy this hidden specification, we can use runtime checking methods to study the consistency of the actual package specification with its body. But because MAP is specified recursively, we cannot apply our recipe. We then discuss briefly how to extend the recipe to interpret the visible specifications of the actual package.

Suppose we are given a theory package for queues rather like the stack theory described in Section 5.2.[7]

Example: *Queue theory specification.*

```
--: generic
--:
--:     type ELEMENT is private;
--:
--: package QUEUE_THEORY is
--:
--:     type QUEUE is private;
--:     NULL_QUEUE : constant QUEUE;

--:     function EMPTY (Q : QUEUE) return BOOLEAN;
--:
--:     function INSERT (Q : QUEUE; E : ELEMENT)
--:     return QUEUE;
--:
--:     function FIRST (Q : QUEUE) return ELEMENT;
--|     where out (EMPTY (Q) → FALSE);
--:
--:     function REMOVE (Q : QUEUE) return QUEUE;
--|     where out (EMPTY (Q) → FALSE);
--:
--:     function EQUAL (Q1, Q2 : QUEUE) return BOOLEAN;
--:
--| axiom for all Q : QUEUE; E : ELEMENT =>
--|     EMPTY (QUEUE'INITIAL),
--|     EMPTY (NULL_QUEUE),
--|     EQUAL ( REMOVE (INSERT (QUEUE'INITIAL, E)),
--|                                            QUEUE'INITIAL ),
--|     EQUAL (FIRST (INSERT (QUEUE'INITIAL, E)), E),
--|     EQUAL (EMPTY (REMOVE (INSERT (Q, E))), EMPTY (Q)),
--|     EQUAL (REMOVE (INSERT (Q, E)), INSERT (REMOVE (Q),E)),
--|     EQUAL (FIRST (INSERT (Q, E)), FIRST (Q));
```

[7]This example is due to Sriram Sankar and Neel Madhav.

```
--:
--: private
--:
--:     type QUEUE_REC;
--:     type QUEUE_PTR is access QUEUE_REC;
--:     type QUEUE_REC is record
--:                            E : ELEMENT;
--:                            PREV, NEXT : QUEUE_PTR;
--:                         end record;
--:     type QUEUE is record
--:                        FRONT, REAR : QUEUE_PTR := null;
--:                     end record;
--|     where in out Q : QUEUE =>
--|                          Q.FRONT = null ↔ Q.REAR = null;
--:     NULL_QUEUE : constant QUEUE := (null, null);
--:
--: end QUEUE_THEORY;
```

Commentary

The theory of queues is specified in the visible part. A theory package provides only a private type and functions and algebraic specifications. No exceptional behavior is specified. If a function gets an argument it cannot possibly process, then it must simply not terminate. Conditions under which a function does not terminate are specified as **out** conditions that can never be true of any state:

```
--|      where out (EMPTY(Q) → FALSE);
```

Unfortunately our theory contains an "Adaism." We have to use an abstract EQUAL function to introduce a concept of equality that is independent of any Ada predefined operator because type QUEUE is **private** but not **limited**. This makes the axioms look a little clumsier than using the infix "=". And we should also add the standard equality axioms applied to EQUAL, but we have omitted them here.

A private part that implements type QUEUE has been included in this virtual theory package. This allows us to construct a body for QUEUE_THEORY. Specifications that use this theory package can be executed. Note that we do not want EQUAL to mean "=" on record type QUEUE.

The following example of an integer queue uses the queue theory.

Example: *Integer queue specification.*

```
--: with QUEUE_THEORY
    package INTEGER_QUEUE is

--      IQT stands for integer queue theory.
--:     package IQT is new QUEUE_THEORY (INTEGER);
--:     use IQT;

        type QUEUE is private;

        QUEUE_EMPTY, QUEUE_FULL : exception;

--      Basic functions.
--:     function MAP (Q : QUEUE) return IQT.QUEUE;
--:     function MAXIMUM_LENGTH (Q : QUEUE)
--:     return NATURAL;
        function LENGTH (Q : QUEUE) return NATURAL;
--      End basic functions.

        function CREATE (MAX_LENGTH : NATURAL)
        return QUEUE;
--|         where
--|             return Q : QUEUE =>
--|                 MAXIMUM_LENGTH (Q) = MAX_LENGTH and
--|                 LENGTH (Q) = 0 and
--|                 IQT.EMPTY (MAP (Q));

        procedure INSERT (Q : in out QUEUE; E : in INTEGER);
--|         where
--|           LENGTH (Q) = MAXIMUM_LENGTH (Q) =>
--|                                            raise QUEUE_FULL,
--|           raise QUEUE_FULL => Q = in Q,
--|           out (EQUAL (MAP (Q), IQT.INSERT
--|                                            (MAP (in Q), E))),
--|           out (MAXIMUM_LENGTH (Q) =
--|                                  MAXIMUM_LENGTH (in Q)),
--|           out (LENGTH (Q) = LENGTH (in Q) +1);

        procedure REMOVE (Q : in out QUEUE;
                          E : out INTEGER);
--|       where
--|           LENGTH (Q) = 0 => raise QUEUE_EMPTY,
--|           raise QUEUE_EMPTY => Q = in Q,
--|           out (EQUAL (MAP (Q), IQT.REMOVE (MAP (in Q)))),
--|           out (E = IQT.FIRST (MAP (in Q))),
--|           out (MAXIMUM_LENGTH (Q) =
--|                                  MAXIMUM_LENGTH (in Q)),
--|           out (LENGTH (Q) = LENGTH (in Q) -1);
```

```
private

    type INTEGER_ARRAY_REC
        is array (INTEGER range <>) of INTEGER;
    type INTEGER_ARRAY is access INTEGER_ARRAY_REC;

    type QUEUE is
            record
                STORE : INTEGER_ARRAY :=
                            new INTEGER_ARRAY_REC(0 .. 0);
                FRONT, BACK : INTEGER := 0;
            end record;
--|         where Q : QUEUE => Q.STORE'FIRST = 0;

end INTEGER_QUEUE;
```

Commentary

INTEGER_QUEUE is specified by association (see Section 5.6.2) with an instance of QUEUE_THEORY called IQT (i. e., integer queue theory). There are three basic functions, two of which map values of the integer queue type into the natural numbers. Function MAP maps values of the actual integer queue type into values of the theory queue type. All specifications of the integer queue are thereby expressed in terms of operations on the integers and theory queues.

A representation of the actual integer queue type is already defined in the private part of this package. Quite complex, it allows for the length of queues to vary during their lifetime by access type allocation.

Now suppose we want to implement a body for the integer queue package. Let us plan to achieve two goals:

1. Ensure that the visible specification is executable, so that we can test the consistency of the specification and body at runtime.

2. Try to use the recipe to guide implementation, even though it does not apply to dependent specifications.

To follow the recipe, we must first give adequate annotations for the basic functions in the proposed new body. But we will relax the "no outside calls" criterion for adequate hidden annotations — e. g., hidden annotations may call operations of the theory. They will probably look like this:

Example: *Annotation of basic functions in the integer queue body.*

```
    package body INTEGER_QUEUE is

--:     function MAXIMUM_LENGTH (Q : QUEUE)
--:     return NATURAL
--|         where return Q.STORE'LAST;
--:     is ... end;

        function LENGTH (Q : QUEUE) return NATURAL
--|         where return if Q.FRONT >= Q.BACK then
--|                          Q.FRONT - Q.BACK
--|                      else Q.FRONT - Q.BACK +
--|                               Q.STORE'LENGTH
--|                      end if;
        is ... end;

--:       function MAP (Q : QUEUE) return IQT.QUEUE
--|           where return
--|               if Q.BACK = Q.FRONT then
--|                   IQT.NULL_QUEUE
--|               else
--|                   IQT.INSERT (MAP (QUEUE' (Q.STORE,
--|                                            Q.FRONT,
--|                       (Q.BACK+1) mod Q.STORE'LENGTH)),
--|                                         Q.STORE (Q.BACK))
--|               end if;
--:       is ... end MAP;

    end INTEGER_QUEUE;
```

Commentary

By calling INSERT of the queue theory package, the annotation of MAP specifies how a theory queue is constructed that corresponds to the data structure representing integer queues. This tells us precisely how the actual record data structure represents an integer queue. For example, the queue data is stored in Q.STORE (it is those elements that are inserted in the theory queue by MAP), Q.BACK is the first element in the queue, and the queue order is the sequential index type order from back to front (expressed by the recursive **return** annotation of MAP). Note that MAP cannot define a correspondence between the data structures representating the two queue types directly because the theory queue structure is hidden from it. Thus, we have to specify it recursively.

We can now implement the three basic functions — consistently with these hidden annotations. Then the visible subprogram specifications of the actual integer queue package are executable — assuming the theory has an Ada body so that calls to IQT.INSERT, etc. are executable. The actual visible subprogram specifications can be used to check the behavior of an implementation.

Thus, hidden recursive specifications of basic functions permit runtime checking to compare consistency of package implementations with visible specifications that depend on other packages.

If we apply the recipe to visible annotations of the integer queue, calls to MAP are replaced (according to the function call rule) by the conditional result annotation (above). The resulting interpretations will not be very helpful as a guide to implementing package INTEGER_QUEUE. Roughly, an interpretation of one of the **out** annotations of INSERT will look like:

```
--|     IQT.EQUAL(if Q.BACK = Q.FRONT then
--|                  IQT.NULL_QUEUE(...)
--|               else IQT.INSERT(MAP...)
--|               end if,
--|               IQT.INSERT(...))
```

Not only does our simple attempt to eliminate calls to MAP fail because the hidden result annotation of MAP is recursive, but the body of an actual integer queue operation is specified by annotations calling IQT. To use these annotations as an implementation guide, we must convert them to adequate specifications involving only manipulations of the actual integer queue record structure.

One simple extension of the recipe to interpret dependent specifications is given in the following guideline.

- **Guideline: Interpreting dependent package specifications.**

If an actual package is specified by association with a theory package, (Section 5.6), *then interpretation of the actual specification may be carried out in two steps.*

1. *Treat the functions of the theory package as if they were basic functions declared in the actual package, and provide adequate hidden annotations for them specifying their operations on the hidden representations of the actual package types.*

2. *Apply the recipe of* Section 9.2.

The guideline embodies a process that is natural to carry out intuitively when implementing packages whose specifications depend on other packages. In the case of INTEGER_QUEUE, all of its operations are specified by mapping to corresponding operations of IQT. Consequently, when a representation for integer queues has been chosen, and the actual integer queue operations are to be implemented, the guideline says :

- *First understand how to interpret the operations of queue theory on the record structure representation for the private type queue of the integer queue package. Then you can interpret the specifications of the integer queue package.*

Thus, the next step in implementing package INTEGER_QUEUE is to give adequate hidden annotations for each of the functions of package IQT, treating them as if they were basic functions declared in INTEGER_QUEUE. This step should be viewed as another way of specifying exactly how queues (the abstract concept) are represented by the Ada record structure of the hidden full type definition for type queue. It requires no more insight than giving the hidden recursive specification for MAP (see previous commentary).

10

Processes for Consistent Implementation of Packages

Topics:

- *rigorous processes for constructing package hidden parts;*
- *processes based on runtime consistency;*
- *processes based on consistency proof.*

Constructing the hidden part of a package is a prime example of what is popularly called a *development process*. It is often a complex process involving many separate steps. Typically, the first step is the choice of data structures. This is followed by construction of subprograms that access global data comprising the package state.

The crucial questions are *what needs to be done*, *in what order*, and *using what techniques*? The primary goal is to construct a hidden part that is consistent with the specification — a *consistent package implementation*.

Broadly speaking, processes for building packages can be divided into two classes according to the techniques they employ: *do–before–think* and *think–before–do*. Here we equate "do" with the activity of programming and "think" with the activity of specification.

A typical do–before–think process is sometimes called "prototyping." A program is written quickly. Observation of its behavior is used to modify and develop the program until a final version is reached which conforms to requirements. For many people, this is an efficient way to express intuitive knowledge and experience in an executable form which can then be analyzed and manipulated. In the absence of powerful specification languages (with support tools), prototyping has become a popular development process.

Think–before–do processes involve starting by specifying the program and then converting specifications to executable code. Such processes are said to be *rigorous* because the various informal approaches that were used in early stages of software development are replaced by techniques that employ formal specifications. In actual fact, the use of specifications *is* is a form of programming with different kinds of information.

Let us consider what our processes for building package hidden parts start with, and how this affects the activities in each process.

- *An Ada package specification is just a list of Ada declarations.*

An Ada package declaration without annotations is simply a list of type declarations (often private), subprogram declarations, and sometimes some exceptions. It contains little information that can be used to guide an implementor. Given an Ada package declaration, a rather loose do–before–think process can be outlined for implementing a hidden part — we refer to it as the *normal Ada process*.

- *An Anna package specification is a guide to implementation.*

A detailed Anna package specification, on the other hand, can provide a plan for the process of constructing the hidden part. For example, the dependency between subprogram specifications indicates a plausible order of implementing subprogram bodies. Propagation annotations tell us which subprograms should propagate which exceptions, and when they should do so. Visible subprogram annotations, when interpreted, provide detailed hidden specifications for the subprogram bodies. And axioms define constraints on the hidden package state.

- *Consistency analysis is part of an implementation process.*

Having put a lot of thought into an Anna package specification, we want to make the best use of it.

Given an Anna package specification, we can define more rigorous think–before–do processes for implementing a hidden part. Annotations in the specification are interpreted and used both to plan the implementation and to check for inconsistencies between specifications and Ada code as early as possible. The main idea is to integrate consistency analysis (either runtime checking or proof) into the implementation process, rather than delaying consistency analysis (as is normally done) to a postimplementation testing phase.

The new processes use consistency analysis to catch implementation errors as early as possible, and stop some kinds of errors from ever happening.

The new processes vary, depending on the method of consistency analysis employed. If runtime checking is used, the process is one that Ada programmers can adapt to easily — it's just a little different from the normal Ada process. If proof methods are used, the process is rigorous. It employs interpretation methods illustrated in Chapter 9 to plan subprogram bodies and analyze consistency of those plans (i. e., full hidden annotations) with package axioms. The rigorous process involves a new kind of "programming" — manipulation and proof of annotations. It emphasizes more *what* programs do and less *how* they do it.

- *Processes depend on automation.*

All these processes depend on support tools. The normal Ada process requires a compiler, and usually a debugger is considered helpful. The processes based on consistency analysis require various Anna tools. Interpretation of visible annotations, runtime checking of annotations, and consistency proof can be performed by automated tools that already exist in prototype forms or are under development.[1]

[1]See Appendix B.

In this chapter we describe processes for developing a package hidden part starting with an Anna package specification. A process based on run-time checking of executable Anna specifications is described first. Then we outline a rigorous process based on consistency proof. We point out which steps in the proof–based process are supported (or soon will be) by current state-of-the-art tools, and which steps must still be regarded as "creative effort" at this time.

10.1 Making the Normal Ada Process More Rigorous

The top–down process of starting with an abstract specification and developing a concrete implementation can be viewed as consisting of three general steps (a particular process will break down each general step into subprocesses):

1. Abstract type representation
2. Algorithm implementation
3. Testing

These three steps are iterated a number of times. Results from testing usually indicate a return to the previous two steps, for example. We refer to this iteration as *regression*.

Figure 10.1 illustrates the normal Ada process. It is a typical *do–before–think* process, whereby code is written first and thinking really starts when tests go wrong. The figure shows the potential to regress back to a previous step by backward arrows. Any step can regress back to a previous one. Also, the steps themselves are large and unstructured — particularly the "implement subprogram bodies" step. Regression within a large step can be similarly large, so the possibility of the process not terminating at all is maximized.

Delaying the testing phase until the end is perhaps the most glaring deficiency of all — lack of techniques and tools for planning and guiding the implementation being others. Testing, because it is delayed until the end of the process, is usually inadequate. In practice, the testing phase really includes all the revisions of the software in response to user complaints about it not working — this is generally categorized under a different process, like "customer support." This situation, where the customer does much of the manufacturer's testing, will have to change if product liability laws are applied to software.

Our objective is to modify the normal Ada process by using Anna specifications to guide and check the process. In the new processes, the amount of regression back to previous steps and also within a step should be reduced.

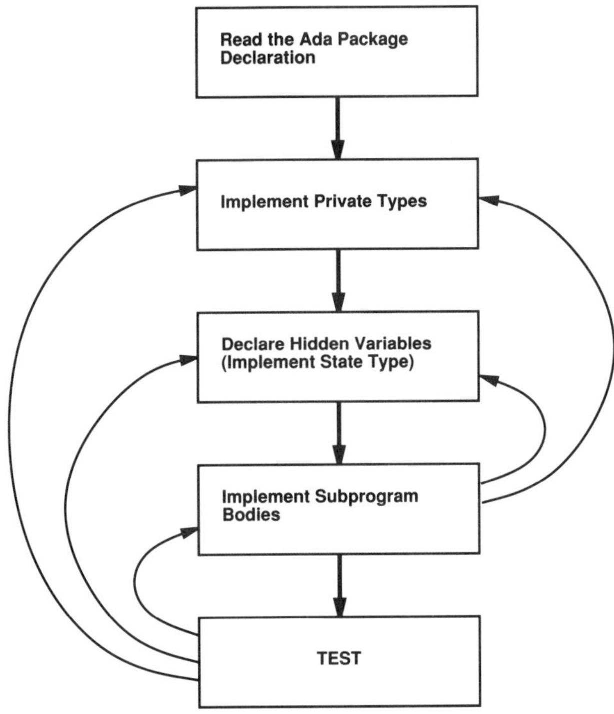

FIGURE 10.1. Ada method.

We will define alternative processes with varying degrees of rigor that differ in three ways from the normal Ada process:

- Abstract type representation is broken down into: (1) representation of data structures and specification of stability, (2) adequate specification of basic functions, (3) implementation of bodies for basic functions, and (4) validation of basic functions.
- Algorithm implementation is broken down into: (1) annotation of hidden (nonbasic) subprogram bodies, (2) implementation of subprogram bodies, and (3) validation of hidden subprogram specifications and bodies as early as possible, thus cutting down the amount of regression.
- The validation methods differ; one uses runtime consistency checking on test data, and another uses consistency proof.

In these processes, hidden specification of basic functions is part of the representation of abstract types. For example, choosing a representation for an abstract type QUEUE not only involves its full data structure definition, e.g., a record containing an array (the data store), two index components (pointers to the front and back of the queue), and a type stability constraint; it also also includes specifications for basic functions such as FIRST, LENGTH, MAX_LENGTH, and EQUAL. All these hidden specifications taken together must be detailed enough to determine how the record structure represents a queue — e.g., which element of the store is the first, which components of the store contain the queue and which ones are garbage, and whether or not it is a "wrap–around" queue.

Having made the abstract type representation decision, the implementation of nonbasic operations such as INSERT and REMOVE is highly constrained. The subprogram bodies must satisfy their visible annotations and the type stability constraint. Any remaining freedom in the implementation will be specified by hidden subprogram annotations. Consistency of each subprogram body can be validated immediately after its implementation.

Getting the basic functions "right" is important in cutting down regression within the step of implementing subprogram bodies. This is because specifications of nonbasic subprograms contain calls to basic functions. We must have confidence that the hidden specifications of basic functions express our intentions for representing abstract data types, and also that their bodies (if any) satisfy the specifications. Then, when inconsistencies arise, we do not have to worry that the visible specifications could be wrong. The search for the cause of the problem is reduced to finding what needs to be changed in the hidden annotations and implementations of the nonbasic subprograms.

Without confidence in the basic functions, an inconsistency will force us to re-examine both the basic functions as well as the nonbasic subprograms.

10.2 A Process Based on Runtime Checking

Figure 10.2 illustrates a process based on runtime checking of annotations. This process emphasizes writing specifications at each step in developing the package hidden part. The kinds of hidden specifications described in Chapter 8 are used, and priority is given to annotating and implementing basic functions — see the guidelines in Section 8.5. However, since the validation method is runtime checking, no tests can be run until some subprogram bodies are implemented. The recipe describing the process follows a strategy of testing as soon as possible to minimize regression.

The first step in Figure 10.2 is needed because the recipe assumes that specifications are logically consistent and also express the informal requirements for the package. Visible specifications should be subjected to analysis to justify this assumption. This analysis may take place in an earlier process, when the package is specified. Alternatively, the analysis step described in the proof–based process (Section 10.3) can be used.

The recipe does not assume that specifications are complete — see below.

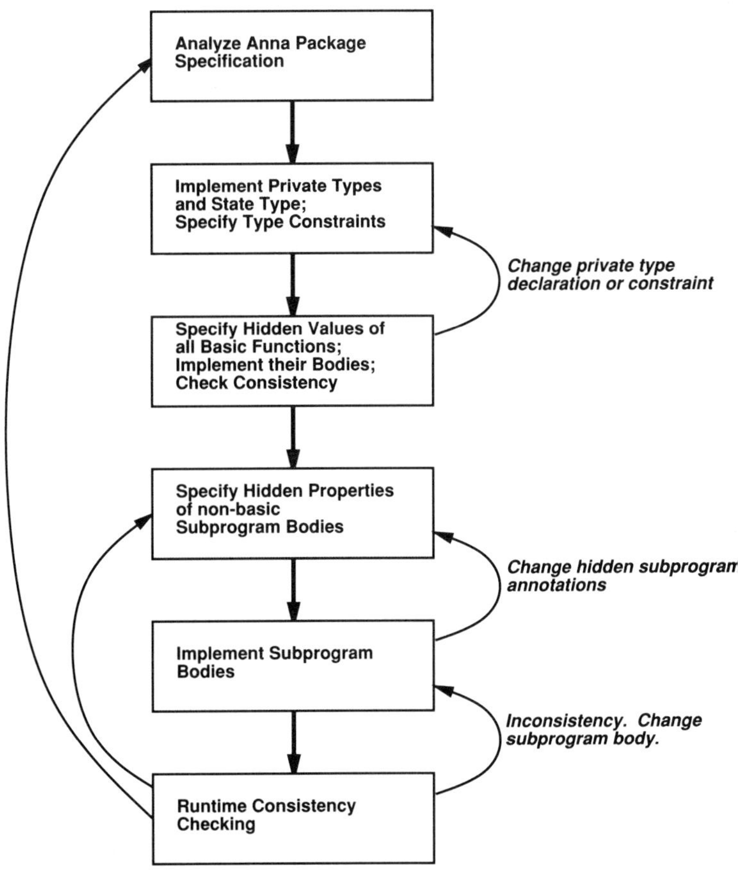

FIGURE 10.2. Runtime checking with Anna.

- **Recipe to construct a package hidden part using runtime checking**

1. **Implement the private types.**
   Ada full type definitions for private types are given together with any subsidiary type definitions. Anna type constraints that express accurate restrictions on the types (i. e., restrictions beyond Ada type constraints) must be given.

2. **Represent the package state.**
   This should be regarded as another private type definition, although the actual Ada text will be a sequence of object declarations — i. e., the components of the current state. State type constraints should be expressed at this step, but weaker object annotations on the hidden

objects can be used instead (see Section 8.3).

3. **Specify, implement, and test basic functions.**
All basic functions are specified by hidden subprogram annotations, and their bodies are implemented. The guidelines of Section 8.5 should be followed. Each basic function is then tested against its hidden annotations.

   The goal of this step is to increase confidence that the basic functions are implemented consistently with their hidden specifications. They will be executed as part of the checks for specifications of nonbasic subprograms.

4. **Specify hidden subprogram bodies.**
Subprogram annotations should be given for the body of each visible (nonbasic) subprogram. These annotations should express how the hidden data structures will be manipulated, and need only deal with special hidden details, not with repeating the visible subprogram annotations. This is an essentially creative step, in the sense that it involves a choice between various implementation options that are left open by the visible annotations.

5. **Implement and test single subprogram bodies.**
The actual subprogram bodies are written and tested, one at a time. This step tests consistency of single subprogram bodies with subprogram annotations (visible and hidden) and hidden type constraints. The goal is to eliminate simple inconsistencies first, so that they are not confused with more complex problems (next step).

6. **Test sets of subprogram bodies.**
Sequences of subprogram calls are executed and checked for consistency with all (hidden and visible) annotations, including axioms.

   This step is necessary because we do not assume that visible or hidden annotations are complete — i.e., although we assume the visible specifications are correct, we may have forgotten to specify some property.

   For example, some axioms or stability conditions may be forgotten. Typically, incompleteness can allow a subprogram to have an effect on the (shared) state that does not lead to a violation of a specification until another subprogram is executed. We note that Figure 10.2 shows a regression from testing back to the visible specification. This occurs if a missing specification is discovered.

end recipe

Commentary

This process must be supported by runtime checking tools for Anna. Some of these tools have already been implemented.[2]

The process itself is a fairly simple variation of the normal Ada process. It can be used even if the package specification depends on other packages, such as virtual theory packages, provided they have executable bodies to allow runtime checking.

Annotating, implementing, and testing the bodies of basic functions are treated as a special step, separate from the nonbasic subprograms. At the end of the first three steps, we should be confident that the data structure representation for abstract types is adequately specified, and that the basic functions are implemented consistently with their hidden specifications.

This recipe really embodies a family of processes. The key ideas are expressed in the following guidelines.

- **Guideline: Plan with hidden annotations before implementation.**

  Type annotations should be used to specify stability constraints on the hidden declarations of the package types. Hidden implementation details should be specified by subprogram annotations before each subprogram body is implemented.

- **Guideline: Test as early as possible.**

  Implementation of subprogram bodies should be scheduled in an order that allows runtime checking against visible and hidden specifications as early as possible. In particular, basic functions should be implemented and checked first.

Processes based on runtime checking do not differ radically from the normal Ada process. The use of annotations is new, the order of implementation is changed, and tests are executed as soon as possible.

The annotations constructed during the implementation of a package hidden part apply to other processes, such as debugging and reuse.

For example, in debugging, annotations at various levels of the package structure can be used with runtime checking to pinpoint the source of an inconsistency. There are various creative methods of doing this that minimize the number of annotations that are tested at various levels in a package to locate an error.[3]

---

[2]See Appendix B.

[3]See papers on Anna methodology in the bibliography.

The specifications (visible and hidden) provide formal documentation for the package and package body, when the implementation process is complete. They can be used to check any subsequent changes to the hidden part of the package. So the process should pay off, not only in developing consistent implementations of packages initially, but also in maintenance and reuse later on.

Finally, in general we do not know bounds on the number of tests, length of test sequences, or nature of test data that are needed to cover all possible inconsistencies. Consequently, although this process is much more likely to result in a consistent package implementation than the normal Ada process, it does not guarantee a consistent implementation. It may not be a satisfactory development process for certain kinds of software applications where consistency is a must.

10.3 A Rigorous Process Based on Consistency Proof

Figure 10.3 illustrates a rigorous process based on consistency proof. The main theme of the process is to reduce the risk of the implementation going off on a path that is inconsistent with the visible specifications. Interpretations of visible specifications are used to guide the implementation by checking consistency with hidden annotations as early as possible. To do this, hidden full specifications for subprogram bodies (Section 9.4) are constructed. They are shown to be consistent and to imply the interpretations of the package axioms. This is done *before* bodies for the subprograms are implemented. The final outcome is a package implementation that is provably consistent with an Anna package specification.

The principle steps of this process are described in the following recipe. To simplify matters, it is assumed that the process starts with an Anna package specification that declares all its user–defined basic concepts.

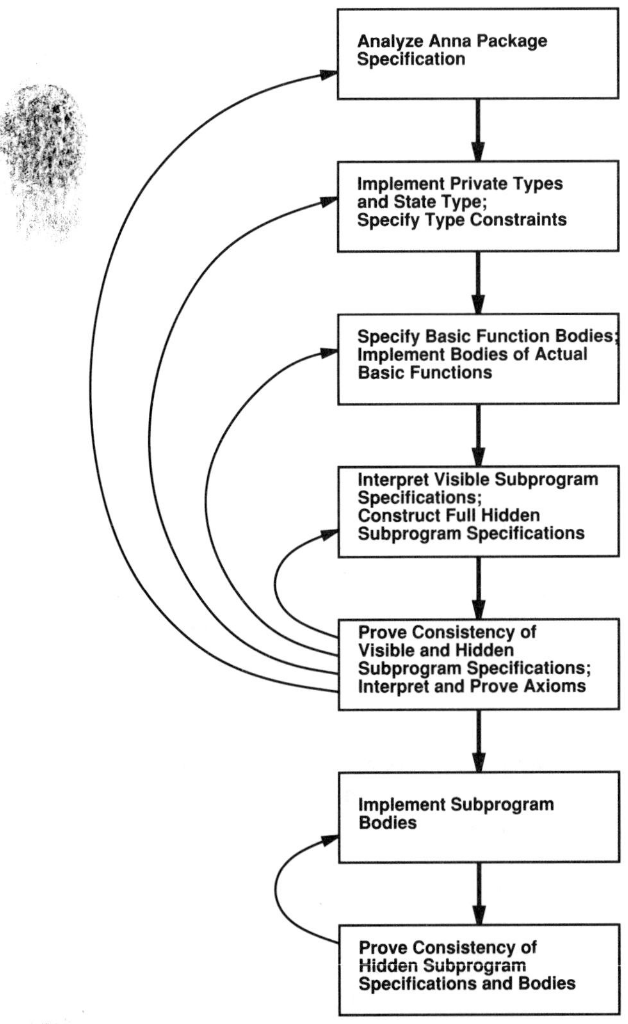

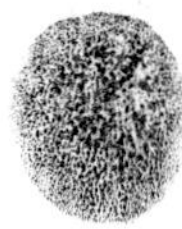

FIGURE 10.3. Consistency proof with Anna.

- **Recipe for constructing a package hidden part using consistency proof**

1. **Analyze the specification.**
   There are three main problems to be looked for before implementation begins.

   (a) *The specification itself may be inconsistent.* Axioms, for example, may be contradictory, or may contradict subprogram annotations. Such situations should be discovered as early as possible.

   (b) *The specification may be incomplete.* A typical problem is the lack of an exception propagation annotation to specify behavior when a possible error arises. Another common case is a missing constraint on a generic parameter. This kind of omission becomes obvious when use of a generic parameter in the specification assumes a property, but the generic formal parameter declaration is not constrained to have that property.

   (c) *The specification may have obscure implications.* A common situation involves the logical consequences of axioms. For example, the axioms may imply that an individual subprogram must return certain parameter values, but these values are not specified in the subprogram annotation. In such situations, it is sometimes a good idea to introduce redundant subprogram annotations to ensure that the subprogram body will be implemented to satisfy all the subtle implications.

2. **Implement the private types.**
   Same as previous recipe, step 1.

3. **Represent the package state.**
   Same as previous recipe, step 2.

4. **Specify the basic concepts of the package specification.**
   All basic functions must be given internal annotations that define their **result** values. At the end of this step, the package has hidden annotations that are *adequate* (Section 9.2) for interpreting the visible specification.

5. **Interpret the visible annotations of each subprogram.**
   This step employs methods described in Chapter 9. The interpreted subprogram annotations act as an implementation guide, outlining *what* the subprogram must do.

6. **Provide hidden subprogram annotations.**
   Subprogram annotations should be given for the body of each visible nonbasic subprogram. As in the previous recipe, these annotations

deal with special hidden details, not with repeating the visible subprogram annotations.

The visible and hidden annotations must be consistent. That is, the interpretation of the visible **in** annotations must be consistent with the hidden **in** annotations, and the hidden **out** annotations must be consistent with the interpretation of the visible **out** annotations.

At this step, local subprograms that are not visible outside the package may also be declared and specified.

At the end of steps 5 and 6, full hidden subprogram specifications will have been constructed for each nonbasic subprogram body.

7. **Interpret and prove package axioms.**
At this step, we have planned the subprogram bodies, but haven't implemented them.

This step employs the recipe in Chapter 9 to interpret package axioms. An axiom is interpreted by using the function call rule to replace calls to visible functions by their full hidden annotations. So, at this step, we are assuming that all subprogram bodies will satisfy their full hidden annotations — when they are implemented.

An interpretation of an axiom is a modified constraint on the package state type, generally looking like (see Section 9.5)

where in out X : P′TYPE => IS_P′TYPE (X) → C (X);

where C (X) is a boolean constraint that contains no program variables. Often, when P′TYPE is trivial, the interpretation is equivalent to C, a fully quantified boolean expression.

Proof of an interpretation of an axiom tells us that all stable states satisfy the axiom, or in the case of a trivial state, that the visible package subprograms, as specified by their full hidden annotations, satisfy the axiom.

Inability to prove an axiom generally indicates that the axiom is not satisfied by some states of the package — or equivalently, some sequences of calls to its subprograms. In this event, we must consider making changes in the hidden part, as planned so far, so that the axiom is satisfied. These changes may include changing some of the hidden subprogram annotations and hidden representation of types, including type declarations, type annotations, and the specifications of basic functions.

Consequently, an axiom should be proof-checked as soon as the hidden annotations have been given for the subprograms it refers to. This strategy of early checking limits the ripple effect of specification changes.

8. **Implement subprogram bodies to satisfy their full hidden specifications.**
   At this point, it is known that the package hidden part, as specified by type and subprogram body annotations, is consistent with the visible package specification. To complete an executable package body, we implement the individual subprogram bodies so that each one satisfies its own full hidden specification (Section 9.4).

End recipe.

This recipe separates the package consistency problem into three parts and deals with consistency as the package is being constructed.

- The first part is the consistency of the visible specification. The methods and tools for building and analyzing specifications are applied (Chapter 5).

- The second part is the consistency between the visible specification and the hidden annotations. This is analyzed as the hidden annotations are constructed and takes place during the choice of abstract type representation, stability constraints, and hidden subprogram annotations. At various stages, full hidden subprogram specifications are constructed. As this is done, consistency between the hidden subprogram annotations and interpretations of visible subprogram annotations is analyzed. Also, consistency with the package axioms is analyzed. This is done by interpreting the axioms and trying to prove them.

- The third part is implementation of a subprogram body to satisfy each full hidden subprogram specification.

The proof-based process described by our recipe can be quite challenging. It will only finish when the programmer has implemented a *consistent* Anna package — which is not a necessary condition for termination of the previous processes.

We can carry out small examples by hand, as illustrated in the next section. But any complex example will need automated tools. Construction of tools for interpreting visible specifications and for manipulating annotations is within the current state-of-the-art. Automated proving, however, is still a developing area, and current provers may not be up to the tasks inherent in this process.

In the absence of suitable automated provers, not all of the consistency analysis activity based on proof that is suggested as part of the process will be practicable. The steps can still be carried out, and interpretations of subprogram annotations can be constructed by automated tools and used to guide implementation. But the number of proofs required may be prohibitively large. Instead, consistency will be tested by runtime checking when the implementation is complete. So essentially we will combine the two processes we have just described.

10.4 An Example: Implementing a Package Body *

The table manager example is used to illustrate development of a package body by the consistency proof process. This package should be familiar to the reader by now, so we can afford to shorten some of the formulas and refer to details given in previous chapters. We begin with a specification that differs slightly from previous ones.

Example: Step 1 – analysis of a specification.

```
   generic

      type DATA is private;
      NULL_DATA   : DATA;
      type PRIORITY is (<>);
--|   0 < PRIORITY'POS (PRIORITY'LAST) –
--|                  PRIORITY'POS (PRIORITY'FIRST) < 255;
      MAX : POSITIVE;

   package TABLE_MANAGER is

      type ITEM is
         record
            D : DATA;
            P : PRIORITY;
         end record;

      NULL_ITEM : constant ITEM :=
                          (NULL_DATA, PRIORITY'LAST);

      TABLE_FULL, TABLE_EMPTY, ILLEGAL_DATA : exception;

--    Basic functions.
--:   function FULL return BOOLEAN;
--:   function MEMBER (X : ITEM) return BOOLEAN;
--:   function "=" (X, Y : TABLE_MANAGER'TYPE)
--:   return BOOLEAN;

--    Definitions.
--:   function EMPTY return BOOLEAN;
--|      where return for all X : ITEM => not MEMBER (X);

--:   function PRECEDES (X, Y : ITEM) return BOOLEAN;
--|      where
--|      return PRIORITY'POS (X.P) < PRIORITY'POS (Y.P);
```

```
--:     function LEAST_PRIORITY(I : ITEM) return BOOLEAN;
--|         where return (for all X : ITEM =>
--|                 MEMBER(X) → X.PRIORITY >= I.PRIORITY);

--      Package visible procedures.
        procedure INSERT(NEW_ITEM : in ITEM);
--|         where
--|             in TABLE_MANAGER.FULL => raise TABLE_FULL,
--|             raise TABLE_FULL =>
--|                     TABLE_MANAGER = in TABLE_MANAGER,
--|             in NEW_ITEM = NULL_ITEM =>
--|                                     raise ILLEGAL_DATA,
--|             raise ILLEGAL_DATA =>
--|                     TABLE_MANAGER = in TABLE_MANAGER,
--|             in NEW_ITEM'DEFINED,
--|             out (
--|              not in TABLE_MANAGER.MEMBER(NEW_ITEM) →
--|                     TABLE_MANAGER.MEMBER(NEW_ITEM)),
--|             out (
--|                 in TABLE_MANAGER.MEMBER(NEW_ITEM) →
--|                   TABLE_MANAGER = in TABLE_MANAGER);

        procedure RETRIEVE(FIRST_ITEM : out ITEM);
--|         where
--|             in TABLE_MANAGER.EMPTY =>
--|                                     raise TABLE_EMPTY,
--|             raise TABLE_EMPTY =>
--|                 in TABLE_MANAGER.EMPTY
--|                     and
--|                 TABLE_MANAGER.EMPTY,
--|             out (in TABLE_MANAGER.MEMBER
--|                                     (FIRST_ITEM)),
--|             out (not TABLE_MANAGER.MEMBER
--|                                     (FIRST_ITEM)),
--|             out (for all X : ITEM =>
--|                     TABLE_MANAGER.MEMBER(X) →
--|                         not PRECEDES(X, FIRST_ITEM));

--|     axiom                                               -- (1)
--|         TABLE_MANAGER'INITIAL.EMPTY,
--|         not TABLE_MANAGER'INITIAL.FULL;

--|     axiom                                               -- (2)
--|         for all TM : TABLE_MANAGER'TYPE =>
--|             not TM.MEMBER(NULL_ITEM);
```

```
--|     axiom                                                    -- (3)
--|         for all TM : TABLE_MANAGER'TYPE;
--|                     I, J : ITEM =>
--|                     TM [INSERT (I) ] . MEMBER (J) =
--|                         if I = J then
--|                             TRUE
--|                         else
--|                             TM . MEMBER (J)
--|                         end if,
--|                     TM [INSERT (I) ; RETRIEVE (J) ] =
--|                         if not TM . LEAST_PRIORITY (I) then
--|                             TM [RETRIEVE (J) ; INSERT (I) ]
--|                         elsif not TM . MEMBER (I) then
--|                             TM
--|                         else
--|                             TM [RETRIEVE (J) ]
--|                         end if;

    end TABLE_MANAGER;
```

Commentary

This version generalizes previous versions (e. g., Section 4.5) by introducing generic parameters. Although type PRIORITY is now a generic parameter, it is still required to be a non-null discrete type and to provide less than 256 values.

Analysis of the specification shows both redundancy and incompleteness. For example, the axioms in (3) imply the **out** annotations of INSERT and RETRIEVE, as noted in Section 4.5 (commentary). If the original specification contains only the axioms, it is a good idea to add the redundant subprogram annotations as an implementation guide for each subprogram.

On the other hand, the role of generic parameter MAX is not specified. This incompleteness should be remedied at this stage. Suppose the writer of the specification tells us that it is intended to define an upper bound on the number of items stored in TABLE_MANAGER. A virtual LENGTH function can be provided to specify this. EMPTY and FULL would be specified by the cases when LENGTH is equal to 0 or MAX. Adding LENGTH and axiomatic annotations for it could lead to a possible inconsistency with axioms (1), which must be checked. Since MAX is positive, we can always assume within the package specification that MAX > 0, which implies that the initial state is empty and not full. For brevity, we omit introduction of LENGTH.

Since there are no Ada private types, the next step is to implement the table manager state and to specify the basic functions.

Example: *Steps 3 and 4 – representing the package state and specifying basic functions.*

```
package body TABLE_MANAGER is

    type TABLE_TYPE is array (0 .. MAX) of ITEM;
    TABLE : TABLE_TYPE := (others => NULL_ITEM);
    LAST_ITEM : INTEGER := -1;

--  State type stability constraint.
--| where
--| in out TM : TABLE_MANAGER'TYPE;
--| for all I, J : TABLE'FIRST .. LAST_ITEM =>
--|     TM.TABLE(I) /= NULL_ITEM and
--|     (I < J → TM.TABLE(I) /= TM.TABLE(J) and
--|                         TM.TABLE(I).P <= TM.TABLE(J).P);


--  Basic subprograms.
--: function FULL return BOOLEAN
--|     where
--|         return LAST_ITEM = MAX;
      is ...

--: function MEMBER(X : ITEM) return BOOLEAN
--|     where
--|         return exist J : TABLE'FIRST .. LAST_ITEM =>
--|                                             TABLE(J) = X;
      is ...

--: function "=" (X, Y : TABLE_MANAGER'TYPE)
--| return BOOLEAN
--|     where
--|     return X.LAST_ITEM = Y.LAST_ITEM and then
--|         for all I : TABLE'FIRST .. X.LAST_ITEM =>
--|                                   X.TABLE(I) = Y.TABLE(I);
      is ...
    ...     --  Bodies of visible subprograms not yet implemented.

end TABLE_MANAGER;
```

Commentary

An implementation of the state has been chosen. A stability constraint is imposed. This constraint will reduce RETRIEVE to a rather simple operation, but it is something the implementor of INSERT cannot afford to forget.

The position of the constraint is the first position where a virtual full state type declaration could be placed. From this point to the end of the package body the standard Ada visibility rules for private types apply to the state type. Components TABLE

and LAST_ITEM of state type variables are visible (Section 8.2). The equality operator "=" on TABLE_MANAGER'TYPE is redefined using the state components of its parameters in the annotation.
The state allows MAX+1 items. This is consistent with the specification — no relationship of MAX to the package is specified.

At this stage, we can interpret and prove some of the axioms, particularly those defining the initial state. Doing this now will tell us if our implementation of the state and the initial values of its components satisfy the axioms specifying the initial state.

For brevity we will replace TABLE'FIRST by its value 0 from now on. The interpretation of

```
TABLE_MANAGER'INITIAL . EMPTY
```

is similar to the example given in Section 9.5:

```
First, we replace EMPTY by its definition:
  for all X : ITEM =>
     not TABLE_MANAGER'INITIAL . MEMBER (X) ;

To interpret this, we replace MEMBER by its result annotation:
  for all X : ITEM =>
     not ( exist J : 0 ..
              I (TABLE_MANAGER'INITIAL) . LAST_ITEM =>
                 I (TABLE_MANAGER'INITIAL) . TABLE (J) = X);

Finally, we replace I (TABLE_MANAGER'INITIAL) by its hidden
aggregate value and apply a logical equivalence rule for quantifiers:
  for all X : ITEM; J : 0 .. -1 =>
              TABLE_TYPE' (others => NULL_ITEM) (J) /= X );
```

which is true because the range of J is empty.

Similarly, the interpretation of **not** TABLE_MANAGER'INITIAL . FULL is:

```
not I (TABLE_MANAGER'INITIAL) . LAST_ITEM = MAX;

-- Substituting the initial value of LAST_ITEM, this reduces to:
     -1 /= MAX.
```

Since the generic parameter declaration requires 0 < MAX, this interpretation is also true.

Now we are ready to plan the implementation of INSERT and RETRIEVE. First we construct interpretations of their visible specifications (step 5). This will define hidden **in** annotations and **out** annotations that the subprogram bodies must satisfy in order to be consistent with the visible specification.

We can then decide (step 6) what additional hidden subprogram annotations must be satisfied as goals towards satisfying the interpreted annotations. The additional hidden annotations specify how these procedures compute on internal variables TABLE and LAST_ITEM. Also, we must make sure that our new hidden annotations do not contradict a visible one.

Example: *Step 5 – interpreting subprogram specifications.*

```
    package body TABLE_MANAGER is
       ...              -- Internal objects, state constraint, and basic
                        -- functions as before.

       procedure INSERT (NEW_ITEM : in ITEM)
--|       where
--|          in FULL    => raise TABLE_FULL,
--|          raise TABLE_FULL => TABLE = in TABLE and
--|                              LAST_ITEM = in LAST_ITEM,

--|          in NEW_ITEM = NULL_ITEM =>
--|                                        raise ILLEGAL_DATA,
--|          raise ILLEGAL_DATA =>
--|                          TABLE = in TABLE and
--|                          LAST_ITEM = in LAST_ITEM,
--|          in NEW_ITEM'DEFINED,
--|          in (for all I, J : 0 .. LAST_ITEM =>
--|             TABLE (I) /= NULL_ITEM and
--|             I < J → TABLE (I) /= TABLE (J) and
--|                     TABLE (I) . P <= TABLE (J) . P),
--|          out (for all I, J : 0 .. LAST_ITEM =>        -- (a)
--|             TABLE (I) /= NULL_ITEM and
--|             I < J → TABLE (I) /= TABLE (J) and
--|                     TABLE (I) . P <= TABLE (J) . P),
--|          out (in MEMBER (NEW_ITEM) →                  -- (b)
--|                TABLE = in TABLE and
--|                LAST_ITEM = in LAST_ITEM ),
--|          out (not in MEMBER (NEW_ITEM) →              -- (c)
--|                    exist I : 0 .. LAST_ITEM =>
--|                             TABLE (I) = NEW_ITEM );
       is
       ...                            -- Body to be implemented.
       end INSERT;

       procedure RETRIEVE (FIRST_ITEM : out ITEM)
--|       where
--|          in LAST_ITEM = -1 => raise TABLE_EMPTY,
--|          raise TABLE_EMPTY =>
--|             in LAST_ITEM = -1 and LAST_ITEM = -1,
--|          in (for all I, J : 0 .. LAST_ITEM =>
--|             TABLE (I) /= NULL_ITEM and
--|             I < J → TABLE (I) /= TABLE (J) and
--|                     TABLE (I) . P <= TABLE (J) . P),
```

```
--|             out (for all I, J : 0 .. LAST_ITEM =>
--|                   TABLE(I) /= NULL_ITEM and
--|                   I < J → TABLE(I) /= TABLE(J) and
--|                            TABLE(I).P <= TABLE(J).P),
--|             out (not exist I : 0 .. LAST_ITEM =>
--|                                 TABLE(I) = FIRST_ITEM),
--|             out (for all X : ITEM =>
--|              (exist I : 0 .. LAST_ITEM => TABLE(I) = X) →
--|                             not PRECEDES(X, FIRST_ITEM));
       is
       ...                                  -- Body to be implemented.
       end RETRIEVE;

    end TABLE_MANAGER;
```

Commentary

These annotations are interpretations of the visible annotations together with the **in** and **out** annotations implied by the stability constraint on the state. These interpretations are constructed at Step 5 of the recipe, so that we can see what internal implementation details are not covered by the visible annotations.

Note that some expressions contain calls to MEMBER, FULL, and EMPTY as abbreviations to simplify some annotations of INSERT or RETRIEVE. The expression **in** MEMBER(NEW_ITEM), for example, is an abbreviation of the corresponding instance of the result annotation of MEMBER:

```
exist I : 0 .. in LAST_ITEM =>
                         in TABLE(I) = NEW_ITEM.
```

Subprogram bodies must be constructed to satisfy these annotations. We consider each set of subprogram annotations in turn. First, assume a null body. If the **in** annotations imply the **out** annotations, the body is obviously trivial — it does not need to do anything. Whenever an **out** annotation is not a logical consequence of the **in** annotations, we must decide what the body has to do to make the **out** annotation true.

One way to plan this decision is to construct more detailed hidden annotations that imply that particular **out** annotation and do not contradict the others. Essentially, this is Step 6 of the recipe.

Consider the annotations for INSERT. There are three **out** annotations, (a), (b), and (c) above. Clearly, (a) and (b) are satisfied by a null body. The antecedent of (c) specifies conditions under which INSERT must change the package state. However, the actual change is specified by an existential quantifier, which says, in effect, "upon termination, NEW_ITEM is one of the components of TABLE," but it does not say which component. This is typical of a visible specification (and its interpretation), since it omits implementation details.

We must think of a way to compute a solution to the existential quantifier. Our first step is to give a more accurate internal annotation. One way to do this is to adopt a new concept:

```
--: function GOOD_INDEX (K : INTEGER; D : ITEM)
--: return BOOLEAN;
--|     where K ≤ MAX,
--|     return
--|     (for all I : 0 .. K => PRECEDES (TABLE (I), D)) and
--|     (for all J : K+1  .. LAST_ITEM =>
--|                                  not PRECEDES (TABLE (J), D));
```

where TABLE is a global parameter. Using GOOD_INDEX, we can annotate more accurately how the body of INSERT will implement its specification:

```
    procedure INSERT (NEW_ITEM : in ITEM)
--|     where
--|         ...
--|         out (not in (MEMBER (NEW_ITEM)) →
--|              (exist I : 0 .. LAST_ITEM =>
--|                  in GOOD_INDEX (I, NEW_ITEM) and
--|                  TABLE (0 .. I) = in TABLE (0 .. I) and
--|                  TABLE (I+2 .. LAST_ITEM) =
--|                          in TABLE (I+1 .. in LAST_ITEM) and
--|                  TABLE (I+1) = NEW_ITEM and
--|                  LAST_ITEM = in LAST_ITEM+1)   );
```

Essentially, this annotation says "find a good index and put the new item in that position while maintaining membership of all other items." In the presence of the strong propagation annotations, this new annotation logically implies annotations (a), (b), and (c) if we assume the stability condition for the **in** state. Therefore, if the body satisfies this annotation and the propagation annotations, it will satisfy its visible specification. Note that the new annotation still has an existential quantifier, but it gives a lot more information about a possible solution.

Similarly, the interpreted specifications of RETRIEVE contain existential quantifiers, which are open to many possible solutions. So our first task is to give a detailed hidden annotation that specifies how RETRIEVE works:

```
    procedure RETRIEVE (FIRST_ITEM : out ITEM)
--|     where
--|         out (FIRST_ITEM = in TABLE (0)),
--|         out (TABLE (0 .. LAST_ITEM−1) =
--|                                  in TABLE (1 .. LAST_ITEM)),
--|         out (LAST_ITEM = in LAST_ITEM−1);
```

Assuming the previous **in** annotations, these more detailed annotations imply the previous **out** annotations. Proving these implications is easy, again providing we assume the state stability constraint.

We have now reached Step 7 of the consistency proof recipe. At this stage, it is possible to interpret axioms (2) and (3) given in the package specification at Step 1. These interpretations can be easily proved. Axiom (2) for example has the form,

```
for all TM : TABLE_MANAGER'TYPE =>
      IS_TABLE_MANAGER'TYPE(TM) →
           for all I : 0 .. TM.LAST_ITEM =>
                        TM.TABLE(I) /= NULL_ITEM.
```

The type predicate premise IS_TABLE_MANAGER'TYPE(TM) is the stability constraint on the state type, which implies that NULL_ITEM is not an element of TM.TABLE.

The first axiom in (3) implies a frame axiom, namely that inserting a new component does not delete any previous members (see Section 4.5). Although this fact is already implied by the internal annotations of INSERT, the proof can be made easier by adding a new (redundant) annotation of INSERT; in abbreviated form, it is simply

```
out (for all X : ITEM => in MEMBER(X) → MEMBER(X)).
```

This would have the effect of adding premises about membership to the interpretation of the axiom, which makes its proof easier. A similar constraint will be required of RETRIEVE, namely that all members except the first item must remain members of the table. But in this case, it follows easily from the new hidden annotation.

We have now reached Step 8. The individual subprogram bodies must be implemented consistently with their full hidden annotations. The hidden full subprogram specifications constructed earlier at steps 5 and 6 are used to plan the bodies. Let us consider INSERT in detail.

Example: *Planning the body of INSERT.*

```
        procedure INSERT(NEW_ITEM : in ITEM)
--|        where
--             Exception propagation.
--|            in FULL   => raise TABLE_FULL,
--|            raise TABLE_FULL => TABLE = in TABLE and
--|                                LAST_ITEM = in LAST_ITEM,

--|            in NEW_ITEM = NULL_ITEM =>
--|                                        raise ILLEGAL_DATA,
--|            raise ILLEGAL_DATA =>
--|                            TABLE = in TABLE and
--|                            LAST_ITEM = in LAST_ITEM,
```

```
--             Input conditions.
--|            in NEW_ITEM'DEFINED,
--|            in (for all I, J : 0 .. LAST_ITEM =>
--|                TABLE(I) /= NULL_ITEM and
--|                I < J → TABLE(I) /= TABLE(J) and
--|                         TABLE(I).P <= TABLE(J).P ),
--             Output conditions.
--|            out (for all I, J : 0 .. LAST_ITEM =>          -- (a)
--|                TABLE(I) /= NULL_ITEM and
--|                I < J → TABLE(I) /= TABLE(J) and
--|                         TABLE(I).P <= TABLE(J).P),
--|            out (in MEMBER(NEW_ITEM) →                     -- (b)
--|                    TABLE = in TABLE and
--|                    LAST_ITEM = in LAST_ITEM ),
--|            out (not in (MEMBER(NEW_ITEM)) →               -- (c)
--|                  (exist I : 0 .. LAST_ITEM =>
--|                    in GOOD_INDEX(I, NEW_ITEM) and
--|                    TABLE(0 .. I) = in TABLE(0 .. I) and
--|                    TABLE(I+2 .. LAST_ITEM) =
--|                        in TABLE(I+1 .. in LAST_ITEM) and
--|                    TABLE(I+1) = NEW_ITEM and
--|                    LAST_ITEM = in LAST_ITEM+1 )   );

      is                                          -- Plan for the body.


-- Tests for exceptional conditions:
-- If conditions are true propagate exceptions, else:
--|         not FULL ard NEW_ITEM /= NULL_DATA;

-- Check input conditions:
-- The first input condition is already a visible annotation and can be omitted.
-- The second input condition is implied by the state type stability constraint
-- and can be omitted.

-- Tactic: output condition (a) is the state type stability constraint;
-- try to achieve (b) and (c) so that (a) remains true.

-- Test for premise of output condition (b):
-- Existentially quantified expression for MEMBER is implemented as a loop
-- to test for membership of NEW_ITEM in TABLE.
-- If found,
--|                MEMBER(NEW_ITEM);
-- The state has not been changed, so constraints of (a) and (b) are satisfied,
-- therefore simply return.
-- If not found,
--|                not MEMBER(NEW_ITEM);
```

```
-- Premise of (c) is true, so achieve goals of (c) :
-- Universally quantified expression for GOOD_INDEX is implemented as a
-- loop to find a GOOD_INDEX for NEW_ITEM:
-- when found, J say, then exit;
--|                GOOD_INDEX (J, NEW_ITEM);
-- Change TABLE and LAST_ITEM to satisfy (a) and (c).

        end INSERT;
```

Commentary

A plan for the body has a clause corresponding to each annotation in the full hidden specification. Assertions about the computation state after various steps in the plan are included in the body. They express goals of the preceding steps in the plan.

First, the exceptional situations are tested, and if the tests are true, the exceptions are propagated. Since no change to the state is made in the tests, the propagation conditions are satisfied.

Next, the input conditions are checked. If **in** annotations are true when the body is entered there is no need to have hidden annotations to check them. The definedness condition is already checked by a visible annotation. The stability condition is implied by the state type modified constraint.

Assuming the exceptional conditions are not satisfied and the input conditions are, we must plan to achieve the **out** annotations. Since **out** annotation (a) is the state type stability constraint, we adopt a strategy to achieve (b) and (c) so as to satisfy (a).

out annotations (b) and (c) depend on the test,

MEMBER (NEW_ITEM).

This test, as we see from the hidden specification of MEMBER, is an existentially quantified boolean expression. As a general rule, quantified expressions transform into loops testing for the boolean expression that is within the scope of the quantifier. For example, the membership test

```
--|     return exist I : 0 .. LAST_ITEM =>
--|                              TABLE (I) = NEW_ITEM;
```

will transform to a loop:

```
         for I in 0 .. LAST_ITEM loop
            if TABLE(I) = NEW_ITEM then
--|            MEMBER(NEW_ITEM);
               return;
            end if;
            exit when NEW_ITEM.P <= TABLE(I).P;
         end loop;
--|     not MEMBER(NEW_ITEM);
```

Here the loop **exit** condition, which terminates the loop search early, is justified by the state stability constraint, which must be true on input, together with the observation that so far the plan does not change the state.
If the loop terminates by executing the exit condition, we know that

not MEMBER(NEW_ITEM).

This is the premise for **out** annotation (c).
Thus, to satisfy **out** annotation (c) we need only find a good index in the table. GOOD_INDEX is interpreted as a quantified expression and would normally be implemented as another loop. However, the state stability constraint implies that the loop control variable I of the first loop already is a good index. Therefore we need only save the value of I.

```
         for I in 0 .. LAST_ITEM loop
            if TABLE(I) = NEW_ITEM then
--|            MEMBER(NEW_ITEM);
               return;
            end if;
            J := I;
            exit when NEW_ITEM.P <= TABLE(J).P;
         end loop;
--|     not MEMBER(NEW_ITEM) and
--|                          GOOD_INDEX(J, NEW_ITEM);
```

The resulting bodies with hidden annotations are shown below.

Example: *Final step – subprogram bodies with hidden annotations.*

```
     package body TABLE_MANAGER is
        ...                         --  Internal objects and basic functions.

--|  where
--|     for all I, J : 0 .. LAST_ITEM =>
--|        TABLE(I) /= NULL_ITEM and
--|        I < J → TABLE(I) /= TABLE(J) and
--|                 TABLE(I).PRIORITY <= TABLE(J).PRIORITY;

--:     function GOOD_INDEX(K : INTEGER; D : ITEM)
--:     return BOOLEAN;
--|        where
--|           (for all I : 0 .. K =>
--|                 PRECEDES(TABLE(I), D)) and
--|           (for all J : K+1 .. LAST_ITEM =>
--|                                not PRECEDES(TABLE(J), D));

        procedure INSERT(NEW_ITEM : in ITEM)
--|        where
--|           out (not in (MEMBER(NEW_ITEM)) →
--|              exist I : 0 .. LAST_ITEM =>
--|                 GOOD_INDEX(I, NEW_ITEM) and
--|                 TABLE(0 .. I-1) =
--|                                  in TABLE(0 .. I-1) and
--|                 TABLE(I+1 .. LAST_ITEM) =
--|                         in TABLE(I .. in LAST_ITEM) and
--|                 TABLE(I) = NEW_ITEM and
--|                 LAST_ITEM = in LAST_ITEM+1);
        is
           J : INTEGER := 0;
        begin
           if LAST_ITEM = MAX then
              raise TABLE_FULL;
           end if;
           if NEW_ITEM = NULL_ITEM then
              raise ILLEGAL_DATA;
           end if;
--|        not FULL and NEW_ITEM /= NULL_ITEM;
--|        NEW_ITEM'DEFINED;
           for I in 0 .. LAST_ITEM loop
              if TABLE(I) = NEW_ITEM then
--|              MEMBER(NEW_ITEM);
                 return;
              end if;
              J := I;
              exit when NEW_ITEM.P <= TABLE(J).P;
           end loop;
```

```
--|         not MEMBER(NEW_ITEM) and
--|                                  GOOD_INDEX(J, NEW_ITEM);
            TABLE(J+1 .. LAST_ITEM+1) :=
                                       TABLE(J .. LAST_ITEM);
            TABLE(J) := NEW_ITEM;
            LAST_ITEM := LAST_ITEM+1;

        end INSERT;

        procedure RETRIEVE(FIRST_ITEM : out ITEM)
--|         where
--|             out (FIRST_ITEM = in TABLE(0)),
--|             out (TABLE(0 .. LAST_ITEM - 1) =
--|                                  in TABLE(1 .. LAST_ITEM)),
--|             out (LAST_ITEM = in LAST_ITEM - 1);
        is
            J : INTEGER := 0;
        begin
            if LAST_ITEM = -1
                then raise TABLE_EMPTY;
            end if;
            FIRST_ITEM := TABLE(0);
            TABLE(0 .. LAST_ITEM-1) :=
                TABLE(1 .. LAST_ITEM);
--|             not MEMBER(FIRST_ITEM);
            LAST_ITEM := LAST_ITEM-1;
        end RETRIEVE;

    end TABLE_MANAGER;
```

Summary

We have described two processes that use formal annotations in developing packages. One is based on runtime checking of annotations; the other on formal consistency proof. Our example illustrates the formal consistency proof process applied to implementing a package body.

The key ideas are (1) to use the formal Anna package specifications as a template to drive the order in which we do things, and (2) to validate consistency between package specification and body as early as possible. Both processes have as an outcome a package that has formal annotations at all structural levels. The formal documentation can be applied to subsequent modifications and general "reuse" of the package (as we note below).

Both processes assume automated help. The construction of interpretations, full hidden subprogram specifications, runtime checking of annotations, and consistency proofs are assumed done by programming environment tools. Without tools to help us with these kinds of activities, there are so many chances for error that the advantages of rigorous programming with specifications will be lost — except on small examples.

- *Suppose the support tools are available; how do the new techniques compare with normal Ada programming?*

Obviously use of this methodology requires training. The programmer will be creating annotation concepts and analyzing the implications of annotations as often as writing Ada text. This may still seem difficult in comparison with just writing Ada text, but it isn't. The programmer is programming with annotations instead of Ada statements. He is expressing what the Ada text is intended to do, rather than simply writing code to do it. It's a different kind of programming, but it isn't any harder. The subconscious process of "figuring out what the program should do" is being made into a conscious process of "expressing what the program should do".

It is probably a good strategy to have a spectrum of rigorous processes, each requiring progressively more rigor. Then people can work at a level of rigor that is acceptable to them. This is illustrated in the three processes we have described above.

- *How do the expected results compare?*

Programming with annotations may take longer than just "programming," but that's because more things are being done at the same time. The proper comparison between rigorous processes and current practices is to include the time (and cost) of programming, testing, debugging, and revision into both processes. Rigorous processes should result in decreased testing and debugging, and fewer errors in software when it is released for use.

In addition, many possibilities are still open for exploration, such as reuse of a development process. A particular instance of a package body development process (e.g., test data used, inconsistencies discovered and fixed, trade-offs in using different specifications) can be archived within a support environment. The annotations can be used to check incremental changes, say to the body of a subprogram, or a data representation. So, we argue that rigorous processes will result in programmers being much more productive over the lifetime of the software.

- *When will environment support tools be available?*

The kinds of tools we need are being built today, most of them in prototype experimental form. The next generation of programming environments should contain production quality versions of these kinds of tools — i.e., tools that give answers quickly, do not "blow up" on large problems, and do not "die" if the programmer does something wrong. With this kind of help, nearly all steps of the rigorous processes are automated, just as compilers automate the code translation process today. The programmer guides the process interactively, and does the things we have labeled as "creative."

Finally, we note that the Ada package is probably the right complexity of unit at which to proposed a new rigorous process based on formal methods. Let us remember that most of the examples in this book are short and simple, serving to illustrate principles and techniques. A real Ada package in a software system is often much more complex. A typical Diana tree package in use on our programming environment project, for example, includes extra tree nodes to represent Anna constructs in addition to Ada constructs. It has a visible specification containing 226 different kinds of tree nodes, and 60 subprograms for manipulating them. Its package state comprises a large table encoding mappings that associate strings with nodes and nodes with attributes. The body contains 160 subprogram bodies and a total of 2200 Ada statements. The package is a critical interface between many other software components of the environment. Its lifetime can be measured in tens of years. The revisions and modifications to it over its lifetime are countless. Maintenance of an up-to-date specification and a body consistent with that specification are critical to the progress of our project. Such problems are typical in software projects today. Controlling them requires new methods, and there can be no doubt that those methods must be automated.

Further Reading

Techniques of applying specifications are being actively researched, and the field as a whole is expanding rapidly. One very active proposal at the moment is the Vienna Development Method, called VDM. Various collections of papers on VDM are available, including the two proceedings of VDM conferences listed below. There are strong similiarities between VDM and some of the processes we have outlined here for Ada packages. The reader should have no trouble applying ideas from VDM to Ada programs using Anna specifications — in fact some of the VDM papers deal with applications to Ada software, and some suggest using Anna.

Another contemporary specification notation is Z (pronounced the European way as "zed"). Some of the ideas of Z and example applications are described in the collection of papers edited by Hayes. There are clear correspondences between concepts in Z and Ada/Anna. For example, Z schemas correspond to generic Anna package specifications. And the standard kinds of types used in Z such as sets and sequences can be defined very simply as theory packages in Anna and used in specifications. The examples of Z specifications in the collection below make good exercises for specification in Ada/Anna.

1. D. Bjorner, C.B. Jones, editors. *VDM'87 — A Formal Method at Work*. Springer-Verlag — Lecture Notes in Computer Science No. 252, 1987.
2. R. Bloomfield, L. Marshall, R. Jones, editors. *VDM'88, VDM — The Way Ahead*. Springer-Verlag — Lecture Notes in Computer Science, No. 328, 1988.
3. Ian Hayes. *Specification Case Studies*. Prentice–Hall International Series in Computer Science, 1987.

Appendix A

Syntax

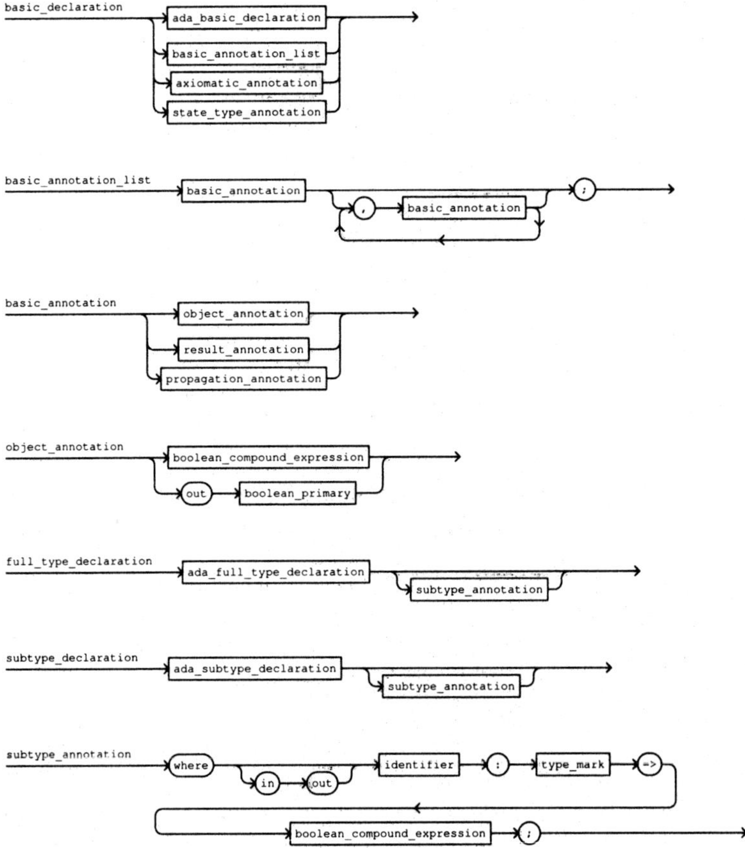

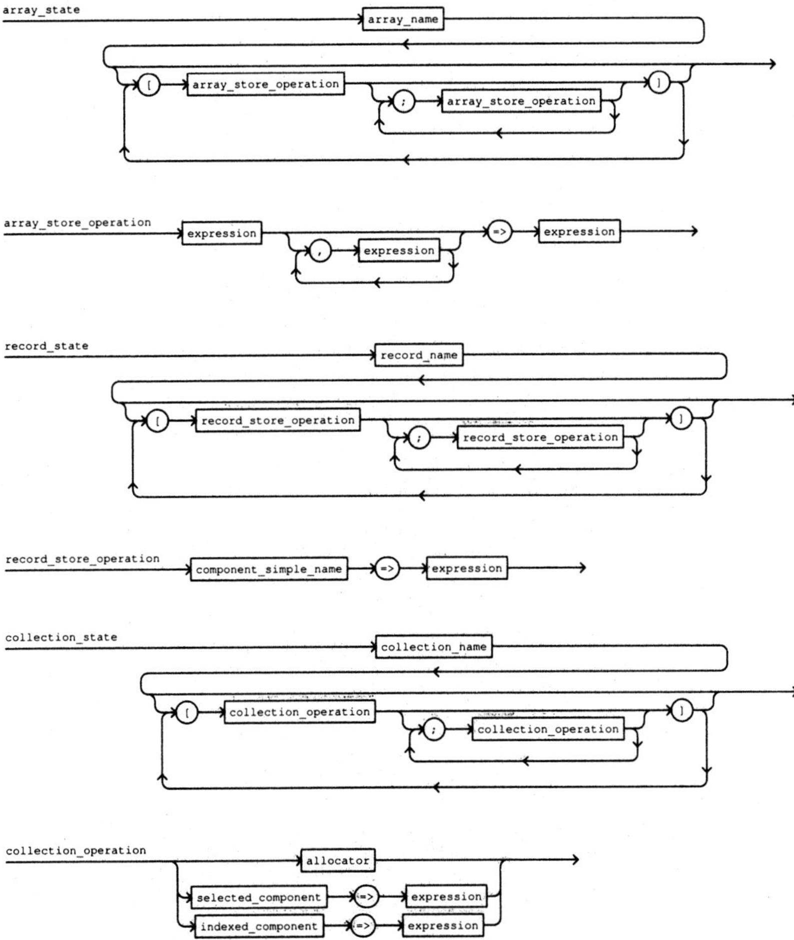

array_state
array_name
[
array_store_operation
;
array_store_operation
]
array_store_operation
expression
,
expression
=>
expression
record_state
record_name
[
record_store_operation
;
record_store_operation
]
record_store_operation
component_simple_name
=>
expression
collection_state
collection_name
[
collection_operation
;
collection_operation
]
collection_operation
allocator
selected_component
=>
expression
indexed_component
=>
expression

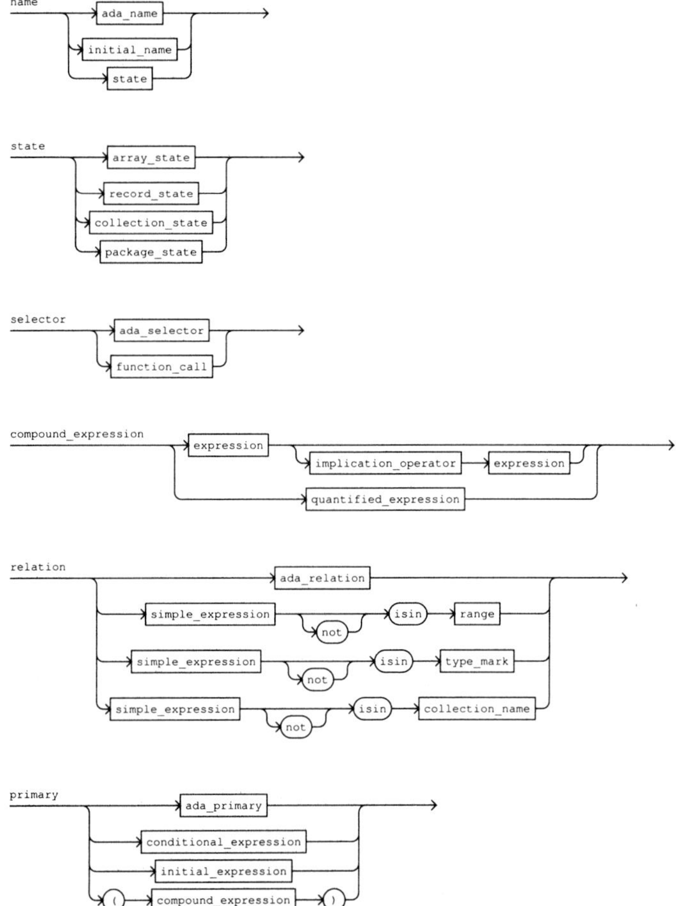

name
ada_name
initial_name
state
state
array_state
record_state
collection_state
package_state
selector
ada_selector
function_call
compound_expression
expression
implication_operator
expression
quantified_expression
relation
ada_relation
simple_expression
not
isin
range
simple_expression
not
isin
type_mark
simple_expression
not
isin
collection_name
primary
ada_primary
conditional_expression
initial_expression
(
compound_expression
)

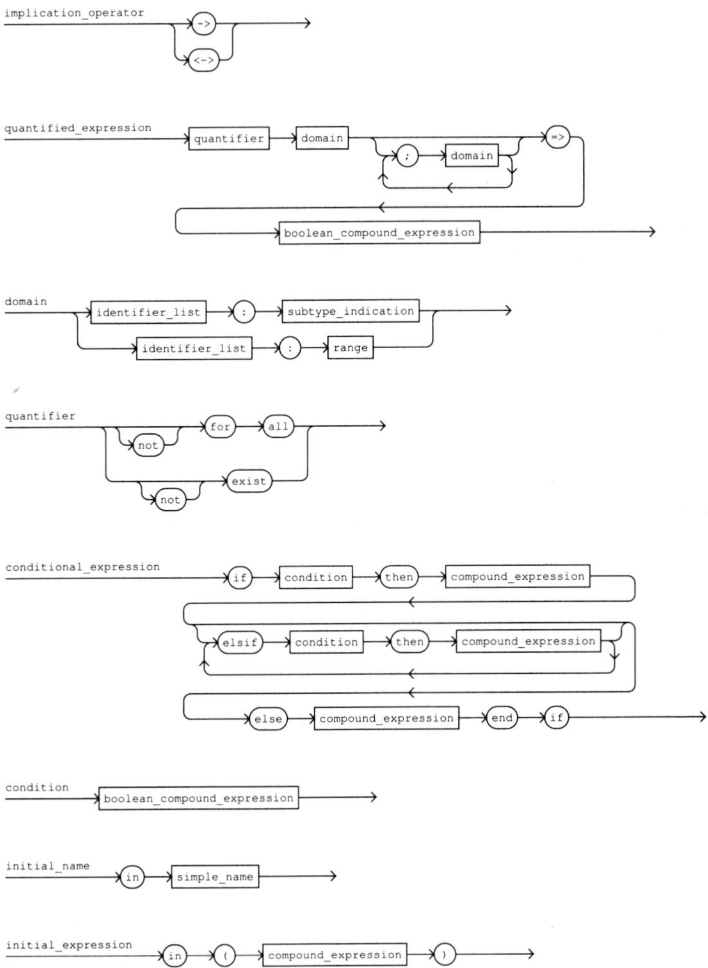
implication_operator
->
<->
quantified_expression
quantifier
domain
=>
;
domain
boolean_compound_expression
domain
identifier_list
:
subtype_indication
identifier_list
:
range
quantifier
not
for
all
not
exist
conditional_expression
if
condition
then
compound_expression
elsif
condition
then
compound_expression
else
compound_expression
end
if
condition
boolean_compound_expression
initial_name
in
simple_name
initial_expression
in
(
compound_expression
)

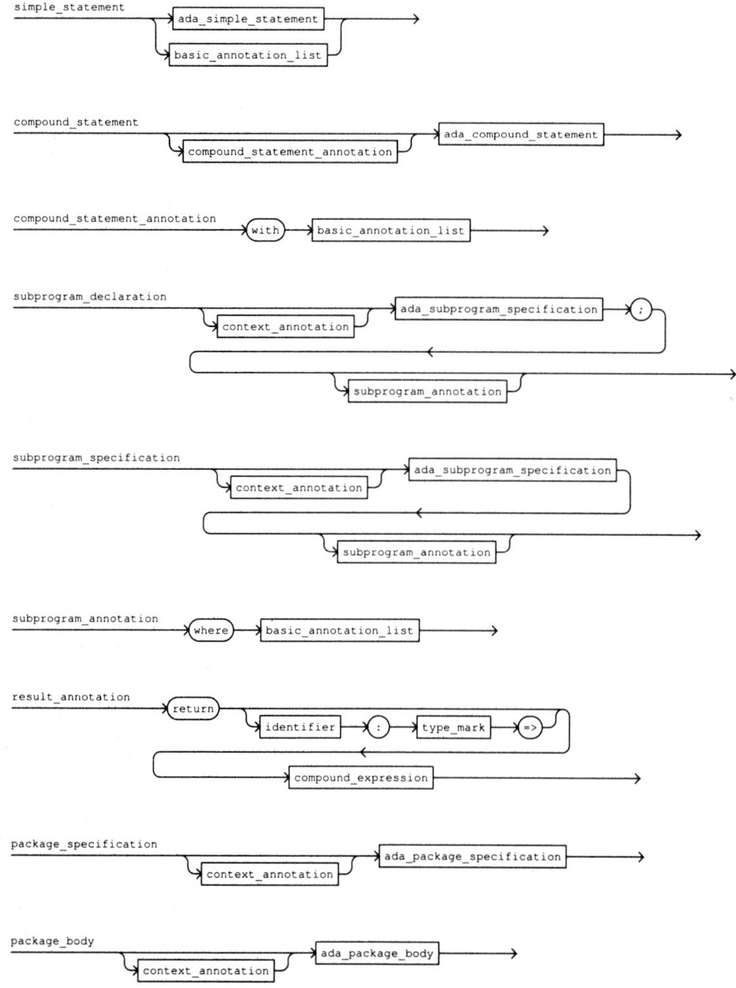
simple_statement
ada_simple_statement
basic_annotation_list
compound_statement
compound_statement_annotation
ada_compound_statement
compound_statement_annotation
with
basic_annotation_list
subprogram_declaration
context_annotation
ada_subprogram_specification
;
subprogram_annotation
subprogram_specification
context_annotation
ada_subprogram_specification
subprogram_annotation
subprogram_annotation
where
basic_annotation_list
result_annotation
return
identifier
:
type_mark
=>
compound_expression
package_specification
context_annotation
ada_package_specification
package_body
context_annotation
ada_package_body

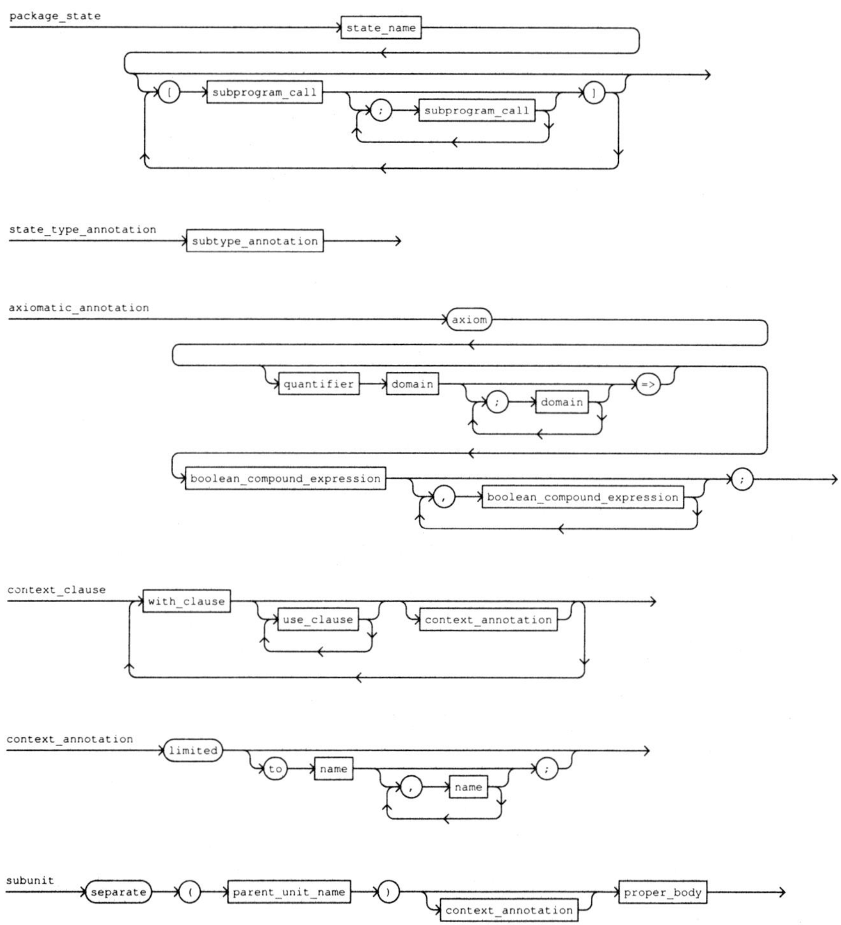
package_state
state_name
[
subprogram_call
;
subprogram_call
]
state_type_annotation
subtype_annotation
axiomatic_annotation
axiom
quantifier
domain
;
domain
=>
boolean_compound_expression
,
boolean_compound_expression
;
context_clause
with_clause
use_clause
context_annotation
context_annotation
limited
to
name
,
name
;
subunit
separate
(
parent_unit_name
)
context_annotation
proper_body

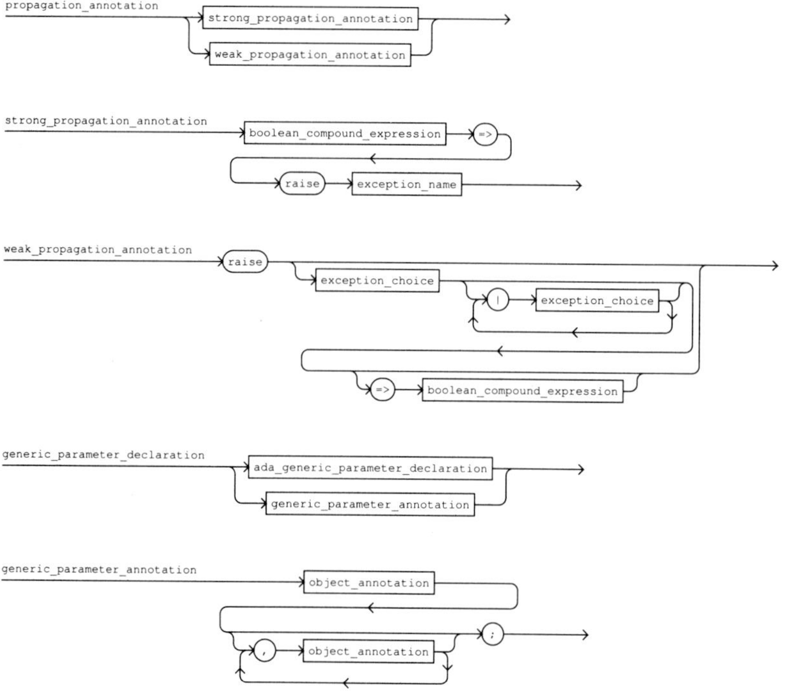
propagation_annotation
strong_propagation_annotation
weak_propagation_annotation
strong_propagation_annotation
boolean_compound_expression
=>
raise
exception_name
weak_propagation_annotation
raise
exception_choice
|
exception_choice
=>
boolean_compound_expression
generic_parameter_declaration
ada_generic_parameter_declaration
generic_parameter_annotation
generic_parameter_annotation
object_annotation
,
object_annotation
;

Appendix B

Tools

Topics:

- *runtime checking tools;*
- *symbolic execution tools.*

This appendix gives a brief description of two tools that currently support applications of Anna. We have pointed out several times in this book that tools are an essential prerequisite to many applications of Anna, so a short discussion of current support tools is appropriate. Because these tools are being experimented with and are changing rapidly, an appendix is the best place for this discussion.

There are two essential aspects of any tool that automates an application of a computer language.

1. The *technology* upon which the tool is based,

2. The *packaging* by which the tool provides a user access to the technology.

Usually the technology is a particular algorithm or theory for computing something. Traditional compilers, for example, generally embody three technologies: (1) parsing of context–free grammars, (2) context–sensitive rule checking, and (3) translation of high-level statements (in some suitable representation) into lower-level machine instructions.

The packaging is often called a "user interface." It constitutes the way in which the technology is made available to the user. Indeed, the analogy between our informal use of "packaging" and the Ada package construct is deliberate; a technology is implemented in the hidden part of a tool and a user has access to it only through the visible operations provided by the tool. Again, for example, most compilers package their technologies in a linear fashion: parse, check-semantics, code-generate, code-optimize. The user is given no control over the sequence.

The purpose of packaging is to make the technology easy to use — it suggests simple and obvious use-processes. Also, of course, the technology is usually hidden for proprietary reasons. Quite often, packaging inhibits innovative uses of a technology, and its integration with other tools and technologies.

So there is a sense in which one may hope to see a new generation of "open" tools in which the packaging of a tool provides detailed access to the technology. This could be achieved by packaging that provides access to separate components of a tool, or by more atomic tools. The result would be to allow individual tools to be combined into a macrotool — called a *process* — by the user. In newer programming environments, for example, the traditional compiler package has disappeared altogether. Its separate technologies are provided by more atomic tools that can be invoked interactively: "parse," "semanticize," "code–gen" can be applied whenever appropriate.

Thus, the two tools we are going to describe here may "look" very different in the future.

The two tools described below are implemented in Ada. They use other tools from an environment of Anna tools. These component tools are all specified as Ada/Anna packages. They include, for example, an abstract syntax tree package for internal representations (a simple extension of the DIANA tree representation for Ada), a context sensitive rule checker for Ada and Anna, and an automated deduction system providing Prolog capabilities.

Anna support tools are independent of any Ada compiler and runtime system. Various experimental versions of them have been ported to a wide variety of computers including multiprocessors. The more advanced versions have fancy packaging, which is dependent on the host support environment, generally for I/O and windowing displays.[1]

B.1 The Anna Runtime Checking System

This tool automates the transformation of annotations into executable Ada checking code and provides a simple user interface for analyzing the causes of inconsistencies at runtime.

• Technology

The runtime checking system uses the checking function approach outlined in Section 2.9. Its basic technology is the translation of annotations into checking functions and calls to those functions. In addition it uses an equality rewrite rule system to check the consistency of package axioms, called *chromatic proving* because a coloring scheme is used to bound potentially infinite loops in the rewriting of terms. When checking algebraic specifications, the corresponding checking functions call the chromatic theorem prover to compute and remember lemmas whose consistency should be checked at different points in the computation.

The various components of this system and the data flow between them are shown in Figure B.1. Annotations are converted to *checking code*, which

[1]Specifically, X–11/3 windows, which are becoming quite standard.

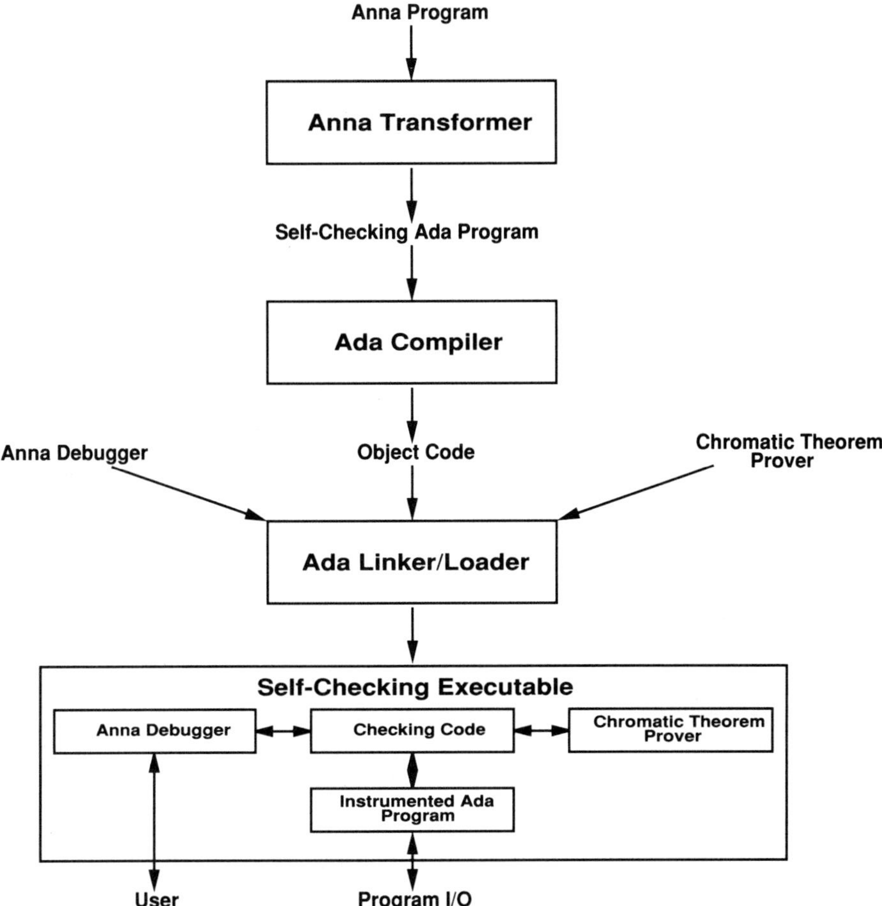

FIGURE B.1. The Anna runtime checking system.

is inserted into the underlying Ada program. This process is performed by a tool called the *Anna transformer*. The result is an Ada program (no Anna) instrumented with checking function declarations and calls to them. The instrumented Ada program makes calls to the checking code every time a specification may potentially be violated. We refer to this version of the Ada/Anna program as a "self–checking" Ada program.

The self–checking Ada program is compiled using a standard Ada compiler and then linked and loaded together with the Anna debugger and the chromatic theorem prover. The result is an executable version of the Anna specifications and underlying Ada program together with an interactive debugger .

• Packaging

Assume that the user has written a driver program as part of the transformed Anna program. The driver accepts subprogram calls from the console and executes the corresponding calls to operations of the underlying program that is being tested. This allows sequences of tests to be performed either interactively or predefined in an input file.

When a *transformed* Anna program is first executed, the Anna debugger takes control and provides a top-level interface between the user and the program being tested. The user can then set up a test strategy by choosing which annotations to check and which to suppress. Control is transferred back to the underlying program (and driver) to execute various tests. If the checking code determines that a violation has taken place, the exception ANNA_ERROR is raised and control is transferred to the Anna debugger . The user can then interact with the Anna debugger to get more information on the nature of the inconsistency. The debugger provides the following capabilities:

- *Diagnostics.*
  Provides diagnostic messages when inconsistent behavior is detected. Diagnostics include the annotation violated and the Ada source text whose execution violated the annotation.

- *Manipulation of annotations.*
  Checking of individual annotations can be suppressed or unsuppressed interactively. Propagation of ANNA_ERROR can also be suppressed when a particular annotation is violated; this allows testing to be continued from the current computation state. These features use annotation names, which can be defined using Ada–like labels.

The programmer interacts with the debugger using menus to choose displayed options with an input device such as a mouse. An example of how the programmer may suppress annotations is shown in Figure B.2. The menu displays the various options the programmer has in interacting with the debugger . On deciding to suppress annotations, another menu displays the set of annotations that can be suppressed. The programmer can now choose the set of annotations to be suppressed and then commit this action.

In addition to the menus of Figure B.2, a window displays the program execution. When an annotation is violated, two more windows are opened; one shows the annotation that was violated, and the other shows the local program text around the statement where it was violated. This scenario is illustrated in Figure B.3

Figure B.3 shows a situation where the user has interactively executed calls to package QUEUE_MANAGER. The PROGRAM_IO window shows a sequence of calls,

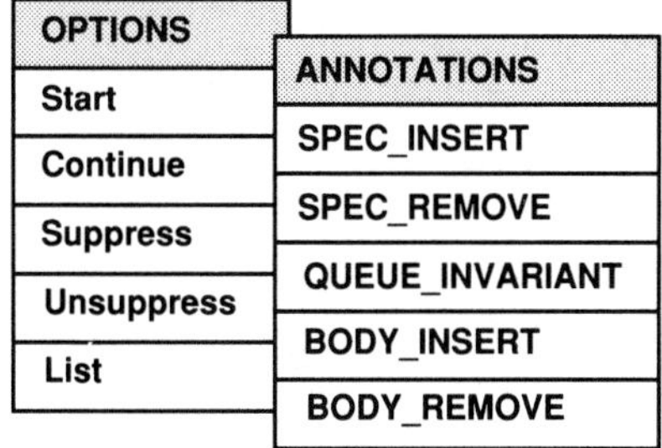

FIGURE B.2. The Anna debugger menus.

```
INSERT (1, Q0);
INSERT (2, Q0);
```

where Q0 is a queue variable declared in the driver program. An inconsistency is detected at the second call. At this point two other windows open. The VIOLATION OF ANNOTATION window shows that an annotation of procedure INSERT was violated — invariance of the top element of Q0 under insertion. The VIOLATION OCCURRED AT window shows the actual statement where the computation violated the annotation.

• **Status**

The Anna runtime checking system is currently capable of handling significantly complex Ada/Anna programs, say several thousands of lines of Ada and Anna, and involving separate compilation units. It supports nearly all of Anna, except for certain kinds of quantified expressions, some uses of package state types, and complicated package axioms. Recipes for using this system, both in testing and debugging, and in prototyping package specifications on actual software projects, are being defined.

B.2 Package Specification Analyzer

The package specification analyzer allows analysis of Anna package specifications by symbolic execution (see Section 5.8). It is intended for use during the specification of a package and *before* the package is implemented. By examining the logical implications of a package specification, the user can check whether the specification matches his own informal expectations of how the package should behave.

• **Technology**

The specification analyzer is based on a method of translating the symbolic execution of a package specification into operations on a set of formulas

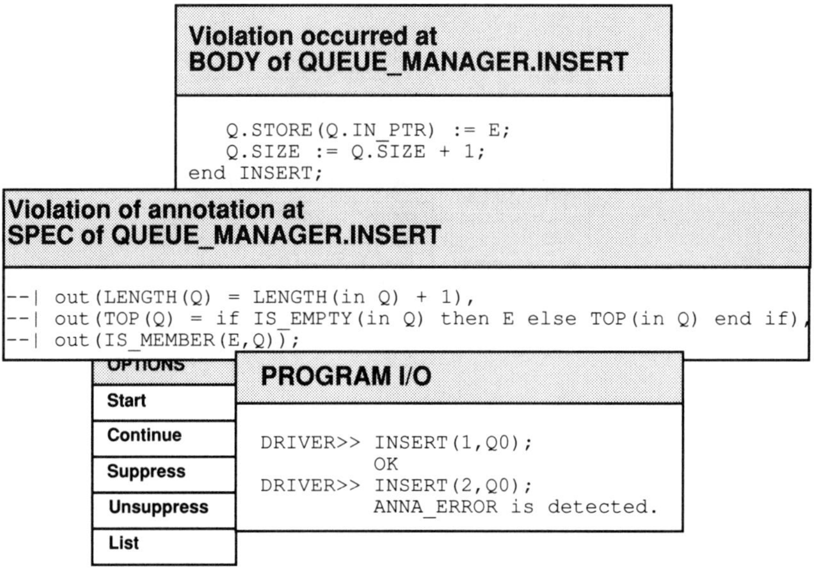

Violation occurred at BODY of QUEUE_MANAGER.INSERT

```
   Q.STORE(Q.IN_PTR) := E;
   Q.SIZE := Q.SIZE + 1;
end INSERT;
```

Violation of annotation at SPEC of QUEUE_MANAGER.INSERT

```
--| out(LENGTH(Q) = LENGTH(in Q) + 1),
--| out(TOP(Q) = if IS_EMPTY(in Q) then E else TOP(in Q) end if),
--| out(IS_MEMBER(E,Q));
```

OPTIONS

- Start
- Continue
- Suppress
- Unsuppress
- List

PROGRAM I/O

```
DRIVER>> INSERT(1,Q0);
         OK
DRIVER>> INSERT(2,Q0);
         ANNA_ERROR is detected.
```

FIGURE B.3. Error reporting by the Anna debugger.

expressed in a many-sorted, first-order predicate logic. We refer to such a set of formulas as a database.

Anna package specifications and computation states are translated into databases. Symbolic execution of Anna subprogram specifications is translated into mappings between databases. Querying the results of symbolic execution is translated into database queries. The mappings and queries involve making deductions from databases (i. e., first order proof).

The translation can be formalized as a set of reduction rules that map Ada/Anna constructs into many-sorted first-order logic expressions. Examples of reduction rules are given below. In each case, an example of the Anna construct is given, along with its representation in first-order logic.

- **Program variable** *maps to* **set of subscripted logic constants.** For example, the Ada variable V is represented by the set of logic constants $\{v_1, v_2, v_3, \ldots\}$. Constant v_n represents the value of variable V in the nth computation state.

- **Anna axiom** *maps to* **first-order logic axiom.** A first-order logic axiom is a formula that is asserted to be true in all databases. For example, the Anna axiom

```
--| axiom for all E : EVEN => E mod 2 = 0;
```

is represented by the following logical formula:

$$(\forall\ e)\ even(e) \quad \rightarrow \quad e\ mod\ 2\ =\ 0$$

The first order formula is added to the database to express a true formula of the computation state. Functions = and *mod* will have first-order formulas that define their properties.

- **Result annotation** *maps to* **first-order logic axiom.**
  For instance, the result annotation of the program fragment

  ```
     function SQR( I : INTEGER ) return INTEGER;
  --|    where return I * I;
  ```

  is represented by the following logical formula:

  $$(\forall\ i)\ integer(i)\ and\ defd\_sqr(i) \quad \rightarrow \quad sqr(i)\ =\ i * i$$

  Because Anna functions are only partially defined, a predicate $defd\_sqr(x)$ is defined by first-order formulas so that it is true if and only if x satisfies the **in** annotations, parameter type constraints, and negated propagation conditions of SQR.

The major components of the specification analyzer are shown in Figure B.4.

Anna environment tools are used to check that inputs satisfy the Ada and Anna language rules. Anna specifications (i. e., their internal representations) are translated into logical formulas. Databases, mappings between datatbases, and queries are handled by a first-order logic subsystem. The logic subsystem is composed out of other packages, including a package providing Prolog capabilities.

- **Packaging**

Figure B.5 illustrates the user's view of the specification analyzer. Given an Anna package specification, the tool allows the user to declare variables of the package types or standard Ada types. The user may interactively execute symbolic operations on the package, as though they are step-by-step executing a program that uses the package. Values passed as parameters of package operations may either be symbolic or literal. In a sense, the user simulates a driver program, but since communication is interactive, the user can determine at each step which operation to execute next.

The specification analyzer defines the database for the *computation state* of the using program and the package. It keeps track of changes to the computation state resulting from symbolic execution by means of a history

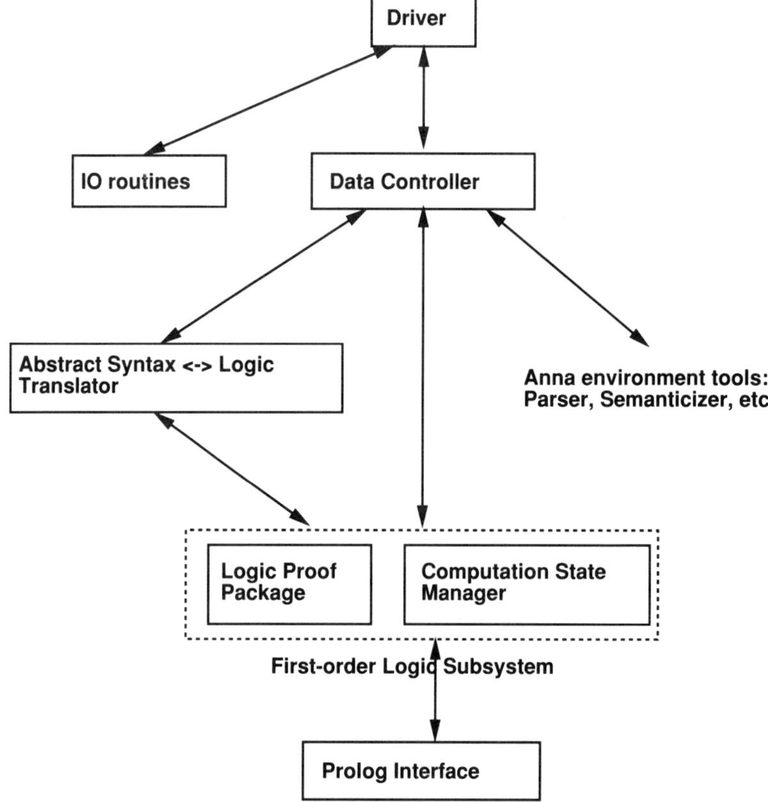

FIGURE B.4. Components of the specification analyzer.

sequence of databases. Each operation executed causes a computation state transformation, potentially resulting in a change to the database representing the current state.

Also available are querying facilities, allowing the user to evaluate any semantically legal Anna expression with respect to the current computation state. This facility is shown in Figure B.5 as a capability to evaluate annotations. If an expression has a value (meaning it is equal to an Ada literal), this value is returned.

Other features of the specification analyzer (not shown in the figure) include:

- The ability to declare and use objects of a defined type interactively. These objects are useful in storing the values of complex expressions.

- The ability to augment the specification by adding new axioms interactively.

- A facility for storing the history of a session.

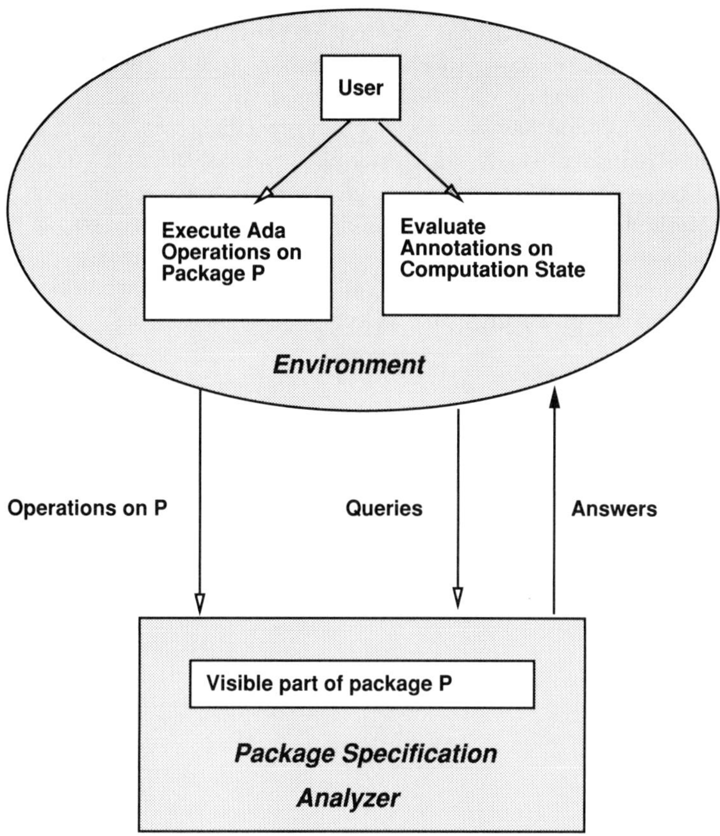

FIGURE B.5. User's view of the specification analyzer.

- A facility to use an external file as input to the specification analyzer, which is useful in regression testing and testing of complex packages requiring a great deal of computing time. Histories of previous tests may be used as input.

Typical scenarios of interactive sessions with the specification analyzer look like the examples of recipe applications given in Section 5.8.

- **Status**

The package specification analyzer is a more experimental tool than the Anna runtime checker. There are two reasons for this.

1. It depends much more on the technology of automated first-order logic theorem proving.

2. It is newer and has not been exposed to as many users and projects.

Typically, complicated sets of axioms cause it to think for a long time — but they have the same effect on us humans too! On package specifications that depend heavily on transformational specifications (i. e., subprogram annotations) and have simple algebraic specifications, it is already a useful tool. It can deal easily with examples such as DIRECT_IO (Section 5.7) and more complicated examples involving separate compilation units.

Methodology of applying symbolic execution in early stages of software development needs to be explored and defined. Such ideas have fewer precedents in traditional programming methods than do runtime checking methods. And use of features such as symbolic regression testing have not been explored yet.

Appendix C

A Short Bibliography

C.1 Anna

B. Krieg-Brückner and D. C. Luckham. Anna: towards a language for annotating Ada programs. *ACM SIGPLAN Notices*, 15(11):128–138, 1980.

B. Krieg-Brückner. Consistency checking in Ada and Anna: a transformational approach. *Ada Letters*, 3(2):46–54, September-October 1983.

D. C. Luckham, S. Sankar, and S. Takahashi. Two-dimensional pinpointing: an application of formal specification to debugging packages. To appear in *IEEE Software.*

D. C. Luckham and F. W. von Henke. An overview of Anna, a specification language for Ada. *IEEE Software*, 2(2):9–23, March 1985.

D. C. Luckham, F. W. von Henke, B. Krieg-Brückner, and O. Owe. *Anna — A Language for Annotating Ada Programs.* Springer-Verlag — Lecture Notes in Computer Science No. 260, July 1987.

G. Mendal, et al. The Anna-1 user guide and installation manual. Computer Systems Laboratory, Stanford University, Stanford, California - 94305. April 1990. Available upon request and by electronic FTP.

M. Mandal and S. Sankar. Concurrent runtime checking of formally specified programs. Stanford University Computer Systems Lab. report.

R. Neff. *Ada/Anna Package Specification Analysis.* PhD thesis, Stanford University, December 1989. Also Stanford University Computer Systems Laboratory Technical Report No. CSL–TR–89–406.

D. S. Rosenblum, S. Sankar, and D. C. Luckham. Concurrent runtime checking of annotated Ada programs. In *Proceedings of the 6th Conference on Foundations of Software Technology and Theoretical Computer Science*, pages 10–35, Springer-Verlag — Lecture Notes in Computer Science No. 241, December 1986. Also Stanford University Computer Systems Laboratory Technical Report No. 86-312.

S. Sankar. *Automatic Runtime Consistency Checking and Debugging of Formally Specified Programs.* PhD thesis, Stanford University, August

1989. Also Stanford University Department of Computer Science Technical Report No. STAN–CS–89–1282, and Computer Systems Laboratory Technical Report No. CSL–TR–89–391.

S. Sankar. A note on the detection of an Ada compiler bug while debugging an Anna program. *ACM SIGPLAN*, 24(6):23–31, 1989.

S. Sankar and D. S. Rosenblum. *The Complete Transformation Methodology for Sequential Runtime Checking of an Anna Subset.* Technical Report 86-301, Computer Systems Laboratory, Stanford University, June 1986. Also Program Analysis and Verification Group Report 30.

S. Sankar, D. S. Rosenblum, and R. B. Neff. An implementation of Anna. In *Ada in Use: Proceedings of the Ada International Conference, Paris*, pages 285–296, Cambridge University Press, May 1985.

C.2 Ada

The Ada Programming Language Reference Manual. US Department of Defense, US Government Printing Office, February 1983. ANSI/MIL-STD-1815A-1983.

J. G. P. Barnes. *Programming in Ada.* Addison-Wesley, 1984.

D. L. Bryan and G. O. Mendal. *Exploring Ada.* Prentice-Hall, 1990.

G. Booch. *Software Engineering with Ada*, 2nd Edition. Benjamin/Cummings, Inc., 1987.

N. H. Cohen. *Ada as a Second Language.* McGraw Hill, 1986.

C.3 Specification Languages

A. L. Ambler, D. I. Good, J. C. Browne, W. F. Burger, R. M. Cohen, C. G. Hoch, and R. E. Wells. GYPSY: a language for specification. *ACM SIGPLAN Notices*, 12(3):1–10, March 1977.

O. J. Dahl and O. Owe. *Generator Induction in Order Sorted Algebras.* Technical Report Research Report No. 122, Institute for Informatics, University of Oslo, Norway, February 1989.

J. V. Guttag, J. J. Horning, and J. M. Wing. The Larch family of specification languages. *IEEE Software*, 2(5):24–36, September 1985.

C. M. Geschke, J. H. Morris Jr., and E. Satterthwaite. Early experience with Mesa. *Communications of the ACM*, 20(8):540–553, August 1977.

D. I. Good and L. C. Ragland. Nucleus — a language for provable programs. In William C. Hetzel, editor, *Program Test Methods*, pages 93–117, Prentice-Hall, 1973.

A. Goldberg and D. Robson. *Smalltalk-80.* Addison-Wesley, 1983.

D. P. Helmbold and D. C. Luckham. TSL: task sequencing language. In *Ada in Use: Proceedings of the Ada International Conference, Paris*, pages 255–274, Cambridge University Press, May 1985.

D. C. Ince. *An Introduction to Discrete Mathematics and Formal System Specification. Oxford Applied Math and Computing Science Series*, Clarendon Press, Oxford, 1988.

B. W. Lampson, J. J. Horning, R. L. London, J. G. Mitchell, and G. L. Popek. Report on the programming language Euclid. *ACM SIGPLAN Notices*, 12(2), February 1977.

B. Liskov, A. Snyder, R. Atkinson, and C. Schaffert. Abstraction mechanisms in CLU. *Communications of the ACM*, 20(8):564–576, August 1977.

B. Meyer. *Object-Oriented Software Construction.* Prentice-Hall, 1988.

D. R. Musser. Abstract data type specification in the AFFIRM system. *IEEE Transactions on Software Engineering*, SE-6(1):24–32, January 1980.

M. Nielsen, K. Havelund, K. R. Wagner, and C. George. The RAISE language, method and tools. In *Proceedings of the VDM Conference*, pages 376–405, Springer-Verlag — Lecture Notes in Computer Science No. 328, 1988.

J. T. Schwartz, R. B. K. Dewar, E. Dubinsky, and E. Schonberg. *Programming with Sets: An Introduction to SETL.* Springer-Verlag, 1986.

J. M. Spivey. *Understanding Z, A Specification Language and its Formal Semantics.* Cambridge Unversity Press, 1988. Tracts in Theorectical Computer Science, Volume 3.

W. A. Wulf, R. L. London, and M. Shaw. An introduction to the construction and verification of Alphard programs. *IEEE Transactions on Software Engineering*, SE-2(4):253–265, December 1976.

C.4 Formal Methods

R. S. Boyer, B. Elspas, and K. N. Levitt. SELECT — a formal system for testing and debugging programs by symbolic execution. In *Proceedings of the International Conference on Reliable Software*, pages 234–245, April 1975.

Dines Bjørner and Cliff B. Jones. *Formal Specification and Software Development.* Prentice-Hall International, 1982.

F. L. Bauer, B. Moller, M. Partsch, and P. Pepper. Formal program construction by transformations — computer-aided, intuition-guided programming. *IEEE Transactions on Software Engineering*, 15(2):165–180, February 1989.

D. Bjørner, C. Jones, editors. *VDM'87 — A Formal Method at Work.* Springer-Verlag — Lecture Notes in Computer Science No. 252, 1987.

O. J. Dahl, E. W. Dijkstra, and C. A. R. Hoare. *Structured Programming.* Academic Press, 1972.

E. W. Dijkstra. *A Discipline of Programming. Series in Automatic Computation*, Prentice-Hall, 1976.

R. W. Floyd. Assigning meanings to programs. In *Proceedings of a Symposium in Applied Mathematics of the American Mathematical Society*, pages 19–32, American Mathematical Society, 1967.

J. V. Guttag and J. J. Horning. The algebraic specification of abstract data types. *Acta Informatica*, 10:27–52, 1978.

J. V. Guttag, E. Horowitz, and D. R. Musser. Abstract data types and software validation. *Communications of the ACM*, 21(12):1048–1064, December 1978.

J. V. Guttag, E. Horowitz, and R. Musser. The design of data type specifications. In R. T. Yeh, editor, *Current Trends in Programming Methodology, Volume 4 — Data Structuring*, chapter 4, pages 60–79, Prentice-Hall, 1978.

N. Gehani and A. D. McGettrick, editors. *Software Specification Techniques.* Addison-Wesley, 1986.

D. I. Good. Provable programming. In *Proceedings of the International Conference on Reliable Software*, pages 411–419, April 1975.

D. Gries. *The Science of Programming.* Texts and Monographs in Computer Science, Springer-Verlag, 1981.

J. V. Guttag. The design of data type specifications. *Communications of the ACM*, 20(6):396–404, June 1977.

J. V. Guttag. Notes on type abstraction (version 2). *IEEE Transactions on Software Engineering*, SE-6(1):13–23, January 1980.

C. A. R. Hoare. An axiomatic basis for computer programming. *Communications of the ACM*, 12(10):576–581, October 1969.

C. A. R. Hoare and N. Wirth. An axiomatic definition of the programming language PASCAL. *Acta Informatica*, 2(4):335–355, 1973.

I. Hayes. *Specification Case Studies.* International Series in Computer Science, Prentice-Hall, 1987.

S. Igarashi, R. L. London, and D. C. Luckham. Automatic program verification I: a logical basis and its implementation. *Acta Informatica*, 4:145–182, 1975.

C. B. Jones. *Systematic software development using VDM.* International Series in Computer Science, Prentice-Hall, 1990.

J. C. King. Proving programs to be correct. *IEEE Transactions on Computers*, C-20(11):1331–1336, November 1971.

S. Katz and Z. Manna. Towards automatic debugging of programs. In *Proceedings of the International Conference on Reliable Software*, pages 143–155, April 1975.

D. C. Luckham, S. M. German, F. W. von Henke, R. A. Karp, P. W. Milne, D. C. Oppen, W. Polak, and W. L. Scherlis. *Stanford Pascal Verifier User Manual.* Technical Report 79-731, Department of Computer Science, Stanford University, March 1979. Also Program Analysis and Verification Group Report 11.

D. C. Luckham. Program verification and verification oriented programming. In *Proceedings of the IFIP Congress, North Holland*, pages 783–794, August 1977.

B. Liskov and S. Zilles. Programming with abstract data types. *SIGPLAN Notices*, 9(4):50–59, April 1974.

B. Liskov and S. Zilles. Specification techniques for data abstraction. *IEEE Transactions on Software Engineering*, SE-1(1):7–19, March 1975.

Z. Manna and R. Waldinger. The logic of computer programming. *IEEE Transactions on Software Engineering*, SE-4(3):199–229, May 1978.

P. Naur. Proof of algorithms by general snapshots. *BIT*, 6(4):310–316, 1966.

M. Nielsen, K. Havelund, K. R. Wagner, and C. George. The RAISE language, method and tools. In *Proceedings of the VDM Conference*, pages 376–405, Springer-Verlag — Lecture Notes in Computer Science No. 328, 1988.

D. L. Parnas. A technique for software module specification with examples. *Communications of the ACM*, 15(5):330–336, May 1972.

C. Rich. Formal representation of plans in the Programmer's Apprentice. In *Proceedings of the Seventh International Joint Conference on Artificial Intelligence (IJCAI)*, pages 1044–1052, 1981.

R. Bloomfield, L. Marshall, and R. Jones, editors. *VDM'88, VDM — The Way Ahead.* Springer-Verlag — Lecture Notes in Computer Science No. 328, 1988,

S. N. Zilles. *Algebraic Specification of Data Types.* Project MAC Progress Report 11, Massachusetts Institute of Technology, 1974.

C.5 Testing

Ada Joint Program Office. Ada validation procedures and guidelines. *Ada Letters*, 7(2):29–57, March–April 1987.

D. L. Bird and C. U. Munoz. Automatic generation of random self-checking test cases. *IBM Systems Journal*, 22(3):229–245, 1983.

B. W. Boehm, R. K. McClean, and D. B. Urfrig. Some experiences with automated aids to the design of large-scale reliable software. In *Proceedings of the International Conference on Reliable Software*, pages 105–113, April 1975.

R. A. DeMillo, R. J. Lipton, and F. G. Sayward. Program mutation: a new approach to program testing. In *Infotech State of the Art Report, Software Testing, Volume 2: Invited Papers*, pages 107–126, Infotech International, 1979.

R. A. DeMillo, W. M. McCracken, R. J. Martin, and J. F. Passafiume. *Software Testing and Evaluation.* Benjamin/Cummings, Inc., 1987.

A. Ersoz, D. M. Andrews, and E. J. McCluskey. *The Watchdog Task: Concurrent Error Detection Using Assertions.* Technical Report 85-267, Computer Systems Laboratory, Stanford University, May 1985.

J. B. Goodenough and S. L. Gerhart. Towards a theory of test data selection. In *Proceedings of the International Conference on Reliable Software*, pages 493–510, April 1975.

S. L. Gerhart and L. Yelowitz. Observations of fallibility in applications of modern programming methodologies. *IEEE Transactions on Software Engineering*, SE-2(3):195–207, September 1976.

W. C. Hetzel, editor. *Program Test Methods. Series in Automatic Computation*, Prentice-Hall, 1973.

W. E. Howden. Algebraic program testing. *Acta Informatica*, 10:53–66, 1978.

Infotech International. *Infotech State of the Art Report, Software Testing Volume 1: Analysis and Bibliography*, 1979.

M. S. Johnson. A software debugging glossary. *ACM SIGPLAN Notices*, 17(2):53–70, February 1982.

J. C. King. A new approach to program testing. In *Proceedings of the International Conference on Reliable Software*, pages 228–233, April 1975.

R. J. Lipton and F. G. Sayward. The status of research on program mutation. In *Digest for the Workshop on Software Testing and Test Documentation*, Ft. Lauderdale, FL, pages 355–373, 1978.

D. J. Lu. Watchdog processors and VLSI. In *Proceedings of the National Electronics Conference (Volume 34)*, pages 240–245, October 1980.

D. J. Lu. Watchdog processors and structural integrity checking. *IEEE Transactions on Computers*, C-31(7):681–685, July 1982.

G. J. Meyers. *The Art of Software Testing.* John Wiley & Sons, 1979.

A. Mili. Self-stabilizing programs: the fault-tolerant capability of self-checking programs. *IEEE Transactions on Computers*, C-31(7):685–689, July 1982. Also see correspondence in *IEEE Transactions on Computers*, C-34(1):97–98, January 1985.

D. L. Parnas. The influence of software structure on reliability. In *Proceedings of the International Conference on Reliable Software*, pages 358–362, April 1975.

B. Randell. System structure for fault tolerance. *IEEE Transactions on Software Engineering*, SE-1(2):220–232, June 1975.

C. V. Ramamoorthy and S. F. Ho. Testing large software with automated software evaluation systems. *IEEE Transactions on Software Engineering*, SE-1(1):46–58, March 1975.

C. V. Ramamoorthy, K. H. Kim, and W. T. Chen. Optimal placement of software monitors aiding systematic testing. *IEEE Transactions on Software Engineering*, SE-1(4):403–411, December 1975.

L. G. Stucki and G. L. Foshee. New assertion concepts for self-metric software validation. In *Proceedings of the International Conference on Reliable Software*, pages 59–65, April 1975.

E. Y. Shapiro. *Algorithmic Program Debugging*. MIT Press, 1983. (An ACM Distinguished Dissertation, 1982).

S. S. Yau and R. C. Cheung. Design of self-checking software. In *Proceedings of the International Conference on Reliable Software*, pages 450–457, April 1975.

R. T. Yeh and K. M. Chandy, editors. *Current Trends in Programming Methodology, Volume 3 — Software Modelling*. Prentice-Hall, Inc., 1978.

R. T. Yeh, editor. *Current Trends in Programming Methodology, Volume 1 — Software Specification and Design*. Prentice-Hall, Inc., 1977.

R. T. Yeh, editor. *Current Trends in Programming Methodology, Volume 2 — Program Validation*. Prentice-Hall, Inc., 1977.

R. T. Yeh, editor. *Current Trends in Programming Methodology, Volume 4 — Data Structuring*. Prentice-Hall, Inc., 1978.

Index

Texts and Monographs in Computer Science

---

continued

R.T. Gregory and E.V. Krishnamurthy
Methods and Applications of Error-Free Computation
1984. XII, 194 pages, 1 illus.

David Gries, Ed.
Programming Methodology: A Collection of Articles by Members of IFIP WG2.3
1978. XIV, 437 pages, 68 illus.

David Gries
The Science of Programming
1981. XV, 366 pages

Micha Hofri
Probabilistic Analysis of Algorithms
1987. XV, 240 pages, 14 illus.

A.J. Kfoury, Robert N. Moll, and Michael A. Arbib
A Programming Approach to Computability
1982. VIII, 251 pages, 36 illus.

E.V. Krishnamurthy
Error-Free Polynomial Matrix Computations
1985. XV, 154 pages

David Luckham
Programming with Specifications: An Introduction to ANNA, A Language for Specifying Ada Programs
1990. XVI, 418 pages, 20 illus.

Ernest G. Manes and Michael A. Arbib
Algebraic Approaches to Program Semantics
1986. XIII, 351 pages

Robert N. Moll, Michael A. Arbib, and A.J. Kfoury
An Introduction to Formal Language Theory
1988. X, 203 pages, 61 illus.

Helmut A. Partsch
Specification and Transformation of Programs
1990. XIII, 493 pages, 44 illus.

Franco P. Preparata and Michael Ian Shamos
Computational Geometry: An Introduction
1988. XII, 390 pages, 231 illus.

Brian Randell, Ed.
The Origins of Digital Computers: Selected Papers, 3rd Edition
1982. XVI, 580 pages, 126 illus.

Texts and Monographs in Computer Science

continued

Thomas W. Reps and Tim Teitelbaum
The Synthesizer Generator: A System for Constructing Language-Based Editors
1989. XIII, 317 pages, 75 illus.

Thomas W. Reps and Tim Teitelbaum
The Synthesizer Generator Reference Manual, 3rd Edition
1989. XI, 171 pages, 79 illus.

Arto Salomaa and Matti Soittola
Automata-Theoretic Aspects of Formal Power Series
1978. X, 171 pages

J.T. Schwartz, R.B.K. Dewar, E. Dubinsky, and E. Schonberg
Programming with Sets: An Introduction to SETL
1986. XV, 493 pages, 31 illus.

Alan T. Sherman
VLSI Placement and Routing: The PI Project
1989. XII, 189 pages, 47 illus.

Santosh K. Shrivastava, Ed.
Reliable Computer Systems
1985. XII, 580 pages, 215 illus.

William M. Waite and Gerhard Goos
Compiler Construction
1984. XIV, 446 pages, 196 illus.

Niklaus Wirth
Programming in Modula-2, 4th Edition
1988. II, 182 pages

Study Edition
Edward Cohen
Programming in the 1990s: An Introduction to the Calculation of Programs
1990. XV, 265 pages